Introductory Macroeconomics

Introductory Macroeconomics

Michael Veseth
UNIVERSITY OF PUGET SOUND

ACADEMIC PRESS
New York London Toronto Sydney San Francisco
A Subsidiary of Harcourt Brace Jovanovich, Publishers

Chapter opening illustrations
and cover illustration by Stuart Leeds

Academic Press, Inc.
111 Fifth Avenue, New York, New York 10003

United Kingdom Edition published by
Academic Press, Inc. (London) Ltd.
24/28 Oval Road, London NWl 7DX

ISBN: 0-12-719550-5
Library of Congress Catalog Card Number: 78-73966

Printed in the United States of America

Table Of Contents

Preface

These are fascinating times to study economics, because economic events have taken on a new importance. Even relatively obscure economic statistics routinely make the front pages. Television news programs employ full-time economic correspondents. Presidents, senators, and congressmen are quizzed as much on their economic stand as other issues. The polls tell us that inflation, not crime or pollution, is the number one problem facing the nation.

To understand how the economic system operates and to make intelligent decisions within that system is not an easy task. Yet it is absolutely crucial that today's students have a thorough working knowledge of the national economy.

This book is designed to help students understand how the economy works and how economic events affect them, and to give them a sound knowledge base for making decisions in the future. It provides an up-to-date picture of our current economic problems and their possible solutions in a clear, understandable form.

WHAT THIS BOOK IS ABOUT

The interest in economics today has been amplified by the changing nature of the economy: we have clearly entered what may be called the Second Era of Modern Macroeconomics. The First Era of Macroeconomics began in the 1930s when we learned that the economy is not self-regulating. Unemployment is a real and pre-sent danger. Nothing automatically assures that high levels of employment will prevail. The study of macroeconomics began as an attempt to understand the problem of high unemployment and to discover ways of achieving and managing prosperity.

The Second Era of Macroeconomics began in the 1970s. Equipped with tools to fight unemployment, we found ourselves plagued by another economic malady, high rates of price inflation. High unemployment rates combined with soaring inflation proved to be a new kind of problem requiring a new brand of medicine. The "old time religion" of macroeconomics was of only limited usefulness.

Most previous macroeconomics texts have concentrated on an analysis of the causes of and cures for high unemployment rates. The causes of inflation and, in particular, the oddly changing relationship between inflation and unemployment, have taken a back seat. This has left students (and instructors) confused and dissatisfied.

This book is designed to take students into the Second Era of Modern Macroeconomics. Both inflation and unemployment need to be analyzed in a real world setting. The causes of recession, rising prices, and worst of all, the *stagflation* which combines joblessness with rising prices, need to be discussed in a clear and understandable fashion.

In order to do this, some new approaches are necessary. The economic models used in this text differ somewhat from those found in *traditional* textbooks in that they focus quite clearly on current problems and deal explicitly with the problem of inflation as well as unemployment. Some of the important features of this text include:

Discussion of current problems. It is not enough to be able to list our economic problems and their potential solutions. In order to deal with these issues effectively on either a national or personal level, today's student must truly understand what our economic problems are, why they are problems, and what their economic impacts can be. A major portion of this text is devoted to understanding the nature of inflation and unemployment and their impacts on nations and on individuals.

Analysis of inflation. A thorough discussion of inflation has been included throughout the text. Every chapter features some discussion of inflation's causes or economic implications. This heavy emphasis on inflation is entirely appropriate. Inflation is today's most severe economic problem. It is also our least understood problem. Today's student must understand how inflation works and the damage that it does.

Economic policy. This text concentrates on understanding the nature of our economic problems and the trade-offs inherent in any solutions of those problems. Thus it concentrates on economic policy rather than economic theory or institutions. This makes the analysis interesting and useful to the student and provides the tools necessary to understand how the economy works.

International economics. National economic policies cannot be discussed in a vacuum. International economic events are no longer buried in the financial pages; today they make front page headlines. Any student who does not understand the basics of international trade and exchange rates is truly ill-equipped to deal with the modern world. Fully one-fourth of this text deals with international economics. International trade and payments, exchange rates, and economic policy are all discussed with the depth necessary for the 1980s.

Understandable presentation. Finally, this text is designed to present economic problems, tools, and theories in a way that is easily understandable so that the important concepts of macroeconomics can be retained for longer than just a semester. Of course not all of the details will *stick* in the reader's mind forever, but the intention here is to provide a basic economic education for a lifetime. Important economic concepts, because they are presented in a way that is easy to understand, should form a lasting base from which to view a changing economic world.

ACKNOWLEDGMENTS

Any work of this nature benefits from the contributions of a host of individuals whose names do not, alas, appear on the title page. I wish to thank the administration of the University of Puget Sound for providing an atmosphere of freedom and creativity in which to think, write, and teach. Thanks must go, as well, to my colleagues at U.P.S., Ernie Combs, Bruce Mann, and Douglas Goodman, who provided constructive criticism throughout the course of this volume's preparation. Editors at Academic Press, Susan J. Anderson and Randi Kashan, and a number of referees contributed greatly to the final draft of this text. A large measure of credit (but no blame) may also be assigned my wife, Sue, who contributed patience and understanding during the long months when the manuscript was in preparation.

Finally, I wish to thank a generation of students at the University of Puget Sound who willingly subjected themselves to experimental material as this text developed. This volume is dedicated to them.

To the Instructor

The first thing that most people ask when they pick up a new text is, "What's so new about this? Why do we need another macroeconomics text when there are so many around already?" These are good questions and they deserve good answers.

A macroeconomics text should be able to really explain the problems that face the economy today. Most current texts, while they present good economics, fail this test.

The typical macro text presents a fairly traditional Keynesian picture of the economy. The principal economic model used is the well-worn Keynesian cross (45-degree-line) model and, in some cases, the IS-LM description of an economy with money. These models are useful and informative but they do not adequately address current problems. The Keynesian cross model was designed to show how economic equilibrium is established and to teach us how we can shift that equilibrium in order to fight unemployment. This is the virtue of the model and also its chief vice: it is designed to help us understand how unemployment occurs. It tells little about inflation.

Today's students want to understand today's problems. They quickly become disillusioned with a macroeconomics course which fights unemployment for the most part and then, at the last minute, throws in a Phillips Curve as an explanation of the relationship between inflation and unemployment. When they press for more details, students are generally told that all of this is too complicated for an introductory course, but that their questions will be answered in the intermediate theory course next Fall.

The problem is that the teaching of macroeconomics has failed to keep pace with economic theory. While instructors and textbook authors have sought out new gimmicks to increase understanding of the traditional models, economists and policy-makers have found that new models are needed to deal with our changing economy. These more realistic and useful pictures of the economy have recently filtered down to the intermediate undergraduate level. The vast majority of undergraduate students, however, are left with the same *traditional* tools and topics that have been around for thirty years.

To really understand how the economy works, we must take into account both of our national economic problems: inflation and unemployment. This text accomplishes this by building a model of the national economy using a simplified version of the aggregate demand-aggregate supply analysis which is now widely used at the intermediate theory level. This model of the economy allows us to understand the causes and cures of inflation, and those of unemployment; to see clearly how these two problems are related and the nature of the trade-offs between them.

The second goal of this text is to make macroeconomics as understandable and exciting for students as it has always been for professors. Many texts make the error of presenting material in a way that prepares students for the next round of theory classes, but does little to help students understand the world today. This method may benefit the minority that go on in economics, but leaves the vast majority out in the cold. This text is written for the majority. Some students take only one class in macroeconomics. They will have just this one chance to really understand how the economy works. This text makes the most of that one chance. Macroeconomics is presented in a clear, readable form. The stress is on applications. Tools, problems, or theories which teach more geometry than economics have been scrapped or revised. The simplified picture of the economy that results actually contains more economics than is found in many more theoretically elegant treatments. The time saved in explaining geometry is efficiently used to discuss important topics in economics.

All of this may be good for the student who does not go into economics, but doesn't it harm the potential economics major? The answer here is a resounding ''NO''. Students who are exposed to this approach learn how the economy works and will understand the nature of our current economic problems. Students exposed to the traditional approach by and large have spent an apprenticeship in manipulating economic models. Both types of students tend to do well in later economics courses. The *traditional* students are equipped with manipulative skills which they can use to help them understand economic models. Students who have learned this newer approach have a better idea of where they are going, so they are better able to use the tools that they pick up along the way. These students are especially well equipped for intermediate theory courses which emphasize aggregate demand and supply.

ORGANIZATION OF THE TEXT

The text is divided into four parts. Most instructors will want to use material from each of the four parts, although individual chapters may be deleted and extra material added to fit the needs of the particular students or courses. In *Part I: Tools and Problems*, the reader is exposed to a discussion of our national economic problems and equipped with the basic tools of supply and demand for use in analyzing those problems. Chapter 1 presents an overview of macroeconomics and recent economic history, focusing on the changing relationship between inflation and unemployment. Chapter 2 develops the supply and demand model of market activity with emphasis on particular applications which will be seen again, in a different context, in later chapters. Chapter 3 looks at the problem of unemployment and attempts to determine what unemployment means, how it is caused, and how serious a problem it is. Chapter 4 ends the first part of the text with a discussion of the economic effects of inflation.

Part II: A Simple Model of the Economy constructs a simple but effective framework of analysis for use in understanding how the national economy works. Chapter 5 develops necessary definitions such as gross national product and Real GNP and shows how they can be used to measure economic activity. Chapter 6 discusses aggregate demand by looking at the circular flow of economic activity, the Keynesian income-expenditure analysis of national income and, finally, aggregate demand in a world that includes inflation. Chapter 7 develops the concept of aggregate supply and looks at how aggregate demand and aggregate supply can be used as a simple but powerful tool to unravel the causes of our economic problems. Chapter 8 examines fiscal policy and applies the aggregate demand-supply model to the analysis of governmental economic policies.

Part III: Money, Credit, and the Economy looks at the role of money in a modern economy. Chapter 9 presents the definitions of money and interest rates and describes the operation of fractional reserve banks. The credit market is introduced in Chapter 10. The determination of interest rates through the interaction of the demands and supplies for credit is discussed along with applications of this analysis to the real world. Chapter 11 compares monetary and fiscal policies and examines the impacts of different schemes for financing government spending. Finally, a simple model of the monetarist view of the economy is presented in Chapter 12. The conclusions of monetarist and traditional theories are compared and discussed.

Part IV: International Economics looks at length at the international forces affecting national economic problems and policies. Chapter 13 looks at international trade and payments. Comparative advantage, tariffs and quotas, and the Balance of Payments and Trade are discussed here. Chapter 14 models the foreign exchange markets and shows how exchange rates are determined. The systems of flexible and fixed exchange rates are discussed, as is exchange rate intervention. Chapter 15 evaluates the effectiveness of various national economic policies when their international impacts are taken into consideration. Chapter 16 ends the text with review of the goals and problems of the national economy and a reminder of the trade-offs that economic policy-makers face.

SPECIAL FEATURES OF THE TEXT

This text has several special features designed to make it more useful to both student and instructor. Eight economic debates are presented in the *Economic Controversies* sections. Here topics such as wage and price controls, the independence of the Federal Reserve, and the relative importance of fighting inflation versus controlling unemployment are debated, with the final analysis of the trade-offs left to the reader. These sections allow the student to apply the principles developed in past chapters to current problems and make good topics for class discussion.

Each chapter begins with a *Preview* which presents a number of questions that will be answered in the coming pages. This gives the student an idea of what is coming and what topics are central to the chapter.

Each chapter ends with a number of important features. A chapter *Summary* lets the reader check to see if all of the principal points of the text have been absorbed. *Discussion Questions* give the student the chance to think about the topics covered in greater depth. These questions provide, as well, a good basis for classroom discussions of the material. A number of objective questions are presented in *Test Yourself*. Answers to these sample questions are at the end of the text. *Suggestions for Further Reading* can also be found at the back of the book. Students who pursue the suggested reading will learn even more about how the economy works and the way that economists think. Instructors can vary the breadth and depth of their courses by use of these readings. A *Glossary* of all important terms appears at the back of the book as well.

These features of the text make it a self-contained guide to macroeconomics that can be used in a wide variety of classroom situations.

Part 1
Tools and Problems

1
Macroeconomic Problems

This chapter will introduce you to economics in general and macroeconomics in particular. It will give you a better feel for our current economic problems and help you understand these problems within a historical context. This chapter will provide the answers to the following important questions:

What is economics?

How does macroeconomics differ from microeconomics?

What are our current macroeconomic goals?

Have we been successful in achieving these goals?

What is the Phillips curve? How does it work?

Why hasn't the Phillips curve worked recently?

Many of our most important social problems are fundamentally economic problems. To understand the world and make intelligent choices, therefore, it is necessary to understand something of economics.

It is astounding to consider how much economic events have come to monopolize our time and influence our lives. The federal government was once primarily a lawmaker and defender. Now much of Congress's time is spent attempting to regulate prosperity and enhance economic welfare. Newspapers that used to count on stories of fires, murders, and kidnappings to increase circulation now rely on inflation predictions and unemployment statistics. Businesses that once spent all of their time worrying about gross profits now worry first about gross national product. Farmers are experts in exchange rates. Private citizens who five years ago didn't know the difference between a prime rate and a prime rib have discovered that they must master some pretty sophisticated economics in order to make even relatively simple decisions with confidence.

Economics is important stuff, and this book is designed to help you understand economic events and policies. It is the goal of this text to increase your understanding of our current economic problems, their causes, and some possible cures. Strong medicines, however, often have undesirable side effects, so a perfect prescription for the economy may not exist. Policies that reduce one economic problem may inflame another, be politically unwise, or have unacceptable social consequences. Pat answers are hard to come by, but an understanding of the options available will help us make more intelligent decisions in the choices that we face.

This chapter will answer some basic questions that many students have regarding economics and macroeconomics, and briefly discuss our national economic goals and problems. We will also take a short trip down memory lane with a small dose of recent economic history to help you understand not only what today's problems are, but how we got here as well.

WHAT IS ECONOMICS?

Suppose you were to pose the question "What is economics?" to a hundred "people on the street" in a major city in an attempt to find out what economics is all about. The results might be something like those shown in Table 1-1.

Most of the people in our hypothetical sample group don't have a very clear idea of what economics is all about. But as luck would have it, one economics professor stumbled into the sample and gave us the textbook

TABLE 1-1

WHAT IS ECONOMICS?

Response	Percentage responding
"Economics is the study of the production and distribution of goods and services in a world of scarce resources."	1
"Economics is like business—how to make a buck."	37
"Economics is all about inflation and unemployment and stuff like that."	23
"Economics is a bunch of charts and graphs."	18
"I really don't know."	15
"Leave me alone or I'll call a cop."	6

definition: "**Economics** is the study of how society chooses to produce and distribute goods and services in a world of scarce resources." Economics is essentially an analysis of choices. How does society choose what to produce and how to allocate the fruits of the production process? Since our resources are limited, we cannot produce all things or satisfy all desires. We face the problem of choice. Economics helps us understand these choices and the trade-offs that are made whenever a choice is made.

Economics: a social science dealing with the production and distribution of goods and services in a world of scarce resources

A lot of the people in our hypothetical poll thought that economics was basically business. In a sense, this answer is correct. In **market economies** like the United States, business firms make most of the production and distribution decisions. Their decisions are made in response to our wishes as expressed in the free market. If society wants skateboards instead of opera, then firms will respond to the profits available in skateboard production and the losses inherent in opera and allocate scarce resources so as to satisfy society's desires. We "vote" for what we want with our dollars in the market.

Market economy: an economic system where production and distribution decisions are made in decentralized markets

In a **command economy** this is not the case. A command economy is one where economic decision making is centralized in a group of planners, not decentralized among individuals and firms as in a market economy. In the command economy needs are decided and choices made by planners, and businesses act merely to carry out the "plan."

Command economy: an economy where production and distribution decisions are made by central planners

A number of people in our imaginary poll said that economics was the study of inflation and unemployment. This is true, too. Inflation and unemployment are the two most visible national economic problems that we face. Much of this book is devoted to an analysis of the causes and cures of inflation and unemployment.

Several people responded that economics is just a bunch of charts and graphs. These poor folks have obviously been exposed to a course in economics somewhere along the line. Economists love charts and graphs because economists love **models**. Economists use models to make the world more understandable. A model is just a simplification. By taking a complex process and reducing it to its simplest forms, we can usefully analyze the actions and interactions that are possible and likely. We can learn more from this simplified picture than we ever could by staring in confusion at the extremely complex processes that the model describes.

This book uses several models in its attempt to uncover the basic workings of the national economy. The first such model, the market model of supply and demand, appears in the next chapter. Our models, because they are simplifications, cannot embody all of the detail of the real world. Something is lost in the translation. But as we go along we will build on these simplifications until, at the end of the text, we will have a simple yet accurate model of the economic process.

Models: simplified descriptions of real-world processes designed to increase the understanding of real-world behavior

MACRO-VERSUS MICROECONOMICS

Microeconomics: the study of individual economic decisions focusing on markets, production, and consumer behavior

Trade-off: occurs when one item or goal must be given up in order to obtain another item or goal

Macroeconomics: the study of the functioning of the national economy

Microeconomics and macroeconomics are not two opposing schools of economics. Instead they are two different ways of viewing economic events.

Microeconomics focuses on individual decisions. Microeconomics asks questions like: How much should a firm produce and sell? What price will be charged? How much labor will the firm hire? How will consumers decide how much to spend and how much to save? The emphasis is on individual choices, the factors which influence these choices, and the **trade-offs** that must be made.

Macroeconomics, on the other hand, looks at the broad issues of the national economy. It examines not individual actions, but the combined impacts of these individual actions. Instead of asking how much an individual firm will sell, macroeconomics tries to determine how much the economy as a whole will produce and sell. Where microeconomics might be interested in what determines the price of oil and makes it rise or fall, macroeconomics is interested in what determines the general level of prices and causes inflation or deflation. Where microeconomics is interested in how many resources a single firm uses, macroeconomics is interested in the national employment and unemployment of resources.

Macro- and microeconomics have much in common; they focus on different parts of the same scene. Microeconomics looks at the trees, macroeconomics watches the forest. Each view is informative and useful. This book concentrates primarily on macroeconomics.

In 1946 Congress officially put the nation into the macroeconomics business. The Employment Act of 1946 set macroeconomic goals for the nation and made the federal government responsible for the achievement of those goals. The Act reads, in part:

The Congress hereby declares that it is the continuing policy and responsibility of the Federal Government to use all practicable means . . . to promote maximum employment, production, and purchasing power.

These goals are difficult to achieve and are sometimes mutually contradictory. We can restate these macroeconomic objectives as follows:

MACROECONOMICS GOALS AND PROBLEMS

GOAL 1: FULL EMPLOYMENT. The first aim of national economic policy is to attain high levels of employment (with resulting low unemployment rates). This is a difficult goal to achieve because unemployment is not a simple problem. The predicament of an out-of-work machinist is much different from that of an unskilled laborer or a college student just entering the job market. Each may be unemployed, but each is unemployed for a different reason. Since unemployment is really many different problems, not just one, it will require many different solutions. We will discuss the problem of unemployment at length in Chapter 3.

GOAL 2: ECONOMIC GROWTH. Full employment is a useless goal if these resources are not put to a productive use. The Depression "make-work" schemes (like digging ditches and then filling them in to provide work for desperate men) helped achieve our first goal, but added nothing to the economy. The economy must grow and production must rise, the Congress tells us, if we are to sustain our level of economic well-being. This goal translates to a goal of rising **real gross national product** (RGNP). Real GNP is a measure of the amount that an economy produces in a year. Economic growth (rising RGNP) may be the best way to improve the welfare of low-income groups within a nation. Studies have shown that the disadvantaged can best increase their share of the national pie when the entire pie is growing. In a growing economy, everyone's slice of the pie can increase at the same time. In a stagnant or shrinking economic world, some must lose so that others gain.

Real gross national product (RGNP): a measure of the total annual production in an economy; the GNP adjusted for inflation by use of the GNP Index

GOAL 3: STABLE PRICES. High employment and rising production may mean little if inflation erodes our gains. A condition of stable prices (low inflation) is clearly necessary in order to achieve the goal of "maximum purchasing power."

This goal is particularly troublesome to achieve. We may be able to directly achieve our first two goals of full employment and economic growth by, say, building hydroelectric dams (which lowers unemployment and increases electrical production), but if, in so doing, we cause prices to rise at a steep rate, how much have we gained?

Inflation is a serious problem because it affects us all. Inflation creates winners and losers and causes us to waste time trying to hedge or protect ourselves from its impact. We will discuss inflation's effects in Chapter 4.

How well have we achieved these macroeconomic goals? How are these goals related? To gain a better understanding of the goals and problems of macroeconomics, let us look at the record. Return with us now for those thrilling years of yesterday! The Lone Economist rides again!

THE GREAT DEPRESSION

Our look at economic history begins in 1929. Despite a fifty-year cushion, the year 1929 still brings to mind a vision of panic and desperation. Black Thursday! Investors leaping from skyscraper windows! Panic in the streets and on the stock exchange.

The year 1929 began the long period that we call the Great Depression. Between 1929 and 1933 real gross national product fell by over 29 percent while unemployment rates rose from 4 percent in 1929 to over 25 percent by 1933. Twenty-five percent unemployment!

We begin this look at economic history with the Great Depression because it was not until this time that macroeconomics was taken very seriously by economists and policy makers. Previously, many economists (the so-called classical economists) held that severe unemployment was unlikely or impossible since any idle worker could always find a job simply by offering to work for a few cents less than the next person. The national economy, it was supposed, was pretty much self-regulating. Macroeconomics was unnecessary.

With the Depression came the realization that the economy lacked a built-in governor and was as likely to proceed slowly (with substantial unemployment) as it was to run along at full steam.

What caused the Great Depression? No one thing, really, but a combination of events. The stock market crash started the process. Wall Street speculators had purchased large quantities of stock on credit. They planned to pay back the loans with the profits from their stock speculation. The only problem was that, if their speculations did not pay off, they had nothing left with which to pay their creditors. As the stock prices began to fall in 1929, these "margin" buyers found that they had to unload huge quantities of stock in order to pay their debts. This caused stock prices to fall further, creating problems for other speculators and, eventually, problems for the banks that had made the loans. It was a pyramid built on a risky, unstable foundation. As stock prices fell, the credit pyramid fell too.

Why was this so important? The stock market crash hurt a large number of people. First, the stock traders themselves were ruined. The banks and other lending institutions that had financed their speculation were weakened or went bankrupt. Thousands of individuals had invested their life savings in stock certificates. As stock prices fell, the value of their shares fell from tens of thousands of dollars to sometimes just a few cents.

The stock market crash made people poor. Their savings were gone, their stocks worthless or sold at distressed prices, their bank accounts often gone, too. They were poor, and they cut back their spending because of the hard times. As the victims of the stock crash spent less, they passed hard times on to the merchants and employers that they dealt with. Since less was being purchased, fewer workers were needed to produce goods and services. Unemployment hit new peaks and prices fell drastically. By 1933 prices were actually falling 5 percent per year.

President Franklin D. Roosevelt, according to popular belief, was

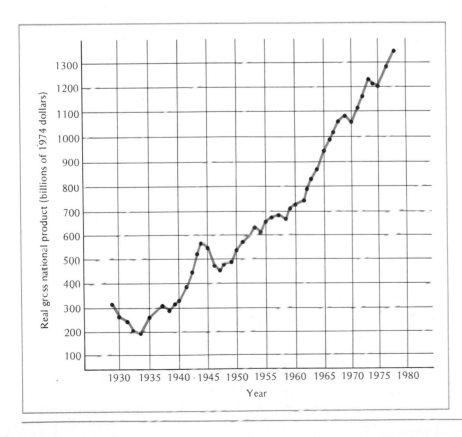

FIGURE 1-1: REAL GROSS NATIONAL PRODUCT, 1929–1977
RGNP increased dramatically over the period shown, but it was not a steady increase. RGNP fell during the 1930s and again immediately after World War II. The 1950s were a roller coaster, with RGNP rising and falling. The 1960s were the longest period of sustained growth in U.S. history. Recessions in the 1970s returned to the pattern of the 1950s, but the causes were different.

responsible for lifting the nation from the Great Depression. In 1933 he closed all the banks for seven days so that they might reopen on a more solid footing. His innovative government spending programs put the unemployed population back to work.

As is usually the case with popular beliefs, the view of FDR as the hero of the Depression is somewhat misleading. Roosevelt did begin and continue many worker programs, but these were more modest than is generally remembered. Roosevelt and the Congress actually strove to keep a balanced federal budget (whereas the prevailing wisdom today is that the federal government should run deficits—spend more than is received in taxes—during economic downturns).

By 1937, unemployment had fallen, but idled workers still amounted to 13 percent of the labor force. The Depression did not go away overnight, and might have lasted considerably longer had it not been for the Second World War. Figure 1-1, which shows RGNP from 1929 to 1977, gives a good picture of the state of the economy during this period.

THE FORTIES

In the 1940s a different economic problem plagued the United States. As production increased for the war effort, inflation became the economic enemy. It is easy to understand how prices could rise during the Second World War. Virtually all workers not in the armed forces were employed producing guns, tanks, and planes. Real gross national product rose to new heights. Workers found themselves with lots of income to spend but few consumer goods to buy, since most of the production was earmarked for the military. With lots of demand and little supply, prices rose and there were shortages of many items (beef, gasoline, rubber). To fight inflation, federal government wage and price controls were instituted and rationing schemes set up to handle the resultant shortages.

Real gross national product fell after 1945 as the country converted from high military output back to a more modest level of consumer production. This fall in production was to be expected. Production rose again in the late 1940s as the millions of dollars saved during wartime were spent on new houses, cars, and refrigerators. The postwar "baby boom" began and the country entered the 1950s.

THE FIFTIES

From an economic point of view, the 1950s are full of interest. Where the thirties were uniformly depressing, and the forties showed high levels of production, the fifties show us the phenomenon of the **business cycle**—

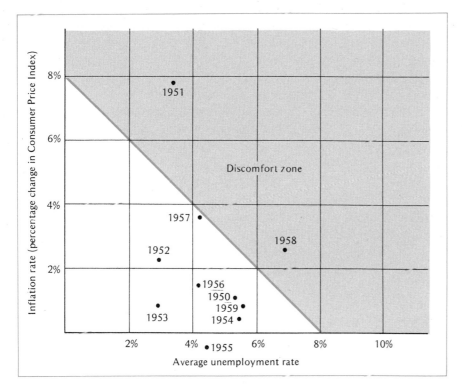

FIGURE 1-2: INFLATION AND
UNEMPLOYMENT, 1950–1959
*Unemployment was high during much
of the 1950s, as the economy twice hit
the bottom of the business cycle.
Inflation was generally low (prices
actually fell in 1955). The Economic
Discomfort Index only entered the
Discomfort Zone twice: in 1951
because of high inflation and in 1958
during the steel strike.*

boom followed by bust, advance by decline, in a regular and consistent cycle. The phenomenon of the business cycle can be seen by examining the path of RGNP in Figure 1-1. Although the overall trend during the 1950s was one of economic growth, **recessions** caused RGNP decline in 1954 and again in 1958.

It is also interesting to examine the progress made in achieving low unemployment rates along with stable prices during the 1950–1959 period. Figure 1-2 shows the inflation rate (the year-to-year change in the Consumer Price Index) plotted against the annual average unemployment rate for the years 1950–1959.

Economists use something called the **Economic Discomfort Index** as a simple way to determine how much "heat" the economy is feeling from its economic problems. Where meteorologists have a Weather Discomfort Index found by summing the temperature plus the relative humidity, economists add the inflation and unemployment rates. Figure 1-2 is divided into two "zones" according to the value of the Economic Discomfort Index—the sum of the inflation and unemployment rates. The area beneath the diagonal line marks off an area of "acceptable" economic performance (although the definition of "acceptable" is open to debate, so this line is

Business cycle: periods of economic expansion followed by high levels of unemployment

Recession: a sustained period of falling RGNP

Economic Discomfort Index: a measure of the magnitude of national economic problems; the sum of the inflation and unemployment rates

purely arbitrary), where the sum of the inflation plus unemployment rates falls in the range 0–8 percent. The second area, the Discomfort Zone, shows those areas where the sum of inflation plus unemployment exceeds 8 percent. When the economy moves into this range, the Economic Discomfort Index is high enough to cause economic and political unrest.

As Figure 1-2 shows, inflation was low and unemployment relatively high during much of the 1950s. Twice, in 1951 and again in 1958, the economy moved into the Discomfort Zone. The cause in 1951 was the high inflation of the Korean War. The cure, to bring inflation back to an acceptable level, was a small dose of wage and price controls. In 1958, the economy was disrupted by a long steel strike which created high levels of unemployment.

The period 1950–1959 was a time of cycles. RGNP rose and fell. The economy moved in and out of the Discomfort Zone with some regularity.

THE SIXTIES

The 1960s present another picture entirely. The sixties were the longest period of sustained economic growth in our history. Figure 1-1 shows that RGNP grew every year during the period 1960–1969 (it also grew in 1959,

FIGURE 1-3: INFLATION AND UNEMPLOYMENT, 1960–1969
The 1960s demonstrated the trade-off between inflation and unemployment. The first half of the decade showed relatively high unemployment, but moderate inflation. As the unemployment rate fell during 1965–1969, the pace of inflation quickened.

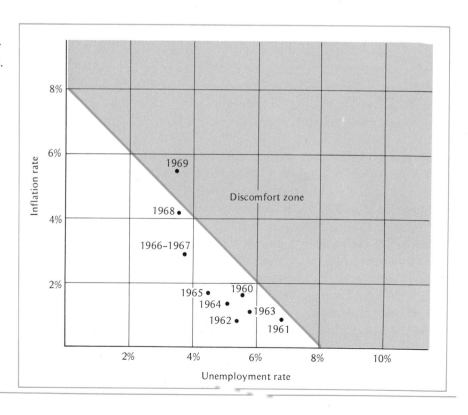

giving a total of eleven years of expansion, but fell in 1970 to end the trend). Real gross national product grew by a total of over 46 percent during the decade. Production rose to satisfy a variety of wants. Consumer spending was high. Government spending on defense materials (for the Vietnam War) and social programs (John Kennedy's New Frontier followed by Lyndon Johnson's Great Society) grew at record rates. The unemployment rate fell to, and then *below*, the target rate of 4 percent.

The economy also managed to stay out of the Discomfort Zone for most of the decade, as shown in Figure 1-3. Only in 1969—when the combination of high defense spending and government spending on social programs finally brought on high inflation—did the Discomfort Index exceed 8 percent.

Economic policy makers made use of a peculiar phenomenon in the sixties. Draw a curve through the points in Figure 1-3. Notice that most of the years fall very close to this line. There appears to be a stable inverse relationship between inflation and unemployment during the 1960s. This relationship is called a **Phillips Curve**, after the British economist A. W. Phillips, who discovered the relationship in the late 1950s.

Phillips Curve: a curve showing an inverse relationship between inflation and unemployment

THE PHILLIPS CURVE

The Phillips Curve, as illustrated in Figure 1-4, suggests that there is a stable short-run trade-off between inflation and unemployment in a modern economy. When actions are taken to reduce unemployment, the trade-off suggests, inflation will result as a side effect. And inflation can be fought only if we are willing to accept higher unemployment rates at the same time.

How does this trade-off take place? The probable basis for the Phillips Curve is something called the **wage-lag theory**. As inflation occurs, this theory states, wage rates do not increase as fast as prices, since wage contracts are negotiated in cycles while prices are free to rise anytime. As a result, inflation tends to temporarily increase producer profits. The price of output rises due to inflation, but worker wages temporarily lag behind, making labor a bargain for employers. As inflation boosts the prices of output, businesses take advantage of the wage lag and hire more workers. Rising inflation rates therefore cause unemployment to fall.

When the inflation rate falls, just the opposite effect is felt. The wage lag works in reverse, and falling inflation rates cause employers to lay off workers, producing higher unemployment rates.

This kind of economic behavior gives us the Phillips Curve, which very well describes the 1960s. As the inflation rate rose in the late 1960s, unemployment fell to levels not seen in years.

The success of the Phillips Curve relationship in the 1960s made

Wage-lag theory: holds that prices rise faster than wages, temporarily increasing employer profits and therefore inducing employers to hire more workers

FIGURE 1-4: THE PHILLIPS CURVE, 1960–1969
The inflation-unemployment trade-off between 1960 and 1969 is shown above. Policy makers believed that the trade-off was stable and that by properly playing inflation against unemployment, it was possible to "fine-tune" the economy and keep it on the Phillips Curve, but out of the Discomfort Zone shown above.

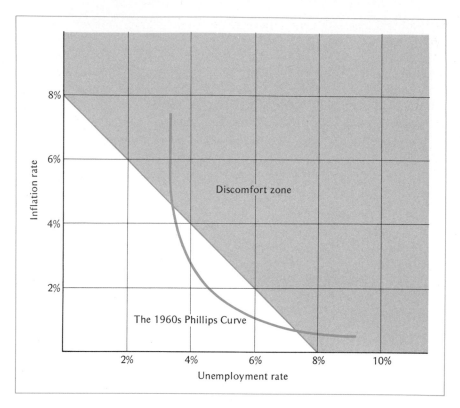

economic policy makers confident that they could manage prosperity. Sustained economic growth was possible, they maintained, and the Discomfort Zone could be avoided if they could "fine-tune" the economy by taking advantage of the Phillips Curve trade-offs. Playing unemployment against inflation could not relieve us of both problems at once, but it would assure us of only moderate levels of each and rapid economic growth in the bargain.

THE SEVENTIES

The 1970s spelled the end of blind faith in the Phillips Curve. The 1970 recession combined high unemployment rates with high inflation rates. The Economic Discomfort Index rose to levels not seen since 1951. The high inflation rates refused to fall even in the face of heavy unemployment. This caused President Richard Nixon to resort, in August 1971, to a general price freeze followed by programs of wage and price controls. These controls caused price increases to moderate during 1972, but did little to alter the public's expectations of inflation. When people expect inflation, they generally get it (see Chapter 4 for more details on inflationary expectations). Inflation in 1973 returned to a rate of over 6 percent.

Stagflation, which is the combination of high unemployment and high inflation, hit with full force in 1974. Many factors contributed to the rise of stagflation. The devaluation of the dollar made imported goods more expensive. Worldwide crop failures drove up the prices of agricultural products. And, not incidentally, the Organization of Petroleum Exporting Countries (OPEC) boosted the world price of crude oil and imposed an embargo on oil shipments to the United States.

All of this had two kinds of impacts on the economy. The first effect was on prices: they rose at unprecedented rates. The Consumer Price Index jumped over 10 percent—entering the dreaded "double-digit inflation" zone. As prices climbed, consumers found that their incomes were not keeping pace with the price increases. Consumer purchasing power declined considerably, causing people to cut back on spending. Cars were fixed up to last one or two more years instead of being traded in on a new model. Purchases of durable goods like freezers and furniture were put off, too. Purchases of many luxury and some necessity items were cut back.

As consumers bought less, industry found that it needed fewer workers because it was producing fewer goods. Layoffs and unemployment occurred, compounding the spending decline. The high prices caused not economic growth, as the Phillips Curve suggested, but recession.

Stagflation: high inflation rates accompanied by high unemployment rates; a stagnant economy with inflation

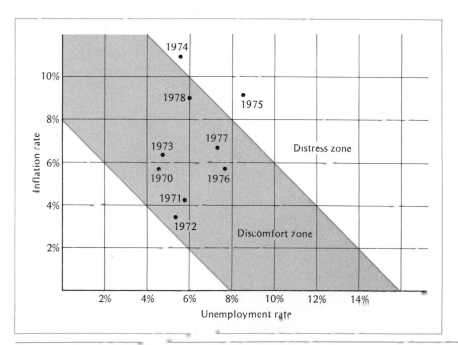

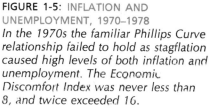

FIGURE 1-5: INFLATION AND UNEMPLOYMENT, 1970–1978
In the 1970s the familiar Phillips Curve relationship failed to hold as stagflation caused high levels of both inflation and unemployment. The Economic Discomfort Index was never less than 8, and twice exceeded 16.

The actions of OPEC not only sent prices skyrocketing, but also resulted in a physical shortage of oil and oil products. Long waits in line for gasoline were only a small part of the problem. Many plants and factories were forced to shut down because of a lack of oil for use as an energy source or raw material. Some coal mines, for example, had to close during the peak of the energy crisis, when the demand for coal was rising, because they could not get gas and oil to run their mining equipment. At hospitals, surgery had to be postponed or cancelled because latex surgical tubing (made from oil products) was not available. The list of disruptions caused by the shortages of oil and related products goes on and on.

The stagflation caused by rising prices coupled with physical shortages boosted the economy out of the Discomfort Zone and into the Distress Zone (going nearly into the Twilight Zone). For a few months, the Discomfort Index soared to over 20 (in July 1975, inflation ran at almost 12 percent, while unemployment approached 9 percent).

Clearly, something had to be done. President Gerald Ford fought inflation with his WIN (Whip Inflation Now) program of voluntary restraints and battled unemployment by giving tax rebates to encourage consumer spending. These programs helped a little, bringing us back into the Discomfort Zone in Figure 1-5, but leaving the economy in a still very disturbed state.

The Carter administration managed to reduce the unemployment rate somewhat, but inflation nevertheless increased. Stagflation was still a very real economic problem.

WHAT HAPPENED TO THE PHILLIPS CURVE?

The comfortable policy recommendations of the 1960s' Phillips Curve seemed to stop working in the 1970s. What happened to the Phillips Curve? Many theories have been put forth to explain the disappearance of the inflation-unemployment trade-off. Two of these theories are the following:

1. The Phillips Curve-type of inflation encountered in the 1960s was based on rising demand ("demand-pull" inflation), whereas the inflation of the 1970s was caused largely by rising costs of production resulting from devaluation, soaring oil prices, and other factors ("cost-push" inflation). Rising demand in the 1960s caused higher prices which, through the wage-lag mechanism, caused employment to rise too. But in the 1970s, rising costs forced firms to cut back production in order to stay in business. Prices rose, but production and employment actually fell as a result.

This cost-push kind of inflation does not obey the Phillips Curve rules, and so the Phillips Curve trade-offs, although still possible in the right situation, were not apparent in the 1970s.

2. Another explanation for the disappearance of the Phillips Curve has to do with the role of expectations in economic decisions. The wage-lag theory, which gives us the Phillips Curve phenomenon, is based on the concept of *unexpected* inflation causing the wage lag and inducing employers to hire more labor. If the inflation is fully anticipated, however, the wage-lag concept may break down.

Suppose, for example, that both employers and workers expect the inflation rate to be 6 percent next year. Then it is likely that a 6 percent wage increase will be built into pay agreements in anticipation of future price increases. If the inflation rate actually turns out to be 6 percent, there is no reason for employment to increase. Wages have not lagged because the inflation was expected. If, on the other hand, the inflation rate for the year turns out to be 10 percent, then the wage-lag concept holds and employment can be expected to rise. The wage-lag phenomenon, then, depends on workers being fooled so that their wages lag behind the "surprise inflation." If workers are more sophisticated about rising prices now, then it may be harder to fool them.

Once people have become accustomed to a certain rate of inflation and expect it to continue, continually higher inflation rates become necessary in order to fight unemployment. If today's inflation rate is 6 percent, prices must rise by 8 or 10 percent before the wage-lag effect will cause the unemployment rate to fall.

This may have caused the disappearance of the Phillips Curve in the early 1970s. As people became more sophisticated about inflation and adjusted their expectations of future price increases, it took higher and higher actual inflation rates to bring unemployment down even a little (examine Figure 1-5 for evidence of this idea).

The Phillips Curve may not be dead, but it is clear that the inflation-unemployment trade-off is not as clearly defined as economists once thought.

The economy is not as easy to manage or describe as it once was. The magic formula of the Phillips Curve no longer holds with accuracy. Economic policy is harder to undertake for a variety of reasons. Consumers, investors, businesses, and labor are now more sophisticated. They hedge, act, and react in response to news and expectations about wages, prices, and governmental policy. This makes prosperity even harder to regulate. The international economy now has a more important effect than ever before on

THE EIGHTIES AND BEYOND

domestic economic well-being. What goes on in Tokyo, Bonn, or Tehran can have an immediate impact in Tulsa, Boston, or Tacoma. Inflation and unemployment now occur together, and policy trade-offs are now harder to make.

Macroeconomics in the 1980s and beyond is a study of a complicated, interrelated world trying to achieve goals which may be mutually inconsistent. Stagflation is the enemy and understanding is our best weapon. It is in this setting that our study begins.

SUMMARY

1. Economics is the study of how society chooses to allocate scarce resources to the production and distribution of goods and services.

2. Macroeconomics is the study of the way the national economy works. Macroeconomics is interested in what determines the amount of total production and the general level of prices. Microeconomics is the study of individual economic decisions. Microeconomics is interested in how individual households, firms, and workers decide how much to produce and spend, and how prices are determined.

3. The Employment Act of 1946 specified three national economic goals: full employment, economic growth, and price stability. These goals are interrelated and difficult to achieve.

4. The economy's track record is not good in achieving the three macroeconomic goals. Recessions have lowered growth rates and caused high unemployment. Inflation has become more, not less, of a problem.

During the 1970s stagflation—the combination of high inflation and high unemployment—moved us even farther away from the goals Congress outlined in 1946.

5. The Phillips Curve shows a historical relationship between inflation and unemployment. The Phillips Curve derives from the wage-lag theory of employment that holds that inflation increases the supply of jobs because wages tend to remain constant while output prices rise. This increases producer profits and promotes higher production and therefore greater employment. When inflation rates rise in this setting, unemployment drops.

6. The Phillips Curve has not lived up to its reputation in recent years. One explanation is that inflation these days may be caused by rising costs, not rising demand. Another explanation is that workers have become too sophisticated to be fooled by the "surprise inflation" necessary for the wage-lag theory to work.

DISCUSSION QUESTIONS

DISCUSSION QUESTIONS

1. What is currently happening to the economy? What is the inflation rate? What is the unemployment rate? What is the level of the Economic Discomfort Index? Is real GNP rising or falling?

2. Where can you go to find out what is happening in the economy? What publications are available? Where are they found in the library?

3. Do you think that we could have another Great Depression today? Why or why not?

4. Does the Phillips Curve still work? How can you determine if an economic theory is valid or not?

5. Who are the important people or groups who make economic policy? What offices do they hold? Are they appointed or elected? What are their political or economic philosophies?

6. What economic policies does the U.S. president currently endorse? Are these policies primarily designed to fight inflation or unemployment?

TEST YOURSELF

State whether the following statements are *true* or *false*. Be able to defend your choice in each case.

1. The Great Depression was caused in part by the rapid inflation of the 1930s.

2. The high employment levels of the World War II period caused shortages of basic commodities. Rationing was necessary in order to keep prices down.

3. Achieving an equitable distribution of income is not one of our "official" national economic goals.

4. The ups and downs of the 1950s' business cycles were predictable and not caused by unforseen economic events.

5. Inflation reduces business profits through the wage-lag phenomenon.

6. The Phillips Curve suggests that it is possible to reduce both inflation and unemployment at the same time.

7. The Phillips Curve accurately described the economic events of the 1950s.

8. The Phillips Curve accurately described the economic events of the 1960s.

9. The Phillips Curve accurately described the economic events of the 1970s.

10. The 1960s was the longest period of sustained economic growth in modern U.S. economic history.

ECONOMIC CONTROVERSIES I: ANOTHER GREAT DEPRESSION?

The 1930s taught politicians, economists, businessmen and women, and workers that a modern economy is not immune from severe economic problems. Catastrophic levels of unemployment are possible. Nothing automatically assures full or even high employment. Since the Great Depression, the economy has experienced several lesser economic downturns. The 1950s gave evidence of a business cycle and the 1970s have taught us, again, that continued prosperity is not always in the cards.

Can we manage prosperity? Is another Great Depression possible? Is it likely? Can it be avoided? These are questions that economists have often debated. In these "Economic Controversies" sections we will present both sides of this and other economic debates and then leave it to the reader to draw conclusions.

Is another Great Depression around the corner? Let's look at both sides of the argument.

THE COMING BUST

One side of this debate argues as follows. Cycles of boom and bust may not be inevitable, but they certainly have been a frequent part of the economic scene and, except for war years, recessions have been as frequent an economic state as has prosperity. A major depression in the future is very likely. There are many reasons for this suspicion.

One set of factors which contributes to the likelihood of a future depression has to do with the way that economic policy is made in the United States. The president,

the Congress, and the Federal Reserve's decision makers are essentially not economic actors, but reactors. That is, they do not take actions designed to affect coming economic events, but rather wait until problems are upon us and then react to them. This creates a dangerous policy lag. For example, instead of taking actions which would prevent inflation, they wait until inflation is here and then push the economy into a recession with anti-inflation policies. When the recession comes around, they inflate prices in trying to boost employment back up. This gives us the boom-bust cycle which has been so common in nonwar years.

Recently the boom-bust cycle has increased in magnitude. Inflation rates are high by historical standards these days, and unemployment is a serious problem, too. In fighting these economic ills, the policy makers are likely to ride an increasingly unstable roller coaster of policy actions until, predictably, the economy is thrown into a major depression.

If this scenario is not enough to make one nervous, recent economic events (calls for balanced budgets, protectionist moves for trade restrictions) mirror, in many ways, the events which helped launch the Great Depression of the 1930s.

The economy could easily be pushed into such a depression by any of a number of "exogenous shocks" that are likely to happen. The term *exogenous shock* refers to some unexpected event which suddenly throws a monkey wrench into the economic works. The 1950s' steel strike was one such "shock," and shocks in the future, although difficult to anticipate, are likely to happen with some frequency. And our system is not well equipped to deal with them. Policy makers respond only slowly to such problems, with the result that the problem can have severe consequences. During the 1970s' oil embargo, for example, policy makers, instead of formulating policies which would moderate the impact of oil shortages and price increases, spent a lot of time holding hearings to find out if there was really an "energy crisis" or if it was just dreamed up by the oil companies to boost profits.

The final reason for believing that a major depression is just around the corner is that inflation is becoming more and more of a problem—a problem that we are finding increasingly difficult to deal with. This presents two dangers. First, the government may intentionally throw the nation into a depression in an attempt to fight high inflation rates. This may sound improbable, but policy makers at the Federal Reserve talk about it as a real possibility.

If the inflation is left unchecked, however, depression is just as likely. Hyperinflation (very high rates of inflation) spells an end to the modern economic system. When inflation is left to compound rapidly, money becomes worthless, making work a fruitless exercise. Without any incentive to produce, but with prices rising rapidly, the economy could quickly reach a

critical mass and literally explode. It has happened before and it is not unreasonable to conclude that it is happening today.

WE CAN MANAGE PROSPERITY

An argument on the other side of this question might go as follows. The prophets of gloom and doom (whose answer to economic problems is to buy cabins in the wilderness stocked with gold and beans in which to wait out the death of modern society) are wrong. To paraphrase Mark Twain, the rumors of the economy's death are much exaggerated. We can manage prosperity, and there is no reason to believe that a depression is on the way.

We shouldn't judge our ability to meet the problems of the economy today by what happened in the 1930s. Economic policy mistakes were clearly made, but we have learned from them. We have read our history books and need not repeat past errors.

We are better able now to deal with our economic problems. For one thing, we now have more sophisticated tools to use in measuring the health of the economy. Econometric computer models of the nation can tell us in advance what is going to happen so that we can deal with problems before they hit us. These predictions of the future are now much used in making economic policy.

We have also responded to the Great Depression by enacting a number of programs which automatically compensate for economic events. The welfare system, unemployment compensation, Social Security payments, countercyclic government grants—all of these "automatic stabilizers" were either nonexistent or less powerful during the Great Depression. Now these programs and others act to automatically reduce the magnitude of any turn in the economy. Automatic programs have lessened the fluctuations in the business cycle and give policy makers the time they need to take wise policy actions.

Our economic system may not be "fail-safe," but it is unlikely to plunge into another depression, either. The economic doomsters don't give policy makers enough credit for knowing what they are doing. Intelligent people making responsible policies can lead the economy to prosperity or, at least, away from depression. Neither do they give the economy enough credit for stability. Our economy is strong and growing. Even if policy makers were as ignorant as the doom-sayers suggest, the basic strength of the economy would probably prevail anyway.

DISCUSSION QUESTIONS

1. Which side of this debate makes more sense to you? Do you see any evidence that we are heading for another Great Depression?

2. If the doom-sayers are correct and a depression is on the way, how could you protect yourself from it? What actions could you take that would minimize the depression's impact on your family? Would these actions make sense if the depression did not come?

3. Can you find evidence to support either argument in the description of recent economic history presented in Chapter 1?

2
Supply and Demand

This chapter constructs one of the most basic of all economic tools: the supply-and-demand model of how markets operate, prices are set, and prices are changed. When finished with this chapter, you should be able to answer the following questions:

What is meant by "demand"?

What factors determine the amounts of goods and services that people demand?

What is meant by "supply"?

What factors determine the quantities supplied?

What is the equilibrium price?

What forces can make prices change?

Why do prices rise?

What is a price ceiling, and what impact does it have on the market?

The beauty of economics is its simplicity. It is at once simple and sophisticated. Economic tools are a lot like the Tinker Toys that you might have played with as a child. Endlessly complicated structures can be built using only a few simple building blocks and some rules concerning how they should be connected. In this chapter we will construct a basic building block of the economist's trade and use it to examine some economic problems.

The analysis of supply and demand occupies a central place in economics. This was demonstrated by the Central Intelligence Agency in the early 1970s. Informed sources report that, in an attempt to gain an advantage in the international espionage game, the CIA decided to enlist the forces of economics on their side (the CIA denies this, of course). Since economics plays such an important role in world decision making, the CIA reasoned that it would be a great advantage to know in advance what was happening to economies around the world. With this in mind, they acquired an extremely powerful electronic computer and set it up, under a curtain of secrecy, beneath the stands of the Purdue University football stadium.

There, surrounded by security guards, CIA agents fed into the electronic brain the economic wisdom of the centuries. Adam Smith, Keynes, Friedman, Samuelson—all of their profound thoughts were carefully programmed into the huge mechanical memory.

The top-secret program was a failure, however. When the moment of truth came; when all of the wisdom of the economics profession had been pumped into the computer, a lone CIA agent asked the fateful question, "What makes the economy run?"

The computer whizzed, burped, and blinked for an hour, and then produced a one-line answer: "Demand and supply always apply."

Market: general term describing the economic institutions where exchanges of goods and services are made

Supply and demand are tools in our attempt to construct a model which describes the way that **markets** work. Markets are economic institutions where goods and services are exchanged. All of us are actively involved in markets. We purchase most of the things that we eat, drink, wear, read, and use in the market for goods and services. We earn income through our participation in the labor market. Financial and equity markets allow us to earn a return on savings. The term *market* is not meant to suggest a specific geographic location where an actual market exists (as, for example, the stock market on Wall Street in New York). The market is simply the collection of all transactions (exchanges) involving a specific good wherever and whenever these transactions take place. Markets allow us to make mutually advantageous exchanges effectively and efficiently.

The basic motivations in a market are conflict and competition. Conflict arises because the two basic sides of the market process have different ends in mind. Sellers (the supply side of the market) are interested in gaining profits which provide them with higher income and allow them to expand their businesses or attract new investors. They are interested in getting the highest possible price for the goods or services that they offer for sale.

Buyers (the demand side of the market) are interested in just the opposite result. They wish to pay the lowest possible price for the goods that they buy. A high price means that they are less able to afford both the good in question and other goods that they must buy. High prices hurt buyers, like business firms, that are also sellers. A farmer, for example, who pays high prices for fertilizer finds his enterprise less profitable than one who purchases fertilizer at a discount. We are all interested in buying cheap and selling dear.

As sellers push for the highest possible price and buyers lobby for bargains, the resulting conflict is resolved only because of the second characteristic of the market: competition.

Both buyers and sellers face competition. A seller who asks too high a price will find himself without customers if other sellers are willing to charge less. Each seller's livelihood is threatened by every other seller. Producers must grasp for any advantage. Often they will try to lure customers by offering goods of a higher quality than those produced by competitors. More often the competition focuses on price.

Buyers, too, face rivals. Goods which are scarce will go to the highest bidder. Individuals who are unable or unwilling to back up their desires with dollars will find themselves "allocated out" of the market. Goods and services will flow where their value (price) is highest. Therefore, prices tend to rise when goods are scarce, and goods in abundance will be cheaper since the competition will bid the price down. This explains why Christmas trees are fairly expensive two weeks before the holiday and cheap two weeks after.

The combination of competition and conflict makes the market work. Sellers attempt to get the highest possible price for their wares, while noting that, if the price is too high, competitors will get all the sales. Buyers haggle to find bargains, but must be aware that the goods will, in the end, go to the highest bidder. These forces set most of the prices that we pay. (In some markets competition breaks down as, for example, when monopolies or governmental price controls exist.) Let us examine these market forces in detail.

Demand: description of the buyer side of the market; examines how the amounts and kinds of goods and services people wish to buy are determined

Demand is the easiest side of the market for most of us to see because this is the part where we seem to be most actively involved. By *demand* we mean a total description of how people feel about the things that they buy—and how these feelings determine how much of any particular good that they

THE CONCEPT OF DEMAND

desire to purchase. Demand, then, is not a purely economic phenomenon. Psychology, sociology, and information theory all are involved in our concept of demand. So are many other, seemingly unrelated factors.

Since demand is such a broad concept, it is useful to begin to simplify it from the start. Demand depends on a virtually endless number of things, but the following list of five determinants of demand will cover most of the important ideas.

1. PRICE.

How much of an item that we wish to purchase depends very much on the price of that item. The price determines how much we can afford to purchase within our budget, and allows comparison with other goods at other prices which may be desired as well. In general, the amount that we wish to purchase is inversely related to the price of the good. That is to say, when prices are low, we respond to the cheap price to purchase more. High prices cause purchases to fall.

The reason for this **inverse relationship** between price and the amount desired is not hard to imagine. Two factors influence the individual purchaser's decisions. The first is that, as the price of any one good rises, consumers tend to buy less of that good and shift purchases to other items that are not rising in price so much. This is called the **substitution effect**, and we see it all around us. In 1976–1977, when coffee prices went through the roof, people cut back on coffee purchases and substituted tea and grain beverages.

Rising prices also cause people to buy less of goods in general because their purchasing power falls—they can't afford to buy as much. This is the **income effect**.

When the price of an item falls, on the other hand, the substitution and income effects cause the amount desired to rise. People tend to substitute cheaper goods for more expensive ones (substitution effect) and will buy more (income effect) because they can afford more at the cheaper price than at the old expensive one.

For these reasons, high prices cause the amount of intended purchases to be low, and low prices cause buyers to demand more goods.

2. INCOME.

Another factor that is as basic to our buying decisions as price is income. In general, the more income we have, the more of any particular item we like to purchase—thus there is a **direct relationship** between income and quantity desired.

There are, of course, a few items concerning which we behave differently. These items are said to have a **negative income effect** in that, as income rises, our desired purchases fall, and vice versa. These goods have low social status or an aura of cheapness. Beans, for example, are

---

Inverse relationship: the relationship that exists between A and B if an increase in A results in a decrease in B (A and B move in opposite directions)

Substitution effect: changes in demand behavior which result from changing prices; as prices change buyers substitute more of relatively cheaper goods and buy less of those with relatively higher prices

Income effect: changes in demand behavior which result from changing prices; as the price of an individual good rises (or falls) buyers find that their fixed incomes are less (or more) able to purchase that good and all others

Direct relationship: the relationship that exists between A and B if they increase or decrease together; that is, an increase in A implies an increase in B

Negative income effect: less demand for a product as a result of an increase in income

purchased less frequently as income rises. Inexpensive subcompact cars also are purchased less, not more, as income rises. When income falls, on the other hand, we tend to buy somewhat more of these inferior goods.

Most goods and services are "normal," however, in that our desire for them responds positively to increases in our purchasing power.

3. PRICES OF OTHER GOODS. The way we feel about buying one item is heavily influenced by the prices of all of the other goods and services available to us. The concept of choice is apparent here. With limited income, the purchase of one item dictates the nonpurchase of something else (the existence of credit only expands this trade-off over a longer time period). Since we must weigh the desirability of each good against all the others, any change in the price of a good alters the delicate balance which has been established.

Some types of goods and services we classify as **substitutes**. Substitutes are goods which satisfy the same need or desire. Water, coffee, tea, and beer are, for example, substitutes for one another (to a greater or lesser extent) since all satisfy our thirst. Fords and Chevys are substitute forms of transportation. Houses and apartments, while different in many respects, are substitute forms of shelter.

> **Substitutes:** goods which perform the same function (e.g., coffee and tea, pens and pencils)

The amount of a good that we wish to purchase tends to vary directly with the price of its substitutes. Thus, for example, the amount of Coke we desire declines if the price of Pepsi falls, and rises if Pepsi becomes more expensive. As the price of the substitute falls, we switch our purchases to the cheaper item. This switching of purchases is strong among goods that are the most alike in their ability to satisfy our desires, and weak among goods which are imperfect substitutes for one another.

Other goods are **complements**—they are used together to satisfy some want or need. The list of complements is endless: bread and butter, toast and jam, or bacon and eggs (just for breakfast), as well as pencils and erasers and economics books and aspirins.

> **Complement:** goods which are used together (e.g., toast and jam, coffee and sugar)

The basic idea of complementarity is that, since the goods are used together, our desire for the two goods rises and falls together, too. When the price of bacon falls, for example, the amount of eggs that are purchased rises since the two are often consumed together. If eggs were to become more expensive, however, less bacon might be sold. There is, then, an inverse relationship between the amount of a particular good that we want and the price of its complementary good or goods.

Merchants, of course, take advantage of the relationship among complements. Stores often put some particular item on sale at a lower price (like, for example, wall paint) in the hope of selling more of the complementary items (brushes, rollers, dropcloths) at their regular prices.

Some sets of complementary goods are not so obvious as those noted above. During the energy crunch of 1973–1974, for example, Big Mac hamburgers were found to be complements of gasoline. How? It turns out that most people use cars to get to fast-food stores. With gasoline expensive and scarce, the number of such hamburger runs was reduced and Ronald McDonald suffered!

4. TASTES AND PREFERENCES. Changes in the nature of our desires (what we want, when we want it, what is fashionable) will have a very direct impact on the kinds and amounts of goods that we wish to buy. As tastes and preferences change, our purchases will change as well.

Sometimes our desires change very gradually. Blue jeans, for example, were once worn largely by workmen who needed the strength and durability of that kind of pants. Slowly, blue jeans gained acceptance among social and economic groups that had previously shunned them. Finally, they became almost a uniform for young people and eventually even appeared in the White House.

But changes in tastes and preferences can be rapid, too. A few years ago a certain type of commercial bread was introduced that claimed to provide fewer calories and more "fiber" per slice than its competitors. People decided that they liked low-calorie fiber, and so sales of that brand of bread quickly increased until it was just about the best-selling bread in the country. Then, however, it was disclosed that the reason that the bread had so much fiber and so few calories was that a key ingredient was a nutritional-quality cellulose fiber which was derived, basically, from sawdust. Sawdust in bread? People got turned off to the idea as quickly as they had embraced it, and the amount sold fell with a splat! As people obtained more information about the product, their taste for it changed.

A similar situation prevailed concerning a brand of bubble gum that was introduced in the 1970s. Small children loved the stuff because it was juicy and made large messes when the bubbles popped. Then, inexplicably, a rumor started that the secret magic ingredient in the gum was spiders' eggs. Spiders' eggs? No, the rumor wasn't true, but that didn't matter. The claim spread kid-to-kid (and mother-to-mother) across the country, and the demand for the gum disappeared.

Most changes in tastes and preferences are less abrupt than these, but may occur for some of the same reasons. As people acquire new information about products, or as styles and living fashions change, the amounts of many different goods purchased can be expected to change as well.

5. EVERYTHING ELSE. Everything else? Sure. A whole world of things can affect our demand for goods and services. Weather, for example. The demand for umbrellas, snow tires, suntan oil, and irrigation water are affected by changes in the weather in fairly obvious ways. Your economics professor is another example of an "everything else." The amounts and kinds of textbooks, tutorial assistance, electricity (for late-night study) and No-Doz tablets you demand all depend on the sort of punishment that your prof decides to inflict on you. An old saying notes that everything, in the end, depends on everything else. It's true in economics, too.

THE DEMAND CURVE

The five factors discussed above describe the general concept of demand. Unfortunately, in reality demand is too complicated a concept to use directly to analyze problems that may occur in the market. For this reason, the concept of demand is simplified by use of a graphical tool: the **demand curve**.

Demand curve: a curve which shows the quantity of a good or service that buyers wish to purchase at every possible price

The demand curve maps the way the quantity demanded of a particular good varies as the price of the good varies. For simplicity, it is assumed that, for a moment, income, the prices of all other goods, tastes and preferences, and (naturally) everything else are fixed or held constant. Then, in this relative vacuum, the effects of just price changes on the quantity demanded can be examined.

A hypothetical demand curve for apples is shown in Figure 2-1. This

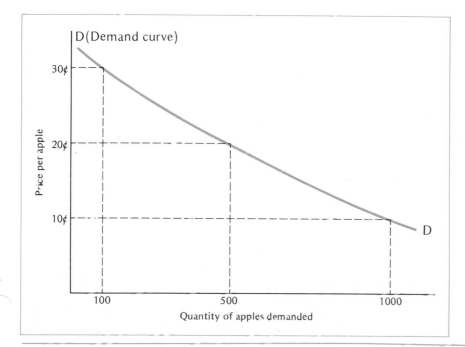

FIGURE 2-1: A DEMAND CURVE FOR APPLES

As the price of apples falls from 30¢ to 10¢, the quantity of apples that people want to purchase increases as the income effect (they can afford to purchase more apples when they cost less) and substitution effect (they substitute cheap apples for more expensive alternative foods) takes place. The demand curve shows the quantity demanded at every price.

graph shows the amount of apples that people wish to purchase at any given price. Such a demand curve could actually be constructed by polling consumers in an area to determine what their likely behavior would be at different apple prices. Whether it is actually compiled and graphed this way or not, however, the demand curve still exists in the sense that the behavior suggested by the demand curve exists.

The demand curve in Figure 2-1 shows that at a relatively low price for apples of 10¢ each, there will be a relatively large quantity of apples demanded—1000 apples. As the price of apples rises to 20¢, fewer apples are sold (only 500). The reasons for this are clear. At 20¢ per apple, some people cannot afford to purchase as many apples as before. They may substitute other foods for the now-more-expensive apples. Or they simply may not be willing to spend that much on apples and so voluntarily withdraw from the market. Essentially, people will only pay 20¢ for an apple if they feel that they get at least 20¢ worth of satisfaction from it. The falling quantity demanded here indicates that only 500 apples give people at least 20¢ worth of satisfaction, while 1000 apples were considered worth a dime each.

At 30¢ each, only 100 apples are desired. The substitution and income effects further reduce quantity demanded as price rises.

In discussing the demand curve, it is important to distinguish between

FIGURE 2-2: INCREASE IN DEMAND
An increase in demand occurs whenever something happens to make a good more desirable. It means that people are willing to purchase more of the item at any given price.

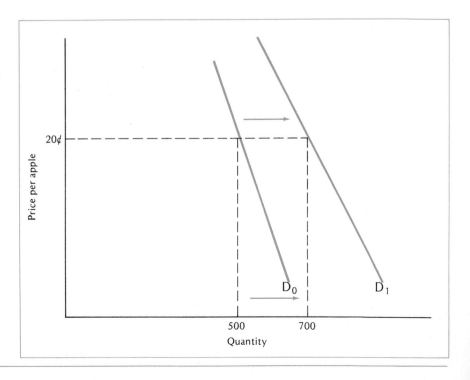

demand (the entire curve) and the quantity demanded (the amount that buyers wish to purchase at any given price). Demand (the concept) will change only when one of the underlying determinants of demand changes. The quantity demanded, however, will change whenever price changes.

To build this demand curve, we were forced to hold constant a whole list of factors—like income and the prices of other goods—which are, in real life, likely to be changing all the time. What effect will a change in one of these parameters have on the demand curve?

We divide the determinants of demand now into two categories: those changes which will increase the quantity which is desired (those which will increase demand) and changes which will reduce the quantity demanded at any price and so reduce demand.

An **increase in demand** is pictured in Figure 2-2. An increase in demand is shown by a shift to the right in the demand curve because this movement indicates that at any given price a larger amount is demanded. In Figure 2-2, for example, a quantity of 500 apples was originally desired at a price of 20¢ each. After the increase in demand (shifting the demand curve from D_0 to D_1) a larger amount, 700 apples, is demanded. (The notations D_0 and D_1 stand respectively for original demand—demand at "time zero"—and new demand; D_2 would denote a second new demand, etc.)

What can cause such an increase in demand? Anything which makes the good in question more desirable or necessary. For example:

☐ An increase in the income of apple eaters.

☐ An increase in the price of pears (an apple substitute).

☐ A decrease in the price of cheddar cheese (which is often consumed together with apples and is therefore a complement).

☐ A medical discovery that an apple a day keeps the doctor away.

☐ A successful advertising campaign by an apple marketing organization which causes people to be more aware of apples.

Demand can also fall when something happens to make a good less desirable. This is illustrated in Figure 2-3 by a shift to the left in the demand curve. Here demand has fallen from D_0 to D_2. At a price of 20¢ per apple, only 300 (as compared to 500) apples are required, with similarly lower quantities demanded at other prices.

A **decrease in demand** can occur due to a wide variety of factors, among them:

☐ A decrease in the incomes of apple eaters.

☐ A fall in the prices of other kinds of fruit.

Increase in demand: a change in income, tastes, or some other determinant of demand which causes the quantity demand of some good to rise at every price (shown by a shift to the right of the demand curve)

Decrease in demand: a change in income, tastes, or some other determinant of demand causing the quantity demanded to be lower at every price (shown by a shift to the left of the demand curve)

FIGURE 2-3: DECREASE IN DEMAND
A decrease in demand occurs when a good becomes less desirable for whatever reasons. A smaller quantity is demanded at every price.

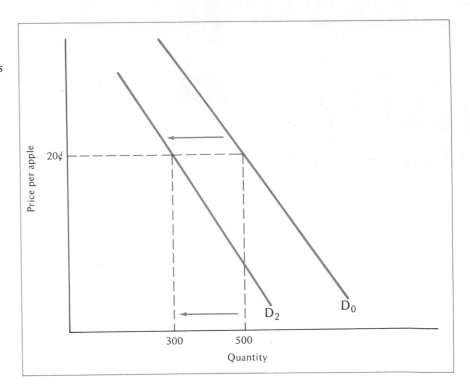

□ A rise in the prices of flour, butter, sugar, and cinnamon (ingredients used in making apple pie and thus possible complements of apples).

□ A rumor that apples cause constipation.

□ A "fad" that involves eating prunes instead of apples (perhaps inspired by the above rumor) in order to avoid doctors.

Demand (and therefore the demand curve), it should be noted, is a description of what buyers would like to do. The demand curve shows us the amounts they would like to purchase at different prices. It does not, by itself, show how much they actually do buy, because only one price prevails in the end. But that one price is influenced heavily by the nature of demand—and by supply.

Supply: a description of the seller side of the market; looks at the factors which determine the amounts and kinds of goods and services offered for sale

THE CONCEPT OF SUPPLY

Supply is a complete description of the way in which producers determine the amount and kinds of goods and services that they wish to produce and offer for sale. While we normally think of ourselves as being primarily demanders—"living" on the demand curve—everyone is actually involved in both demanding goods and in supplying something, such as time, talent, know-how, and experience. Even people who are unemployed or who don't "work" for whatever reason are involved in supplying some of these services at home (we call these "nonmarket" activities, however, since they don't earn a paycheck).

Like demand, the concept of supply can be a very complicated one, but a little intuition will go a long way toward helping us understand the factors that determine how much of something is offered for sale.

While the supply decision depends on a multitude of factors, it is useful to look at just five which are the most important.

1. PRICE.

The price that can be received for a product has, quite obviously, a great deal to do with the amount of that good which is made available for sale. We generally assume that there is a direct relationship between price and the amount produced—higher price induces greater production and lower prices reduce the amount made available. Why is this so? Let's suppose that the price of pizza were to suddenly rise by a dollar in your area. How would the pizza producers respond to this? First, note that pizza making is now more profitable. Assuming that nothing has happened to increase the costs of making pizza pies, each pizza now earns a dollar more profit. This will induce greedy pizza barons to expand production. Local junk food shops may start selling pizza as well as burgers and fries in an attempt to gain a cut of the profits, too. And smart businessmen might open up new pizza places, too, to gain some of the profits.

All of these actions will result in more pizza being offered for sale. Higher price induces greedy sellers to produce more goods to satisfy our wants. They do this because of higher profits (although these profits may be short-lived as the new pizza makers begin to compete with one another for business).

Lower prices have just the opposite effect. Lower prices will cut profits and so cause producers to look for something else to sell, selling less of the lower-priced item in the process.

2. PRICES OF INPUTS.

Inputs are just goods and services which are used to make other goods and services. Flour, water, shortening, yeast, heat, and labor are inputs, for example, in the production of bread. Inputs make **outputs.**

The costs of these inputs have a great deal to do with the amount of any good offered for sale. As input costs rise, it becomes less profitable to produce a good, so smart sellers will produce a little less and look around for a more profitable line. When input costs fall, on the other hand, profits rise and so production goes up.

Inputs: factors of production; goods and services which are used in the production of other goods and services (e.g., labor, raw materials)

Outputs: the goods and services which firms produce

Examples of the effect of input prices on the quantity supplied are not hard to find. When the minimum wage rises, for example, this has a substantial impact on the sellers of fast foods (who traditionally employ lots of young workers at about the minimum wage). As wage rates rise, the fast-food business becomes less profitable. Many sellers respond to this by hiring fewer workers and reducing the hours that their business is open, opening at eleven o'clock instead of ten and closing at nine instead of eleven. In this way, they reduce costs during low-profit hours and so keep profits as high as possible. But they also sell fewer burgers, fries, and chicken this way. The higher input prices cause them to lower the quantity of fast food they wish to supply.

3. AVAILABILITY OF INPUTS. Not only does the cost of inputs affect the supply decision, often the mere availability of inputs is a determining factor. A large number of inputs are necessary for even relatively minor production operations. A professor, for example, wouldn't seem to need very many tools in order to produce education services (or, in some cases, sleep). Yet most profs would be hard-pressed to operate without such basic inputs as blackboards, chalk, heat, lights, chairs, texts, and . . . oh, yes . . . students!

Inputs are a very necessary part of the supply process, yet they are often unavailable. Stores frequently run out of sale items. Factories cannot sell goods for lack of trucks or rail cars to bring them to a market. Airlines cannot sell as many tickets as they would like to for lack of seats aboard their planes. Crops go unharvested because workers, machines, or fuels are unavailable. The list goes on and on. Even your local sports team probably has trouble selling as many tickets as it would like for lack of the proper input in terms of a quarterback, center, goalie, or first baseman.

The availability of the proper kinds of inputs at the right time with the correct skills or properties has a large impact on the amounts and kinds of goods offered for sale.

4. TECHNOLOGY. **Technology**—the way inputs are combined to produce outputs—is at the very heart of the concept of supply. Changes in technology affect the goods produced and sold as well as the demands for the various kinds of inputs involved.

Technology: the process by which inputs are combined to produce goods and services; changes in technology involve changes in the production process

Changes in technology are very important because improved technology allows us to produce more things with the same resources (i.e., makes things cheaper) or to produce better things. Much of the growth in American industry can be attributed to improved technologies.

You probably own a symbol of the power of changing technology: a hand calculator. Just a few years ago such things as small electronic calculators did not exist. A room-size electronic Univac was necessary to perform the kinds of calculations that even inexpensive portable machines now perform instantly. When small calculators first appeared on the market, they were complicated, expensive to produce, and very costly (selling for more than $200 each for models that were not very powerful compared to today's products). Now, because of advanced technology, you can buy a simple add-subtract-multiply-divide model for less than $10 and very sophisticated ones for only a little more.

The power of improving technology is not to be denied, and it shows up in the unlikeliest of places. Even the familiar hamburger has benefited from the march of science. Burger shops that were once slow and inefficient, operated by one or two people, have now made way for the modern McDonald's and similar chains that use specialization of labor, modern machinery (such as sensors to determine when french fries are golden brown), and automatic soft-drink dispensers to increase the amounts and kinds of fast foods that they can sell.

5. EVERYTHING ELSE. All sorts of other things can affect the process of production and sale. You should have no trouble coming up with dozens of examples, but here are two to start things off.

The weather is a very basic "everything else" that can affect the supply decision. Weather has a very large impact on the amounts of agricultural goods that are made available each year. Too much rain, not enough rain, too much heat, not enough heat—all these situations can reduce agricultural yields and so reduce the supply of fruits and vegetables.

A second example of "everything else" is government regulation. The government has broad powers to regulate the production and distribution of goods and services to protect the public interest. Goods can rise and fall in price, appear or disappear from store shelves, or change in design in response to changing government regulations. This "everything else" is coming to have a large impact on the goods that we purchase. Environmental regulations, for example, have significantly affected the supplies of automobiles, coal, clean air and water, and nuclear power, to list just a few items.

Supply curve: a graphical device showing the relationship between price and the quantity supplied, all other factors held constant

The **supply curve** is a simplification of the concept of supply which allows us to more clearly see the consequences of a change in one of the determinants of supply on the market process. The supply curve holds the costs and availability of inputs constant; assumes no change in technology

THE SUPPLY CURVE

FIGURE 2-4: A SUPPLY CURVE FOR
APPLES
*The supply curve shows how the
amount of goods offered for sale varies
with the price that those goods sell for.
Higher prices mean higher profits, all
else being equal, and so encourage
firms to produce. The quantity supplied
is high, then, when prices are high,
and it declines as the selling price falls.*

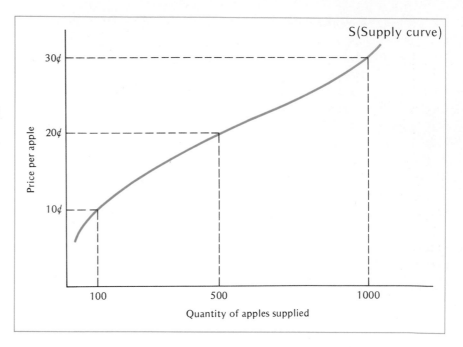

or "anything else"; and examines the relationship between the quantity
supplied and the price at which the goods are sold.

There are many possible shapes that a supply curve can take on. Figure
2-4 shows the normal representation of a supply curve for apples. This curve
is upward-sloping, showing that as the market price of apples rises, more
and more apples are offered for sale. Conversely, if the price of apples falls,
fewer apple growers find this business profitable and so fewer apples are
made available.

This upward-sloping supply curve probably characterizes the supply
situation in most industries. In general, higher prices are needed, at least in
the short run, in order to induce increased production, and lower prices
cause less to be supplied.

Although the upward-sloping supply curve may hold in most cases, it
does not describe all industries or businesses. In some cases, the maximum
amount that can be offered for sale is physically limited. In this case, the
supply curve is vertical, like the one in Figure 2-5, which shows the supply
curve for apples in January. Since the apple crop is already in, there is no
way to secure additional apples, regardless of the price. The supply of
apples in the short run is fixed, resulting in the vertical supply curve which
states, graphically, that the amount of apples available cannot increase, no
matter how high the price goes.

What kinds of supply curves have this vertical shape? Many agricultural

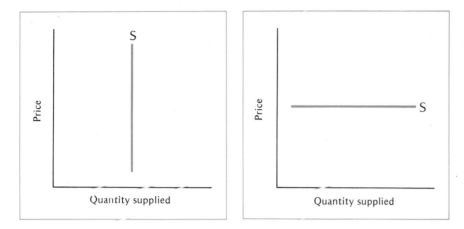

FIGURE 2-5: FIXED SUPPLY
When there is a physical limitation to the amount that is available, the supply curve takes on this shape.

FIGURE 2-6: HORIZONTAL SUPPLY
Since there is a great deal of excess capacity in this industry, production will rise to meet consumer demand without the motivation of rising price.

goods have inflexible supplies. Natural resources also are often physically limited in the short run (although in the long run new sources can be developed).

Figure 2-6 shows the opposite case. Here the supply curve is horizontal, showing that any desired quantity of apples will be supplied at the going price. This type of supply curve describes an industry with excess productive capacity—one that is not producing up to its potential. This is perhaps the only case where a larger quantity can be obtained without price increases.

How can this be? Consider, for example, an apple rancher who is not harvesting all of his crop because he cannot find buyers for his fruit (this is the idea of excess capacity—a business able to produce more than it can currently sell). The apple farmer would gladly increase the quantity of apples that he supplies at the going price just because this is more profitable to him than seeing the fruit fall to the ground and rot. Increases in the amount supplied, then, can take place without a motivating increase in price.

The amount of any good or service that a firm will provide depends mostly upon the price of that good, the costs of production (prices of inputs, technology), and the amount and availability of inputs necessary to the production process. Anything which acts to change the costs of production or the availability of inputs causes the supply relationship to change.

CHANGES IN SUPPLY

FIGURE 2-7: INCREASE IN SUPPLY
Supply rises (a larger quantity is supplied at any price) when goods become cheaper to make, more profitable, or easier to make.

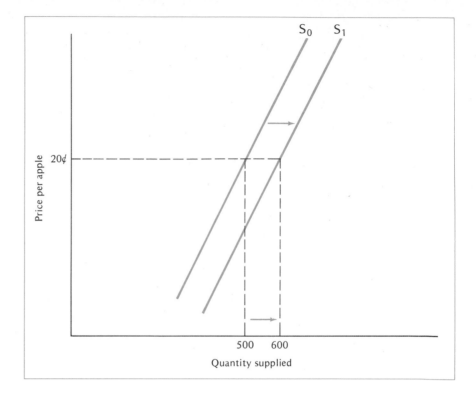

Increase in supply: a change in the costs of production, technology, or some other determinant of supply which causes the quantity supplied to increase at every price (shown by a shift to the right of the supply curve)

Changes which make production cheaper, or that increase the amounts of goods that can be produced with the same resources are said to cause supply to increase. An **increase in supply** is pictured in Figure 2-7 as a shift to the right in the supply curve. An increase in supply could be caused by numerous factors, among them the following:

☐ Reduced labor costs (which make production more profitable and so cause more to be produced).

☐ Reduced raw material costs (which have the same effect on profits and production).

☐ Increased availability of inputs (which make it easier to produce if there have been some shortages in the past).

☐ A labor-saving invention which reduces costs.

☐ The lifting of a government regulation which had added to costs.

An increase in supply is defined to be a change in one of the determinants of supply which induces producers to increase the quantity supplied at any

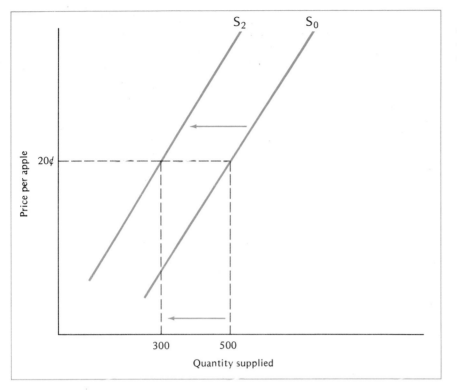

FIGURE 2-8: DECREASE IN SUPPLY
Supply falls when a good becomes more costly to produce or less profitable to make and sell.

price. Note here we distinguish between the concept of supply—which is a description of the entire supply process—and the quantity which is supplied at any given price. Quantity supplied rises whenever price rises. Supply rises only when something has happened—like a reduction in the costs of production—to alter the supply relationship.

A **decrease in supply** occurs whenever something happens to either increase the costs of production or hamper the ability to produce (as in the case of a shortage of necessary inputs). A decrease in supply is defined to be a situation where the quantity which is supplied is decreased at any price. A decrease in supply is pictured in Figure 2-8 as a shift to the left in the supply curve.

Many factors can cause supply to fall, among them the following:

☐ An increase in the price of vital raw materials (which reduces profit and so discourages production).

☐ A strike which reduces the availability of labor.

☐ An increase in the taxes which business must pay.

☐ The imposition of costly environmental regulations.

Decrease in supply: a change in costs of production, technology, or some other determinant of supply causing the quantity supplied to be less at every price (shown by a shift to the left of the supply curve)

Supply changes whenever one of the underlying determinants of supply changes. Note that the supply curve shows the amounts of goods that producers would *like* to sell at particular prices. There is no guarantee that the public will cooperate and purchase these amounts. In the end, that decision is made by the market.

THE MARKET AT WORK

The *market* is where all of the action is. In the market, the conflict and cooperation that characterize the process of exchange come to the fore.

To fully understand how markets work, it is useful to think for a moment of an imaginary market where all of the forces at work in the real world come to bear in more obvious ways. So pretend for a moment that you have been transported to a medieval street market. There is a large crowd milling around the marketplace waiting for the buying and selling to begin.

On one side of the street are the producers. They make up the supply curve for this market. Each knows how much of the day's goods—apples—can be profitably sold at any given price. The supply curve that they form is shown in Figure 2-9.

FIGURE 2-9: THE MARKET FOR APPLES
The supply and demand curves show how many apples people would like to buy and sell at different prices. The market determines the final amounts and selling price.

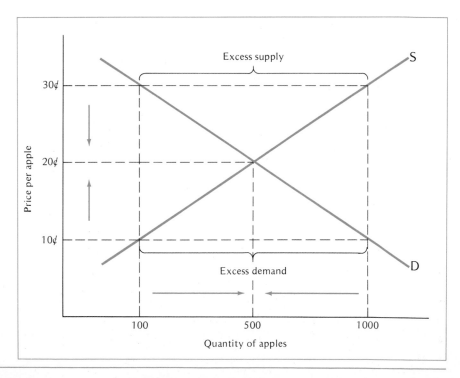

On the other side of the street are the buyers. There are many of them, too, with widely different preferences, and each has decided how many apples to buy at any given price. They make up the demand curve.

In the middle of the street, standing on a soapbox, is the auctioneer. His job is to call out prices. He will continue to call out prices until all of the buyers and all of the sellers are satisfied with the results of the exchanges that take place at that price. When everyone is happy with the price he calls out, he can go home.

The market opens at 10:00 A.M. sharp, and the auctioneer calls out his first price, 30¢ per apple, and buyers and sellers form huddles and examine the results of the call.

At a price of 30¢, the apple growers are willing to sell 1000 apples (see Figure 2-9). Thirty cents is a comparatively high price for this market, so most of the growers are willing to sell most of their apples (although some are still holding out for a higher price). But since the price is so high, the consumers are only interested in buying 100 apples. There is a **surplus** or **excess supply** equal to 900 apples. Some of the sellers quickly calculate that, at this high price, there will be no (or too few) buyers for their apples and they will be left holding the bag. Since they want to do business, the holders of the surplus apples offer to put them "on sale" and demand that the auctioneer call out a lower price.

Surplus: the quantity supplied exceeds the quantity demanded

Excess supply: the quantity supplied at a particular price exceeds the quantity demanded at that price

Since some of the suppliers are very agitated about the lack of demand for apples at this high price, the auctioneer quickly calls out a much lower one: 10¢ per apple.

At 10¢ per apple, apples are cheap, and the buyers announce that they are willing to purchase 1000 of them. But the sellers are not so pleased. At such a low price it does not pay most of them to produce apples, and many of the producers find that it would be more profitable to produce something else or to hold their apples and hope for a better price later. Those few producers who have particularly profitable harvesting methods are willing to sell at this price—but this amounts to only 100 apples.

A quick tally indicates that, at this price, there is going to be a **shortage** or **excess demand** of apples. People want to buy 1000 apples, but there will be only 100 available, creating a potential shortage of 900 apples. Some of the apple buyers, realizing that at 10¢ an apple they will go home empty-handed, offer to pay a higher price to receive apples and demand that a higher price be called.

Shortage: the quantity demanded exceeds the quantity supplied

Excess demand: the quantity demanded at a particular price exceeds the quantity supplied at that price

The auctioneer spends most of the next two hours calling out prices between 10¢ and 30¢ per apple, but each time there is either a surplus (and some of the producers offer to sell their excess apples for less) or a shortage (and some of the buyers indicate that they are willing to pay more in order to get apples).

Eventually, however, the auctioneer calls out a price of 20¢ per apple. At this price something unique happens. The producers discover, in their huddle, that they are willing to sell a total of 500 apples (some of the producers, unwilling to sell for such a low price, start to leave). On the other side of the road, the buyers discover that, together, they are willing to buy 500 apples (and some of them, unwilling to pay this much, start to leave as well).

At the price of 20¢ per apple, the quantity that producers are willing to sell exactly equals the amount that consumers are willing to buy. There is no shortage, and no surplus either. The auctioneer has found a price that will "clear the market."

This is actually how markets work in the real world, although the buyers and sellers do not necessarily all gather in one place, and no actual auctioneer exists. The goal of the market is to find a market-clearing price, which economists call the **equilibrium price**.

Equilibrium price: the one price where the quantity supplied equals the quantity demanded

The market responds to shortages and surpluses. When too much of a good is offered for sale, a surplus is created and the goods are put "on sale," causing the price to fall. When not enough is produced, buyers "bribe" the sellers to produce more by offering them a higher price.

Eventually, the equilibrium price is found such that no surplus or shortage exists, and that price holds. In compact and highly organized markets (like the New York Stock Exchange), this price is arrived at quickly and easily. In other, less organized markets (like the market for used cars), the price is found eventually.

The magical property of the equilibrium price is that it is the only price at which the quantity demanded is equal to the quantity supplied. While buyers would prefer a lower price and sellers would be pleased if they could charge more, at the equilibrium both buyers and sellers can be accommodated.

Shortages occur when the quantity demanded exceeds the quantity supplied. Shortages occur whenever something happens to increase the amount that buyers wish to purchase, or to reduce the amount offered for sale. In either case, a shortage is a sign that the price is too low. When the shortage becomes apparent, market forces bid up the price to its equilibrium level.

Surpluses signify the opposite situation. A surplus exists when the quantity demanded is less than the quantity supplied. This can happen when something occurs to reduce the amount that people wish to purchase, or to increase the amount that sellers offer for sale. Surpluses indicate that price is too high. In response to the excess supply, sellers tend to "bid down" the price of their goods in search of a market-clearing situation. The equilibrium price is arrived at eventually.

The forces of supply and demand exert substantial influence over our lives. The efficient functioning of markets—and what can happen when markets break down—is best illustrated by looking at a market that we are all involved in, directly or indirectly, and which is increasingly in the news: the energy market.

Energy is, of course, one of the basic necessities of modern life. We use power for heat, light, to cook and clean, and power is a required part of most jobs. Despite our heavy dependence on power for work and play, we sometimes take it for granted. But this dependence has been graphically demonstrated to us several times in recent years when exceptionally hard winters have hit most of the nation. Let's examine the economics of such situations.

To begin with, we will look at just one part of the energy market—the demand and supply for electrical energy. Electricity is used for heating, air conditioning, industrial power, and a variety of other uses. During a heavy winter, like those in the late 1970s, the demand for electrical energy increases. As temperatures fall and snow drifts pile high, more and more electricity is needed for space heating and other uses. In short, the demand for electricity rises (the demand curve for electricity shifts to the right).

What impact does this have on energy prices and production? There are three possible cases, illustrated by Figures 2-10, 2-11, and 2-12. The first case would occur if there were excess capacity in electrical generation for a particular region. If the present facilities can generate all of the power needed, then an increase in demand can be satisfied with no increase in price. This situation actually happens in the electrical energy industry, because generators work at set output levels, and excess production cannot be saved but must be earthed to get rid of it.

This situation is very interesting, but it has not been the case recently. While excess capacity may occur in some parts of the country, most areas are operating very close to their maximum. Therefore in many areas a situation prevails like that shown in Figure 2-11. Electrical production here is taking place right at the finite physical limit. Current generating capacities are fully utilized, and it is therefore impossible to supply even an additional kilowatt-hour of power.

An increase in the demand for electricity in this fixed-supply market results in no increase in electrical supply. As demand increases beyond the finite limit, shortages of power take place. Brownouts or blackouts may occur. Since, in the short run, no additional power is available, the only solution is conservation in order to make the existing supply of power go around. Voluntary conservation may be tried, but this is not likely to be effective. As a result, electrical rates are increased (surcharges are imposed

FIGURE 2-10: INCREASING DEMAND
WITH EXCESS CAPACITY
*Because there is already an excess
capacity to produce electricity, the
increased demand can be met without
an increase in price.*

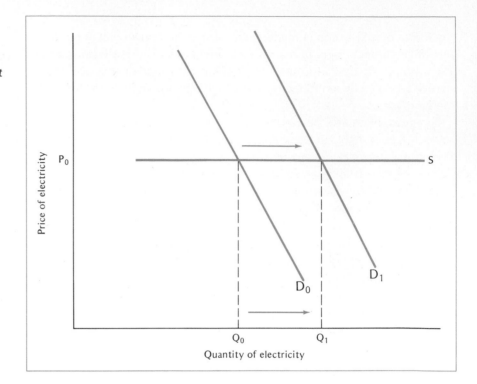

on electric bills). The increase in the price of electricity induces buyers to
lower their thermostats or otherwise cut back on energy uses. As the rise in
price takes place, the fall in electrical use reduces the shortage until finally,
at the equilibrium price, no shortage exists. Price movements have allocated
the scarce power supply to those who need or want it most and stretched the
supply to satisfy electrical users.

The supply of electricity may not be completely limited, however. Often
additional amounts of electricity can be obtained from outside sources
through power networks or by firing up old, outdated, and inefficient
generators, but at higher costs. This is the case shown by Figure 2-12. Here
the supply curve is upward-sloping, showing that more electricity can be
obtained at higher prices. The higher prices are necessary because the cost
of the imported electricity is higher or because the additional power is
generated by ancient plants that have higher operating costs.

In this kind of market, the increased winter demand for energy again
creates a power shortage at the existing price for electricity. If the price
remains at the original level, the power shortage also remains, and power
rationing or some similar scheme has to be devised to allocate the scarce

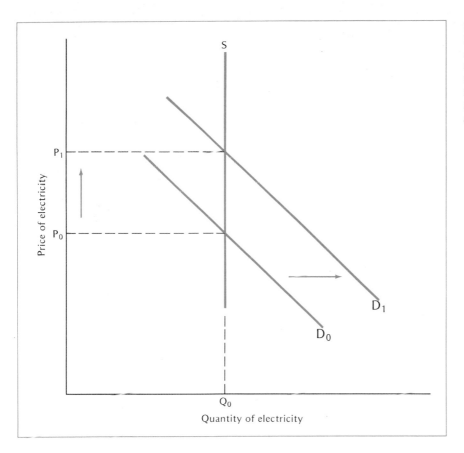

FIGURE 2-11: RISING DEMAND FOR
ELECTRICITY WITH FIXED SUPPLY
*Because the supply of electricity has
reached its short-run limit, there is no
way for the quantity supplied to rise to
match the higher demand. Prices must
rise to ration the scarce electricity
among those who need it.*

electricity. An increase in the price of electricity (again through a surcharge
or some other device) tends to reduce the power shortage in two ways. First,
as price rises, outside sources (or more expensive sources) of energy can be
brought in to satisfy demand. The quantity of electricity supplied increases.
Also, as the cost of power goes up, consumers begin to conserve the more
expensive energy. The quantity of electricity demanded begins to fall back
from its initial cold-weather increase.

With the quantity demanded falling and the amount supplied increasing,
soon the energy shortage is brought under control. Consumers may not be
pleased with the higher prices, but they seem to be an economic necessity if
the shortage is to be resolved.

Occurrences in one market have a way of spilling over into the markets
for other products, and this is the case in energy markets. As the price of
electricity rises, consumers begin to search for alternate energy sources that

FIGURE 2-12: RISE IN DEMAND WITH
INCREASED-COST ELECTRICITY
*In this example, additional amounts of
energy are available, but at higher
costs. The rising demand can be met,
but the price rises at the same time that
increased quantity is supplied. The
higher price induces conservation
among those not willing to bear the
higher electricity costs.*

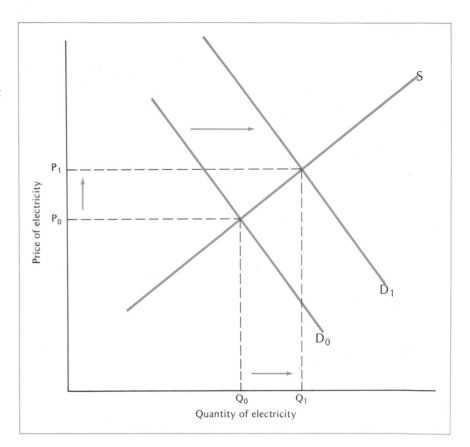

save money. Some invest in solar heating systems. Others purchase wood
stoves. And some electricity users switch to natural-gas systems. Let us
examine the impact of this substitution on the market.

As the price of electricity rises in Figure 2-12, some people begin to
substitute natural gas for electricity as an energy source. This causes an
increase in the demand for natural gas, as shown in Figure 2-13. The
increased use of gas will put a strain on the supply of this commodity as
well, and the market forces suggest that the price of natural gas will rise so
that more natural gas can be supplied.

This, however, is one situation where the answer that the market gives is
not necessarily the one that prevails in the real world. While the market
response to an increase in demand normally is rising price and quantity,
sometimes governmental restrictions prevent the market from performing its
tasks.

The price of natural gas is regulated by the federal government. The

Price ceiling: a maximum legal price (set by the
government, not by market forces)

government sets a **price ceiling**—a maximum price that may be charged for
natural gas which crosses state lines (intrastate sales of natural gas are not

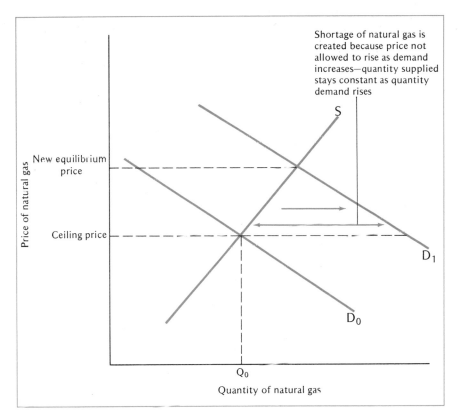

Shortage of natural gas is created because price not allowed to rise as demand increases—quantity supplied stays constant as quantity demand rises

New equilibrium price

Ceiling price

Price of natural gas

S

D_1

D_0

Q_0

Quantity of natural gas

FIGURE 2-13: INCREASE IN DEMAND WITH PRICE CEILING
As demand rises, the price should rise as well to induce increased production and conservation. Here, however, the price is controlled and may not rise. Production does not rise, and the amount demanded increases. A shortage is created which must be solved through rationing, since the price is not allowed to clear the market.

subject to these federal controls, and so are normally priced higher). These price controls dramatically affect the natural-gas market.

As demand for natural gas rises in a price-controlled market, the amount that consumers desire increases, but the price available for producers does not. With no increase in price, sellers have no incentive to increase production. As a result, permanent shortages of gas occur. Consumers have no reason to conserve because the price of natural gas remains low, encouraging use. Producers have no incentive to produce more gas because there is no increase in price to cover their costs. The shortage does *not* disappear, and other methods like rationing must be used to allocate the limited supplies of this energy source. This, in fact, has occurred many times, with the normal rationing method being to allocate natural gas first to households (to prevent anyone freezing to death as an indirect result of the price regulations), but reducing the amounts available for industrial use. This policy has resulted in situations where people are warm but unemployed. This, in turn, has led to a call for the deregulation of natural gas.

If price controls on natural gas (and other commodities) are bad, why do we have them? This may be more a political than an economic question. Price ceilings lead to lower prices for those who can obtain the goods in question, and to great inconvenience or suffering to those who must go without. Apparently, the needs of the first group are seen to outweigh those of the second. This, at least, is the trade-off that price controls make.

INFLATION: A PREVIEW

Inflation, which will be discussed in Chapter 4, is a situation where prices in general are rising for some reason. To get a feel for what might make all prices rise, it is instructive to examine what would make prices in one market go up. The concepts that we learn here will come in handy later.

All things being equal, there are only two basic types of changes which can make the price of a good rise. Price rises, first of all, if there is an increase in the demand for the item. This type of price increase, graphed in Figure 2-14, we can call a **demand-pull** price increase. As people wish to purchase more and more of something, they create a shortage of it. The market's solution to the shortage is for price to rise since the rising price diminishes the shortage in two ways: it lowers the quantity demanded and induces sellers to produce more of the good in short supply. In the

Demand-pull: price increases which result from an increase in demand

FIGURE 2-14: DEMAND-PULL INFLATION
Prices are shown here to rise because higher demand creates shortages which serve to bid up price in this market.

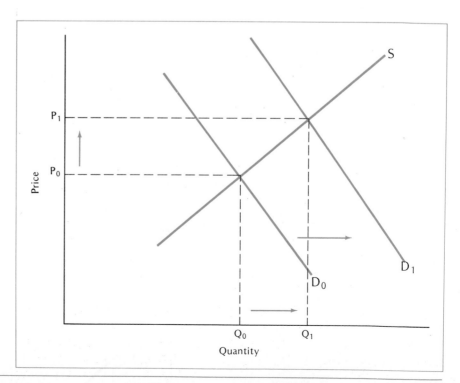

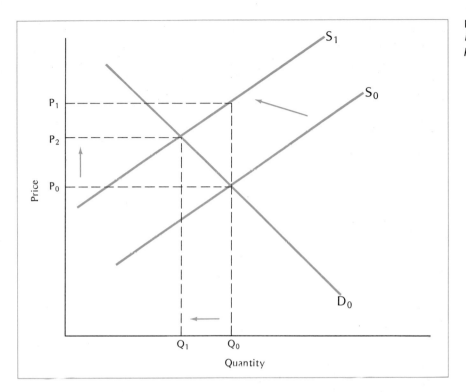

FIGURE 2-15: COST-PUSH INFLATION
Rising costs cause firms to raise the price. At the higher price, less is sold.

demand-pull situation, prices rise, but the higher prices bring with them greater production. This, perhaps, justifies the price increases.

The second case is shown in Figure 2-15. A decrease in supply (caused by, say, an increase in the costs of production) results in a **cost-push** price increase. The end here is the same—higher prices—but there are many differences, too.

As the costs of production rise (due to increased input costs, taxes, or more costly regulations) the firm attempts to pass these higher costs along to its customers in terms of higher prices. Thus the firm initially attempts to raise its price from P_0 to P_1. But at this new higher price, the quantity demanded falls below the quantity supplied. The attempt to pass through the increased costs results in a temporary surplus. In response to this surplus, some suppliers cut their prices to get rid of the excess merchandise, causing other firms to supply less. The process ends when the price has fallen down to P_2, at which point the quantities supplied and demanded are again equal and no shortages or surpluses prevail.

Note the impact of cost-push inflation. Prices rise (although by less than they did initially), but quantity has fallen, since only a lesser amount can be sold at the cost-induced higher price. Consumers are getting less and paying more. All of this because of increased costs of production. As you can see,

Cost-push: price increases which are brought about through a decrease in supply typically caused by increased costs of production

this cost-push situation is not a pleasant one, but one that happens frequently in real-world markets.

In the real world, the demands for most (but not all) things are rising most of the time due to general increases in income, standard of living, and population. Since, as we have seen, increasing demand results in increases in price, is inflation a necessity? In other words, must prices always rise in a world of rising demand?

The answer to this question is no. Although there are many forces which tend to cause prices to rise, it is not necessary for prices to climb continually, even in the face of normally rising demand. There are two situations where increasing demand can be met without higher prices. The first case was already discussed in regard to Figure 2-10. When there are many unemployed resources (excess capacity) in an industry, an increase in

FIGURE 2-16: BALANCED GROWTH IN DEMAND AND SUPPLY
If demand and supply grow together, the rise in supply meets the growing needs. Since no shortage is created, there is no reason for price to rise. Quantity increases without rising price.

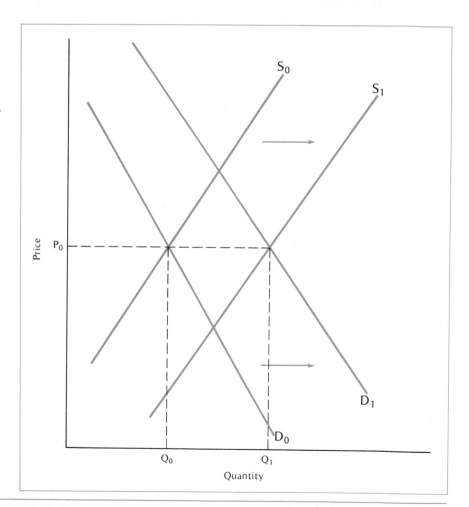

demand need not cause increased price. We cannot, however, hope to always find spare capacity in industries, since this would call for high unemployment rates. Is there, then, some other way to beat inflation?

Rising demand can also be met without rising prices if, as shown in Figure 2-16, the increases in demand are met with similar increases in supply. When the rising demand for goods is matched by an increased ability to produce them, no shortage is created. We can call this particular situation **balanced growth** of supply and demand, and it is, of course, a very desirable situation for a market to be in. The key feature in this balanced growth of supply and demand is the increase in supply. What can cause supply to rise? Lower input prices can do the job. So can improved technology and increased productivity. These things allow us to meet demand without forcing prices up.

Balanced growth: increases in demand accompanied by increasing supply; allows the larger quantities demanded to be satisfied without price increases

REVIEW OF MARKET ACTIONS

The model of supply and demand is a very rich one that allows us to model all sorts of market situations. Demand depends primarily on price, income, the prices of other goods, and tastes and preferences. Supply depends largely on price, the costs of production, availability of inputs, and technology. Demand curves show us the quantities that buyers would like to purchase at different prices. The supply curve tells the sellers' intended actions at differing prices. The equilibrium price is the unique price at which the quantity that sellers offer for sale is equal to the amount that buyers want to purchase. The study of markets is mostly a study of how and what can change the equilibrium price.

Since the model is so simple, we can summarize the basic market movements in the following few paragraphs (assume here a "normal" upward-sloping supply curve):

An increase in demand occurs whenever the quantity that people wish to buy of a good increases at any price. The increase in demand causes a shortage of that good, bidding up its price. The higher price induces higher production. We can summarize this chain-reaction as follows:

$$\uparrow D \rightarrow \uparrow P \text{ and } \uparrow Q$$

An increase in supply occurs whenever something happens to make a good more profitable to produce, and therefore causes more of it to be offered for sale. The increase in the amount supplied causes a surplus of the good. To get rid of the surplus, sellers put the item "on sale," and its price falls. The result is

$$\uparrow S \rightarrow \uparrow Q \text{ and } \downarrow P$$

A decrease in demand occurs whenever a good becomes less desirable—as, for example, when some substitute item falls in price. The falling demand creates a surplus of the good. As dealers' shelves and stockrooms fill up, sellers get wise to the surplus and offer a lower price to clear out the goods. The lower price, of course, discourages further production of the item involved. The result of a fall in demand is

$$\downarrow D \rightarrow \downarrow P \rightarrow \downarrow Q$$

A decrease in supply will have the opposite effect. As costs rise, businesses attempt to pass these higher costs on to consumers in the form of higher prices. At the higher prices, less is purchased, so that quantity falls. The result is

$$\downarrow S \rightarrow \uparrow P \rightarrow \downarrow Q$$

An increase in demand accompanied by a decrease in supply causes prices to rise substantially. The increase in demand causes prices to be bid up. The fall in supply means that firms are attempting to pass increased costs of production on to consumers. Together they cause a large increase in price. The direction of the change in quantity is not easily determined. Increasing demand tends to cause quantity to rise, but falling supply causes it to shrink. The change in quantity depends on the relative magnitudes of the changes in supply and demand.

A decrease in demand followed by an increase in supply lowers price, but the impact on the equilibrium quantity is indeterminant. Falling demand tends to bid down price, while rising supply floods the market with even more goods. A very large surplus is created, and so price falls. The directions of the change in quantity, however, depends upon the relative magnitudes of the supply and demand changes.

An increase in both demand and supply (balanced growth) causes, as we have already seen, a large increase in the equilibrium quantity, but little of or no change in price. Likewise, a fall in both supply and demand causes a large fall in the equilibrium quantity, with the change in price depending upon which is relatively larger, the decrease in supply or the fall in demand.

Price floor: a minimum legal price

The preceding results obtain only when the market is free to perform its allocation task without regulations. When price ceilings (maximum legal prices) or **price floors** (minimum prices) are set, the ability of the market to do away with surpluses and shortages is severely limited. Prices may not adjust as we have seen here, and permanent disequilibria is possible.

SUMMARY

1. Every market has two sides: buyers and sellers. The buyers' side of the market is called "demand." Demand is a description of how people decide how many and what kinds of goods and services to purchase. The demand curve shows the

amount of intended purchases at every price.

2. Many factors can influence demand. The quantity purchased depends largely on the price of the good in question, but it is also influenced by the income of buyers, the prices of other goods, tastes, preferences and styles, and a world of other factors. The demand curve holds all of these factors fixed except price. When the other factors (such as income) change, the demand curve "shifts" to show that the amount demanded at each price has changed.

3. The sellers' side of the market is called "supply." Supply is a description of how sellers determine the amounts and kinds of goods to offer for sale. The supply curve shows the quantity supplied at every price.

4. Many factors influence the amount of a good offered for sale. The price of the good involved has an important effect on the quantity supplied (although this can vary from market to market—as shown by the three types of supply curves illustrated in the text). Besides price, the costs and availability of inputs, technology, and other factors such as government regulations affect the amounts and kinds of goods offered for sale. When these underlying factors change, the supply curve shifts.

5. Equilibrium price is that one price where the quantity demanded equals the quantity supplied. It is called "equilibrium" because it is the only stable price. At the equilibrium price there are no forces acting on the market to cause price to change. Away from the equilibrium price there are shortages (when the price is below equilibrium) or surpluses (when price exceeds the equilibrium price) which bring the market price back to equilibrium.

6. Prices change as the result of market reactions to shortages and surpluses. When the quantity demand exceeds the quantity supplied (shortage), the market price is bid up by buyers competing for scarce goods. When the quantity supplied exceeds the quantity demanded (surplus), sellers bid down the market price in an attempt to sell their abundant goods.

7. Rising prices are caused by basically two kinds of economic events. Demand-pull price increases are caused by rising demand which forces up prices but results in higher production. Cost-push price increases, on the other hand, are caused by rising costs of production and result in higher prices but lower output.

8. A price ceiling is a legal maximum price. This kind of price control can cause permanent shortages of goods and services if demand increases or costs rise while the price ceiling is in effect.

DISCUSSION QUESTIONS

1. Suppose that you are interested in the supply of beer. Draw a hypothetical beer supply curve. Why is it shaped the way you have drawn it? What effect will the following situations have on your beer supply curve?

   ☐ A fall in the price of hops.
   ☐ An increase in the price of aluminum cans.
   ☐ A fall in the price of pizza.
   ☐ The invention of an improved bottling machine.

2. Suppose you are interested in the demand for prunes. Draw a hypothetical prune demand curve. Why is it shaped the way you have drawn it? What affect will the following situations have on your prune demand curve?

   ☐ Scientists discover that eating prunes slows aging.
   ☐ The price of Ex-Lax falls.
   ☐ There is an increase in the incomes of prune eaters.
   ☐ The price of prunes falls.

3. Suppose that we are looking at the market for pizza in the local area. What affect would each of the following situations have on demand? on supply? on price? on the quantity produced and sold?

   ☐ A decrease in the price of mozzarella cheese.
   ☐ An increase in the number of pizza palaces.
   ☐ A decrease in the price of beer.
   ☐ An increase in the price of hamburgers.
   ☐ An increase in the number of college students.

4. Do markets in the real world work like markets in the textbook do? Explain your answer.

5. Describe the way a market reacts to surpluses and shortages. Can you recall experiences when you have observed markets behaving this way?

6. Under what conditions does an increase in demand *not* result in a price increase?

7. Under what conditions does an increase in demand *not* bring about increased production?

8. Suppose that demand for a good increased a little while supply increased a great deal. What would happen to price and quantity at equilibrium? What would happen if demand fell substantially and supply fell by relatively less?

9. Price controls are particularly troublesome when costs increase to make goods more expensive to produce. Many apartments in New York are price-controlled—maximum rents are set and not frequently raised. In addition, landlords are often precluded from converting their buildings to condominiums or selling them for other uses. The maximum price is set, and landlords are forced to supply a certain amount of housing services.

What is the impact in this case, of an increase in the cost of renting apartments (a decrease in the apartment supply curve)? Will the adjustment take place through changes in price, quantity, or quality?

10. In what cases would a price floor (minimum price) make sense? Can you think of any markets where minimum prices prevail? What would happen in such a market if demand were to fall?

In each of the following questions, indicate whether the statement is *true* or *false*. Be able to defend your answer.

1. If there is a surplus of cars on the market, sellers tend to bid up the price of cars.

2. Indoor plants and ceramic pots are complements. If the price of plants rises, then we can expect the demand for pots to fall.

3. Steak and hamburger are substitutes. If the price of steak rises, we can expect the price of hamburger to fall.

4. An increase in the price of donuts causes the demand for donuts to fall (shift the donut demand curve to the left).

5. The quantity supplied of a good rises when the price of that good rises.

6. An increase in the demand for tuna always causes an increase in the price of tuna.

7. An increase in the demand for tuna causes an increase in the quantity of tuna supplied.

8. If the demand for concert tickets rises at the same time that the supply of concert tickets is reduced, we can expect the equilibrium price of concert tickets to rise.

9. An increase in demand can only be met without an increase in price when the supply curve is horizontal.

10. Price ceilings remove the forces which tend to cause price increases.

3
The
Problem
of
Unemployment

Unemployment is one of our major economic problems. Although we know a lot about the unemployment problem, it has remained a difficult problem to solve. This chapter will answer many questions about the problem of unemployment including:

What does the unemployment rate mean?

What is the unemployment record?

What are the causes of unemployment?

What does "full employment" mean?

How do minimum-wage laws affect the unemployment problem?

How serious is the unemployment problem?

Unemployment is a serious problem in a modern economy. Although unemployment directly affects only a relatively small proportion of the population (in 1977 just 6.8 million people were unemployed in the United States out of a total of over 220 million), the shock waves that are caused by unemployment affect a much larger group.

For the unemployed individual, both income and self-esteem may suffer. For the economy, there is a double burden. First, potential output is lost because scarce and valuable resources (people) are not being used to their fullest. Economists estimate that total production is reduced by about 3 percent for every percentage point that joblessness rises above the full-employment level. This means that in 1977 unemployment cost the nation the equivalent of between $40 and $60 billion in lost production and income. In addition, resources must be taken away from competing uses and spent trying to solve the unemployment problem or cushioning its impact. This loss is great. In 1975 over $16 billion was spent on unemployment compensation alone. Clearly, unemployment is a serious economic and social problem and reducing unemployment is an important national goal.

The goal of low unemployment is not one that has always been successfully achieved in the United States. As can be seen in Figure 3-1, the United States has endured relatively high unemployment rates for most of the post–World War II period. Only in the early 1950s and the late 1960s (in both cases during war periods) did the unemployment rate fall below 4

FIGURE 3-1: THE UNEMPLOYMENT RECORD

The unemployment record for the period 1950–1978 is not very encouraging. Only twice—in the early 1950s (during the Korean War) and again in the late 1960s (during the Vietnam War) did the unemployment rate dip below 4 percent.

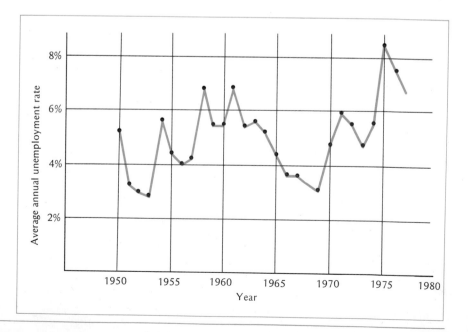

percent. In 1958–1961 the unemployment rate hovered at about 6 percent, and unemployment peaked at over 8 percent in 1975, remaining over 6 percent for several years thereafter.

In this chapter we will take a close look at the problem of unemployment. We will explore the meaning of the unemployment rates and look at some of the causes of unemployment. The concept of full employment will be explained, and finally we will look behind the unemployment figures to see how serious the unemployment problem really is.

THE UNEMPLOYMENT RATE

The severity of the unemployment problem is usually measured by the **unemployment rate.** But what is the unemployment rate? What does it mean when the unemployment rate is 6 percent? Six percent of what? Of the population?

Unemployment rate: a measure of unemployment calculated by dividing the number of unemployed individuals by the size of the labor force

The unemployment rate, as calculated by the federal government, is the ratio of the number of people unemployed to the total number of people in the labor force. Definitions are important here. A person is considered to be an **unemployed worker,** for the purpose of this statistic, when he or she is willing and able to work and actively seeking work, but cannot find a job at the going wage rate. How is this number determined? The unemployed are not actually counted, but are estimated through a monthly national survey conducted by the Department of Labor using scientific sampling techniques designed to assure accuracy.

Unemployed worker: a person willing and able to work, actively seeking work, but unable to find a job at the going wage rate

The **labor force** is defined to be all of those people who are actively involved in supplying labor. That is, it is composed of all of those who are actually working, plus those who are actively seeking work (the unemployed). In 1977 the civilian labor force numbered 97.4 million out of a working-age population of over 158 million. The official unemployment rate for 1977 is found by dividing the average number of unemployed people for 1977 (6.8 million) by the size of the labor force (97.4 million), giving an unemployment rate of 7 percent.

Labor force: all those involved in the labor market; those working plus those actively seeking work

Note that there are, mathematically, two ways for the unemployment rate to rise. The first is if some people who are currently employed get fired or laid off. In this case, the size of the labor force remains constant, but the number of individuals unemployed (the fraction's numerator) rises. The unemployment rate also goes up, however, if people who were previously not in the labor force (like students or housewives) decide to start looking for work. This increases both the size of the labor force and the number of people unemployed, causing the unemployment statistics to get worse.

This second cause of rising unemployment rates—new entrants into the labor force—is one of the principle causes of our current unemployment problem. More people want to work these days. Between 1967 and 1977, the labor force grew by over 26 percent, while the working-age population was growing by less than 20 percent. A larger and larger proportion of working age people are getting out and looking for work. In many cases they lack experience or skills necessary to successfully compete in the job market.

Why has the labor force grown so rapidly? The changing role of women in the economy is one factor. Women have broken away from old nonmarket jobs as housewives and begun to seek careers of their own. This movement has been reinforced by the impact of heavy inflation rates on the American household. Many families have come to discover that it now takes two paychecks to maintain their chosen standard of living. Better child-care facilities have contributed to this movement, too. Increasing numbers of young people are joining the job hunt, as well. The problem of unemployment is, in some respects, the problem of creating jobs for these new members of the labor force.

It is important to realize that the unemployment rate does not reflect all of the unemployment problem. There are two groups which suffer an unemployment problem but which are not included in the calculation of the unemployment rate. These groups are the following:

1. THE UNDEREMPLOYED. The Labor Department counts a person as being employed if the worker earned any wages or salary during the period in question. Part-time workers (who may be seeking full-time work) and people working in temporary jobs (like an engineer pumping gas while looking for a job in his field) are counted as fully employed even though they may be searching for a job and, in this sense, are **underemployed workers.** Their jobs are just stop-gap measures to earn an income until they can find a job that fits their talents and needs. These people are neither fully employed nor really unemployed (in a technical sense), but they are clearly part of the unemployment problem. Their time and talents are not being fully utilized by the economy.

Underemployed worker: part-time workers who seek full-time jobs or people employed at occupations which do not use their training or skills

2. THE DISCOURAGED WORKERS. People who have been unemployed for a long time often get discouraged and stop looking for work. Any number of explanations can be found for their continuing inability to find work. But when they give up looking, they officially drop out of the labor force and are no longer "unemployed" (because they are not actively seeking work). These hard-core unemployed people represent a real economic and social problem which does not show up in the unemployment rates. Indeed, when **discouraged workers** drop out of the labor force, the unemployment rate actually goes down, suggesting that the problem has gotten better, not worse.

Discouraged workers: people who become discouraged with employment prospects and leave the labor force

Unemployment statistics, then, are not perfect measures of the extent of the unemployment problem, although they are good general indicators of the relative severity of the unemployment problem in the economy.

THE LABOR MARKET

In order to understand some of the basic causes of unemployment, it is necessary to understand how the labor market works. The labor market is the market where labor is exchanged for income. It is the job market. A hypothetical job market is pictured in Figure 3-2.

The supply of labor is made up of people who choose whether and how much they would like to work. The supply curve is upward-sloping, indicating a positive wage response—more people will choose to work more hours as the wage they receive increases. This labor-supply curve represents the number of people who are offering their services in exchange

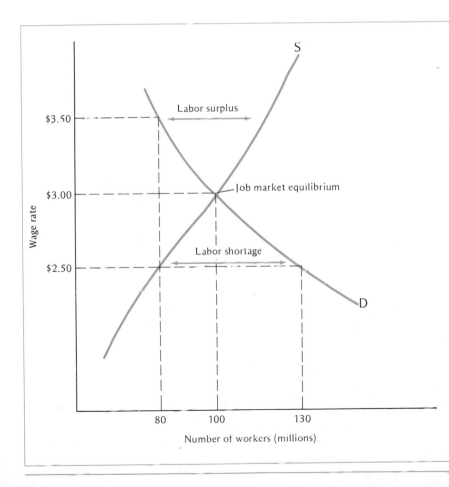

FIGURE 3-2: THE LABOR MARKET
At the wage rate of $3.00 per hour, the amount of labor supplied and demanded is equal. At all other wage rates, labor shortages or surpluses act to push the wage rate toward $3.00.

Productivity: the relative ability of a resource to produce goods and services; often measured by the amount of production per man-hour

Aggregate demand (AD): desired total purchases of goods and services in an economy

for wages. The supply of labor has increased (the labor supply has shifted to the right) steadily over the past few years. The increase has come because of increases in the population and increases in the proportion of the population that is seeking employment.

The demand curve for labor comes from businesses who want and need workers. What determines the number of workers that are hired and the wage that the employer is willing to pay them? Two things are obvious: the demand for the business' output and worker **productivity,** or the ability of the worker to contribute to production.

The demand for workers is directly related to **aggregate demand (AD)**—the demand for all goods and services. When aggregate (or total) demand rises, producers need more workers to make the goods to satisfy their customers. The demand for labor therefore rises and employment rises, too. During economic downturns (when aggregate demand falls) the demand for labor falls and unemployment results.

Labor demand also hinges on the productivity of labor. In essence, an employer is only willing to hire additional workers if it appears that they will add at least as much to production as it will cost to pay their wages. In this way, an employer would be willing to pay $3.00 per hour to any worker who can produce at least $3.00 per hour or more worth of additional goods (obviously the most productive workers—those that can add the most to production—will be hired first). An individual who can add just $2.75 worth of production per hour will be unemployed if the going wage rate is $3.00. It simply would be unprofitable to hire this person. At a wage of $2.50 per hour, however, this individual would have a job (assuming sufficient aggregate demand).

The demand curve for labor is therefore downward-sloping. As the wage rate falls, more and more workers are sought, because their skills can be profitably used by business. As the wage rate rises, on the other hand, only those people with the highest productivity are kept on, and the quantity of labor demanded falls.

The relationship between the demand for labor and the productivity of labor accounts for the wage-lag effect discussed in Chapter 1. As inflation occurs, the price of an employer's production rises. This increase in the price of output translates into an increase in the value of worker production. A worker who can produce 100 hamburgers per hour is worth a higher wage when hamburgers sell for $1.00 than when they sell for 85¢. Inflation, therefore, increases the value of workers' added production (productivity) and so causes the demand for labor to increase (shift to the right). The increased demand for labor brings about higher total employment. The Phillips Curve relationship between inflation and unemployment follows.

In Figure 3-2, the equilibrium average wage rate is shown to be $3.00. At this wage, the amount of labor demanded (the number of workers who add $3.00 or more per hour to production) is equal to the amount of labor supplied (the number of people who are willing to work for $3.00). At any wage rate above $3.00, there will be a surplus of labor. The excess of job seekers will, in theory, bid down the wage and restore equilibrium. At a wage below the equilibrium, employers attempt to hire more labor and cause the wage rate to rise. The forces of demand and supply work here just as they did in the markets discussed in Chapter 2.

Given this labor-market setting, what are the causes of unemployment? To fully answer this question it must be realized that unemployment can result from many different types of economic problems. There are at least three different types of unemployment, each with a different set of roots: cyclical unemployment is caused by the ups and downs of business cycles; structural unemployment results from a poor matching of job requirements and worker skills; frictional unemployment stems from a variety of institutional factors which keep the labor market from operating efficiently.

CYCLICAL UNEMPLOYMENT

Assume for a moment that the supply of labor in Figure 3-2 is constant as is approximately the case for short periods of time. If the supply of labor does not change, then the number of workers employed will vary directly with the demand for labor. If worker productivity does not change very much, either, in the short run, then unemployment will rise and fall as the total demand for goods and services—aggregate demand—rises and falls. The unemployment which results from falling aggregate demand is called **cyclical unemployment.**

Cyclical unemployment is not hard to understand. During a recession, for example, consumers normally buy fewer things like new cars. They fix up old goods and generally delay major purchases until the employment picture is brighter. Manufacturers who are selling fewer cars, refrigerators, and TV sets shut down factories and lay off workers until the demand for their output is revived. This causes cyclical unemployment. When the economy has improved and sales of all these items become stronger, cyclical unemployment is reduced.

Cyclical unemployment is a serious problem. This problem is made even worse by the existence of **"sticky" wages.** The term sticky wages refers to wages that, because of institutional factors like minimum-wage laws and labor agreements, are set for relatively long periods of time. When market conditions change, these wages cannot respond to these changes. When decreases in aggregate demand indicate that wages should fall, for example, the existence of these sticky wages keeps wage rates high. Why won't they

Cyclical unemployment: unemployment resulting from decreases in AD

Sticky wages: inflexible wages; wage rates that do not change in response to changing labor market conditions

FIGURE 3-3: DECREASE IN THE DEMAND FOR LABOR WITH STICKY WAGES
Because wages here are "sticky"—set by a labor contract, for example—they cannot fall in response to a surplus of labor. Since employers cannot cut wages, they must cut employment instead—resulting in higher unemployment.

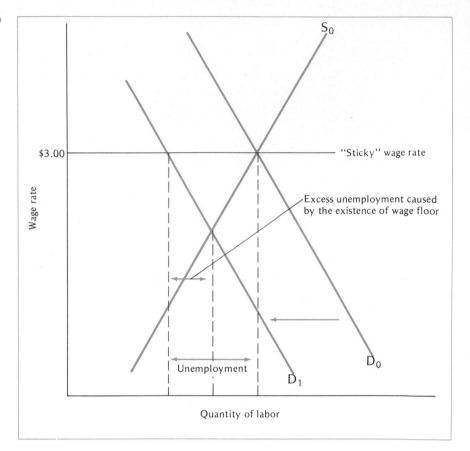

fall? Wages are not all set in the market anymore. Workers have long-term labor contracts, cost-of-living protection, and union rules, all of which restrict their ability to "bid down" wages. This often results in a floor on wages, as shown in Figure 3-3, which prevents workers from offering to take a pay cut instead of becoming unemployed.

When a recession causes the demand for labor to fall, employers must lower their costs of production one of two ways: they can either lay off many people, or they can lay off a few and employ the rest at lower wages. A **wage floor** (often caused by a union rule or labor contract) takes away the second option. Since workers can't take a pay cut (or can, but won't), employment falls, and many people who are willing and ready to work are put out of a job—they become unemployed.

A related cause of high unemployment rates are governmental **minimum-wage laws.** These laws seem to be helping low-paid workers by guaranteeing them relatively high pay for their labor, but this is not their real

Wage floor: minimum-wage rate caused by minimum-wage laws or sticky wages in a particular labor market

Minimum-wage laws: federal laws which specify a minimum legal wage for workers in a variety of job categories

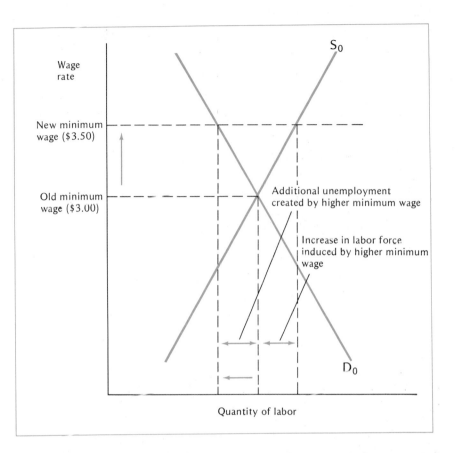

FIGURE 3-4: EFFECT OF AN INCREASE IN
THE MINIMUM WAGE
*A rise in the minimum wage results in
unemployment for some current
workers (whose labor is not worth
$3.00) and a rise in income for those
who are able to retain their jobs.*

effect. Suppose that the minimum wage is raised from, say, $3.00 to $3.50 per hour. This situation is shown in Figure 3-4. If the market for this particular type of labor was in equilibrium before the increase in the legal minimum wage, then this new law will create a surplus of labor (more people will start looking for work in response to the higher wage rate). At the higher minimum wage, there is a larger amount of labor offered. However, at this high wage, employers find that they cannot afford to employ all the workers they had before, much less put any additional people to work. At the higher wage, low-productivity workers are unprofitable and are laid off. Employment falls; the unemployment rate rises. Those workers who have retained their jobs are better off—they are making higher wages. But a smaller number of people have paid for this benefit with their jobs. Their labor, suddenly overpriced because of legislative actions, is no longer demanded, and their time is now spent in the unemployment line (if they are eligible for benefits), not on the production line.

Cyclical unemployment may be inevitable, even with intelligent government policies, but the existence of inflexible wages in labor markets tends to make cyclical unemployment a greater problem than would otherwise be the case.

STRUCTURAL UNEMPLOYMENT

Structural unemployment: unemployment resulting from a poor matching of worker skills and job needs

Structural unemployment refers to the problem faced by people who lack the proper skills with which to compete in today's job market. Structural unemployment can exist even when there are many jobs available if the skills and talents required for the vacant jobs are different from those that jobless workers possess.

In a growing economy, some industries are always expanding rapidly and hiring more workers, while some are contracting and cutting their employment. Unemployed workers need to acquire new skills—to "retool"—if they are to again enter the ranks of the employed. Such training is costly and often difficult to find. Those people who most need the training are exactly those who are least able to afford it and least likely to secure loans to pay for it. A related problem is that training programs often fail to meet the needs of those enrolled. There have been many cases of job programs which have taken people with unmarketable skills and trained them for new jobs which are also unavailable. These individuals merely became unemployable at a better class of jobs.

How serious is the structural unemployment problem? Opinions differ here. Clearly for some groups which lack necessary job skills completely (as many teenaged workers do), the problem is severe. But many of those unemployed workers that fall into the "structural" classification are voluntarily unemployed. They may be able to find jobs such as janitors or manual laborers, but choose to remain unemployed and wait for better-paying jobs to open up. This kind of voluntary unemployment is a problem, but less of one than that faced by people whose skills are such that finding any job, even a low-paying or low-status one, is impossible.

FRICTIONAL UNEMPLOYMENT

Frictional unemployment: unemployment resulting from imperfections in the labor market such as poor information about jobs and lack of worker mobility

Even when aggregate demand is high, a certain amount of unemployment results among workers with needed skills because of inefficiencies in the labor market. The labor market often has trouble fitting willing workers into vacant jobs. A number of labor market problems which result in high levels of such **frictional unemployment** are the following:

1. IMPERFECT INFORMATION. For an unemployed person, the most expensive (and most important) budget item is information. Unemployed people generally lack information about what types of jobs are available, where those jobs are, and the training needed to qualify for them.

There are several sources of this necessary information, such as unemployment offices, employment agencies, union hiring halls, and newspapers. But some, like the employment agency, are costly, and others, like the newspaper classified ads and state job offices, offer only incomplete listings limited to relatively small geographic or occupational areas. The most effective source of job leads actually turns out to be the least sophisticated one: word-of-mouth information from friends and relatives. As a result, an unemployed janitor may be out of work for months, while a job for a janitor waits unfilled in the same city or county. Getting unemployed workers and unfilled jobs together is a difficult proposition, and the poor informational systems currently in use make it even harder.

Students suffer from a different kind of "information gap." College students often train for a career, not knowing if jobs will be available in that occupation when they enter the labor market. In the early 1970s, for example, many college students took degrees in education because they had heard that there was a need for teachers. This need turned out to be more apparent than real. Because of this poor information, there is now an unemployed surplus of schoolteachers in most areas.

Because information of this type is so poor, the college student is forced to gamble when choosing a particular type of college training. Students who pick a major which provides training for a specific job run the risk that the demand for that particular job will disappear before graduation or soon thereafter. This gamble may help explain the current emphasis on many campuses for more general "lifetime" training. A general education—emphasizing basic skills such as reading, writing, and thinking—is one way to hedge one's bets, since this type of education prepares the student for a number of occupations, not all of which are likely to disappear at once.

Economics is such a broad field of study. Economists perform a variety of useful services and are readily adaptable to changing demands. End of commercial.

Clearly, getting information is costly and time-consuming. Improving information concerning job openings and career opportunities would yield dividends in terms of lower unemployment in the economy.

2. BARRIERS TO OCCUPATIONAL ENTRY. Sometimes people are unable to get jobs for which they are qualified and needed because they are unable to penetrate a particular job market due to restrictions placed on entry to that field.

Unions set up rules that sometimes make it difficult for nonmembers to get jobs—and difficult for them to join the union as well. Barbers, embalmers, pharmacists, dentists, architects, and many others must pass state licensing exams before they can practice their trades. Lawyers must do well on bar exams, or their employment opportunities are restricted. Some good teachers who lack a Ph.D. find that getting or holding a college teaching position is difficult.

Barriers to occupational entry: institutional factors which limit or restrict employment in various occupations

In many cases good workers cannot take jobs which they are qualified for because, while they have the necessary skills, they lack the needed "credentials." Many of these **barriers to occupational entry** (like the licensing of barbers) are designed to protect the public from shoddy products and services. Unfortunately, many times the licensing boards are made up of people with a vested interest in restricting the supply of a particular good or service so that the income of the protected group can be kept high. By restricting entry into an occupational area, those already holding jobs earn higher wages. This is fine for them, but the system also causes unemployment among those who are denied entry to the labor market in this way.

3. DISCRIMINATION.

The rational employer hires workers on the basis of their skills and their productivity. Unfortunately, many employers have, consciously or unconsciously, developed an image of the way that their workers should look, act, and dress. Individuals who don't fit into this mold—because they are members of racial minorities, women, products of a different ethnic background, or just young—often don't get the jobs for which they are qualified for this reason. This causes unemployment to be high among these groups and contributes to the overall unemployment problem.

4. LACK OF MOBILITY.

Workers often remain unemployed and unfilled jobs remain vacant because they are separated by long (and sometimes not-so-long) distances. These distances reduce the information flow between employer and job seeker, but they create another problem as well. Families are often unwilling to pull up roots and move from pockets of high unemployment to areas where job prospects are better. This lack of mobility both hurts the workers who can't find a job because they are in the wrong city or region and keeps industries from expanding as quickly as would otherwise be the case because of local shortages of workers. Worker mobility has increased in the United States in recent years as the economy has grown, but lack of mobility is still a major cause of frictional unemployment.

When people lose their jobs, the lost income can cause considerable damage to their standard of living and economic well-being. The unemployment insurance system is designed to reduce the hardship caused by unemployment. The unemployment insurance system works like this: In most industries (some occupations are not covered by unemployment insurance), employers pay a small state tax based upon the wages they pay. These taxes are collected and form a pool out of which unemployment compensation benefits are paid.

To be eligible for unemployment compensation, one needs to have worked for a specified minimum amount of time in an occupation covered by the unemployment program. The unemployed worker receives a periodic payment equal to a percentage of the lost wages (the percentage varies from state to state).

The existence of unemployment insurance surely helps reduce the severity of the unemployment problem, but it also may contribute to higher unemployment rates. Workers who are collecting unemployment compensation behave differently than workers who do not receive these payments. First, they are often unwilling to bid down the wage rate—to accept low-paying jobs. Why accept a job paying $100 per week when unemployment insurance pays $75 and the unemployment payments are not taxable? Wages must be higher to induce these individuals to take jobs. Only when their benefits run out (in six months or a year) are they likely to consider these low-paying jobs.

The existence of unemployment insurance also contributes to higher structural unemployment rates because it allows people to stay unemployed longer as they search for better jobs. Without unemployment benefits, a jobless worker might jump at the first job he found, even if it didn't exactly fit his talents or needs. With unemployment insurance, this person can perhaps afford to search longer for just the right job.

To the extent that this longer job search results in a better matching of people and works, it is a good thing. But because It results in lower production in the meantime and hIgher taxes for those who contribute to the unemployment insurance program, this phenomenon is undesirable.

UNEMPLOYMENT INSURANCE

Full employment: the maximum possible employment rate in a healthy economy

Economists and policy makers talk about the economic goal of **full employment,** but what does this mean? One hundred percent employment? Zero percent unemployment?

No, a zero unemployment rate is impossible. The market imperfections just discussed, plus "normal" unemployment which takes place as people

THE GOAL OF FULL EMPLOYMENT

routinely move from one job to another, from one occupation to another, or move from city to city will always give us some unemployment, even in a well-functioning economy.

Full employment is said to prevail when the only unemployment is of the minimal structural and frictional kind. Even increases in aggregate demand or productivity may not be able to reduce the unemployment rate once full employment is reached—simply because labor market imperfections, and not other factors, are causing the joblessness.

How do we know when we have hit full employment? In the 1960s there was some agreement that full employment occurred when the unemployment rate was down to about 4 percent (the economy therefore reached full employment in the late 1960s). These days the definition of full employment is not so clear. Our rapidly expanding labor force is not very homogeneous—women and young workers have different problems entering the job force than experienced workers have finding new jobs. As a result, the frictional unemployment rate seems to have risen. Full employment may well occur at a 5 or even a 6 percent unemployment rate these days.

The definition of full employment cannot be exact. One of former President Gerald Ford's economic advisors even went so far as to tell Congress that he would define full employment as being whatever the unemployment rate turned out to be at election time!

The goal of full employment should not be interpreted as a chase to achieve some particular numerical unemployment goal, since some economic problems would remain even at a low average unemployment rate. Our goals should be to attain high levels of employment and to solve the problems of those who are not able to contribute to the productive economy. To really understand this goal, we must better understand the unemployment problem.

HOW SERIOUS IS THE UNEMPLOYMENT PROBLEM?

To understand the nature of the unemployment problem at any given time, it is not enough just to know what the unemployment rate is. The unemployment rate is important, to be sure, but its meaning changes over time as the definition of full employment changes. Focusing on the unemployment rate is not enough, as well, because it gives the impression that unemployment is just one problem, possibly with a single solution, when in fact it can be many problems all of which are called "unemployment" for convenience.

To really understand how serious the unemployment problem is, we must find the answer to four separate questions:

1. HOW MANY ARE UNEMPLOYED? This is the only one of the four questions where the unemployment rate published in the newspaper is of much help. The unemployment rate, by telling us how many people are out of work, gives us a tool to use in estimating the extent of hardship that unemployment is causing in the country.

In 1976, for example, the unemployment rate was 7.7 percent. This translates to about 7.3 million people out of work, but the story does not end here. Unemployed people have families who also suffer from the lowered income. The figure of 7.3 million workers unemployed means that families totaling perhaps as many as 18 million people were without a crucial income source. This is roughly equal to the combined populations of Alaska, Washington, Oregon, Idaho, Montana, Nevada, Utah, Arizona, New Mexico, North and South Dakota, Colorado, and Nebraska. Clearly, unemployment is a serious problem affecting a large portion of the economy.

This is the most obvious way to gauge the impact of unemployment, but it may lead us to the view that there is only one problem here. The remaining three questions will help us pinpoint other problems and possibly suggest solutions.

2. WHO ARE THE UNEMPLOYED? A 7 percent unemployment rate does not mean that about 1 out of every 14 workers everywhere is unemployed. Far from it. Unemployment varies by geographical area, and it also is different for different groups within the population. Figure 3-5 shows the unemployment rates for different components of the labor force.

The unemployment figures shown here for 1977 and 1967 display several relationships which have been fairly stable over the years. Unemployment is relatively lower among males and whites, and relatively higher among women, teenagers, and nonwhites.

Teenagers have traditionally had the highest unemployment rates, and this represents a serious problem. These are people who are trying to effectively enter the labor market. Their high rate of failure to do this may affect them most of their lives. Their problem may be lack of proper training, or perhaps a lack of low-paying "starting" jobs caused by high minimum wages which prevent employers from taking on young, inexperienced workers. This is a particular type of problem, and the kinds of governmental policies which would help older, experienced workers find jobs may, indeed, have failed to help young workers enter the productive economy. The solution here may be better training for young workers, or less legislation designed to boost wages higher than these inexperienced workers can reasonably expect to receive.

The higher unemployment rates for females and nonwhites represent

FIGURE 3-5: WHO ARE THE
UNEMPLOYED?

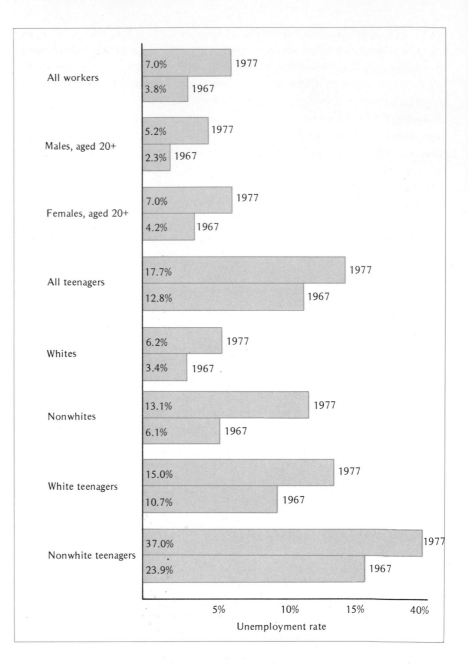

another problem. Lack of training may again be a problem, but it is likely
that discrimination enters the picture here and prevents qualified workers
from receiving the jobs that they need. This is a different type of problem
requiring a different solution.

The higher overall unemployment rates in 1977 suggest that there was insufficient aggregate demand compared to the high-employment year 1967. Additional policies to stimulate employment, uncalled for in 1967, were needed to put the economy to work.

3. HOW LONG HAVE PEOPLE BEEN UNEMPLOYED? Unemployment can be an inconvenience, a serious problem, or a life-shattering experience, depending on its duration—how long unemployment lasts. If we want to understand the unemployment problem, we must know how long the unemployed have been unable to find a job.

Figure 3-6 gives us an idea of the way that this problem has changed. In 1977, 72 percent of those unemployed had been without a job for fourteen weeks or less, while the "hard-core" unemployed (those who had been without employment for six months or more) accounted for 15 percent of the total.

Ten years before, however, fully 85 percent of the unemployed had been

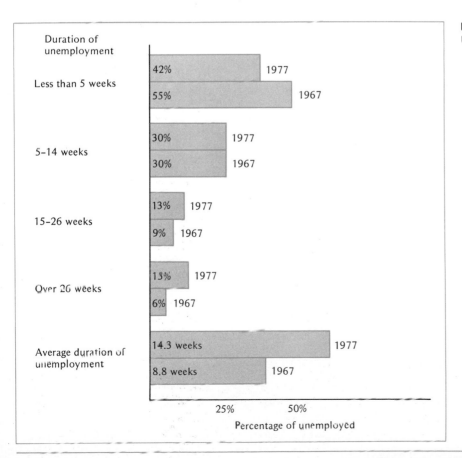

FIGURE 3-6: HOW LONG ARE THEY UNEMPLOYED?

out of a job for only a relatively short period, while the hard-core unemployed accounted for only 6 percent of the total.

The message here is clear. A greater proportion of the unemployed were out of work for longer periods in 1977—they suffered a more severe unemployment problem, in this sense, than did jobless workers in 1967. The average duration of unemployment was over 60 percent longer in 1977 than in 1967.

4. WHY ARE PEOPLE UNEMPLOYED? There are essentially four ways to become unemployed. You can quit an existing job (a job leaver), be fired or laid off (a job loser), return to the job market after having left it to do something else (a reentrant), or suddenly start looking for work for the first time because, say, you have graduated from school (a new entrant into the labor force). Of these types of unemployed workers, the plight of the job loser may be the most critical, and that of the new entrant the most difficult to solve.

Figure 3-7 shows the types of unemployment for the years 1977 and 1967. The differences here are small but important. Note that, in 1977, the numbers of job losers were relatively high and the amount of reentrants

FIGURE 3-7: WHY ARE THEY UNEMPLOYED?

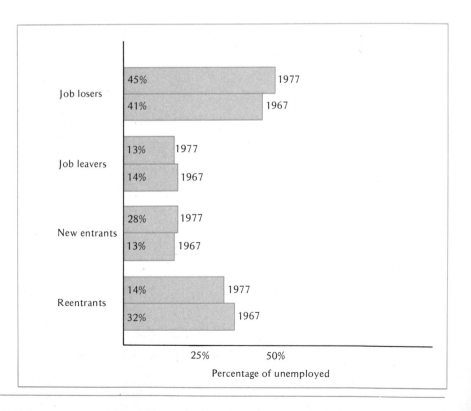

relatively low. This indicates, again, insufficient total demand for output, causing almost half of the unemployed to be job losers and discouraging others from reentering the labor force. The proportion of new entrants is higher in 1977, because of greater labor-force participation—more and more people were moving away from nonmarket activities and looking for work.

Unemployment is really a very complicated problem, and one that is not likely to be solved easily or quickly. One of the problems that we have in dealing with unemployment is that there is a tendency to view the unemployed as a uniform group and to try to find one solution to their problem. Unemployment is more usefully viewed as a "layer cake." Different groups—the layers—experience different unemployment rates for different reasons. One policy will not solve all of their problems. Market imperfections form the icing which holds all of the groups in unemployment. There are no quick and easy answers here, only ways of understanding the problems and some of the answers they suggest.

SUMMARY

1. The unemployment rate tells the proportion of the labor force (those actively involved in working or looking for work) who are currently unable to find employment. The unemployment rate gives a good idea of the number of people out of work, but it fails to count a number of groups who are part of the unemployment problem even though they are not officially "unemployed."

2. The unemployment record is dismal. Unemployment rates have remained fairly high. Only twice since 1950 (during the Korean and Vietnam Wars) has the unemployment rate fallen below 4 percent.

3. There are a number of causes of unemployment. Falling demand for final goods, slowing growth in productivity, and large increases in the labor force have caused the unemployment rate to rise in recent years. Sticky wages, lack of information, poor labor mobility and other factors have also contributed to the high "frictional" unemployment rate.

4. Full employment is the lowest unemployment rate that even a healthy economy could reasonably hope to achieve. Because of imperfections in the labor market, a zero percent unemployment rate is impossible to achieve. Full employment now probably occurs at an unemployment rate in the range of 5 to 6 percent.

5. Minimum-wage laws aggrevate the unemployment problem, particularly for relatively unskilled workers and young people. Minimum-wage laws assure

a higher wage for those who retain their jobs, but they cause substantial unemployment.

6. The unemployment rate tells just part of the story about unemployment. In order to really understand how serious the unemployment situation is, one must ask not only how many are unemployed, but also who are the unemployed, how long have they been unemployed, and why are they unemployed.

DISCUSSION QUESTIONS

1. Define unemployment. Unemployment is said to result from certain market imperfections. What are these market imperfections and how do they result in unemployment?

2. Define the following terms and explain how they differ:

   ☐ Full employment
   ☐ Frictional employment
   ☐ Underemployment

3. Suppose that teenagers were subject to a lower legal minimum wage than experienced workers. What impact do you think this would have on the unemployment problem? Explain.

4. What do you think would happen if minimum-wage laws were repealed? Would the result be good or bad? Explain.

5. What is the nature of our current unemployment problem? (Hint: You can find the answers to the preceding four unemployment questions in a publication called *Economic Indicators* published monthly by the President's Council of Economic Advisors and available in your college library).

TEST YOURSELF

Determine whether each of the following statements is *true* or *false*. Be able to defend your choice.

1. The unemployment rate falls when the number of people employed increases.

2. The so-called *discouraged workers* who have dropped out of the labor force are not included in the unemployment rate.

3. Suppose that the population is 100 million people. Of this group, 45 million are working and 5 million are actively seeking a job. The unemployment rate is therefore 5 percent.

4. The existence of unemployment insurance helps lower the unemployment rate.

5. If workers become more productive, the demand for their labor increases.

6. Minimum-wage laws help make teenagers better off than they would be without minimum-wage legislation.

7. Unemployment compensation causes higher levels of struc-

tural unemployment.

8. Full employment has not been often achieved in the United States in recent years.

9. Teenagers have the highest unemployment rate of any group in the population.

10. An unemployment rate of 6 percent in 1965 and an unemployment rate of 6 percent in 1985 would have the same economic meaning.

4
Understanding
Inflation

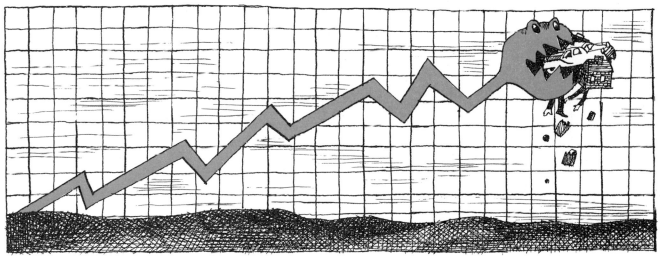

This chapter is designed to help you understand what inflation is and why it is a national economic problem. This chapter will answer many questions that you may have about inflation, including the following:

What is inflation?

What is the record on inflation?

How does inflation affect the economy?

Who loses from inflation? Does anyone gain?

How can one hedge against inflation's impact?

How is inflation measured?

What are the different measures of inflation and what do they measure?

Inflation: a substantial, sustained increase in the general level of prices

Inflation is like the caterpillar's magic mushroom in *Alice in Wonderland*. "One side will make you grow taller and the other side will make you grow shorter," the caterpillar told Alice.

Inflation has the same dual impact on the economy as eating the mushroom had on Alice. On the one hand, inflation increases our wages and makes the things we own worth more dollars than before. Inflation makes these **money values** grow taller. At the same time, however, inflation reduces the *real value* of our income. Each dollar grows smaller and smaller in terms of the goods and services that can be bought.

Money value: the value of an item as measured by the amount of current dollars required to purchase that item

Inflation, then, makes us at once both richer and poorer. The question is, as Alice said: "And now which is which?"

WHAT IS INFLATION?

Inflation is defined to be a substantial, sustained increase in the general level of prices. This definition is important because all price increases are not inflation. Changes in individual prices resulting from individual market conditions do not constitute inflation. Inflation is said to occur when a large number of prices around the economy are rising together, creating an increase in the average price (however calculated) of the things that we buy. The **inflation rate** tells us how fast this average price is rising.

Inflation rate: the rate of increase in prices as measured by a price index

Deflation: a substantial, sustained decrease in the general level of prices

Deflation is the extreme opposite of inflation. Deflation would mean a substantial, sustained decrease in the general level of prices. Deflation has occurred in the past, often during periods of economic despair (like the Great Depression). Deflation is not, as some would have it, a desirable economic goal. With prices of output falling, it would be only a short period until wages fall, too. Many of the detrimental economic impacts of inflation which we will discuss in this chapter would occur during a deflationary period. Our goal is not to actually cause prices to fall, but rather to end their rise—**price stability**.

Price stability: a national economic goal; a situation where inflation rates are close to zero

Inflation is not a new concept to any of us. Inflation has become a built-in factor in our expectations and economic decisions. A less familiar concept is the national economic goal of price stability. Consider for a moment what is meant by price stability. In an economy without inflation, the prices of goods wouldn't be expected to rise every year. Individual prices would rise (and fall!) in response to individual market conditions—supply and demand factors. A no-inflation economy would be one where next year's cars would cost about as much as this year's models. Tuition would be pretty much the same during your senior as during your freshman year. Cost-of-living pay increases would not be very important because prices would not be expected to rise. And incredibly, things like Hershey bars would neither shrink nor rise in price from one year to the next.

This idea of price stability is foreign to most of us. We are more accustomed to the world of rising prices and shrinking candy bars. This chapter won't explain what causes inflation (the causes of inflation will be dealt with in Part II). It will discuss, instead, what inflation does. It will look at the economic impacts of inflation, the winners and losers that inflation generates, and the **price indices** that are used to measure inflation. Throughout this study, our goals will be to understand just why inflation is a problem and how it affects individuals, businesses, and governments.

Price index (indices): mathematical estimators of inflation which compare the price of a fixed market basket of items for different years

How have we done in achieving our goal of price stability in the United States? The record has been quite dismal in recent years. Figure 4-1 shows the inflation rate for the period 1950–1978.

Inflation rates in the 1950s varied widely. Prices rose at a nearly 8 percent annual rate between 1950 and 1951, but actually fell (deflation!) for the last time in recent history in 1954–1955. On the whole, the average annual inflation rate was about 2 percent for the decade of the 1950s. Two percent

THE INFLATION RECORD

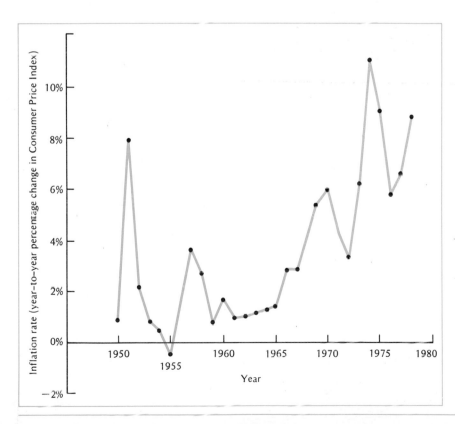

FIGURE 4-1: AVERAGE ANNUAL INFLATION RATES, 1950–1978
Although inflation rates were highly volatile in this period (rising and falling dramatically), the overall trend was toward higher inflation rates. During the 1950s the average yearly inflation rate was just 2.0 percent. This increased to an average of 2.3 percent in the 1960s and jumped to over 5.2 percent in the period 1970–1978.

inflation probably seems very mild to most of us who are used to much higher rates, but in the 1950s it was considered a real problem. "Creeping inflation," as it was called, was thought to be a threat to prosperity. It may well be, but we would surely trade that problem for the current inflation dilemma.

The 1960s were a period of relatively low but rising inflation rates. The ailing economy of the late 1950s left little reason for large price increases. But as rising government spending caused demand-pull inflationary pressures, the price level rose in the second half of the decade. The average annual inflation rate for the 1960s was still low—just 2.3 percent—but rising ominously.

The 1970s saw inflation rise to even higher levels. Prices rose at double-digit rates during 1974–1975, and were increasing rapidly at the end of the decade. The average annual inflation rate of the 1960s was more than doubled during the decade of the 1970s. Creeping inflation was no longer the problem—"galloping inflation" had now become the enemy.

ECONOMIC EFFECTS OF INFLATION

Inflation, like unemployment, is a national economic problem. But exactly why is it such a major concern? To understand this, one must first understand the purpose of money in the economy. Money is used as a measure of value, like inches are used as a measure of length or ounces as a measure of weight.

If a bottle of wine costs $4 and a new car costs $5000, it is clear that the greater cost of the car means that it is more valuable than the wine, using the dollar as a unit of measure. Inflation shrinks our unit of measure. If prices rise an average of 10 percent, this means that it now takes $110 to "measure" the same value that $100 would have measured before. Economists say that inflation reduces the **purchasing power** of the dollar because each dollar can now be exchanged for less value than before.

This shrinking of the dollar creates a number of problems of a very serious nature. It is a problem for at least six reasons:

Purchasing power: the value of money as measured by the amount of goods and services that money will buy

1. INFLATION HURTS PEOPLE LIVING ON FIXED INCOMES.

Retired people living on fixed pensions and others who have incomes which do not rise with the general level of prices will find that, as inflation shrinks the size of their dollars, it shrinks the amount of goods and services which they can purchase. Inflation robs them of their standard of living.

While this is a major problem today, it is less of a problem than it used to be because policy makers have recognized this situation and acted to "index" Social Security and other types of previously fixed payments.

Indexation means tying payments to some sort of inflation index. Social Security payments now rise in step with prices, protecting retired people from inflation. Unfortunately, not all fixed incomes are indexed, and the inflation thief still steals from many households.

Indexation: programs which tie wages, values, and/or taxes to a price index

2. INFLATION AFFECTS BORROWERS AND LENDERS. Would you be willing to lend someone $100 for a year at an interest rate of 5 percent if you expected the inflation rate to be 10 percent for that period? Most people wouldn't. You would receive back $105 at the end of the year, but because the dollar has shrunk by 10 percent, the $105 that you receive would purchase fewer goods and services than the $100 that you originally lent.

Because of this phenomenon, the rate of inflation tends to get "built into" the interest rate. If you are willing to lend money at 5 percent interest without inflation, you would want to receive at least 15 percent interest if you expect a 10 percent inflation rate. You need to do this in order to protect the purchasing power of the loan repayment.

An economist named Irving Fisher formulated the following equation to summarize the impact of inflation on interest rates:

$$i_n = i_r + P_e$$

where i_n is the nominal (actual) rate of interest that you would pay or receive, i_r is the "real" interest rate (adjusted for inflation), and P_e is the expected rate of inflation for the period of the loan. As the anticipated rate of inflation rises, so does the interest rate.

Suppose the real interest rate (i_r) on some type of loan is 5 percent and that this real interest rate is constant. Then the amount that you must pay for the loan (i_n) depends directly on the inflation rate. If 5 percent inflation is expected, the loan will cost you 10 percent interest. If prices are thought to be rising by 10 percent, the interest rate will rise to 15 percent! In each case, the lender will have to ask for higher interest rates in order to keep the value of his repayments from being shrunk by the inflation.

Inflation, therefore, tends to drive up interest rates. This alone would not be a very large problem, if we could accurately predict the rate of inflation. But the actual rate of inflation and the expected one are often different, and this creates problems.

Suppose you expected a 10 percent rate of inflation, and so borrowed money at 15 percent interest to purchase a car. Now suppose that the actual rate of inflation turned out to be only 7 percent. What has happened? Because inflation has been unexpectedly low, the amount of actual purchasing power that you are paying to the lender is greater than you had anticipated. Unexpectedly low inflation rates tend to hurt borrowers who make greater payments, adjusted for inflation, than anticipated and benefit lenders who will receive more than they had bargained for.

Unexpectedly high inflation rates have just the opposite effect. If the inflation rate had turned out to be 20 percent, you would be paying back smaller dollars than expected. The lender would lose because he would receive payments which are smaller in real terms than the money originally lent. Unexpectedly high inflation rates tend to hurt lenders and benefit borrowers.

Most people are both lenders (they "lend" their money to banks and insurance companies) and borrowers (for things like houses and cars) and so must deal with both sides of this problem.

3. INFLATION DISCOURAGES SAVING. Saving is very important to a modern, growing economy, since savings provide funds to be used for new houses and business investments. Inflation tends to discourage saving because savings accounts are generally not protected from inflation; people quickly discover that if they save their money, it loses value in the bank, but if they spend it now they can get full value.

Why does money lose value in banks during inflationary times? This occurs because the government regulates the rate of interest that banks can pay to savers. Depending on the type of account and bank involved, the interest rate is set roughly at between 4 and 7 percent by the government. Bank interest rates are not allowed to rise much in response to inflation. As a result, money stored in a 5 percent savings account during a 10 percent inflation will lose 5 percent of its purchasing power each year. This discourages people from saving and hurts people with money in the bank.

4. INFLATION DISRUPTS THE BALANCE BETWEEN THE PUBLIC AND PRIVATE SECTORS. The **public sector** tends to grow more rapidly than the **private sector** during periods of high inflation. How does inflation cause this? The main source of revenue for the federal government is the income tax. Because it is progressive (imposing higher tax rates on higher incomes), the income tax will generate an "inflation tax" as prices rise.

The inflation tax works like this. As prices go up, most workers try to get a cost-of-living pay increase in order to keep about the same purchasing power. If they are successful, they receive more dollars, although each of these dollars is a little smaller in terms of what it will purchase. Unfortunately, taxes are not levied on purchasing power, but on the number of dollars that you have, so that if prices go up by 10 percent and your income goes up by 10 percent—just staying even—income taxes will actually rise by about 12 percent, faster than either prices or income! The result is that inflation

Public sector: the government part of the economy; includes federal, state, and local governments

Private sector: the nongovernment part of the economy; private industry generates large amounts of revenue for the public sector, fueling Big Government.

There is a way to avoid this. A form of indexing would adjust the tax burden to reflect purchasing power, not just dollar amounts. Indexation of the income tax would stop the inflation tax. Canada and a few other countries have adopted indexed tax systems, but in the United States the topic is still being discussed.

5. INFLATION'S DEADWEIGHT LOSS.

Inflation imposes what economists sometimes call a **deadweight loss** on the economy. We say that a deadweight loss occurs when scarce resources are put to work *not* to produce goods and services that make us better off, but are wasted or used to undertake activities that merely serve to keep us from being worse off.

Deadweight loss: the loss due to wasted resources

During high-inflation periods, a lot of effort goes into just coping with the problem of inflation. Consumers spend more time, labor, and gasoline shopping for bargains, trying to avoid the impact of inflation. Investors spend more time hedging or protecting themselves from inflation than in making profitable investments. People run back and forth between savings banks and checking account banks, trying to squeeze the last drop of interest from each dollar before its purchasing power shrinks even more.

An example of deadweight loss is plainly visible everytime you go to the grocery store. More and more time is now spent not in stocking shelves or checking out customers, but in marking higher prices on goods already on the shelves. Ironically, since inflation causes prices to rise, and since the rising prices mean that time must be spent putting new prices on old goods, higher costs of marking the goods are passed on to the consumer, causing prices to rise even more.

This has even brought about a new grocery store technology. In the past, many stores stamped prices onto canned goods with ink. This works fine, but prices are hard to change, since the ink must be wiped off, the can cleaned, and the new price restamped. To save time, most stores now use small paper labels that are designed so that they cannot be successfully peeled off once they are in place. This permits stores to raise prices just by putting a new price sticker over the old one. For some items, the stack of stickers can get pretty thick, giving us a new inflation measure—the depth of price stickers on canned goods!

6. INFLATION IS SELF-PERPETUATING.

Inflation can be a self-fulfilling prophecy. Once people have experienced inflation for a while, it becomes a part of their expectations. If they expect inflation next year, workers will seek higher wage increases to protect themselves from the higher prices. Now, because of the higher wages, it costs more to produce things, so businesses pass the higher costs on to the consumers. This results in higher market prices and, voilà, inflation!

Economists believe that expectations have a lot to do with the problem of inflation, and in fact the real goal of anti-inflationary policies such as wage and price controls is often simply to make people think that the problem is under control so that they will stop expecting inflation.

The logic here is as follows. If people believe that inflation has been stopped, they will stop lobbying for large pay increases. With wages held down, the cost of doing business will level off and prices should stay stable. Wage and price controls are designed to give people "faith" in stable prices. Faith in this case may be, as Mark Twain said, believing what you know ain't so.

THE ROLE OF EXPECTATIONS

Who wins and who loses in periods of rapid price inflation depends on, among other things, whether that inflation is expected or comes as a surprise.

Even in a world where all inflation is fully anticipated, some groups within the economy would still lose, others win. Suppose, for example, that we expected inflation of about 5 percent over the next several years and that in fact the inflation rate turned out to be 5 percent. Who would be hurt or would benefit from the inflation?

Borrowers and lenders would neither win nor lose. If the inflation rate is perfectly predicted, then it should be accurately built into the nominal interest rate. Since interest rates are 5 percent higher in anticipation of 5 percent inflation, the 5 percent price increase hurts neither side of the bargain. Workers with cost-of-living clauses written into their pay contracts will be unaffected, too, because their wages should rise in step with prices.

Several groups would lose, however. Anyone who holds cash or has money stored in a checking account will lose 5 percent purchasing power each year. Money holders are always hurt by inflation. People who have savings stored in accounts earning less than 5 percent interest will also find their savings worth less and less each year. Individuals with fixed incomes also lose.

Taxpayers lose, too, since their higher wages will be taxed at higher nominal rates because of the structure of the progressive income tax.

Winners? Banks which pay low, government-controlled interest rates on savings accounts win if they can lend out these funds at inflation-induced higher interest rates. The government sector wins as well, because it collects more than 5 percent more income tax dollars when prices rise by 5 percent.

While fully expected inflation would still create winners and losers, it would have the advantage that we could adjust our habits to cope with rising prices. Holding onto only a minimum amount of cash and investing savings in places where it would earn a return higher than the inflation rate would go a long way toward protecting an individual from price increases.

Most inflations are not fully expected. In fact, the real problem with inflation is that it is so unexpected. Looking at the inflation record shown in Figure 4-1, it is hard to imagine anyone accurately predicting the ups and downs in the inflation rate that have taken place recently. What happens, then, when the inflation rate comes as a surprise?

There are two cases to be examined when dealing with unexpected inflation. Inflation, after all, can be unexpectedly high or unexpectedly low. The winners and losers are different in each case.

If inflation is unexpectedly high, people with fixed incomes, people with low-interest savings accounts, and anyone with cash holdings will stand to lose. Lenders also lose. They made loans on the basis of a lower inflation rate and so receive a lower real return on their money. Borrowers win when inflation is unexpectedly high because they pay back less purchasing power than they had bargained for.

Workers, in general, lose, too. If they receive a 5 percent pay increase and then suffer a 7 percent inflation, their **real incomes**—incomes whose measurement is adjusted for inflation—have actually fallen. They have 5 percent more dollars, but each dollar buys 7 percent less than it used to. In total, they can purchase an average of 2 percent fewer goods and services than before inflation.

Real income: a measure of the amount of goods and services that income will buy; income adjusted for the impact of rising prices

Unexpectedly low inflation will change the distribution of costs and benefits. If the inflation rate turns out to be lower than expected, borrowers become losers. They counted upon paying back loans with inflation-shortened dollars. Instead, they must pay up with dollars of relatively high purchasing power. They pay back more, in real terms, than they bargained for. Lenders win since they receive a larger-than-expected amount of purchasing power in return for their initial loan.

Workers who have negotiated high pay increases in anticipation of inflation are better off. They find that their wages have gone up faster than prices and so their real incomes have risen.

People who have spent a lot of time and trouble hedging against the expected high inflation rates by, say, lowering their cash holdings by buying gold and real estate may lose, too. They might have spent too much money hedging against the inflation which did not happen.

WINNERS AND LOSERS

Since different groups can win or lose in the inflation race, depending upon how well the inflation is anticipated, the accuracy of inflationary expectations is very important. Inflation has been anything but predictable, however.

Recent studies have indicated that, while the public is becoming more sophisticated about inflation, they are most often surprised by the size of the inflation rate. If inflation is higher than we expected, exactly who wins and who loses? People with fixed incomes and those who hold large amounts of cash lose. Taxpayers lose, too, as do workers who underestimated the size of the pay increases necessary to keep up with inflation.

Borrowers win (some of them were paying 5 percent interest on house loans in 1974 when inflation was over 10 percent). And lenders lose. But who are these borrowers and lenders?

The borrowers tend to be younger people. With small savings accounts and cash balances but large debts in the form of home mortgages and car and tuition loans, young people are well insulated from inflation. Though they may not know it, these groups do relatively well.

Lenders lose because of the unanticipated high inflation. Who are the lenders? Banks? No, banks really only act as intermediaries. The real lenders are the people who lent their money to the banks in the form of savings deposits. These tend to be older families with less debt and more savings. This group is hit particularly hard by inflation.

Inflation, then, has some rather unexpected impacts. While cash holders, taxpayers, and many workers lose, to a greater or lesser extent, because of the surprise inflation there has been an inflation-induced redistribution of purchasing power away from older families (who lose because of their large savings accounts) to younger families (who win because of their high debt).

THE POWER OF COMPOUND INFLATION

One of the things that makes inflation such a compelling problem is its ability to greatly distort values in only relatively short periods of time. Even modest inflation rates can result in shocking prices after a while because inflation causes prices to grow like compound interest. A small inflation rate, continued for a long time, can pack quite a wallop.

To get a feel for the impact of compound inflation rates, let us suppose that inflation were to continue at a constant 5 percent for a period of years. What would happen to the prices that we pay? Table 4-1 suggests the possible outcome.

An economics book that costs just $10.00 today would rise to $12.76 within 5 years, to over $33.00 within 25 years, and in 45 years, when

TABLE 4-1

THE IMPACT OF 5 PERCENT INFLATION

Item	Price Today	Price in:			
		5 years	10 years	25 years	45 years
Hamburger	$ .85	$ 1.08	$ 1.38	$ 2.87	$ 7.65
Textbook	10.00	12.76	16.28	33.80	90.00
Economy car	5,000.00	6,380.00	8,140.00	16,900.00	45,000.00
Luxury car	12,000.00	15,312.00	19,536.00	40,560.00	108,000.00
New house	60,000.00	76,560.00	97,680.00	202,800.00	540,000.00

today's student retires, that $10.00 text would sell for $90.00 The moral: Save this book!

After 45 years, still with a 5 percent annual inflation rate, an 85¢ hamburger would cost $7.65, an economy car would be priced at $45,000, and a luxury car would run more than $100,000 (fortunately, your trade-in would be worth more, too). Newly constructed houses today can easily cost $60,000, which makes it hard for young families to afford them. But the grandchildren of today's student would, with a 5 percent inflation rate, be looking at the same house with a $540,000 price tag! Incomes will be rising along with prices if this 5 percent inflation should occur, but would they rise as fast as prices? That is anybody's guess.

These hypothetical price increases may be shocking, but they are nothing compared with the impact of the **hyperinflations** that have struck several countries in the past. In Germany in the 1920s, for example, prices rose not at a 5 percent per year rate, but (for a while) faster than 5 percent per hour! Prices rose so fast that people actually needed to take wheelbarrows full of currency to the store to buy a sack of groceries. Workers demanded, and got, the right to be paid three times a day. When they got paid at 10:00 A.M., they ran out and spent the money immediately, knowing that it would be worth considerably less by noon.

Hyperinflation: very high rates of price inflation

If high inflation rates are here to stay, then it is important for us to be able to cope with them so as to minimize the damage that they inflict. One school of thought, in fact, is that national economic policy should give up the fight against inflation, work hard to lick the unemployment problem instead, and develop programs to cope with the effects of inflation without necessarily worrying about the inflation rate itself.

There are two levels at which we need to cope with inflation: nationally and individually. The policy prescriptions are different in each case.

COPING WITH INFLATION

At the national level, continuing high inflation rates cause some policy makers to call for a national program of indexation. Indexation, in this broad sense, would be a program where all wages, payments, and values would be tied to some price index. The goal would be to lessen the detrimental effects of inflation by increasing everyone's wages, interest payments, and bank account balances, through government action, to keep pace with inflation.

By increasing all wages and values in step with inflation, the argument for indexation goes, the inequities that inflation brings about could be lessened. Programs of indexation have been tried in various high-inflation countries like Brazil.

There are several problems with the inflation-proofing scheme, however. The first is that it is impossible to actually index away all of inflation's undesirable effects. In the end, indexation would not end the creation of winners and losers, it would probably just create different winners and losers. In addition, indexation programs, because they make living with high inflation more comfortable, would be likely to actually increase the inflation rates. Our inflationary expectations would be increased, causing more inflation and additional economic distortions. With inflation rising even faster, the remaining winners and losers would be more heavily affected by rising prices.

A last problem would be selection of the inflation index. There are different ways of measuring inflation, and the choice of the inflation-measurement mechanism benefits some and hurts others. This is likely to be a political decision, with labor unions lobbying for inflation indices which might overestimate inflation (and so result in higher pay increases for union members) and employers pushing for conservative inflation measures which would limit wage rises.

If a national indexation policy is unlikely to effectively cope with the problem of inflation (and might generate additional problems instead), is there anything that individuals can do to protect themselves from the ravages of inflation? A glance back at the section on the economic effects of inflation suggests a few basic strategies.

First of all, it is wise to note that the people who are always hurt by inflation, whether expected or unanticipated, are people with large cash holdings and folks receiving more or less fixed incomes. It is therefore wise to avoid being numbered in these groups. Let's look at fixed incomes first. Who receives fixed incomes? This group is not just made up of retired people with fixed-payment pensions. A lot of people who receive interest income are in this boat. By putting money into long-term savings accounts (called certificates of deposit), they are agreeing to receive fixed interest payments for several years, regardless of the changes in the interest or inflation rates. This can be a risky business in times of high inflation. A first strategy, then, is to find investments that earn a high enough return, but which increase the return as prices rise. The stock market has the potential to do this, as do some recently developed variable-interest bank account programs.

To minimize cash holdings does not mean that one should put all money into checking accounts (since checking account balances are damaged by inflation just as severely as dollar bills). Rather, one should attempt to keep only the minimum necessary amounts in no-interest holdings (like cash and checking accounts) and put the rest of it to work earning interest and protecting itself from inflation. One new wrinkle here is the **negotiable order of withdrawal (NOW) accounts** that many savings banks are offering these days. NOW accounts provide checklike convenience while earning interest on deposits.

Negotiable order of withdrawal (NOW): a special type of bank account which allows depositors to earn interest on what are essentially checking accounts

Having avoided being a cash holder or a recipient of fixed payments, what is left? Since borrowers are winners during surprise inflation, it would be wise to borrow money, hoping that inflation will reduce the real value of the repayments. Also worthy of note is that real assets (houses, real estate, gold) tend to rise in value at least as fast as inflation. People who have borrowed money to use to buy houses in years past have faired relatively well in the fight against inflation.

Finally, perhaps the best defense against inflation is to be cheap. Shopping for bargains and buying large quantities of goods when their prices fall can be a good hedge against inflation. A case of pork and beans in the cupboard may, in the end, be the best protection against inflation there is.

All of these hedges are, however, just ways of trying to minimize the damage that inflation causes. It is probably impossible to actually inflation-proof a country or a family. The goal of price stability remains important.

Why is it necessary to actually measure the inflation rate? Who cares if inflation is going at 5 percent instead of 7 percent? Aren't the economic impacts the same whether we know the exact number or not?

It is important to be able to correctly determine the inflation rate for two reasons. The first is that the fate of many people's economic well-being now depends upon the inflation numbers. Workers with cost-of-living pay clauses, government employees, Social Security recipients—these all receive payments which rise based on the measured inflation rate. A small change in the inflation rate can mean billions of dollars of increased payments by businesses and governments. With so much money hanging in the balance, it is clearly important that inflation be measured accurately. In

MEASURING INFLATION

addition, it is also important that we measure inflation so that we can determine how much of a problem it is and how well we are doing in our fight against it.

If you want to fully understand what the inflation rates published in the newspapers mean, you must first understand how they are calculated. This sounds like an excuse to make you memorize a complicated mathematical procedure, but it is really more than that. As was seen when we looked at the unemployment rate, economic statistics often say more or less than it seems. The same is true for inflation statistics.

There are a lot of different ways you can choose to measure inflation. You could go to the nearest grocery store and write down the price of each item in the store (this would be a considerable task in itself) and then go back six months later and compare the prices. If more prices had gone up than had gone down, you might conclude that prices were rising, but you could not really tell how much.

You might, instead, add up what it would cost to purchase one item of everything in the store, and then go back later and see how much one of everything would cost. You could then compare the two totals, and that would give you some idea of the rate of inflation. But it would not give a very useful measure, since no one buys just one of everything, and you would be ignoring some items, such as clothing, transportation, and housing, which are pretty important to the average person.

Base year: an arbitrarily chosen year that all other years are compared with in the construction of a price index for measuring inflation

Market basket: a list of kinds and quantities of goods and services which is used in the calculation of the inflation rate

Or you could measure inflation the way the government does. The Commerce Department begins by picking a **base year** on which to build its price comparisons. The government inflation measurers then put together a long list of goods and services which make up a standard **market basket** which represents the kinds and amounts of goods that some "average family" might buy in a typical month or year. They find out how much this market basket costs in the base year, and then price these same goods again in later periods. They compare the total cost of the market basket in the current year with how much it cost in the base year, and determine the inflation rate mathematically.

This process is easier to see in an example. Suppose that we had gone out, surveyed college students, and arrived at the amounts and kinds of things that an "average" student purchased in 1970. This market basket is shown in Table 4-2. As you might expect, this average student spends his income mostly on economics texts and other forms of junk food.

Having found what students buy, and how much, we now find out the prices of the stuff they buy. If a student buys four six-packs of beer at $1.25 each, plus three pizzas at $3.00 each, and so on, the 1970 market basket adds up to $34.50 in 1970 prices.

Next, we see how much the same market basket of goods and services

TABLE 4-2

A HYPOTHETICAL PRICE INDEX

| | 1970 | | 1977 | |
	Price	Amount Purchased	Price	Amount Purchased
Item				
Beer	$1.25	4	$ 1.60	5
Pizza	3.00	3	4.00	4
Hamburgers	.50	10	.65	6
French fries	.35	10	.50	6
Coke	.20	10	.30	6
Economics texts	5.00	2	10.00	1

Cost of 1970 budget = $34.50
(in 1970 prices)

Cost of 1970 budget = $52.90
(in 1977 prices)

$$\text{Inflation} = \left(\frac{\$52.90}{\$34.50} - 1 \right) \times 100 = 53.3\%$$

costs in a later year, 1977. Because of inflation, most things cost more, and when we add up the total cost of the 1970 quantities at 1977 prices (four cartons of beer at $1.60 each, plus three pizzas at $4.00 each, and so on), the total cost is $52.90.

The inflation rate can be computed using the formula:

$$\text{Inflation rate} = \frac{\text{Cost of 1970 goods in 1977 prices}}{\text{Cost of 1970 goods in 1970 prices}} - 1 \times 100$$

As Table 4-2 shows, the same goods cost 53.3 percent more to buy in 1977, so the inflation rate between 1970 and 1977 was 53.3 percent.

Obviously, the government economists measure more prices than this, but their technique is the same, and interestingly enough, their conclusions would be the same as ours here. Prices did, in fact, rise by over 50 percent over the years between 1970 and 1977. This represents a compounded annual inflation rate of 5.5 percent for the seven-year period. This is a relatively high inflation rate and a serious problem.

A second glance at Table 4-2 points out a rather disturbing fact: while we have been calculating our inflation rate based on what the average college student purchased in 1970, by 1977 the buying habits of those students had changed. In 1977 the average student bought more beer and pizza and fewer french fries and economics texts. This is one of the several problems with any sort of price index. In order for the process to be meaningful, the base quantities of the market basket must be held constant. If, as was the case here, people change their buying habits over time, the price index becomes a less accurate measure of inflation.

The inflation index does not measure changes in the cost of living, but only changes in the prices of certain goods. The student's market basket of goods cost 53 percent more to buy in 1977 than in 1970, but what happened to the cost of living? To find this out we will have to carefully study what also happened to the goods purchased in each year. Since there is no guarantee that the 1977 student confined his purchases to just these four items (as the 1970 student did), the inflation rate measured here cannot accurately tell us what has happened to the actual cost of living for students. The inflation rate tells what has happened to prices, but gives only a general idea as to what has happened to the cost of living.

People can buy different things, and they can buy them in different places, and this can also affect the accuracy of the inflation measure. The **Consumer Price Index,** for example, is constructed using a market basket which basically reflects buying habits in 1972–1973 (this is updated occasionally, but it takes a long time because government statisticians insist on comprehensive studies of consumer behavior).

In 1972–1973, most people shopped in retail stores—neighborhood drugstores, grocery chains, and so on. These days, people spend more of their money at "discount" stores—discount drugstores, "mark-it-yourself" grocery stores, and even garage sales. People had big cars in 1972–1973 and bought huge amounts of gas for them at full-service gas stations. Now that gasoline prices have doubled, people are driving more miserly cars and many are saving money by pumping their own gas, too. The price index does not give people credit for shopping at cheaper stores when inflation hits or for changing their buying habits to take advantage of bargains. As a result, it tends to overstate the inflation rate somewhat.

There is another problem which the price index faces. Since different groups have different buying habits, any price index must be formulated for some particular group. People who do not happen to fall into that socioeconomic class should understand that the inflation index provides only a general indication of the impact of inflation on their lives. It is not meant to exactly reflect inflation's effect on all groups. For this reason, it is really inappropriate to use one inflation measure to index Social Security payments, auto workers' wages, and government salaries, since the buying habits of the three groups are probably much different.

A final problem is that the quality of goods is likely to change over a period of time, and the price index is unable to compensate for this fact. Cars today are far different from cars in 1960, and the improvement in quality accounts for some of the increase in their price. But in calculating

Consumer Price Index (CPI): a measure of inflation based on a market basket of goods and services purchased by urban households

the inflation rate, only the increase in price can be measured. Additionally, people buy things today (like pocket calculators and TV Ping Pong games) which did not even exist a few years ago. The market basket cannot change to include these new products.

There are three measures of inflation currently in use in the United States. They measure inflation for different groups based on different market baskets. Each is useful, but no one is a perfect measure of inflation.

THREE INFLATION MEASURES

1. THE CONSUMER PRICE INDEX (CPI). The Consumer Price Index (CPI) is the most widely used measure of inflation. It is designed, as its name implies, to measure the prices that consumers pay, based on a market basket compiled for a "typical" family. The index is calculated from 1967 on, with the index for 1967 arbitrarily set at 100; succeeding years' indexes are greater than 100, showing that inflation has taken place (no surprise!). The Consumer Price Index was revised in January 1978, and there are now really *two* CPIs, not one. The CPI-W is a revision of the original CPI and looks at prices paid for goods that a typical lower-income urban clerical worker's family might buy. This market basket reflects only the buying habits of a relatively small part of the economy, since it is restricted to the behavior of low-income families living in cities.

The CPI-U is the broadest measure of inflation available for consumers. It still concentrates on urban dwellers. (If you live on a farm, then none of these indexes does a very good job of describing the inflation that you face.) But the market basket for the CPI-U is picked to be an average of *all* urban households. Since a larger cross-section of families were surveyed in formulating the CPI-U, the buying habits of moderate- and high-income families, previously ignored, are now part of the inflation index.

Besides bringing out these new indices, the Labor Department is also changing the way that they take consumer surveys so that the different CPIs can be updated more often and thus kept more accurate in the future.

Because the CPI was designed to reflect inflation's impact on very specific groups, it cannot exactly estimate the effects of inflation on everyone. It is, however, a pretty fair general measure, since several hundred prices are added into the index every month.

Four times a year the federal government also releases inflation figures for fifty-six large metropolitan areas, so you can get a good idea of how inflation is hitting your particular area by watching for these statistics.

2. THE WHOLESALE PRICE INDEX (WPI). The **Wholesale Price**

Wholesale Price Index (WPI): a measure of the prices of goods used in business

Index (WPI) measures the price that businesses pay. Since it measures the prices of all kinds of business goods (although it does not measure the price of labor), it is a very broad measure of inflation's impact on the cost of doing business, but does not indicate how inflation has hit any particular firm or industry.

The WPI is useful in another way. The WPI is what economists call a **leading indicator**. It tends to tell us what will happen to consumer prices in the future, and can therefore be used as a predictive tool. If the WPI goes up at an annual rate of 10 percent in January, for example, this means that business costs are rising rapidly. We can pretty much expect that businesses will try to pass these higher costs along to consumers in the form of higher prices a little later. A large increase in the WPI in January therefore tells us to expect large rises in the CPI in March and April. So if you want to know what is going to happen to the prices that you pay, it is a very good idea to keep an eye on the WPI.

Leading indicator: an economic statistic which foretells future changes in the economy

3. GNP IMPLICIT PRICE DEFLATOR INDEX (GNP INDEX). The **Gross National Product Implicit Price Deflator Index** (GNP Index) is the very broadest index of inflation for the economy. It was invented to be used as an index to adjust the gross national product figures for inflation.

The GNP Index is the economist's friend. While it cannot measure inflation's impact on any specific group, it does measure a large number of prices. It measures a very large market basket—essentially all new goods. Because it looks at the prices of so many goods, it is the best indicator of the effect of inflation on the entire economy, but is not useful for determining inflation's impact on any particular group or industry.

Gross National Product Implicit Price Deflator (GNP Index): a measure of the prices of final goods, used to adjust the GNP statistics for inflation

REAL VERSUS NOMINAL VALUES

Nominal value: the number of current dollars required to purchase an item

Real value: values adjusted for the impact of rising prices so as to allow the comparison of values over time

Since the dollar shrinks in value due to inflation, it is difficult to compare dollar amounts or values from year to year or over time. Just because a house has a higher price in 1975 than it had in 1965, for example, does not indicate that it has increased in value in real terms—"real" here meaning adjusted for inflation.

Price indices are useful here in that they can help us make the conversion from **nominal** (money) to **real** (adjusted-for-inflation) **values**.

An example will make this process easier to see. Suppose that a farmer earned $12,000 in 1974 and that his pay increased to $13,500 by 1976. Did he get an increase in income in real terms or did inflation wipe out the increased number of dollars, leaving him with less purchasing power? We can determine this by "deflating" the 1976 salary using the following formula:

$$\text{Value in 1974 dollars} = \text{Value in 1976 dollars} \times \frac{\text{CPI for 1974}}{\text{CPI for 1976}}$$

The farmer's real income (measured in 1974 dollars) can now be calculated easily. The CPI in 1974 was 147.7 (1967 = 100) and the CPI for 1976 was 169.1. The farmer's real income in 1976, then, was equal to

$$\text{Value in 1974 dollars} = \$13,500 \times \frac{147.7}{169.1} = \$11,791$$

This tells us that $13,500 measured in small 1976 dollars would have bought only $11,791 worth of goods and services as measured in 1974 dollars. Our conclusion is that, while the farmer was able to increase his money income between 1974 and 1976, his real income actually declined! His money income rose, but prices rose higher, and his purchasing power thus decreased.

This little example shows declining real income, and this is what actually happened to most households during the years from 1969 to 1976. People received more and more money, but prices rose faster and people ended up with less purchasing power than they had at the start. Declining real incomes is one of the uncomfortable possibilities during periods of rapid price inflation. The whole idea of indexation, which has already been mentioned several times, was concocted in order to preserve real incomes and tax burdens during periods of rapid inflation.

SUMMARY

1. Inflation is a substantial, sustained increase in the general level of prices.

2. Inflation rates have varied widely over the last thirty years. Prices actually fell briefly in the mid-1950s, and low inflation rates prevailed during the early 1960s. Inflation rates in recent years have been much higher, indicating that inflation is a more serious national problem these days.

3. Inflation affects the economy in many ways. It hurts people living on fixed incomes. It disrupts exchanges between borrowers and lenders because of its impact on the interest rate. Inflation tends to discourage saving. Inflation creates problems with our tax system which has resulted in an unintended "inflation tax."

4. Most inflation in recent years has been "surprise inflation"— inflation which was higher than anticipated. In cases of unexpectedly high inflation rates, people on relatively fixed in-

comes, lenders, money holders, and taxpayers tend to lose. Borrowers, governments, and people whose incomes vary with the inflation rate, while still affected by the price increases, have tended to gain.

5. People who hold money or hold fixed-value assets tend to lose when high inflation rates strike. One way to hedge against inflation, then, would be to hold little money and invest in variable-income assets (like land and property) instead of fixed-value assets (like savings accounts). Being thrifty is also a good hedge against price increases.

6. Inflation is measured using price indices. A price index looks at the total cost of a fixed market basket of goods in different years. By comparing the costs of these goods, conclusions can be drawn concerning changes in the general level of prices.

7. There are three main measures of inflation in the United States. The Consumer Price Index (CPI) looks at retail prices paid by urban consumers. This is the most accurate measure of the impact of inflation on consumers, although all price indices suffer from a variety of measurement problems. The Wholesale Price Index (WPI) measures the prices that businesses pay. It is a leading indicator of inflation because it generally foretells changes in the CPI. The Gross National Product Implicit Price Deflator Index (GNP Index) measures the prices of all new goods. It is the broadest measure of inflation available.

DISCUSSION QUESTIONS

1. Using 1970 as the base year, calculate the rate of inflation in the hypothetical economy outlined below. If a worker made $100 per week in 1970 and $125 per week in 1977, would he be better off?

2. It is also possible to calculate inflation in a different way by using the current year's market basket (in the example above, 1977) as the base on which to make the calculation. What is the inflation rate in Question 1, above, if inflation is calculated in this fashion? Are there any advantages to this method? Can you think of a reason why the

Good	1970		1977	
	Price	Quantity	Price	Quantity
Beer	$1.25	10	$1.50	7
Pizza	3.50	8	4.00	6
Tums	.25	6	.20	6

government does not measure inflation this way instead of the way described in the text?

3. Suppose that you expected a 20 percent inflation rate over the next year. Would this alter your behavior? How? Why? Suppose that you expected a zero percent inflation rate. How would your behavior change in this case? Why? What do you expect the inflation rate to be for the next year?

4. List the winners and losers from an unexpectedly high inflation. Explain why each group wins or loses. How would your list change if inflation were unexpectedly low?

5. The opposite of inflation is deflation—a fall in the general level of prices. If inflation is bad, can deflation be good? Can you think of any problems that deflation causes? Make a list of the winners and losers that deflation creates.

6. Listed below is the CPI for several selected years. Use this information to answer the questions that follow.

Year	CPI
1967	100.0
1969	109.8
1971	121.3
1973	133.1
1975	161.2
1977	181.5

a. In which two-year period did the United States have the highest inflation?

b. If an individual made $100 per week in 1969 and $150 per week in 1975, would that person be better off in 1975 or not?

c. If someone made $200 weekly in 1971, how much would he or she have to be making in 1975 to have the same purchasing power?

Determine whether each of the following statements is *true* or *false*. Be able to defend your choice.

1. In 1977, coffee prices rose in the United States due to poor coffee harvests in Brazil. These price increases were examples in inflation.

2. Everyone is hurt about the same by inflation.

3. Savers (people with money in savings accounts at banks) have failed to beat inflation during recent years because the return on their savings has averaged less than the inflation rate.

4. Borrowers are most hurt by inflation because it tends to drive up the interest rates that they pay.

5. Borrowers gain during a period of deflation because interest rates fall.

6. Unexpectedly low inflation

rates hurt borrowers more than lenders.

7. Indexation would soften the blow of inflation, but would not solve the problem of inflation.

8. The Consumer Price Index tends to rise and fall along with the Wholesale Price Index (the WPI generally "leads" the CPI by a few months).

9. The CPI is a measure of the cost of living of urban households.

10. Gasoline cost about 30¢ per gallon in 1955. In 1978 its price had risen to about 75¢. In 1955 the CPI was about 80, and by 1978 it had risen to about 190. Based on these numbers, it is possible to conclude that the real price of gasoline actually fell between 1955 and 1978.

ECONOMIC CONTROVERSIES II: INFLATION OR UNEMPLOYMENT?

Economists often disagree about basic social, political and economic issues. These disagreements usually don't result from differences in basic economic beliefs, but rather stem from differences in personal values. Rational people may disagree concerning the question of which problems are the most important and which solutions are the best, even when they share common views of how the economy operates and economic tools work. Differences in values or philosophies account for the tendency of economists to draw different conclusions from the same set of facts.

The question of inflation versus unemployment has stirred much debate within the economics profession and among policy makers and concerned citizens. If there is a Phillips Curve trade-off (as discussed in Chapter 1), then one economic goal must be sacrificed in order to achieve the other. If the Phillips Curve trade-off does not always hold, it is still the case that policy makers generally choose to fight just one fire at a time. A choice must still be made: which problem is more important, inflation or unemployment?

This question is particularly interesting because it has a political as well as an economic side. Republicans have traditionally viewed inflation rates as more of a threat to the economy than unemployment. Democrats, on the other hand, have been stereotyped as fearing joblessness more than soaring prices. These labels are oversimplifications, to be sure, but the labels may still be valid in the public eye. Voters may cast ballots for these basic philosophies as much as for the candidates in many races. Let's examine each point of view.

WINNERS AND LOSERS

One of the reasons for disagreement concerning the relative importance of inflation and unemployment as economic problems is that each of these diseases affects different groups to different degrees. So to assess the relative importance of these two problems, we are forced to make the uncomfortable judgment as to whether Mr. A's illness is worse than Ms. B's and, in addition, whether Mrs. C's gain is sufficient to justify the losses suffered by both A and B. In making this determination we leave the world of *positive economics*, which deals with statements that can be proven either true or false, and enter the world of *normative judgments*, which are matters of opinion or individual values.

Unemployment creates no winners and imposes two kinds of loss: private and social. The private burden of unemployment falls on the unemployed worker. The burden here takes the form of lower income, reduced standard of living, and loss of self-esteem and confidence.

The social costs of unemployment are many. First there are direct costs to governments. Governments (and therefore taxpayers) suffer lower tax collections and higher expenditures when unemployment strikes. Tax collections go down because out-of-work people generally pay little or no income tax. But government spending must rise to pay for unemployment benefits and job-training programs. This increased burden is, of course, shifted onto the remaining employed taxpayers who will bear higher tax rates as a result.

Lost production also is a social cost. When workers remain unemployed, their talents and skills are unused. Less is produced to satisfy society's wants, needs, and desires.

Finally, crime and conflict may result from unemployment, and this imposes a burden on society. This is particularly likely if the unemployment is heavily concentrated in one ethnic or social group.

Inflation's winners and losers have been discussed in some detail in Chapter 4, so a summary here will suffice. Inflation strikes all parts of the population to the extent that we are all money holders who watch our dollars wither away when prices rise. Still, some groups are particularly hard-hit. Lenders, we have noted, include all people with savings. During periods of unexpected inflation this group is hard-hit; they lend their dollars to banks and other financial institutions at low interest rates and watch their savings erode.

Taxpayers are also damaged by inflation. Rising prices distort the income tax structure and impose higher tax rates. Tax rates for individual workers can actually rise during heavy inflation even while real incomes are falling (the tax burden will rise so long as money income is rising).

Inflation benefits some groups, such as borrowers. To the extent that households fall into both the winner and loser categories, the net impact of inflation is probably somewhat less than might otherwise be the case.

UNEMPLOYMENT IS MORE IMPORTANT

Many people feel that high unemployment rates must be more important than inflation for the simple reason that unemployment is a human (as opposed to a financial) problem. The unemployment burden falls directly on people, lowering their standard of living and increasing the gap between the rich and the poor in an economy which is noted for its unequal distribution of its wealth. In a prosperous system such as ours, how can we justify poverty and unemployment?

Unemployment is a more serious problem than inflation because the principal effects of joblessness are heavily concentrated in a relatively small group. No one suffers as much from inflation as the jobless suffer from unemployment. Inflation spreads its burden more evenly and perhaps more equitably. That unemployment strikes the disadvantaged groups within our economy—especially blacks and women—harder than others makes it a particularly important concern.

The people who are hurt by inflation are those who have the most to begin with: people with lots of money and savings. Unemployment harms those who are least able to bear the burden: low-income families often possessing few marketable skills. The unemployed desperately need help. Those most hurt by inflation are better able to help themselves.

Finally, it should be noted that people are pretty much able to protect themselves from inflation by hedging against its impact. It is more difficult to hedge against the effects of unemployment.

FIGHT INFLATION FIRST

Inflation must be considered the more important of these economic problems. It affects all of us and distorts economic decisions all around the economy. The severity of high unemployment is overrated. The unemployed bear a rather variable private cost. For many, the loss in income due to unemployment is not very great because of the many social welfare programs which have been designed to cope with this problem. Indeed, much of the unemployment around us is of a voluntary nature. People remain unemployed in order to search for even better jobs or to take a taxpayer-financed vacation. This is not true in every case, of course, but it occurs often enough to make the argument of "devastating unemployment" largely invalid. The suffering, in general, is overrated.

The unemployment rates also act to overstate the problem here. Much of our current unemployment is of a very-short-term nature. A worker is laid off from his job for a few weeks and then returns to it with only a very modest interruption in work. In fact, many of these interruptions are so predictable that workers treat them as involuntary vacations and plan vacations around them. Many other countries do not even officially consider this unemployment—they treat these layoffs as "worker furloughs" instead.

Inflation, on the other hand, is a very significant dilemma. Even relatively modest inflation rates have devastating compound effects. The impact of inflation on the income tax alone creates great inequities. Add to this the losses suffered by savers and others and it is clear that inflation is the more important problem.

A final argument is perhaps the most important. History has taught us that unemployment eventually goes away. Governments don't fall because of high unemployment rates. Inflation, however, tends to feed on itself. It grows and grows and becomes hyperinflation, which can destroy the economic system. Inflation causes political unrest, too. At its worst, inflation can be a fatal disease. Inflation is the plague of the modern world and must be treated with respect.

DISCUSSION QUESTIONS

1. Which side of this argument do you agree with? Can you find faults in either side's position?
2. Are the poor hurt most by inflation or by unemployment? Which problem has hit your family the hardest?
3. Do current government policies seem aimed more at fighting inflation or unemployment?

Part 2
A Simple Model of the Economy

5
Measuring
Economic
Activity

This chapter develops some basic concepts and definitions which will be used again later in the text. This chapter will answer a number of questions, including the following:

Why is it necessary to measure economic activity?

What is gross national product?

Is GNP a good measure of our national welfare?

What is real gross national product?

What is per capita real gross national product?

How has the economy performed in recent years as measured by these different measures?

What causes inflation? How can we solve the unemployment problem? What determines the level of economic activity? How can we achieve our macroeconomic goals?

These are very basic, very important questions that will be answered in simple terms in this and the next three chapters. Part II of the text constructs a working model of the national economy that can be used to analyze our economic problems and goals. But before this can be done, it will first be necessary to develop some basic definitions of economic activity, tools that are used to accurately measure economic progress.

It is important to be able to measure the level of national economic activity for three basic reasons. First, policy makers need to know how well the economy is doing so as to judge their past success and the need for future economic policies. They need to find out if national economic goals are being achieved and, if not, the nature of the policy gap remaining. Business people need to know how the economy is doing for other reasons. Businesses are involved in selling goods and services. They need to measure economic activity so that they may accurately plan production, inventory, and advertising programs. Firms that sell nationally need to know how much income will be generated in the economy so that they can better guess how much of that income will be spent on their products. Finally, we all are concerned about our economic well-being. We need a measure that will allow us to determine if Americans are doing better or worse in their race for material satisfaction.

The measures of economic activity currently available do not perfectly satisfy any of these requirements, but they can help us understand how well the economy is working. This chapter will look at three useful economic statistics: *gross national product*, *real gross national product*, and *per capita gross national product*. The analysis of these three measures of economic activity may not be particularly exciting, but these measures are very useful in understanding the economy.

GROSS NATIONAL PRODUCT

Gross national product (GNP): the total market value in current prices of all final goods and services produced in a year; a basic measure of current market economic activity

Gross national product (GNP) is the basic measure of national economic health. It is used by both businesses and government policy makers in arriving at important decisions. It is oft-quoted but little understood.

Gross national product is defined to be the total market value (measured in current prices) of all final goods and services produced in an economy in a year. All of the parts of this definition are important. Note first that GNP is a measure of current production. It gauges not how much we have, but how much we added to our holdings (produced) in the current period.

Since it is impossible to physically add up all of our production (5 million cars plus 2 million boats, and so on), GNP instead adds up the total value of all current production. How can values be assigned to different goods? The prices of the goods (their market value) acts as a measure of relative value. The value of all current production is calculated by adding up the total market values of all new goods and services. This gives a good measure of the value of the new production that has taken place in the economy in a year.

Some examples may help the reader understand the concept of GNP. Whenever a good or service is produced (with some exceptions that will be noted later), this increases the amount of GNP:

- ☐ Mr. Smith pays $5.00 for a haircut ($5.00 enters GNP as the value of the service of haircutting).
- ☐ Ms. Jones purchases a new car for $6,000 (the $6,000 enters GNP as the value of the new car which was produced plus the value of the service of auto retailing).
- ☐ The federal government pays $5 million for a new computer (the $5 million value of the computer is a part of GNP).
- ☐ A bakery spends $10,000 for a new oven (the $10,000 value of this business investment adds to GNP, too).
- ☐ A Canadian business spends $500 on a U.S. typewriter (the foreign payment results in production in the United States valued at $500, so U.S. GNP will rise by $500—the value of the production).

Looking at the preceeding examples, it is easy to get the idea that GNP is simply the total amount of sales made involving U.S. goods in a year. Actually, however, total sales is much different than GNP. There are a number of types of sales which are made which do not, in fact, contribute to economic activity as measured by the gross national product.

When a bakery purchases a new oven, as was noted above, this enters GNP because the bakery's purchase has resulted in the production of a new good. This oven is a **final good** in that the bakery is the final purchaser of the item and will not resell it. However, when that same bakery buys flour (for use in making bread) this sale is not included in GNP. Flour, in this case, is what is called an **intermediate good**—a thing which is made into something else. Why isn't the flour counted? Suppose that the flour (and the water and yeast and shortening) that goes into the loaf of bread were all counted, and then that the bread was also counted when it was sold. This would result in an inflated measure of total production. The flour would be counted once as flour, and then again as part of the value of the bread.

In order for GNP to be a good measure of current production, it must count all production once, but avoid **double-counting**. To do this, the

Final good: a good which is purchased by its ultimate user

Intermediate good: items produced at one stage in production that are then used to produce other goods

Double-counting: a potential error in GNP statistics which occurs when production is counted more than once

government statisticians count only the final goods (goods sold to their final or ultimate users). Thus they count the bread but not the flour. Flour sold to a home baker, however, is counted since the person who buys the flour in the supermarket for use at home is the final user of that flour.

The line between intermediate goods and final goods is sometimes hard to draw, and because GNP is essentially an accounting procedure, arbitrary lines are often used to separate the two. For example, a car dealer is basically in business to buy cars from a manufacturer and sell them to customers. So when a car dealer purchases cars from the manufacturer, this transaction is normally considered an intermediate sale and not counted in GNP (although the final sale of the car by the dealer does enter the GNP accounts). However, the GNP books close on December 31. So if the dealer has any of these cars on his lot on December 31, he is counted as the "final" purchaser of those cars for that year. They enter GNP at the price that the dealer paid for them. When he finally sells them next year, only his profit—the current production of the sales service—enters GNP. All other stocks of goods meant for resale or kept for use in production are treated this way on the GNP books.

Another example: Suppose that you purchased a *used* car. Does this enter GNP? Well, part of it does. Let's suppose that you paid $500 for a much-used '57 Chevy. Essentially, the deal does not enter GNP because the car was produced in 1957. It was counted in 1957, and counting it again this year would amount to the double-counting of the car. Yet a part of your $500 payment would show up in GNP. Suppose that you bought the car from a dealer and that the dealer made $50 profit on the deal. That $50 would enter GNP as the value of the service—auto vending—that the dealer provided.

What about the stock market? When someone buys stock on Wall Street, this contributes to GNP, right? Wrong. When a share of stock is purchased, nothing new is produced in the economy (except the stockbroker's commission, which will enter GNP as a payment for a service). Stock sales are really, in GNP terms, just exchanges. You give me a piece of paper (the stock certificate) and I give you a different piece of paper (my check). We have simply exchanged pieces of paper. No goods or services (except, as noted, the stockbroker's service) have been produced. None of this, therefore, enters the GNP accounts. What about when new stock certificates are issued? No, even then the stock sale does not count. If IBM issues $1 million in new stock, for example, the $1 million enters GNP when IBM spends the money on new goods and services, not when "investors" spend it on the stock certificates.

This brings us to an important distinction. When we use the term *investment* in conversation, we are normally talking about holdings of stocks, bonds, and so on. But the economist defines investment somewhat differently. **Investment spending** is defined to be business purchases of goods and services that increase the ability of the firm to produce. That is, investment in the economic sense is business spending on final goods and services. These expenditures add to GNP. **Financial investment**, however, does not add to GNP. Financial investors purchase stocks and bonds. "Economic" investors purchase machines, plants, inventories. When investment is discussed in this book, it will refer to this second, GNP-type of investment spending.

In the above examples, certain items (used cars, intermediate goods, stocks and bonds) were left out of GNP to avoid double-counting so that GNP could accurately measure current production. But GNP does not (and doesn't pretend to) measure all production. It only measures economic activity which takes place through established legal markets. Production which bypasses these markets also escapes GNP detection. The proceeds of crime, for example, are not counted in GNP (and so GNP underestimates total production by ignoring this apparently growing source of economic activity).

More importantly, perhaps, GNP fails to count production which is not actually sold. If an artist paints a picture and gives it away, the act of production does not enter GNP. If the picture were sold, however, GNP would go up. People who paint their own houses, fix their own cars, and calculate their own income taxes are also involved in producing goods and services, but they don't add to GNP. Only the things which they buy (paint, brushes, car parts, aspirins) enter the GNP books. If they had hired others to perform these tasks, however, the value of the labor would have entered GNP as well.

Gross national product, then, measures current market economic activity. Not all sales, nor even all production, is counted, but still the figure is important since income is produced whenever goods or services are produced. Thus businesses and government are concerned about the size of the gross national product.

Investment spending: purchases of plant, equipment, machinery, and other items which increase a firm's ability to produce

Financial investment: the purchase of stocks, bonds, and other financial instruments; an exchange of previously existing goods

Gross national product does a good job of measuring market economic activity. As such, it is very useful to people who want or need to know how much production and income is generated by the economy. It is not, however, a very useful tool in viewing changes in our economic well-being. Gross national product is not, as some people seem to feel, a measure of gross national happiness or well-being.

There are several reasons for this. First, GNP measures only material things and so can't really measure how well off we are. More to the point,

GNP AS A MEASURE OF WELL-BEING

however, is the fact that GNP actually rises when events take place which make us less well off than we were before. Floods, earthquakes, and wars are all examples of undesirable events. Each makes GNP rise, however. Production of guns, tanks, and coffins adds to GNP. Expenditures to rebuild the damage caused by fires, storms, and other natural disasters all have the effect of raising GNP, too.

Since GNP will rise in response to good things (like increased production of needed consumer goods) or bad things (as in response to wars), it is clearly of no use as an indicator of economic or social well-being.

THREE VIEWS OF GNP

Production: the act of using inputs (such as land, labor, and machinery) in order to produce goods and services

Value-added: the amount of value added by the productive process; sale price of an item minus the costs of production

While gross national product is simply a measure of one thing—market economic activity—it can be interpreted different ways and used for different purposes. An analysis of three views of GNP is instructive.

Gross national product is, first of all, a measure of **production**. When a $1.00 loaf of bread enters the gross national product, this indicates that the economy has produced additional output worth $1.00. This is the way that we have viewed GNP up to now.

But GNP is also a measure of the additional value that our efforts have produced. When an item is made worth more than it was before, the incremental worth is called the **value-added**. How does GNP measure the amount of value-added by the economy? Table 5-1 helps explain the idea.

Table 5-1 follows the steps necessary to produce a $1.00 loaf of bread. The farmer grows the wheat and sells it to a miller who sells flour to a baker who sells bread to a merchant who sells the bread to its final user—the consumer. Gross national product counts only this final transaction and does not add in the sale of intermediate goods. Notice, however, an interesting pattern concerning the steps taken along the way.

The farmer begins with simple basic resources (suppose, for the sake of example, that the seed and other necessary items are provided free by God).

TABLE 5-1

GNP AS A MEASURE OF VALUE-ADDED

Firm	Input Purchase Price	Output Selling Price	Value-Added	Total Value-Added
Farmer	$0	$ .20	$.20	$ .20
Miller	.20	.30	.10	.30
Baker	.30	.80	.50	.80
Merchant	.80	1.00	.20	1.00

Total value-added = Value of total production = $1.00

He sells enough wheat to make one loaf of bread to the miller for 20¢. The farmer has added 20¢ of value to the basic resources he began with.

The miller takes 20¢ worth of wheat and processes it into flour, which is then sold for 30¢. The value of the work that the miller has provided is plainly worth 10¢, since that is what he is paid over and above the cost of the wheat input.

The baker buys the flour for 30¢ and sells it as bread for 80¢. He adds 50¢ in value in the process. The merchant then takes the 80¢ loaf of bread and sells it for $1.00. The value he has added—in terms of convenience and other services—is equal to 20¢.

In each step along the way, each producer has taken inputs and made them more valuable by changing them in some way. Each has added value to the raw materials that we started with.

What is the total of all of this work? The farmer added 20¢ of value, the miller added 10¢, the baker added 50¢, and the merchant added 20¢. In total, $1.00 of value was added to the resources. The dollar that we count as final production, then, also represents the dollar of value that has been added to the existing natural resources. The total for GNP also tells us the total amount of value-added that has been produced, at all stages of production, in the economy in a year.

Finally, GNP is also a comprehensive measure of national **income**. Every dollar that is spent on new production of goods or services is, eventually, a dollar of income to someone in the economy. The dollar spent on a loaf of bread, for example, will in the end be entirely used in providing income for the farmer, the miller, the baker, and merchant, and all of those that work for them or who supply inputs for them. Every dollar of spending is translated into a dollar of wages, factor payments, rental income, or profits. Nothing can be left (where would it go?).

The gross national product, therefore, measures not only production, but also value-added and the amount of income generated in the economy, too.

Income: the receipts of a firm or household derived from wages, rents, or business profits

It is important not to take economic statistics like the GNP completely at face value, however. The GNP pretends to be, for example, an accounting of all current market production in our large economy. Who counts all of it? Does a government agent sit in every factory and store adding up all of the production?

Of course, GNP is just an estimate of the amount of production that takes place, although it is, all things considered, a very good estimate. Still, it is important to bear in mind that such broad economic statistics must,

A GRAIN OF SALT

inevitably, be wrong in the sense that GNP will always actually be different from the amount given in the GNP tables.

This sort of error is common to all broad measures of production. And the error can be important in some cases. In Bulgaria, for example, pig production used to be a very important part of the economic structure. A pig census was taken every January 1 in order to gauge the health of the pig industry. Hence, on January 1, 1910, the Bulgarian pig population was officially numbered at 527,311 pigs (imagine for a moment actually counting over half a million pigs!). On the first of January 1920, the pig census showed a total of 1,089,699 pigs in Bulgaria—an increase of over 100 percent in pig production. Obviously, pig farmers in Bulgaria had experienced rapid growth over this ten-year period. The economy was prospering! Or was it?

Also during this ten-year period Bulgaria had officially moved from the old Gregorian calendar to the new Julian one—the difference was thirteen days. The pig census was taken according to the new calendar, but religious holidays were still celebrated according to the old dates. As a result, the pig census which originally took place one week *after* Christmas was now taking place one week *before*. And Bulgarians often eat pork for Christmas.

The mistake is clear. In 1920 there were not really twice as many pigs. Rather, the statisticians were counting "doomed" pigs along with the rest. In two weeks' time the pig population would have been cut in half. The Bulgarian pig count, then, was a sham, and the conclusion that the pig industry was booming was false.

Published GNP figures in the United States are not as silly as the GNP (gross national pig) count in Bulgaria, but it is still a good idea to take them with a grain of salt all the same.

REAL GROSS NATIONAL PRODUCT

Gross national product may be a good way to size up short-term changes in economic activity, but it suffers from one very major flaw. Because it measures production in terms of current prices, GNP will rise either when production rises or when inflation causes prices to rise. That is, GNP measures both the price and output changes that are taking place.

To get a better fix on what is happening to production alone, economists have developed the economic measure of the *real gross national product* (RGNP or real GNP). Real GNP is simply the GNP converted into constant dollars by using the GNP Implicit Price Deflator Index discussed in Chapter 4. By making the "real" conversion, it is possible to separate the changes in price from the changes in total output. The resulting RGNP allows us to compare total production over time.

The conversion to RGNP as a measure of output is very important, as

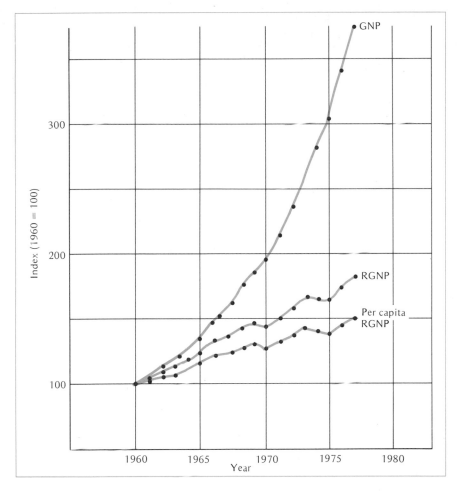

FIGURE 5-1: MEASURES OF ECONOMIC ACTIVITY, 1960–1977
Gross national product grew at exponential rates during this period: it increased every year during the time shown. Real GNP paints a less prosperous picture: it grew at a much slower rate and even declined in 1970, 1973, and 1974. Growth in per capita RGNP was uneven as well, and its rate of growth was even smaller.

illustrated by Figure 5-1. Here both GNP and RGNP are plotted by setting the 1960 values of each equal to 100. As can be seen, over the period 1960–1977 GNP grew nearly fourfold: it actually went from $506 billion in 1960 to over $1890 billion in 1977. This is a tremendous growth rate.

Much of this apparent economic growth, however, was merely the result of rapidly rising prices, not increased output. To conclude that production more than tripled in the United States during this period is much the same sort of mistake that the Bulgarian pig counters made. While GNP increased by about 273 percent over this period, RGNP grew only by about 80 percent (from $736.8 billion in 1960 to $1337 billion in 1977—both amounts measured in 1972 dollars).

Real GNP is our best measure of national economic output. Because we are able to factor out the effects of inflation, we are left with a very good measure of what is actually produced. When RGNP goes up, this suggests that more is being produced and, therefore, more workers are needed and employment is rising. When RGNP falls, this means that production is falling and unemployment rates are rising. Thus, RGNP will be our basic measure of overall changes in the economy.

PER CAPITA RGNP

Per capita RGNP: a measure of production available for each person in a country; RGNP divided by total population of a country

For all of its advantages, RGNP has one remaining fault: it looks at the amount produced over a period of time, but the number of people among whom this production will be divided is not constant. A rising population tends to cause RGNP to rise, and similarly, RGNP must grow at least as fast as the population in order to maintain the average real income available to each of us.

Per capita RGNP is found by dividing RGNP by the size of the nation's population. It tells us the amount of production or income generated per person. It reflects, in very general terms, the standard of living.

Figure 5-1 shows that per capita RGNP increased less than either GNP or RGNP during the period 1960–1977. While GNP was increasing over threefold and RGNP was rising by over 80 percent, per capita RGNP grew by a total of only 50 percent, an average growth rate of only about 3 percent per year. In 1960, per capita RGNP (measured in 1972 dollars) was $4077, and by 1977 it had risen to $6169.

Per capita RGNP is perhaps our best measure of economic progress in that it corrects for both changes in prices and changes in population. It is not, however, a measure of welfare or satisfaction. It is also important to note that it measures only average real income. An increase in per capita RGNP may not actually be very much of an improvement if the distribution of the RGNP is faulty—going all to one group or completely bypassing some part of the population. Finally, per capita RGNP measures only our average ability to meet material wants and needs. It says nothing about a world of other satisfactions that may be wanting.

INTERNATIONAL COMPARISONS

Because per capita RGNP gives a good measure of the economic standard of living and because per capita RGNP figures are available for many countries, it is tempting to use these to make international welfare comparisons. Table 5-2, for example, shows estimates of per capita RGNP amounts for twenty countries for the year 1972. The differences are shocking. People in the United States are shown to have average incomes of over $5500 per capita, while in some parts of the world per capita RGNP is less than $100. Clearly, the poor must be very poor indeed.

But this is not really an accurate use of the RGNP figures. While these statistics are useful in a general sense, they lie here. It is important not to rush to the conclusion, for example, that people in the United States are twice as well off as people in the United Kingdom because the U.S. per capita RGNP is twice as large.

There are two problems here. First, per capita RGNP measures only material welfare. In countries that value concepts of family or honor over goods and services, the RGNP will have little to do with well-being.

Second, and more importantly, per capita RGNP is a measure of market activities. A farmer in a less developed country may produce a great deal of food, clothing, and other goods and services. This production, however, is only counted in RGNP in the unlikely case that he sells any of it. If he barters to get what he wants, or produces for only himself and his family's needs, then there is no contribution to RGNP registered. Thus, the low per capita RGNP scores registered here reflect, in part, simply a larger amount of nonmarket activities in less developed countries.

It is also well to note that per capita RGNP seems to rise when countries become increasingly urbanized. As people move off the farm and go to work in the city, they find that they must buy and pay for goods and services that were previously either free (as would be the case with fruit) or that they produced themselves or bartered for (food, clothes, haircuts) at no money cost.

As the urbanization and specialization processes take place, welfare may not rise (it may actually fall) and production need not increase (the economy may actually be producing fewer goods and services, particularly if the urban immigrants are unemployed). But per capita RGNP is sure to rise simply because more of the kinds of things that it measures will be sold.

Quantitative comparisons using RGNP, then, are to be undertaken with caution. We can tell that there is a difference in economic well-being among nations, but the extent of that difference is difficult to determine with these figures alone.

Many groups within the economy are interested in securing measures of aggregate economic performance. Gross national product is the basic measure of national economic activity. It measures current market production of goods and services in a year. Thus, GNP may be thought of as a measure of production, or an indicator of national income or value-added.

Because GNP can be distorted by changing prices, real gross national product is a better measure of economic performance. Real GNP is calculated by deflating the GNP figures using the GNP Implicit Price

TABLE 5-2

PER CAPITA RGNP IN SELECTED COUNTRIES

Country	Per Capita RGNP ($U.S.)
United States	$5590
Sweden	4480
Canada	4440
France	3620
West Germany	3390
United Kingdom	2600
Japan	2180
Italy	1960
USSR	1530
Spain	1210
Yugoslavia	810
Portugal	780
Mexico	750
Brazil	530
Cuba	450
Turkey	370
Morocco	270
Philippines	220
China	170
Afghanistan	80

Source: *World Bank Atlas 1974.*

Deflator Index. Real GNP is the overall best measure of national economic output.

Real GNP does not take into account changes in the size of the population which can account for growth in output. Per capita RGNP (found by dividing RGNP by the population) gives a standard way to measure material living standards. It is useful in gauging economic growth, but should not be used to make comparisons of international well-being.

SUMMARY

1. Many groups need to measure national economic activity. Policy makers need to know the condition of the economy so as to judge the need for and effectiveness of economic policies. Businesses need to know so that they can make wise investment, sales, and production decisions. Concerned citizens need a measure of economic growth in order to better judge the nation's progress toward meeting its material needs.

2. Gross national product is a measure of the total value of all goods and services produced in an economy in a year. It is a basic measure of market economic activity.

3. Gross national product is not a good measure of national well-being because it rises and falls when prices (not just amounts of production) change, and GNP can rise when disasters actually reduce well-being.

4. Real GNP is a better measure of annual production because it adjusts for changing prices. Real GNP is GNP deflated using the GNP Implicit Price Deflator Index discussed in Chapter 4.

5. Per capita RGNP is an even better measure of production because it adjusts for changing populations. It is a measure of the amount produced per person in the economy. It is also, therefore, an estimate of income per person.

6. Looking just at GNP, it is possible to conclude that economic growth has been substantial in recent years. Using the measures of RGNP or per capita RGNP, however, we find that the economy has grown only relatively slowly.

1. Determine which of the following transactions would be counted in GNP and briefly state why each is or is not part of GNP:

☐ Joel Smith buys a stamp from the post office.

☐ Joe L. Smith buys a birthday present for Joel Smith.

☐ Jo Lee Smith buys typing paper for use in her stenographer business.

☐ Jim Smith pays for a motel room while on vacation.

☐ Jack Smith purchases a house.

☐ John Smith pays his electricity bill.

2. In this chapter we have talked exclusively about measures of *economic* activity. Would it be possible to measure societal well-being in order to determine if we are happier today than we were in years past or to compare nations? What kind of things would you measure in such an index of well-being?

3. If the population is growing at a rate of 5 percent per year, how fast does GNP have to grow in order to maintain a constant per capita RGNP?

4. Suppose that, in some less developed nation, the following facts hold:

DISCUSSION QUESTIONS

Year	GNP	Population	Price Index
1970	$100 million	1 million	100
1975	$120 million	1.5 million	110
1980	$150 million	2.0 million	130

a. What has happened to GNP over this period?

b. What has happened to RGNP over this period?

c. What has happened to per capita RGNP?

Determine whether each of the following statements is *true* or *false*. Be able to defend your choice.

1. Gross national product measures total sales in an economy in a year.

2. Gross national product measures total production in an economy in a year.

3. A government purchase of a tank for the army would be included in GNP.

4. The purchase of a theatre ticket would be included in GNP.

5. The purchase of a U.S. Savings Bond would be included in GNP.

6. An increase in RGNP normally implies an increase in GNP.

7. An increase in RGNP normally implies an increase in total production.

TEST YOURSELF

8. An increase in per capita RGNP normally implies an increase in average real income for the population.

9. The national economic goal of economic growth means that GNP should grow each year.

10. Real GNP can be used to make comparisons of the standard of living among nations.

6
Aggregate Demand

This chapter presents an introduction to the way the economy works, unemployment is created and fought, and the factors which can make the national income rise, fall, or stay the same. This chapter will answer a number of questions including:

What is aggregate demand?

What is the relationship between total spending and national income?

How do saving and investment, government spending and taxes, imports and exports affect the economy?

What is the macroeconomic equilibrium? Is the equilibrium a good place for the economy to be?

What is consumption spending and how is it related to income?

How does the inflation affect the demand for goods and services?

It is time to begin our task of modeling the national economy. To do this, it is necessary to strip the economy to its bare bones and analyze the most basic of national economic interactions. Then, through a cumulative process, we will arrive at a fairly sophisticated understanding of the workings of the national economy.

It is convenient, to begin with, to separate the national economic process into two components much as the microeconomic market was divided into the forces of demand and supply. Aggregate demand (AD) is defined to be the total amount of goods and services that households, businesses, and governments wish to purchase in some time period. Aggregate demand is a basic driving force in the economy. Most national economic policies are designed to influence AD, raising or lowering the level of total demand so as to fight unemployment or lower inflationary pressures.

Equally as important as aggregate demand is the **aggregate supply** (AS). Aggregate supply is the amount of total production for the nation for some time period. Aggregate supply has been, for some years, the forgotten part of the economy. No longer is this the case. Now we must be as concerned with our ability to produce goods and services (AS) as we are with our ability to purchase them (AD).

This chapter will deal with the concept of aggregate demand from a number of perspectives. The analysis of aggregate supply and a look at the simple workings of the economy will be left for Chapter 7.

Aggregate supply (AS): the total production of goods and services in an economy

SPENDING AND INCOME

Spending is the source of all economic activity. Consumer spending, business spending, and government spending all contribute to the total spending flow. When spending takes place, two forces are set in motion. First, a reverse flow of goods and services is created. When you or I spend our income, we receive things in return (this is, of course, why we spend). In addition, an income flow is set forth. Our spending results in income for the producers and sellers of the goods and services that we buy. This gives us a basic economic law: *spending creates income*. Our first analysis of the economy, then, should be to simply trace spending flows so as to see how income is generated.

There is a **circular flow model** of spending and income in the economy, as illustrated in Figure 6-1. In this picture, the economic world has been divided into just two parts or **sectors**—households and businesses. There is a primary spending flow which moves from households to businesses. Consumers buy goods and services from the business sector. This generates income for business and prompts the production of the goods and services that consuming householders want. Businesses, however, do not keep their

Circular flow model: highlights the circular flow of spending and income between the business and household sectors of the economy; built on the concept that spending creates income

Sectors: parts of the economy which respond differently to economic events or are related by similar problems or activities

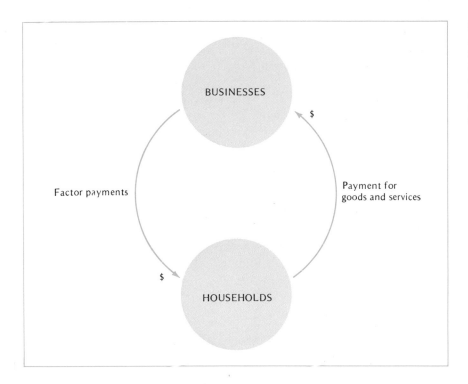

BUSINESSES

$

Factor payments

Payment for
goods and services

$

HOUSEHOLDS

FIGURE 6-1: THE CIRCULAR FLOW
*Household spending for goods and
services creates the income for
businesses which is eventually recycled
as payments for labor, rent, and profits.
Each sector of the economy depends
upon and benefits from the actions of
others. Spending creates income.*

income. They must purchase time, talent, and know-how from the householders. This provides income for the households, and assures a supply of labor, talent, and ideas for the business sector.

Note the interdependence present here. Consumer spending creates income for the business sector. Business spending provides income for consumers. Each gains by the other's actions.

While this basic circular flow of spending and income prevails, the real world adds complications to our simple picture. There are a number of other sectors of the economy which tend to supply **injections** into the spending/ Income stream or produce **leakages** from the stream which cause spending and income to be less. These leakages and injections are illustrated in Figure 6-2.

The first obvious complication results from the actions of the **financial sector**. Most people do not spend all of their incomes. Some part of it is squirreled away in the institutions that make up the financial sector, often as a savings account. This saving (nonspending) represents a leakage from the spending/income stream. Since spending causes income, it follows that saving reduces spending and income. What we save does not go on to produce income for the businesses we deal with.

Injections: factors which increase spending flows

Leakages: factors which tend to reduce total spending

Financial sector: the part of the economy which specifically deals with borrowing, lending, and exchanges of assets

FIGURE 6-2: THE CIRCULAR FLOW, INJECTIONS, AND LEAKAGES

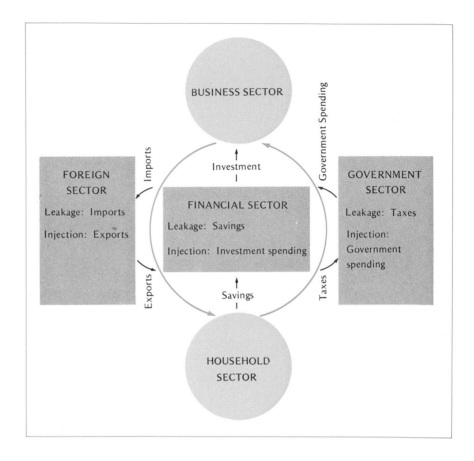

But the financial sector also provides an injection. Savings do not sit idly by, but are put to work through investment spending. Investment spending tends to increase the amount of total spending in the economy and so increases national income.

The financial sector, then, reduces total spending by way of the saving leakage and produces the investment spending injection. But these two flows need not be equal. There is no reason for the amount that people wish to save to be exactly equal to the amount that investors wish to spend on business goods and services. The financial sector can be either a net injection (causing spending and income to grow) or a net leakage (reducing total spending and income).

The government sector is the next part of the economy for us to consider. The government draws a very large leakage from the spending/income flow—taxes. When we send our money to governments (federal, state, or local), our ability to spend is reduced by the amount of our taxes. Taxes are a leakage from the spending/income flow, but the government can balance the equation. Government spending is the obvious injection. When the government buys goods and services, its spending creates income for both business and households. Government spending is a large and important part of the circular flow picture.

The government sector provides an injection—government spending—and the leakage of taxes. Again, there is no guarantee that leakages and injections will balance. Indeed, since the 1950s the federal government has generally been a net injection. Government spending has often exceeded tax proceeds by billions of dollars.

Finally, we have the foreign sector of the economy. Foreign households, businesses, and governments inject spending into our economy when they buy things from us. These foreign purchases are called **exports**. The more that buyers in other countries spend on our goods, the larger is the spending and income generated in this country.

Exports: goods sold to the residents of other countries

In the same sense, **imports**—our purchases of foreign goods and services—tend to increase total spending in other countries and implicitly reduce total income and spending at home. Exports are an injection, then, and imports represent a leakage. When we import goods, we get the items (cars, oil, coffee) and the foreign producers get our income. The opposite occurs when we export goods to the residents of other lands.

Imports: purchases of goods from foreign countries

MACROECONOMIC EQUILIBRIUM

This rather simple-looking picture of economic activity is actually very useful in describing some of the basic forces which can work to shape economic events. The leakages out of and injections into the spending/income stream are as follows:

Injections	Leakages
1. Investment spending	1. Savings
2. Government spending	2. Taxes
3. Exports	3. Imports

When the *total* amount of leakages equals the *total* of the injections, the economy will be in a **macroeconomic equilibrium**. Total spending will equal total income. Income will neither rise nor fall. Every dollar that is received as income is eventually spent by someone, since the amount that leaks out of the spending income stream is eventually used to provide an injection somewhere else. The combined leakages from taxes, savings, and imports are used to create the injections of investment, government spending, and exports. Total income and total spending are equal.

Macroeconomic equilibrium: when desired total spending equals income; at this point total spending and income neither rise nor fall

FIGURE 6-3: THE GROSS NATIONAL
BATHTUB

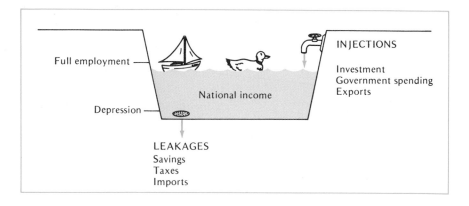

To see this, think of the economy as a bathtub (the "gross national bathtub" is pictured in Figure 6-3). Here we measure the amount of spending and income by the amount of water in the tub. Injections tend to increase the spending/income level like water pouring into the bathtub. The leakages act like drains to lower the spending/income totals.

When the leakages and injections are just equal, the amount of spending flowing into the bathtub equals the amount flowing out. The spending/income level neither rises nor falls, so long as the inflows and outflows remain constant.

This bathtub model is convenient because it suggests some clear policy actions that can be taken. Suppose, for example, that you wanted to increase the level of national income (increase the level of water in the imaginary bathtub). How can this be done? It is easy to see. The equilibrium level of money income will rise whenever the total injections exceed the total leakages. National incomes can be made to increase, then, by either increasing one of the injections, like government spending, or decreasing one of the leakages, like taxes. Either of these kinds of policies can be counted upon to stimulate the economy by increasing the net spending/income flows.

On the other hand, suppose that you wanted to lower the level of economic activity in order to, say, fight inflation using a Phillips Curve trade-off. National income will fall whenever the leakages out of the spending/income stream exceed the injections into it. The economy can be slowed down, therefore, by either increasing the leakages (e.g., raising taxes) or decreasing an injection (e.g., lowering government spending).

The amount of economic activity in the economy is determined by the amount of spending which is produced and by the nature of the leakages and injections which are created.

The spending-income model of national economic activity which has just been presented was first developed by the economist John Maynard Keynes (pronounced "Canes") who lived from 1883 to 1946. It is thus called the **Keynesian model** of the economy. Keynes pointed out that the inevitable forces of spending and income would always push the economy toward some equilibrium level of total spending-income. But is the equilibrium level necessarily desirable? Keynes's answer was no. Keynes held (and history has backed him up) that the equilibrium can occur at full employment, moderate unemployment, or even deep depression with equal chance. Prosperity is not guaranteed, Keynes held; rather, it is only one of many possible outcomes.

If the macroeconomic equilibrium does not assure prosperity, are we doomed to high unemployment rates? Again Keynes's answer was in the negative. By manipulating the leakages and injections (through government spending and taxation policies or other policies designed to affect businesses or consumer spending and saving decisions) the macroeconomic equilibrium can be manipulated toward any desired level.

Much of the post–World War II economic policy has attempted to regulate aggregate demand so as to achieve full employment. This quest for prosperity has not always been successful because there is more to the economy than just leakages and injections.

The simple Keynesian model of economic activity gives us a good general feel for how the economy works, but we can acquire a more refined understanding by looking closely at the determinants of total spending. For this purpose, total spending can be divided into four parts: consumption, investment, government, and net export spending. This division will prove enlightening because each of these types of spending is motivated by different desires and depends on different factors.

IS EQUILIBRIUM GOOD?

Keynesian model: the model of macroeconomic activity developed by John Maynard Keynes which concentrates on total spending as the determinant of the equilibrium level of national income

---

Consumer spending on goods and services makes up the largest single part of aggregate demand. **Consumption spending**, as shown in Figure 6-4, amounted to over $1.2 trillion in 1977, accounting for almost two-thirds of total spending in the economy.

What determines the total amount of consumption spending? Many factors enter in. Life styles, the outlook for the future, the availability of credit—all these things and more can cause consumption spending to rise or fall. The most important determinant of consumer spending, however, is the level of national income. Consumption spending rises and falls with the level of income in the economy.

CONSUMPTION SPENDING

Consumption spending: spending by households on consumer items

FIGURE 6-4: COMPONENTS OF
AGGREGATE DEMAND, 1977

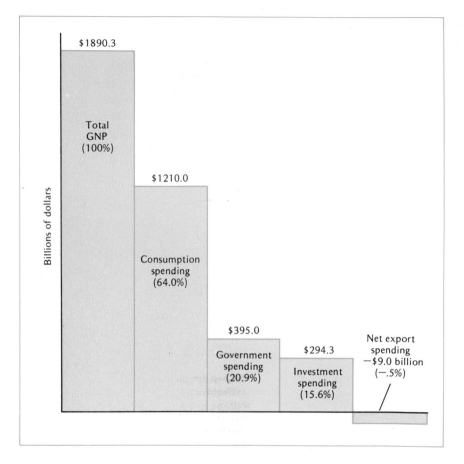

This relationship between income and consumption spending takes an interesting form. Households tend to spend a relatively high percentage of their total income. The fraction of total income spent on consumption is called the **average propensity to consume**, or APC. Households tend, in the aggregate, to behave differently with increases or decreases in their income than they do with their income as a whole. We call the relationship between *changes* in income and *changes* in consumption spending the **marginal propensity to consume** (MPC). The marginal propensity to consume is defined, mathematically, to be equal to the *change* in consumption spending divided by the *change* in income (the APC is equal to *total* consumption spending divided by *total* income). The MPC is found to have two interesting qualities. It is constant in the short run, and it is less than the average propensity to consume. Nationally, people tend to spend over 90 percent of their total incomes on consumption items (this gives an APC of over 90 percent). The MPC, however, is generally thought to be in the range

Average propensity to consume (APC): the fraction of total income which goes to consumption spending

Marginal propensity to consume (MPC): the proportion of any change in income which becomes a change in consumption

of 60 percent to 75 percent (depending on the definitions of income and consumption spending used to calculate the MPC).

What does all of this mean? It suggests that consumers behave, as a group, in a very particular way. Suppose that a household has total income of $1000 per month. Typically, this family might spend $900 of this sum on consumer goods and save the remaining $100 (for the sake of simplicity in this example, we will assume no tax payments or suppose that taxes are paid by the employer). This family then has an average propensity to consume of 90 percent, since nine-tenths of total income goes to consumption and one-tenth is saved.

What would happen if this household's income were to suddenly rise by $100 per month? Economists have found that consumer spending would rise by less than $100. In fact, it would probably only rise by about $60 (assuming an MPC of 60 percent), with the remaining $40 going to increased savings. Total consumption spending would rise to $960, and savings would increase to $140 to account for the $1000 in income.

Why should this behavior prevail? Many explanations have been offered. Consumers may save more of increments to income because they are not sure if the increase is permanent. They do not want to take on major new expenditures (buy a new house or car) or increase their standard of living if the rise in income is only temporary. Therefore, they treat the rise in income as a windfall gain and save a relatively large (40 percent) proportion of it. This kind of "permanent income" behavior generates the MPC phenomenon.

What would occur, on the other hand, if income were to *fall* by $100 per month? The same logic suggests that spending on consumer goods would not fall by the full amount of the fall in income. Rather, consumption spending would decline by 60 percent of the fall in income (falling from $900 to $840) and saving would be reduced to make up the difference (saving would decline from $100 per month to just $60).

Why this pattern? Again, the typical household may not be convinced that the $100 fall in income is permanent. They do not wish to cut expenditures drastically or lower their standard of living until they are sure that the fall in income is real. Therefore, they reduce savings to prop up consumer spending until they know for sure what is happening to income. If the change in income is eventually viewed as permanent, then consumption and saving patterns will be readjusted.

All of this makes sense. Unemployed people cut savings or "dissave" rather than give up their standard of living, and folks who get raises do not normally run out and spend all of the increased pay. In total, the phenomenon of the constant short-run marginal propensity to consume seems clearly to exist.

INVESTMENT SPENDING

Investment spending refers to the amount of plant, equipment, inventories, and capital goods (like machines and computers) that businesses desire to purchase in a given period. Investment spending does *not* include financial investments like stocks and bonds, since these "investments" do not directly result in the production of goods and services.

Investment spending is a relatively small component of aggregate demand—accounting for only 15 percent of total spending in 1977—but it is still very important. When businesses invest, this tends to increase the productive capacity of the economy in the future. Investment spending is very important in determining the rate of economic growth. Investment spending, like financial investments, yields dividends in the future, but the dividends are real (jobs, goods, and services) and important to the national economic health.

The level of investment spending for the nation as a whole is determined by a number of things. Improved technologies tend to cause investment spending to rise, as manufacturers convert to more economical production methods or tool up for new product lines. Rising demand in general tends to cause businesses to expand over time to take advantage of new and larger markets.

The level of interest rates also has a major impact on investment, as we shall see in detail in Part III. Most businesses borrow money in order to undertake investments. Low interest rates make borrowing cheap, and so make it inexpensive and profitable to invest. Higher interest rates have just the opposite effect, tending to make investments costlier, less profitable, and therefore discouraging them.

Investment spending is the least predictable component of aggregate demand. Investment spending can rise or fall by large amounts from year to year as businesses respond to changes in prices, outlooks, and market conditions. This can create problems, of course, since fluctuations in investment spending translate into changing aggregate demand and national income.

GOVERNMENT SPENDING

Government spending at the federal, state, and local levels is a large and important component of total spending (it amounted to 21 percent of total spending in 1977). Governments buy a variety of goods—tanks and bombs, paper and Xerox machines, buildings, and, yes, red tape—but most of government spending goes for services—administrators, secretaries, bureaucrats, teachers, policemen, road crews, and so on.

It is clear that government spending has a large effect on aggregate demand both directly, through governmental purchases of goods and services, and indirectly, through the impact of government policies like taxes and transfers on consumers and businesses. We will explore the impact of government on the economy in greater detail in Chapter 8.

NET EXPORT SPENDING

The way that the economy interacts with the rest of the world also has an impact on the level of income and spending. When we sell goods and services to the residents of other nations, these exports cause income in the economy to rise. Exports are the amounts of goods and services that foreigners demand from us.

Imports, on the other hand, are the items (like oil and coffee) that we purchase from people in other lands. Imports tend to reduce total spending at home and increase it in the other countries. Net exports (exports minus imports) is the net amount of additional spending that is generated in our economy through foreign trade. As we can see in Figure 6-4, net exports were negative in 1977, indicating that we bought $9 billion worth of goods and services more from the rest of the world than they bought from us. The net impact on aggregate demand, then, was negative, but relatively small.

This is an important area to watch. Just after the oil embargo of 1973–1974, for example, the cost of oil imports rose steeply, and aggregate demand fell as a result.

The level of **net exports** depends on a lot of things. Our demand for goods which *must* be imported (like coffee and tea) affects net exports, as do more complicated things like changes in the exchange rates among trading nations. We will take an in-depth look at the international sector of the economy in Part IV of this text.

Net exports: the net injection from the foreign sector of the economy: exports minus imports

THE AGGREGATE DEMAND CURVE

Thus far this discussion has concentrated on the determinants of the amount of total spending and income within the economy. We have analyzed the amount that people wish to spend, but we have thus far ignored one important aspect of the real world: prices.

All of the analysis of spending and income that we have done has been looking at these flows in nominal or money terms—unadjusted for inflation. As was seen when economic growth as measured in GNP and by RGNP was compared in Chapter 5, looking at the world without taking into account the affects of inflation can be very misleading. It is therefore crucial to analyze the real quantity of desired total spending in the economy.

When total spending increases, this can have one of three effects. Either the quantity purchased can rise (more spending, buying more goods), or the quantity of goods and services received may remain the same as the prices of those goods rise to absorb the higher spending, or the increased spending may be divided between both larger quantities and higher prices.

We are all familiar with this idea. In a world where inflation is a reality, increased spending (more dollars spent) does not necessarily mean that more goods are acquired. Indeed, we are often faced with the prospect of spending more and getting less.

At the start of this chapter, we defined aggregate demand to be the amount of goods and services that households, businesses, and governments wish to purchase. The amount of goods and services that are sought depends upon two principal factors: the level of total spending and the general level of prices in the economy. We have already examined the way in which total spending is determined. Figure 6-5 shows how aggregate demand (the quantity that the spending purchases) varies with the price level.

As the price level (PL) rises from PL_0 to PL_1 in Figure 6-5, the amount of goods and services that consumers, businesses, and governments wish to purchase declines from $RGNP_0$ to $RGNP_1$ (we measure the quantity of goods and services using RGNP since this yardstick will show changes in the quantity purchased alone, and not be affected by changes in the price level). There are several reasons for this declining quantity of aggregate demand. The first explanation is the declining **real-income effect**. As prices rise,

Real income effect: a change in the quantity of AD which results from a change in the price level altering real incomes

FIGURE 6-5: THE AGGREGATE DEMAND CURVE
As inflation brings about a rise in the price level from PL_0 to PL_1, the amount of goods and services that consumers, businesses, and government wish to purchase falls from $RGNP_0$ to $RGNP_1$ because of the real income, real balances, and other effects.

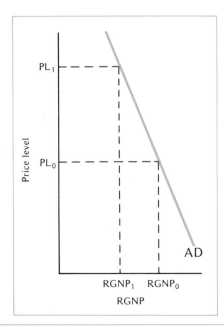

economic agents find that their paychecks purchase fewer goods and services. Their real incomes have declined, so the amount of RGNP that they can afford to buy has fallen, too.

Consumers may also experience a **real-balance effect**. As the price level rises, inflation reduces the worth of assets with fixed nominal values like savings accounts. The "real" bank balance has been reduced. A family who was saving for some specific reason (down payment on a house, a vacation cabin, college tuition, etc.) would find that inflation had left them even further from their savings goal. They will spend less and save more to rebuild that real bank balance. This, of course, causes an increase in leakages (saving) and so the amount of goods and services that are purchased must fall.

Real-balance effect: a change in the quantity of AD which results from prices changing the real value of savings, thus inducing a change in saving and spending habits

Businesses may reduce investment spending in response to the higher interest rates that the inflation is likely to cause. Governments may try to buy less when the price level rises in order to keep from inflaming the inflation problem.

All these factors combined suggest the existence of the kind of downward-sloping aggregate demand curve shown in Figure 6-5. Rising price levels tend to reduce the amounts of goods and services purchased in real terms.

CHANGES IN AGGREGATE DEMAND

Anything which tends to change the amount of total spending within the economy will have the impact of changing aggregate demand, too, and shifting the aggregate demand curve. Figure 6-6 illustrates an increase in aggregate demand. Suppose, for example, that government spending increases in order to, say, provide more public day care centers. This increase in government spending will cause an increase in total spending, and so bring about a rise in aggregate demand. The aggregate demand curve will shift to the right as shown in Figure 6-6, indicating that more goods and services (RGNP) are demanded at every price level.

An increase in aggregate demand can be caused by a large number of factors, including the following:

☐ A tax cut, which increases consumer spending.
☐ An increase in Social Security benefits, which increases spending of retired individuals.
☐ An increase in government defense outlays.
☐ Investment spending for nuclear power plants.
☐ Increased exports of wheat to India.

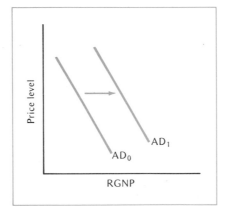

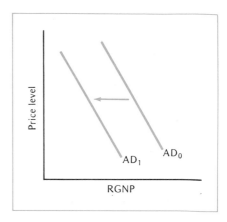

FIGURE 6-6: INCREASE IN AD
An increase in aggregate demand can be caused by increased consumer spending, investment, government purchases, or increased foreign demand.

FIGURE 6-7: DECREASE IN AD
A decrease in AD can come about because of falling consumption, investment, or government or foreign demand.

A fall in total spending will bring about a fall in aggregate demand, as shown in Figure 6-7. As total spending decreases because, say, a tax increase causes consumers to reduce consumption spending, the amount of goods and services purchased declines as well. The aggregate demand curve shifts to the left to show that fewer goods and services are demanded at any price level.

Anything which causes the amount of total spending within the economy to fall will bring about a decrease in AD. Decreased AD can be brought about by the following:

☐ Consumers fear a depression and so save more in anticipation of hard times ahead.

☐ Increased taxes cause consumption spending to fall.

☐ Government cuts spending for education.

☐ High interest rates cause businesses to lower investment spending.

☐ Spending on oil imports increases.

☐ Changes in the exchange rate cause exports to fall.

The amount of goods and services that consumers, businesses, and governments intend to purchase, then, varies both with the level of income and total spending in the economy and with the prevailing general level of prices. A change in the price level will cause a movement along the AD curve. A change in total spending will produce a shift in the entire AD curve.

In Figures 6-5 through 6-8, we have drawn the AD curve with a fairly steep slope in order to show how changes in the price level produce changes in the amounts of goods and services demanded. It is important to note, however, that the effect of price is not really so large as these graphs indicate, at least in the short run.

SLOPE OF THE AD CURVE

In the real world, the amounts of goods and services that are purchased depends less on the price level than on income and factors such as standard of living. In the short run, aggregate demand depends more on these factors and less on the price level. This suggests that the AD curve should be drawn more nearly vertical to indicate that AD does not change very much when prices change. Over longer periods of time, of course, people adjust their buying habits in response to changing prices, and the slope of the AD curve may change.

We began this chapter trying to answer the question, What determines the amount of goods and services that people wish to purchase, in the aggregate, in the economy? In answering this query, we have looked at the economic process in many lights.

Spending creates income, so when we look at spending we are also looking at the determination of the level of national income. Spending and income rise and fall in response to changes in the injections (investment, government, export spending) and leakages (saving, taxes, imports) which take place.

Spending, however, can go to purchase new goods or to pay inflated prices on the amount of goods already in the market basket. We must therefore take the impact of changing price levels into consideration when looking at aggregate demand. The analysis of spending, income, and prices, then, must all go on at once.

A relatively simple tool, the aggregate demand curve, summarizes all of this for us. The AD curve shows how the purchases of goods and services vary with the price level, given a constant amount of total spending. When spending and income change, the aggregate demand curve will change as well.

We have built half of our model of the national economy. It is now left for us to construct the twin concept of aggregate supply.

APPENDIX: THE KEYNESIAN 45-DEGREE-LINE MODEL

Additional insights concerning the circular-flow and bathtub models of the economy can be obtained by taking a different view of the forces at work affecting total income and total spending. This brief appendix presents an introduction to the traditional **Keynesian 45-degree-line model** of the economy.

The 45-degree-line model is designed to show the relationship between total spending and total income graphically. The relationship between income and consumption spending is shown in Figure 6-8. The consumption line (C-line) has all of the properties of consumer spending that were discussed earlier in the chapter. The C-line is upward-sloping to indicate that consumption spending increases and decreases as income rises and falls. The slope of the consumption line is constant (it is a straight line). This reflects the assumption of a constant marginal propensity to consume (MPC). Recall that the MPC is defined to be the change in consumption spending (the vertical distance in Figure 6-8) divided by the change in income (the horizontal distance in Figure 6-8). The MPC is the rise of the C-line divided by its run or, simply, the slope of the consumption line.

Keynesian 45-degree-line model: a model of economic activity based on the ideas of John Maynard Keynes which uses a 45° line to show the macroeconomic equilibrium

FIGURE 6-8: THE CONSUMPTION FUNCTION
Consumption spending rises with income according to the relationship given by the marginal propensity to consume. A fixed proportion of any increase (or decrease) in income is allocated to consumption spending.

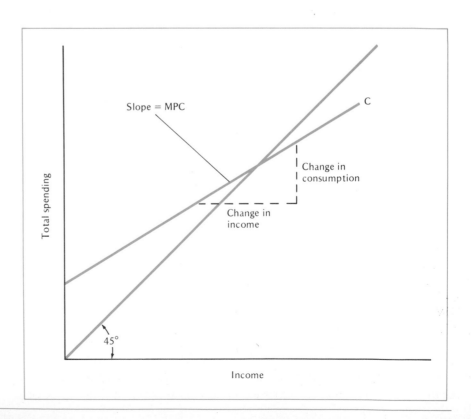

Figure 6-8 also includes a 45-degree line (from which this model takes its name). This line forms a ray where total spending (measured on the vertical axis) equals total income (measured on the horizontal axis). The 45-degree line, then, shows all of the points where total income equals total spending. These are the macroeconomic equilibrium points.

At the level of income where the consumption line crosses the 45-degree line, consumption spending equals total income. Since all income is spent, none is saved. At levels of income below this intersection, consumption spending (the vertical distance to the consumption line) exceeds income (the vertical distance to the 45° line). Since more is spent than is received in income, dissaving occurs (people draw down saving or borrow from others). When income is above the level indicated by the crossing lines, income (as measured by the vertical distance to the 45-degree line) exceeds consumption spending (the distance to the consumption line), and positive saving occurs.

Consumption spending is not, of course, the only component of total spending. We must therefore add the remaining components of aggregate demand. Assume for a moment that the injections into our spending stream are held constant. That is, investment (I), government spending (G), and net exports (X) are temporarily fixed. Consumption spending (C) is not fixed since it rises and falls with changes in national income. We can now determine the level of total spending (and national income) where the bathtub model spending/income equilibrium will prevail.

Figure 6-9 shows a basic graphical framework. Besides the consumption line (from Figure 6-8), a line has been added showing how the level of total spending (C + I + G + X) varies with the level of national income. Since the injections are assumed to be constant, they are simply added vertically to the consumption line.

The macroeconomic equilibrium occurs here at income level Y* in Figure 6-9. At this level of income and spending, every dollar of national income is spent by someone, and total income equals total spending. Leakages are just equal to injections (investment, government, and net export spending). This can be easily seen if we note that, graphically, the leakages are equal to the vertical difference between the C-line and the 45-degree income line (the difference between consumption and income). Injections are equal to the vertical difference between the C-line and the total spending (C + I + G + X) line. At income level Y*, these two distances are equal.

At any level of income less than Y*, forces will be at work causing income to rise (think back to the bathtub model for intuitive help). At lower levels of national income, less will be saved (smaller leakages), but the amount that will be injected into the economy is still the same. The excess of

*Total spending equals total income at
income level Y*. Since leakages equal
injections, income and spending
neither rise nor fall. At income levels
below Y*, injections exceed leakages,
causing income to rise. At incomes
greater than Y*, leakages exceed
injections, causing income to fall.*

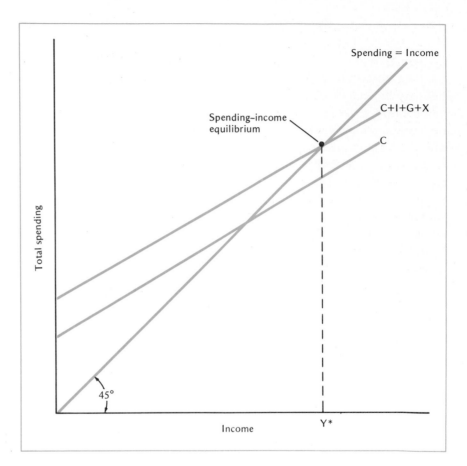

injections over leakages will cause the level of national income to grow, and
the growth will continue until Y* is reached.

At income levels greater than Y*, on the other hand, savings will be
higher because income is higher. This will cause the savings leakage to be
greater than the sum of the injections. When leakages exceed injections it is
only logical for total spending and income to fall, causing income to return
to the equilibrium level of Y*.

Up to now we have assumed investment, government, and net export
spending to be constant. This will not be the case for long. Anything which
has the impact of increasing injections (or lowering leakages) tends to cause
the equilibrium levels of spending an income to rise, as shown in Figure
6-10. Here, government spending has increased from G to G'. As
government spending increases, this disturbs the balance of leakages and
injections which prevailed at income level Y*. Now, suddenly, injections
exceed leakages, causing the level of income to rise as the increased

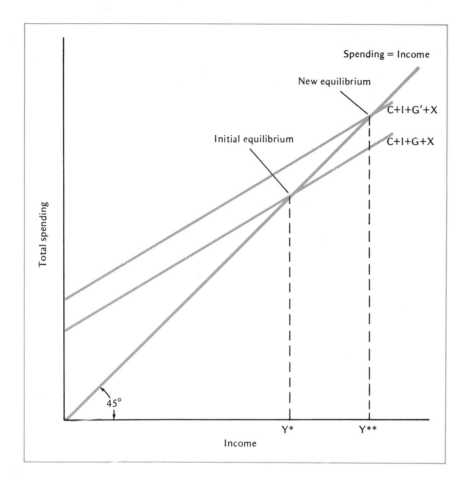

FIGURE 6-10: IMPACT OF INCREASED GOVERNMENT SPENDING
As government spending rises from G to G', this disturbs the spending-income equilibrium which had prevailed at Y*. Since government spending has increased injections, income will rise until increased saving balances leakages and injections at income level Y**.

spending causes increased income. The rising income level causes the savings leakage to rise, too. The equilibrium will be restored eventually at a new, higher level of spending and income denoted Y** in the diagram.

Higher government spending causes higher total spending and therefore higher equilibrium income. The same type of movement would occur if investment or export spending were to increase, or if something caused a sudden increase in consumer spending or decrease in taxes.

Spending and income would fall, following the same lines of reasoning, if injections fell or leakages increased. If investment spending were to suddenly decrease, for example, this would cause injections to be temporarily less than leakages. Spending and income would fall until the savings leakage had fallen to the new lower level of injections, at which time equilibrium would be again established at a lower level of spending and income.

Lower investment spending would lower total spending and so reduce the equilibrium level of national income.

The circular-flow concept and the bathtub and 45-degree-line models all demonstrate the same basic concepts. Spending and income are determined together within the economy. Spending creates income. Income will rise or fall as total spending rises and falls in response to changes in the injections which make spending rise and leakages which reduce total spending and income.

SUMMARY

1. Aggregate demand is a measure of the desired total quantity of goods and services that is demanded throughout the economy in some period of time. The aggregate demand curve shows how that total demand for goods and services (measured by RGNP) varies with the price level.

2. Total spending and total income are identical in the sense that income is created by spending. Policies that are designed to raise or lower the national income must do this by raising or lowering total spending. The spending-income relationship is illustrated by the circular-flow diagram.

3. Saving, taxes, and imports are all leakages from the circular flow of spending and income. That is, because they reduce current spending, they reduce total income. Investment spending, government spending, and purchases of exports (by foreigners) are all injections into the circular flow in that, by increasing total spending, they tend to increase total income.

4. The macroeconomic equilibrium (the equilibrium level of total spending) occurs when total leakages equal total injections. When this occurs, total spending equals total income and so income will neither rise nor fall. The macroeconomic equilibrium is not "good" in the sense that equilibrium occurs at full or even high employment. Indeed, equilibrium can occur at high levels of unemployment. Many national economic policies are designed to alter the macroeconomic equilibrium so as to reduce unemployment.

5. Consumption spending is the amount of spending that households undertake for consumer goods (as opposed to investment or government spending). Consumption spending and income seem to be related by the constant marginal propensity to consume (MPC). The constant MPC simply states that people will tend to increase or decrease consumption spending by a constant proportion of any increase or decrease in their incomes.

6. Changes in the price level affect the amounts of goods and services that are demanded. Aggregate demand is inversely related to the price level (i.e., inflation reduces the demand for goods and services and a lower price level would increase total desired purchases).

---

1. Make a list of ways that the government sector can cause total spending in the economy to rise in order to fight unemployment. How many of these ways are currently being used?

2. Another name for net exports spending is the *balance of trade*. What impact does a deficit in the balance of trade (negative net exports) have on total spending, income, and aggregate demand?

3. Joe Smith earns $500 per week. Suppose that the Smith family's APC is 80 percent. How much do they spend and save? Suppose that their MPC is 70 percent. What would happen to spending and saving (and their APC) if income were to rise by $100 per week? Does this make sense?

4. An increase in total spending can go for either increased quantities of goods and services, higher prices, or both. Can you show how this works for an individual market using supply and demand curves?

5. Why is the aggregate demand curve downward-sloping? What would an upward-sloping AD curve mean? What would a vertical AD curve mean? What would a horizontal AD curve mean? Which shape makes the most sense?

6. For individual families, saving is a good thing because it helps us allocate our income over time and so gives us a more desirable consumption pattern. In the aggregate, however, the "paradox of thrift" prevails. Use the circular-flow and bathtub models to determine what would happen if *all* families increased savings and no corresponding increase in investment appeared.

Indicate whether each of the following statements is *true* or *false*. Be able to defend your choice.

1. Increases in total spending cause income to rise.

2. Higher taxes cause national income to fall.

3. When consumers save more of their income they stimulate the economy and increase total spending and income.

4. Total income rises when total

spending exceeds total income.

5. Macroeconomic equilibrium occurs when saving equals investment, government spending equals taxes, and imports equal exports.

6. The marginal propensity to consume falls as income rises.

7. The average propensity to consume falls as income rises.

8. Macroeconomic equilibrium occurs when full employment is achieved.

9. Inflation is an increase in the price level.

10. Increases in the price level reduce real income and so reduce the quantity of aggregate demand.

7
Aggregate Supply and the Economy

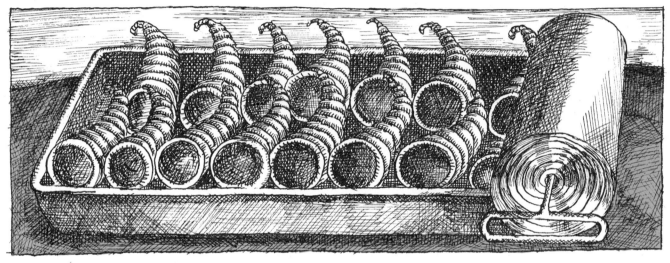

This chapter puts together a simple model of the national economy and uses that model to examine some important questions in macroeconomics. Some questions that will be answered here include:

What is aggregate supply?

What factors affect the aggregate supply?

What is the relationship between changes in the price level and total production?

What are the causes of unemployment?

What are the causes of inflation?

How can both inflation and unemployment be fought at the same time?

Every market is made up of two sides: buyers and sellers. It should not surprise us, then, that when we analyze the sum of all of these markets we again have to treat the interactions of the buyers and sellers: aggregate demand and supply.

In this chapter we will look at what determines the amount of goods that are produced in the economy and the relationship between production and the general level of prices. We will then be able to model the working of the national economy and determine, in simple terms, the causes of inflation and unemployment and evaluate some policies designed to fight one or both of these problems.

AGGREGATE SUPPLY

Aggregate supply is the total production of goods and services available in the economy in some time period. Aggregate supply is to the supply of goods in individual markets as aggregate demand is to market demand. Aggregate supply is essentially the sum of all of the market supplies in the economy.

Aggregate supply is a more difficult concept to grasp than aggregate demand because, while we can easily imagine the factors which might affect the total amount of goods and services that we want to purchase, what determines, in total, how much is produced? To understand this we must realize that there are several fundamental influences which are common to the production of goods and services in all parts of the economy (over and above those which might affect individual markets). Some of these important determinants of the aggregate supply are the following:

1. THE PRICE LEVEL. Just as firms in individual markets will respond to an increase in the price of output by producing more, so increases in the general level of prices (inflation) will affect firms throughout the economy. As the price level rises, firms everywhere will begin to experience higher shortrun profits. This occurs largely because of the wage-lag effect discussed in Chapter 1. Inflation causes the prices of both inputs and outputs to rise. But since the prices of output often increase faster than the cost of inputs like labor (which may be fixed in price by contractural agreement), higher prices tend to temporarily increase profits. More goods and services are produced in response to these higher profit levels.

There is another way to view the relationship between output and the price level. It may be the case that businesses around the economy experience **diminishing returns**. That is, because they must use less productive machines, labor, and materials when increasing production, firms in general may find that the cost of additional goods and services is

Diminishing returns: the phenomenon that prevails when, as more resources are used in production, their average productivity tends to fall

higher than that of current production. In order to induce firms to produce more, then, it is necessary to pay them more so as to cover their higher costs.

Either way that you look at it, though, higher prices—inflation—and higher quantity of aggregate supply generally go together (with two exceptions which we shall see later).

2. PRODUCTIVE CAPACITY OF THE ECONOMY. The physical ability to produce goods and services plays a very important part in the determination of the amount of aggregate supply. By physical **capacity** is meant the amounts and kinds of plants, machines, factories, mines, and stores where goods and services are produced. Since all of these physical items are necessary to production for individual firms or the economy as a whole, their availability or scarcity makes a big difference in aggregate supply.

Capacity: the physical ability of the economy to produce, normally measured by the amount of plants, equipment, machinery, and the like available for use

The productive capacity of the economy is built up through the process of investment. Investment spending, over the long run, replaces worn-out factories and machines and adds new ones which may be more efficient or more productive. This expands the economy's ability to produce and increases the aggregate supply. A lack of investment, on the other hand, can cause the amount of total supply to fall. This happens because of **depreciation**. Depreciation is most often thought of as a business tax deduction. Depreciation, from a tax standpoint, is the amount of money that a business firm can deduct, when calculating taxes, because of the deterioration of their physical productive goods. Since machines, trucks, and buildings wear out over time, firms are allowed to deduct the value of these losses.

Depreciation: the wearing down of machines and other productive resources

Depreciation is a real phenomenon, too. As machines get older and buildings are worn out, a large amount of investment is required just to keep them running. Some investment spending, then, goes just to keep the present capacity working. **Net investment** is the amount that we add to the nation's productive capacity over and above the amount that is spent battling the effects of depreciation.

Net investment: total investment spending minus the amount of investment which went to keep existing capacity in use (i.e., total investment minus depreciation); the amount of investment which goes to expand total production

Investment is very important to the aggregate supply. During the Great Depression business firms were not very optimistic and so invested little in their future. Net investment was *negative*—more machines wore out than were put in place. The productive capacity of the economy declined.

Investment spending is important to the long-run health of the economy for two reasons. In the short run (as we saw in looking at aggregate demand), investment spending, like any other type of spending, creates jobs and incomes around the economy. In the long run, unlike other types of spending, it also adds to the productive capacity of the economy and so creates the firms, plants, and industries which will supply jobs down the road. Investment spending is one key to economic growth, and we will return to view its importance many times in future chapters.

3. TECHNOLOGY. A product of investment is technology. Improving technology allows us to use resources more efficiently and so produce more for less or increase the quality of that which is produced.

Improvements in technology have been very important to the growth of the American economy. Inventions like the electric lamp and the cotton gin and innovations like the production line have increased the aggregate supply manyfold over the years. Indeed, in many ways, the growth of the economy in the past has been tied to the appearance of new inventions which have increased the aggregate supply.

Most of the inventions that we think of seem far in the past, but the force of improving technology is still with us. The solution of the energy problem (and the increase in aggregate supply that would result) is in many ways a problem of finding and developing the right technology.

To generate this new technology, however, requires investment. Investment not in machines, but in research and development. Governments, business, and private individuals spend billions trying to produce the technology of the future. The impact of their actions will be felt significantly in the aggregate supply.

4. SIZE OF THE LABOR FORCE. In many ways the ability of the economy to produce is determined by the number of workers who are available to carry out the production. The machine age may be here, but it seems to have made the worker even more important.

Increases in the labor force can create some short-term problems, such as unemployment if workers are not quickly and efficiently assimilated into the productive economy. But over the long run, increases in the labor force produce the additional goods and services necessary for economy growth. Recent rises in the labor force participation rate (the proportion of working-age people involved in the labor force) suggests that people are concerned about the problem of economic growth, at least on an individual basis. By working they can have and produce more goods and services. For the individual, this can result in an increased standard of living. For the economy, however, the increase is in aggregate supply.

5. PRODUCTIVITY OF THE LABOR FORCE. As important as the size of the labor force is its ability to actually produce goods and services. Increases in *productivity* or amount produced by each resource unit can be brought about in several ways.

Investment spending is one way to increase productivity. By creating better machines or more efficient processes, it is possible for one worker to do the job of many, creating more and more goods and services. This process of mechanization results in some unemployment in the short run, as certain jobs are made obsolete by progress, but tends to create new jobs around the economy in the long run. The trade-off here is short-term unemployment for some individuals for an increase in the long run aggregate supply for the economy.

Investment in human capital is another way to increase productivity. As we invest in ourselves through education, training, and experience, we are able to do more and do it better. The economy gains through these private activities.

Investment in human capital: investments in training and education which increase worker productivity

Technological innovations also have the effect of increasing productivity. Adam Smith, the father of economics, told of the innovation of **specialization** in a pin factory. A group of workers could make many more pins by reducing the production process into a number of discrete steps and then specializing in just one aspect of the job instead of building each pin from scratch individually.

Specialization: the principle of having a person or industry perform just one or a few tasks and so become very good at that task, which tends to increase productivity

Adam Smith's pin factory seems primitive to us now, but the concepts of **division of labor** and specialization are still being used to increase productivity. In some fast-food chains, for example, the standard procedure is now to have different people take orders, call them out, cook them, assemble the orders, and finally deliver the goods to the customer. Many more people are at work, compared to the old system of a single cook doing it all, but through this process, more hamburgers and hot dogs are produced, too.

Division of labor: a way of increasing productivity by breaking a complicated process into a number of simple steps and then treating each step as a specialized job

6. AVAILABILITY AND COST OF INPUTS. The availability and cost of inputs are important to the output of an individual firm, and to the aggregate supply as well. When important basic inputs like energy, natural resources, steel, or oil are scarce or their prices change, this sends impacts rippling out through the economy well beyond the ring of the initial users of these particular products. We can see how important these factors of production are to the economy by noting the dramatic impacts that have resulted when the cost or availability of some basic input has been interrupted. The recession of 1958–1959 was brought on by a steel strike which reduced the availability of this vital resource. The oil embargo and rising oil costs were at least partially responsible for the recession of 1974. And when, during the Truman administration, train workers voted to strike and so reduce the amount of transportation services available, the president threatened to call out the troops to man the engines and keep the trains running. Trains were that important to the national economy.

When something happens to price or output in an industry which serves as one of the basic building blocks of the economy, the impact on total supply can be dramatic. Increases in these same resources, however, cause the aggregate supply to rise.

7. GOVERNMENT REGULATIONS.

Finally, the government can exert influence over the productive part of the economy to cause aggregate supply to either rise or to fall. We are perhaps most familiar with the latter case. Governmental pollution control rules may be necessary in order to preserve the environment, but they generally result in a reduction of supply. This is not to say the environmental controls are always bad. But we must understand the trade-off that is being made, and often that trade-off is clean air for less aggregate supply. Is the trade-off a good one? That probably depends on who you are and whether it is your air or your job at stake.

The government also performs many activities that tend to increase the aggregate supply. Job-training programs, when they are well run, have the effect of increasing both the size and productivity of the labor force. Government research programs may produce innovations that are useful to private industry. The space program, for example, has made communications satellites a reality, increasing our supply of information dramatically.

There are obviously many determinants of aggregate supply that we could talk about. Some, like changes in the price level or government regulations, result in fairly quick changes in the amount produced. Others, like investment or technological innovations, require considerable time before their impact on aggregate supply is felt.

A growing aggregate supply is important to the economy. Therefore, the cultivation of those factors that make supply rise is crucial, and a close examination of factors which limit aggregate supply is important.

THE AGGREGATE SUPPLY CURVE

The aggregate supply (AS) curve shows the relationship between the level of total output of goods and services (measured by RGNP) and the general level of prices in the economy. As the price level rises due to inflation, the amount of total output will change as well. But unlike the aggregate demand (AD) curve which we discussed in Chapter 6, there is more than one possible shape to the AS curve. In general, the aggregate supply curve will take on one of three different shapes, depending upon the state of the national economy.

1. THE DEPRESSION ECONOMY.

An economy in the midst of a depression or recession is plagued with large surpluses of unemployed

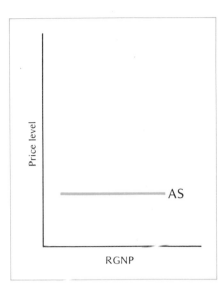

FIGURE 7-1: THE DEPRESSION
ECONOMY
*The aggregate supply curve is flat
during major business downturns
because there are large amounts of
resources unemployed. This excess
economic capacity can be used to
increase production without necessarily
increasing prices.*

resources—machines, factories, natural resources, and workers. Because there is so much unemployment of highly productive resources, firms which wish to expand will not have to bid up input prices in order to acquire the resources necessary to expand production.

This fact—the existence of highly productive unemployed resources available at no increase in cost—gives rise to the **depression AS** curve shown in Figure 7-1. This curve is horizontal, showing that more output may be obtained without an increase in the price level. The economy as a whole can expand without the motivating force of higher prices simply because, with so much excess capacity, firms gladly increase output at current prices whenever there is demand for their products.

Depression AS: the AS situation which prevails when there are large amounts of unemployed resources in the economy, making increased production possible without higher prices

2. THE FULL-EMPLOYMENT ECONOMY. In the depression economy, increases in output may be possible without price increases because of the large supply of unemployed productive resources. In the **full-employment AS economy**, however, just the opposite case holds. Here, all resources are fully used. Whenever one firm expands production, resources are taken away from other firms, causing factor prices (wage rates, machine prices, rents, and the like) to rise in the process. The result is the kind of AS curve shown in Figure 7-2.

Full-employment AS: the AS situation which prevails when all resources are in use, making increases in total production impossible and attempts to increase output result only in higher prices

The "full-employment" AS curve is vertical. It shows that the maximum amount of production possible (in the short run) is being produced. It is impossible to produce more. Any attempt at higher production will only lead to higher prices. The reason is clear. In order to get the additional labor

FIGURE 7-2: THE FULL-EMPLOYMENT
ECONOMY
*When the economy reaches full
employment, the aggregate supply
curve becomes vertical. Since all
resources are fully utilized here, any
attempt to increase output results only
in rapid inflation.*

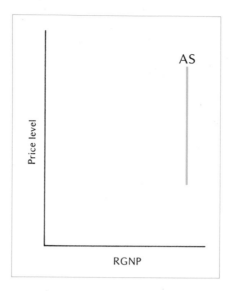

or materials, expanding firms have to offer to pay more for them, bidding up costs and causing prices in general to rise.

Attempts to expand total output here are fruitless and result in pure inflation—inflation where higher prices do not also bring higher production because the economy's production limit has been reached.

3. THE BOTTLENECK ECONOMY. Depressions and full employment have been the exception rather than the rule during most of our economic history. The more common type of economy that we have faced is here called a **bottleneck AS economy**, as shown in Figure 7-3. This type of economy experiences some substantial unemployment, but nothing nearly as severe as was the case in the depression economy. Some resources are unemployed, but most are working. As a result, aggregate output can be increased, but only with an increase in the price level.

Why is this called a "bottleneck" economy? In economics we say that bottlenecks occur in markets when goods cannot flow freely from sellers to buyers because of inefficiencies in the market process like imperfect mobility of labor or temporary shortages which are caused when demand rises faster than suppliers anticipated. These bottlenecks prevent production lines from flowing as fast as desired (much as a real bottleneck—as on a soda bottle—prevents the liquid in the bottle from flowing out smoothly). They also serve to increase the costs of production because temporary shortages that bottlenecks cause tend to force the prices of the scarce goods higher.

An example will help illustrate the problem of bottlenecks. In an expanding economy there may be an increasing demand for wood products

Bottleneck AS: the AS situation which prevails when there is substantial, but not severe, unemployment in an economy

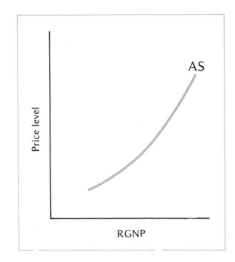

FIGURE 7-3: THE BOTTLENECK ECONOMY

In this aggregate supply situation, there are some unemployed resources, but not so many as in the depression case. Output can be expanded, but the resulting bottlenecks and inefficiencies cause the price level to rise. Inflation must accompany increases in RGNP here.

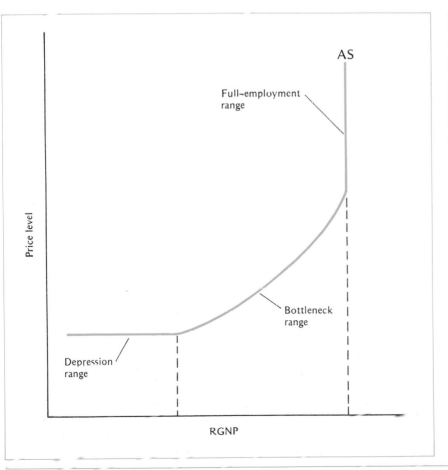

FIGURE 7-4: THE LONG-RUN AGGREGATE SUPPLY CURVE

In the short run the economy is usually in one or another of the three ranges shown here. In the long run the aggregate supply curve contains all three characteristics and the economy moves from one range to another as economic growth or decline take place.

(to build houses and other items). But it may not be possible immediately to meet the increased demand for lumber because of weather factors which prevent logging operations from working full time, a lack of sawmill operators, or any number of other factors. In the short run, then, these production backups will mean a shortage of the needed wood products. Production increases, but the costs go up, too, because of the scarcity of needed factors of production. In an economy not experiencing either full employment or depression, these kinds of bottlenecks are common, with the result that higher production comes at higher cost.

The result of all of this is the upward-sloping AS curve shown in Figure 7-3. Increased output is possible for the economy as a whole, but it must be motivated by a higher general level of prices. This upward-sloping AS curve is the type of economy that we are most used to facing.

Each of these three types of AS curves is really only a part of a total AS curve illustrated in Figure 7-4. At very low levels of RGNP, the economy enters the depression economy AS curve. As production rises, eventually the bottleneck area is reached. Finally, at high levels of RGNP, the roadblock of full employment prevents additional increases in national output, at least in the short-run.

CHANGES IN AGGREGATE SUPPLY

The aggregate supply curve is fixed in the short run, but it can respond to changes in costs, technology, or input prices and supplies over time. The two basic types of changes in the AS curve are shown in Figures 7-5 and 7-6, using a bottleneck AS curve for purposes of illustration.

An increase in AS, as shown in Figure 7-5, will come about, in the short run, whenever production costs fall or input availability increases to generate higher profits and so induce higher total production. Such things as increased supplies (or lower prices) of basic inputs such as steel, aluminum, or energy generate the rightward shift in the AS curve shown here.

This type of AS movement could also be caused, in the long run, by slower-acting factors such as improving technology, increases in the productivity or supply of labor, or the impact of high levels of investment spending.

A decrease in aggregate supply indicates that fewer goods and services are produced in total at each price level. This is illustrated in Figure 7-6. In the short run, such a decrease in AS is most normally caused by the sudden increase in price or reduction in availability of some vital input. Strikes in major sectors of the economy and the 1973–1974 oil embargo, for example, have caused sudden decreases in the aggregate supply as illustrated here.

In the longer run, aggregate supply can also fall if investment spending

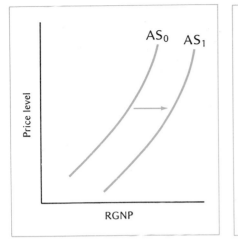

FIGURE 7-5: INCREASED AGGREGATE SUPPLY
Increasing aggregate supply can be caused by anything which increases the total ability of the economy to produce. Rising productivity of resources, increases in the capital stock of the economy, and technological improvements account for much of the normal rise in aggregate supply.

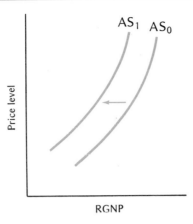

FIGURE 7-6: A DECREASE IN AGGREGATE SUPPLY
A decrease in aggregate supply will occur when something happens that lowers the ability of businesses in general to produce or that increases their costs of production. The OPEC oil embargo of 1973–1974 reduced AS. Government regulations which lower productivity can also cause AS to fall.

fails to keep up with depreciation or if government regulations make production more costly or less efficient.

In general, then, an increase in the aggregate supply (shift to the right in the AS curve) is caused by anything which increases the ability to produce or lowers the costs of production. These are factors such as the following:

☐ An increase in labor productivity.

☐ An increase in the size of labor force.

☐ A discovery of increased supply of inexpensive energy.

☐ A lifting of government regulations which were costly to business.

☐ Improved technology in key industries such as steel or transportation.

Anything which increases the general cost of production or lowers the ability of the economy to produce will cause the aggregate supply to fall and the AS curve to shift to the left. These are factors such as the following:

☐ A fall in labor productivity.

☐ Higher prices for oil.

☐ Reduced supply of natural resources.

☐ Governmental regulations which increase cost to businesses.

MACROECONOMIC EQUILIBRIUM

Aggregate demand pictures for us the total desired purchases of goods and services in the economy, and the aggregate supply is the total amount produced. When we put these two ideas together, we obtain a clear picture of the forces at work in the national economy.

There is one price level at which the amount of total production equals the amount which consumers, businesses, and governments wish to purchase. This is shown in Figure 7-7 as the crossing of the AD and AS curves with a price level of 100 (the base for the price level is arbitrary—we will be concerned with increases and decreases in the level of prices) and a level of RGNP equal to $1500 billion. At this equilibrium price level and RGNP, the total amount produced equals the total amount of goods and services demanded. At price levels other than this one, the economy will not be in macroeconomic equilibrium, and there will be forces at work causing the amount demanded, amount produced, and price level all to change. Let's examine how these forces work.

Suppose, first of all, that the economy were temporarily at a general level of prices that was below the level determined by the macroeconomic equilibrium—a price level such as 95 in Figure 7-7. Because the price level is relatively low here, there is a high aggregate demand. Consumers, businesses, and governments wish to purchase large amounts of goods and services because their real incomes are high. Aggregate supply, on the other hand, is relatively low. Firms cannot and will not increase production to meet the high demand at this price level. A shortage of goods and services exists.

The solution to this problem is fairly clear: in response to the shortage of goods and services, the price level will be bid up, inducing greater aggregate production and lowering the amount of goods and services demanded, moving the economy toward the macroeconomic equilibrium at a price level of 100. This is easy to say, but we are talking about actions which will be taken all around the economy. How do we know that this process will take place?

The mechanism by which the economy adjusts to a shortage of goods and

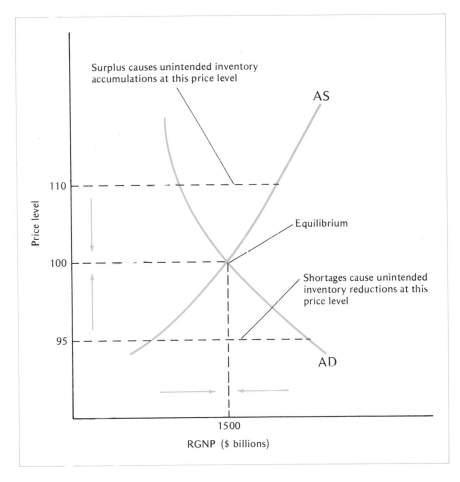

Surplus causes unintended inventory accumulations at this price level

AS

Equilibrium

Shortages cause unintended inventory reductions at this price level

AD

110

100

95

Price level

1500

RGNP ($ billions)

FIGURE 7-7: THE NATIONAL ECONOMIC "MARKET"
The interactions of aggregate supply and demand determine the national economic equilibrium. If the economy should be out of equilibrium, the forces of shortage and surplus act to restore the balance.

services depends heavily on adjustments in **inventories**. Inventories are stockpiles of goods that firms keep on hand in anticipation of selling or of using them to make goods to sell in the future. Inventory levels depend on the amount that firms expect to sell or produce in the near future.

When there is a shortage of goods and services such as the one illustrated in Figure 7-7, the initial impact is felt on inventory levels. As consumers, businesses, and governments purchase amounts greater than the aggregate supply, sellers will find their inventory stockpiles falling. This is how we know that there is excess aggregate demand in the economy—if the total level of inventories is falling, this suggests that buyers are making more purchases than sellers expected and were ready to supply.

As inventory levels fall, sellers will increase their orders in order to replenish the shelves. The new orders translate into new production. If, however, the economy faces the kinds of bottlenecks which characterize the

Inventories: stocks of goods which firms keep on hand in anticipation of future sale or use in production

AS curve shown in Figure 7-7, this increased production will come with increased costs. Higher prices will have to be paid for the additional goods. Since a shortage prevails, these higher prices will be paid, and the increasing quantity of aggregate supply will be produced.

In response to the shortage, then, inventories fall, new orders rise, and production and the price level rise as well. Eventually the rising production (induced by the higher prices) and the falling quantity of aggregate demand (which the higher prices cause) will result in a movement to the equilibrium levels of RGNP and the price level. Inflation here is necessary for the restoration of equilibrium.

If the price level is too high, the opposite types of forces will affect the economy. At a price level of 110 in Figure 7-7, for example, there is a surplus of goods and services. Firms are willing to produce lots of goods at this high price level, but consumers, businesses, and governments are less able or willing to purchase these goods because of real income and real balances effects. As a result, there is an aggregate surplus of goods in the economy.

Again, we can tell that this is the case by looking at the inventory accumulations around the economy. Because the price level is too high, goods will not sell as fast as planned, and the economy will experience unintended inventory accumulations. With more and more goods stacking up on the shelves, sellers will reduce orders for the future and so less will be produced. The lower production should, in theory, lead to lower prices (as firms cut prices trying to regain customers) and the economy returns to the equilibrium levels of RGNP and the price level.

This theoretical deflation may not actually occur in the real world. In reality, many parts of the economy are plagued by sticky prices, as shown in Figure 7-8. While prices and the price level may rise in response to national shortages, it may be more difficult for the price level to fall in response to surpluses. Deflation, you will recall, has not been seen in the United States since the 1950s, despite several periods of very high unemployment.

Why are prices unable to fall? Inflexible wages are probably part of the answer, as are a variety of other prices which are fixed in the short run by contracts or marketing practices. Some prices, of course, do actually fall in times of surplus goods, and many firms will issue rebates or circulate discount coupons that in effect cut price (although these kinds of price cuts don't show up in the inflation index). But many firms are more or less locked into prices and respond, instead, by lowering production levels instead of cutting price. There are perhaps enough industries that adjust with quantity instead of price these days to generate the phenomenon shown in Figure 7-8. Here the price level is above that of the macroeconomic equilibrium. But because prices are sticky, the price level does not fall (although some

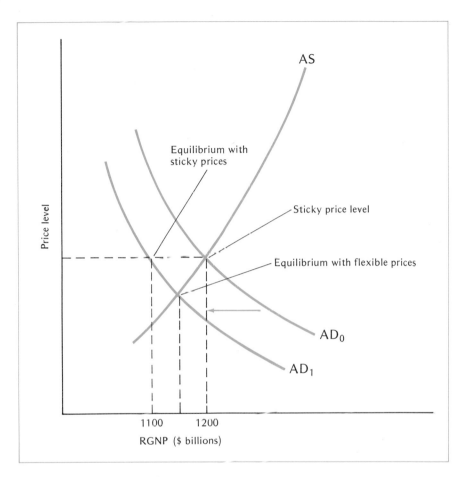

FIGURE 7-8: STICKY PRICES AND AS
When prices are not flexible downward, this affects the determination of equilibrium. Here aggregate demand is falling and equilibrium prices and output should fall as well. But since prices will not drop due to institutional factors, production stays the same temporarily while the quantity of demand drops. The initial $100 billion surplus remains until production drops to the level of aggregate demand. Since prices cannot fall, output falls instead.

individual prices may fall and others rise). Instead, the quantity of aggregate supply simply falls to meet the aggregate demand at the prevailing—above-equilibrium—price level. Output falls to $1100 billion RGNP—$100 billion below the equilibrium.

Over the long run in this situation prices may fall, or demand may rise and restore equilibrium at the prevailing general level of prices. But in the short run, the price level is likely to get stuck and, as we saw in Chapter 3 when we looked at minimum wages, the inflexible prices generate a larger fall in RGNP and employment than would be the case without the sticky-price level. As inventories build up, firms merely cut production and wait for the stockpiles to be bought. Because the prices they pay or receive may be tied by formal or implicit contracts, the price level cannot adjust, in the short term, to the surplus situation.

INVENTORY ADJUSTMENTS

Unintended inventory accumulations: increases in inventories which occur when demand falls behind production

Unintended inventory reductions: decreases in inventory levels which occur when demand rises above supply

Leading indicators: economic statistics which foretell future changes in the economy

Throughout these adjustment processes, it has been the level of inventories which has been the key to understanding what is going on. When there are aggregate surpluses in the economy, this first shows up in terms of **unintended inventory accumulations**. The high inventory levels suggest that, in the future, production will decline causing RGNP to fall and unemployment to climb.

When aggregate shortages prevail, on the other hand, inventories will fall as firms encounter **unintended inventory reductions**. They will respond to the falling level of inventories by ordering more to restock their shelves, causing production and RGNP to rise and the unemployment rate to fall.

The level of inventories, then, may usefully be considered a **leading indicator** of economic activity. Falling inventories suggests that the economy will pick up steam in the future. Rising inventories, though, foretell rising unemployment rates.

Inventory levels are the second example of a leading indicator that we have encountered. The first was the wholesale price index (WPI) discussed in Chapter 4. Changes in the WPI, you will recall, foretell changes in the level of consumer prices. This happens because changes in wholesale prices (the prices of inventory goods) take place as this inventory adjustment process is going on. Both of these leading indicators basically look at what is happening to the seller one step before goods reach the consumer. Since these two economic statistics give us a look into the future, it is important to keep an eye on the WPI and inventory levels in order to determine what is happening now around the economy and what will likely prevail in the future.

CAUSES OF UNEMPLOYMENT

Now that we have the basic AD-AS model in working condition, we can begin to analyze some of the causes and cures for our economic problems. Let us start with a look at some of the macroeconomic causes of high unemployment rates.

High unemployment rates can result in two ways. The first, which we touched upon in Chapter 3, is falling aggregate demand. This case is shown in Figure 7-9. Aggregate demand will decline whenever one of the basic spending components (consumption, investment, government, or net export spending) falls. Let us assume, for example, that a tax increase has lowered consumer spending. This would cause a shift to the left in the AD curve shown in Figure 7-9. As consumer spending falls, inventories begin to accumulate around the economy. Businesses are not selling as much as they had anticipated, and the excess goods pile up. In response to the higher-than-anticipated inventory levels, sellers will reduce new orders

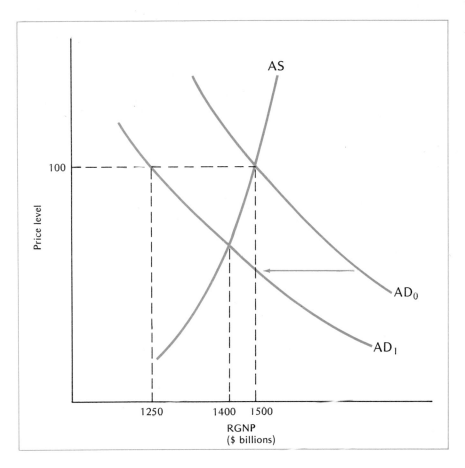

FIGURE 7-9: UNEMPLOYMENT AND STICKY PRICES
Falling aggregate demand creates unemployment. But the amount of unemployment created depends upon the flexibility of prices. In this example, if prices are flexible, production will fall from $1500 billion to $1400 billion. Since prices will not fall, however, production instead falls to $1250, with the resulting much higher number of unemployed.

which will eventually translate into a smaller amount of output and lower employment. The drop in RGNP tells us that less is being produced and fewer workers are employed.

It is important to note here that, in many ways, the severity of the unemployment caused by this fall in aggregate demand will depend upon how readily prices are able to fall. If prices are free to fall, for example, RGNP would only fall from $1500 billion to $1400 billion, with relatively little unemployment. If the price level cannot fall, however, Figure 7-9 shows RGNP falling all the way to $1250 billion. This large fall in total output would result from firms cutting production rather than paying lower wages or selling for lower prices. Inflexible prices, it is clear, can be a major macroeconomic cause of unemployment over and above that which would otherwise prevail on a national level.

Falling demand is an obvious cause of unemployment, but jobs can be lost through less direct means. Suppose, for example, that a heavy tax on

AGGREGATE SUPPLY AND THE ECONOMY

FIGURE 7-10: COST-PUSH INFLATION AS A CAUSE OF UNEMPLOYMENT
Rising costs can cause a reduction in aggregate supply. As rising costs become rising prices, the quantity of aggregate demand falls, creating unemployment.

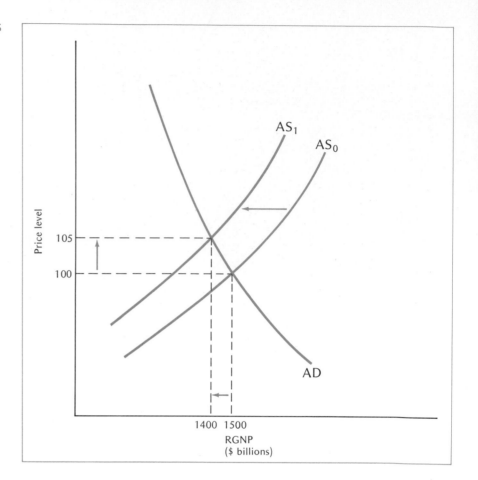

energy were imposed by Congress in an attempt to induce energy conservation in the United States and end our dependence on foreign energy suppliers. This could have the impact shown in Figure 7-10.

As higher energy prices are felt around the economy, they first affect the business sector. Firms which use energy will find that their costs of production are suddenly higher. This will affect aggregate supply. Some firms will attempt to pass the higher costs on to their customers. At the higher prices, however, less will be purchased. These firms, then, will find that they cannot sell as much as before and will cut production.

Other firms which are unable to raise prices because of competitive market conditions will find that the higher energy costs cut their profits. The lower profits will discourage production, again causing the amount produced to fall.

Either way, the result is a fall in aggregate supply as shown in Figure 7-10. As AS falls, the resultant shortage of goods bids up the price level causing

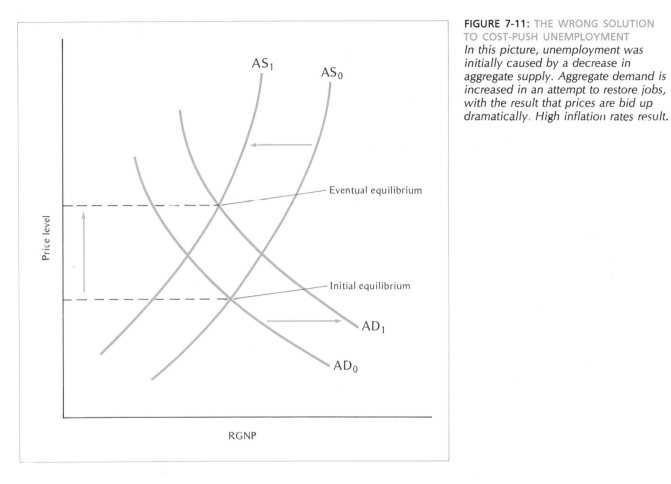

FIGURE 7-11: THE WRONG SOLUTION TO COST-PUSH UNEMPLOYMENT
In this picture, unemployment was initially caused by a decrease in aggregate supply. Aggregate demand is increased in an attempt to restore jobs, with the result that prices are bid up dramatically. High inflation rates result.

inflation. Because less is purchased at the higher price level, RGNP falls, and the unemployment rate soars.

Unemployment can be caused, as we have seen, by falling aggregate demand or declining aggregate supply. The first problem is the easier to solve. If unemployment is caused by lack of demand, then the government sector can step in by lowering taxes, increasing spending, or transfer payments to bridge the gap. Unemployment caused by rising costs of production is not so easy to deal with, however. Investment spending can be increased fairly quickly, but increasing aggregate supply this way can take some time. Government programs which are intended to increase productivity or stimulate investment spending are not likely to have their impact overnight. This kind of unemployment problem is deadly. The unemployment could, of course, be solved by merely taking actions to increase aggregate demand as aggregate supply falls (illustrated in Figure 7-11), but the result is very high inflation rates as the price level climbs.

CAUSES OF INFLATION

Inflation can likewise be caused by two very different types of events, with different impacts upon the economy. Cost-push inflation occurs when something dramatically reduces aggregate supply, like an oil embargo or a major strike in a basic industry. The impact on the economy was shown in Figure 7-10. As supply falls, the price level is bid up, creating substantial inflation. Notice that *both* inflation and unemployment are created when aggregate supply falls.

Inflation can also be caused by rising aggregate demand as pictured in Figure 7-12. This demand-pull inflation results in higher prices, but differs from cost-push inflation in that RGNP *rises* and unemployment rates *fall*. As more spending enters the economy, inventories are temporarily depleted and production rises, causing employment to rise, too. As RGNP rises, the price level is bid up. Inflation is created, but the inflation at least brings with it higher production and employment.

All inflation may be bad, but cost-push is clearly the worse of the two evils because it creates both inflation and unemployment. Demand-pull

FIGURE 7-12: DEMAND-PULL INFLATION
An increase in aggregate demand in the "bottleneck" economy causes both inflation and an increase in RGNP.

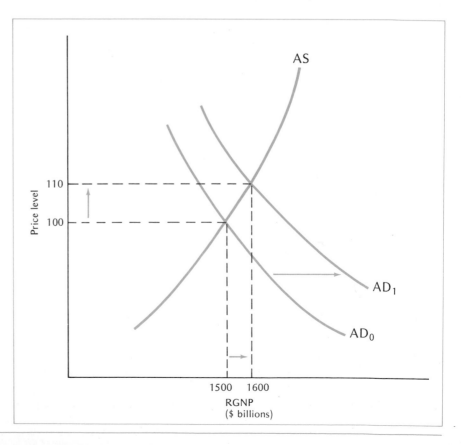

may be the lesser of the two evils because higher prices bring higher incomes in this type of inflation.

Which type of inflation have we experienced in the past? A look back to the historical survey in Chapter 1 will help us understand the past so that we can deal with the future. Demand-pull inflation combines higher prices with lower unemployment. This is the type of inflation that prevailed during much of the 1950s (except, notably, 1957–1958) and almost all of the 1960s. Demand-pull inflation generates the Phillips Curve–type phenomenon illustrated in Figure 1-4. In these periods, it seems, demand-side changes accounted for much of the changes in prices and RGNP.

Cost-push inflation was the problem in the 1970s. Looking back to Figure 1-5, it can be seen that both inflation and unemployment increased during the early 1970s. This is brought on by cost-push inflationary pressures. Although a Phillips Curve–type relationship can still hold when aggregate demand changes, increasing costs (brought on by rising agricultural prices, the oil embargo, and other factors) caused reductions in aggregate supply. This caused the Phillips Curve to "shift" out as the cost-push inflation took place.

Reducing inflation rates is not an easy task. One way to keep the price level from rising would be to reduce aggregate demand. Prices might not fall, but they would at least rise at a slower rate. This option, however, is likely to produce large numbers of unemployed people. Increasing aggregate supply, the other principal solution, is a long-term proposition. Since increasing aggregate supply takes time, it may not appeal to politicians and policy makers who require solutions in the short term.

How can we achieve our economic goals of stable prices and low unemployment rates? The traditional way of dealing with these economic problems (the "old-time religion") has been to fight only one problem at a time while working very hard to cushion the economy from the detrimental side effects of the actions that are taken.

Inflation fighting, for example, has been accomplished by "biting the bullet" (to use a term that President Gerald Ford made popular) and reducing aggregate demand. When aggregate demand falls, as we saw in Figure 7-9, increases in the price level are reduced or halted, but with a large increase in the unemployment rate. Traditional policies have held that this action may be appropriate when inflation rates are high so long as welfare and unemployment programs are sufficient to prevent large-scale suffering. The unemployed bear the burden of reducing the inflation rate for the entire economy.

THE OLD-TIME RELIGION

Such actions designed to simply give up an economic goal are not always appropriate, however. In particular, if cost-push inflation is at the root of the inflation problem, then "biting the bullet" and reducing AD is likely to result in *very* high unemployment rates as both aggregate supply and aggregate demand fall. Stable prices are possible, but the cost is too high. In this case, traditional policies suggest giving up a different goal. Fight unemployment, the prescription reads, and use wage price controls to lessen the inflationary impact.

WAGE AND PRICE CONTROLS

Wage and price controls: government programs which attempt to fight inflation by regulating price and wage increases

One theory of economic policy suggests that the dual goals of high employment and stable prices should be achieved by taking government actions designed to increase aggregate demand while holding down prices by using **wage and price controls**. Wage and price controls act much like the price ceilings that are found in some individual markets. Essentially, the government sets maximum prices which can be charged in most markets, with price increases or wage raises being subject to government review.

Wage and price controls have several problems. The first is that they tend to produce physical shortages of goods. This is illustrated in Figure 7-13. As aggregate demand rises (due to, say, a tax cut designed to reduce unemployment), the amount of goods and services that consumers, businesses, and governments wish to purchase rises. Unfortunately, there is no incentive for businesses to increase their production of goods and services because their prices are held constant by law. A shortage of goods results.

How can this shortage be dealt with? Rising prices could handle the problem, as we saw in Chapter 2 when talking about a shortage of natural gas. But the idea here is to keep prices down. As a result, rationing is necessary in many important markets. Rationing is inefficient. Try to imagine a rationing program which would distribute a scarce resource equitably and efficiently. It probably cannot be done.

Wage and price controls can be defended on two grounds. The first is that, while the shortages that they would cause may be unfair, they may still be preferable to the damage that inflation would cause. Wage and price controls may be effective if they can lower expectations of inflation. If, for example, cost-push inflation was brought on by worker wage demands in anticipation of high inflation rates, then price controls might help the problem if they were to make workers believe that prices would not rise so fast in the future.

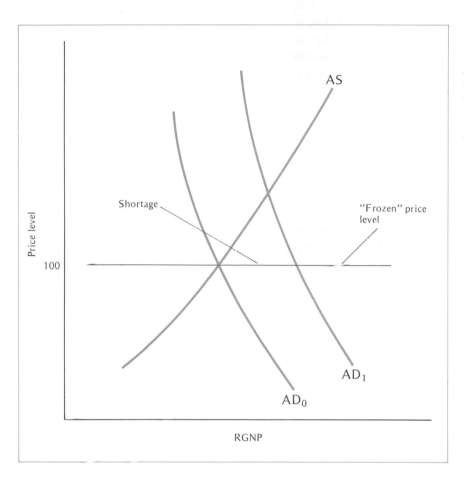

FIGURE 7-13: THE IMPACT OF WAGE AND PRICE CONTROLS
Here wages and prices are frozen at a price level of 100. Because prices cannot increase, an increase in aggregate demand cannot be met. Firms cannot increase output with higher prices. The result is a physical shortage of goods and services (or reductions in quality and service which impose effective price increases).

If wage and price controls create as many problems as they solve, then another solution might be, again, to concentrate on the fight against unemployment and handle the inflation problem through a program of indexation. Rather than trying to hold down prices, the goal would be to keep all wages and values rising at the same rate as prices so that no one would be hurt by the impacts of inflation. The problem here, however, is that inflation harms so many people in so many different ways that is is virtually impossible to fully insulate the economy from its impacts.

There is also the problem of the nature of the inflation which is created. Suppose, for example, that the unemployment is caused by cost-push inflation as pictured in Figure 7-10. Fighting this unemployment by increasing aggregate demand would give us the very high inflation rates shown in Figure 7-11. This inflation could bring on another round of cost-push and create a cycle of higher prices and wages. Even a very good

INDEXATION

indexation scheme may not be able to handle such rapidly rising prices. As a result, other solutions such as wage and price controls may be called in later anyway.

INCREASING AGGREGATE SUPPLY

Ultimately, the achievement of the goals of high employment and stable prices will depend upon growth in aggregate supply. Over the long haul, aggregate demand should continue to grow as our economy grows. Economic growth with low inflation is a real possibility, however, only if the aggregate supply is able to keep pace with rising aggregate demand. This requires continued high levels of investment spending (to keep the economic capacity growing), innovations in technology, and a minimum of government rules and regulations which impose higher costs of production.

A balanced growth of aggregate demand and supply, as shown in Figure 7-14, promises economic growth with stable prices over the long run. In the short run, however, many problems still exist. Elected policy makers often

FIGURE 7-14: BALANCED GROWTH OF AD AND AS
When both aggregate demand and aggregate supply increase at the same time and by the same rate, increases in output are possible without inflation.

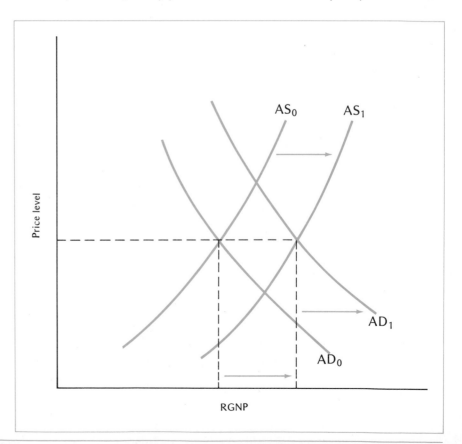

face the problem of long-run solutions to economic problems, but the necessity of solving these problems in the short run for political reasons.

Growth in aggregate supply remains a sound policy for long-run economic growth. Since the long run may be very far away and we are impatient, we must search for appropriate short-run policies to achieve our goals as well.

Economic policies can be popular or detested, depending upon the state of the economy and the distribution of gains and losses from the policies pursued. To see this, let us analyze three instances in history where government spending was increased, with different results in each case due to the different states of the economy.

President Franklin Roosevelt increased government spending in 1932 in response to the Great Depression and his actions were roundly applauded at the ballot box. Why was this the case? Figure 7-15 gives us a hint. Because a "depression" economy prevailed in 1932—when many skilled resources were idled—an increase in aggregate demand could be met with higher production without inflation. Here, economic growth, which put part of the population back to work, did not require a sacrifice by those already working in terms of higher prices at the grocery store. As a result, this was a policy where some won but nobody had to lose. Economic growth without inflation was and is a popular policy.

WINNERS AND LOSERS FROM ECONOMIC POLICIES

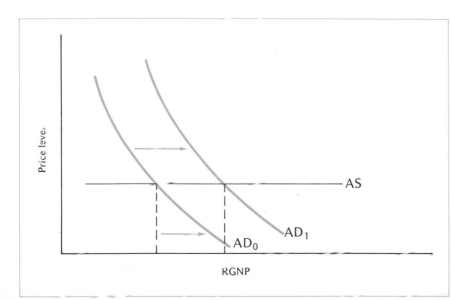

FIGURE 7-15: INCREASING DEMAND, 1932
During the Depression, increasing aggregate demand was a popular government policy. Since no inflation was caused, the unemployed won but no one had to lose.

FIGURE 7-16: INCREASING DEMAND, 1967
Here the economy is fully employed. The government policy to increase aggregate demand made no one better off and imposed inflation.

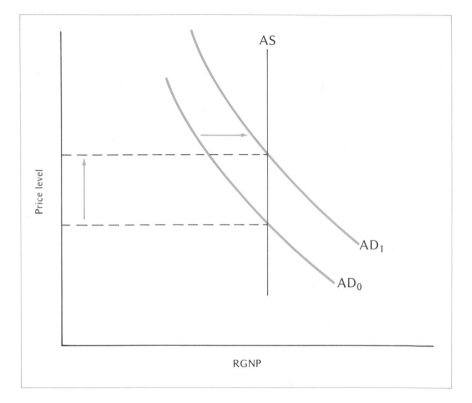

In the late 1960s, President Lyndon Johnson tried the same idea, but with markedly different results (see Figure 7-16). Whereas Roosevelt faced a depression economy when he increased government spending, Johnson's economy was already operating at or near full employment. In this situation an increase in output was virtually impossible. Increased government spending resulted largely in increased prices. As the government caused production to rise in some areas, it necessitated cutbacks elsewhere because of the finite nature of the resources being used.

The difference is clear. Johnson imposed additional burdens on the economy that Roosevelt did not. When Johnson increased government spending, all parts of the economy paid higher prices as a result. This is not a policy which will produce high popularity. In addition, some people had to give up resources in order to allow others to expand their economic activities. This creation of winners and losers is also likely to produce political dissension.

Finally, we can look at the policies which made President John Kennedy relatively popular, and made the early Johnson years successful as well. When the economy is in a "bottleneck" state, as shown in Figure 7-17, an

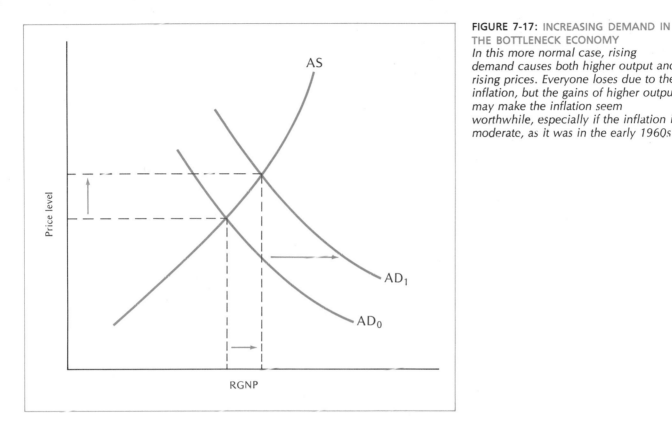

FIGURE 7-17: INCREASING DEMAND IN THE BOTTLENECK ECONOMY
In this more normal case, rising demand causes both higher output and rising prices. Everyone loses due to the inflation, but the gains of higher output may make the inflation seem worthwhile, especially if the inflation is moderate, as it was in the early 1960s.

increase in aggregate demand results in rising RGNP and moderately rising prices. People are gaining because their incomes are rising, making them happy with the economic situation. The cost of this prosperity—higher prices—is spread out among a large number of people. A few—the unemployed—gain substantially, while a larger number are hurt only a little by the higher prices. All is not perfect here, but this policy can be popular, so long as the inflation does not get out of hand.

The effectiveness of government spending, then, depends largely upon the type of economy which prevails when the spending is undertaken. We will learn more about the problems of fiscal policy in the next chapter.

SUMMARY

1. Aggregate supply (AS) is the amount of total production available in the economy. Aggregate supply depends on a number of factors, including the price level, the productive capacity of the economy, technology, the size and skills of the labor force, and the productivity of the labor force. The aggre-

gate supply curve shows how total output varies with the price level, all else being equal.

2. There are three possible relationships between the price level and the quantity of total output depending upon the state of the economy. In a "depression" economy, increases in production do not require higher prices because of the large number of unemployed highly productive resources. In a "full-employment" economy, higher total production is impossible because virtually all resources are fully used. Attempts to increase production result in higher prices. In a more common "bottleneck" economy, higher production is possible, but only at higher price levels.

3. Unemployment can be caused by either falling aggregate demand (which can be cured by increasing total spending flows) or declining aggregate supply (which is best fought by increasing investment spending or taking actions to increase productivity). If a particular type of unemployment is fought with the wrong tools (for example, fighting supply-caused unemployment with higher aggregate demand), the impact on the economy can be severe—very high inflation rates can result.

4. Inflation can also be caused in two ways. Demand-pull inflation brings higher prices but also increases total production. Cost-push inflation brings inflation and high unemployment rates.

5. Many schemes have been suggested to fight both inflation and unemployment. Wage and price controls may control inflation, but they tend to cause physical shortages of goods and services. Indexation is an idea whose time may have come, but it cannot hope to fully inflation-proof all parts of the economy. Increasing aggregate supply by encouraging investment spending is a long-term solution to both of our national economic problems, but takes time to work.

DISCUSSION QUESTIONS

1. What would a downward-sloping aggregate supply curve mean? Is this type of economy likely?

2. What impact would an increase in investment spending have on the economy in the short run? In the long run? Are the two answers different?

3. Suppose that oil were to become very much more expensive, but that the amount which was spent on imported oil increased because oil is such a necessity. What would be the impact of this on aggregate demand? On aggregate supply? On the economy? Does this help explain the economic problems resulting from the

1973–1974 oil embargo and the subsequent increase in oil prices?

4. To see some of the problems caused by wage and price controls, suppose that tuition at your school were to be frozen by Congress. In response to this, your school determines that it has to cut enrollment by 10 percent. Devise an equitable way to determine who stays and who must go (i.e., who is rationed the educational service and who is allocated out of the market?).

5. In discussing inflation, we noted that inflationary expectations induce workers, consumers, businesses, and everyone else to behave as if inflation were going to occur in the future and so act to protect themselves from it by gaining wage increases and so on. How do these activities affect aggregate demand and supply (and the economy)? Would wage and price controls necessarily alter this pattern? Why or why not?

6. We discussed the Phillips Curve in Chapter 1. The Phillips Curve shows a trade-off between inflation and unemployment. Use AD-AS curve analysis to determine what kinds of situations are described by the Phillips Curve. When does the Phillips Curve *not* work?

7. Use AD-AS analysis to determine the types of changes that must have been going on in the economy during the 1950s, 1960s, and 1970s (review the historical data in Chapter 1 for information concerning these periods).

8. The wholesale price index and the level of inventory accumulations are leading indicators of what is happening to the economy. Using these two statistics, we can determine what is going on with respect to aggregate demand and aggregate supply and guess what the future holds for the economy. Find out what has been happening to the WPI and inventories recently. What can you conclude about the path that the economy is taking?

TEST YOURSELF

Indicate whether each of the following statements is *true* or *false*. Be able to defend your choice.

1. Aggregate supply shows the amount of goods and services that people would like to have.

2. Any level of investment spending will cause aggregate supply to increase.

3. An increase in aggregate demand will not necessarily cause increasing prices.

4. Rising aggregate demand causes rising RGNP.

5. It is impossible to fight both inflation and unemployment at the same time by manipulating

aggregate demand.

6. The best way to fight unemployment caused by insufficient aggregate demand is through reductions in aggregate supply.

7. Wage and price controls create shortages which may be worse than the inflation that the controls reduce.

8. Sticky prices are a cause of unemployment.

9. Increases in investment spending tend to cause rising aggregate demand in the short run and rising aggregate supply in the long run.

10. Indexation would tend to increase aggregate supply.

ECONOMIC CONTROVERSIES III: WAGE AND PRICE CONTROLS

The solution to the inflation problem may ultimately lie in the long-run growth of aggregate supply. But as Keynes said, in the long run we are all dead; much damage is caused in the short run. Calls for wage and price controls are often heard when inflation rates start to climb in the short run, regardless of long-run policies. The idea behind wage and price controls is to use the police power of the state to artificially hold down prices during inflation emergencies.

Wage and price controls have been with us for a long time. The Roman emperor Diocletian resorted to perhaps the most brutal form of price controls: he cut off the hands of those who boosted prices. Government controls in recent years have been less drastic, but they have been used with relative frequency, particularly during war years.

The wage and price controls that were instituted during President Richard Nixon's term of office are useful in gaining an understanding of how these controls work. Wages and prices were frozen by presidential edict on August 15, 1971.

During the ninety-day freeze, a wage board and a price review panel were set up to hear requests for increases in these areas. Rules were circulated concerning who would need government permission to change prices and by how much prices and wages could rise. Slowly, over the period, the control noose was loosened and the economy returned to relatively free markets.

The debate over wage and price controls has raged for many years. Here are samples of the pro and con arguments that have been used.

CONTROLS ARE USEFUL

Many arguments can be brought forth in favor of wage and price controls. Recent attempts at antiinflationary policies have been relatively ineffective. Fighting inflation may require the kinds of long-term commitment that we are not willing to make if we must suffer from inflation in the short run. We therefore must have a way of absolutely controlling inflation, and this way is wage and price controls. Administered effectively, wage and price controls can have minimal effect on the economy while holding down the general level of prices.

Wage and price controls will not only hold down prices in the short run, they can also be effective in stopping long-run inflation by lowering inflationary expectations. These days, people have in-born expectations concerning inflation. These expectations are at the root of our current problems. When people expect prices to rise in the future, they act in ways guaranteed to cause those rising prices. We will never be able to stop inflation until we can bring these expectations under control. It is unlikely that they will go away by themselves, but they may disappear if wage and price controls are instituted. By holding down prices in the short run, controls can get people used to stable prices. Then, when the controls are eventually lifted, expectations will not be there to automatically cause more inflation. By reducing inflationary expectations, wage and price controls can significantly improve our ability to fight inflation.

While it is true that wage and price controls, like any other set of government rules and regulations, are likely to create winners and losers within the economy, it is important to remember that inflation causes gains and losses, too. With controls it will be possible to rationally pick the winners and losers and to see that no one gains or loses too much. Inflation, on the other hand, strikes with no feeling and hits some groups particularly hard.

Controls may produce shortages, it is true, but these problems can be dealt with effectively and equitably. Whatever problems that the controls cause are likely to be less damaging than the inflation that they will replace.

The final and most important argument for wage and price controls is that it is unemployment, not inflation, which is our most important economic problem. While we should be concentrating on fighting unemployment, we are diverted from this battle by the problem of inflation. Attempts to hold down prices through government policies can actually end up worsening the unemployment problem. We need to have wage and price controls so that we can finally quit worrying about prices and get down to the job of solving the problems of the jobless and the poor in our economy.

PRICE CONTROLS ARE BAD

The arguments in favor of price and wage controls may sound good, but one need only look at the record to understand why controls will fail to accomplish their objectives. Wage and price controls tend to disrupt the economy. Businesses cannot undertake normal production activities because they first must seek approval of their actions. This slows down the economy and may actually cause unemployment. Investors are unwilling to commit resources to the future due to the uncertainty that the government controls create. This lack of investment can cause a decrease in aggregate supply and so increase the chance for long-run inflation. How can a program which may cause both inflation and unemployment be beneficial?

In a system of wage and price controls it is government decision makers who basically allocate resources within the economy by controlling prices. How can any board have as much knowledge and respond as efficiently as freely operating markets? Periods of wage and price controls have generally given us shortages, queues, and black markets.

Controls don't succeed in lowering the expectations of inflation, either. Because controls are only imposed in emergencies and for short periods of time, people do not believe that stable prices will prevail. The controls are short-lived because they are so basically unacceptable to the economy. Expectations are not really changed by these programs, they are merely delayed and compounded. Workers, businesses, and others bide their time, waiting for the controls to be lifted so that they can boost wages and prices when the controls are re-moved. Inflation is postponed, not reduced.

In fact, just the threat of wage and price controls can be enough to actually cause more inflation! In 1978 there was much talk about the possibility of controls in the future. In response to these rumors, many industries were observed to make quick price increases so that the high prices would be on the books in case prices were eventually frozen. Their actions formed the basis for cost-push inflation. Is this what the controls were intended to do?

The final con argument is that wage and price controls have been basically ineffective in the past. Even Diocletian's "off with their hands" edict failed to hold down prices. Prices actually rose during Nixon's control period by about 4 percent per year. And prices jumped higher when the controls were lifted.

Given the fact that the controls don't work, it is unreasonable to subject ourselves to all of the detrimental impacts that they cause.

DISCUSSION QUESTIONS

1. Do you favor or oppose wage and price controls? Can you find faults with the arguments on either side of this argument?

2. Suppose that you have been appointed Wage and Price Czar. You must decide which wages and prices will be allowed to rise. How would you choose? Try to develop objective criteria for your actions.

3. Evaluate the argument that controls would reduce inflationary expectations.

8
Fiscal Policy

This chapter adds the government sector into the aggregate demand–aggregate supply model of the economy and examines the tools of fiscal policy. This chapter will answer many questions concerning government activities, including the following:

What is fiscal policy?

How do government spending, taxation, and transfer payments policies affect the national economy?

How effective are fiscal policies in solving our national economic problems?

Are all taxes the same in their impact on the economy?

Who pays the major taxes in our economy?

What is deficit spending?

How big of a problem is the national debt?

Fiscal policy: economic policies involving government spending, taxing, and transfer payment activities

This chapter is about **fiscal policy**. What is fiscal policy? The term derives from a Latin word which means basket or purse. The *fisc* is the government's purse—its treasury. The idea of fiscal policy, then, is all tied up in the government's pursestrings. It has to do with government spending policies, taxation, and debt. In this chapter we will look at the macroeconomic role of the government in the United States. We will explore the consequences of government spending and taxation policies on the national economy and try to learn more about how those policies work.

THE ROLE OF GOVERNMENT

Governments perform many functions in the United States. It is important to use the plural form governments because, despite our preoccupation with the government in Washington, D.C., our federal system is made up of many partners. There are, in fact, over 38,000 separate units of state, county, and local government in the United States. While the federal government may be the largest single unit of government, the combined state and local governments are in some ways more important. State and local governments now spend more money than the federal government and collect almost as much in taxes.

This discussion of fiscal policy will focus on the actions of the federal government, however, because it has the responsibility for conducting macroeconomic policies in the United States. Individual state and local governments, while important for the services that they provide, do not have much impact on inflation and unemployment rates because they are small relative to the whole (although changes in their combined policies certainly will affect the economy).

Government has many roles in a modern economy. Governmental actions run the gamut from national defense to welfare to education to garbage collection. In general, however, we can divide all government activities into three areas. The **allocation function** of government includes all government activities which supply us with goods and services. Economic theory suggests that the private market will not supply sufficient quantities of **public goods** (like national defense) or of other items (like parklands, educational services, or electrical power) where private and public costs and benefits differ. The government steps in, then, to assure a sufficient production of these important public services. State and local governments are particularly important in the allocation function since many of their activities are designed to supply needed goods and services (police, fire, and education services, for example).

Allocation function: government activities designed to provide the appropriate amounts and mix of private and public goods

Public goods: goods which, once produced, yield benefits which are (or can be) shared by all

Distribution function: government activities designed to produce an acceptable distribution of income

The government also has a **distribution function**—to see that an acceptable distribution of income and wealth prevails. Many tax policies and such programs as unemployment insurance, Social Security, and welfare payments fall into the distribution function of government.

Finally, the **stabilization function** of government dictates that the government take actions to stabilize the economy and to meet our national economic goals of full employment, stable prices, and economic growth.

Stabilization function: government activities designed to promote full employment, stable prices, and economic growth

This chapter concentrates on the stabilization role of government, but it is important to realize that government must constantly work to further all three functions, and actions taken in one area must necessarily have impacts on the others. A policy like minimum wages, for example, might help in some way to improve the distribution of income. But it also, as we have seen, serves to increase the unemployment problem. The decision to supply more or less governmental services will affect stabilization policy and the distribution of income, too.

Finally, government actions designed to fight inflation or unemployment will alter the distribution of income and probably affect the allocations of both public and private goods and services, too. Government's job is very difficult, and the existence of so many levels and types of governments makes the task even more complicated.

To perform these functions, the government sector has many tools. Government spending for goods and services is an obvious one, since government spending directly affects the aggregate demand and can be targeted to provide services and affect income distribution. Taxation can also be used to achieve goals in all three areas of government. Transfer payments are useful here, too, and manipulation of governmental debt is important to the entire process.

We have already learned something about the impact of government spending on the economy. We know, for example, that if government spending is increased, this will tend to increase aggregate demand (since increased government spending causes increased total spending) and the increase in AD will cause RGNP to grow, or prices to rise, or both depending upon the condition of aggregate supply. There are, however, two additional facts about government spending that are important to understand:

1. If government spending increases by, say, $10 billion, aggregate demand will increase by *far more* than $10 billion;

2. We can *predict* what the total increase in AD will be for any given increase in government spending.

GOVERNMENT SPENDING

When the government injects spending into the economy, that money does not just pay for airplanes or tanks or Xerox machines and then disappear. The increase in government spending (or investment or consumption spending, for that matter) will cascade through the economy and "multiply" into a large increase in aggregate demand before it is through.

How does this happen? The easiest way to explain the process is with an example like the one presented in Table 8-1. When the government purchases $100,000 worth of red tape (yes, they really do use it!), this increase in spending creates income for a large group of people throughout the economy. Workers in tape factories, truck drivers, suppliers of raw materials to the tape makers, the owners of tape factories, and a variety of other people gain income because the government has decided to increase

TABLE 8-1

THE MULTIPLIER GAME: GOVERNMENT SPENDING
(MPC = 60%)

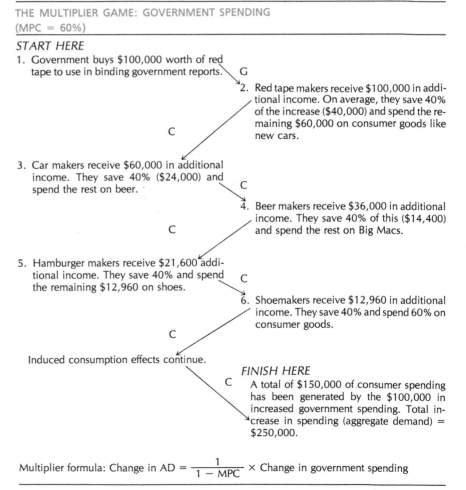

START HERE

1. Government buys $100,000 worth of red tape to use in binding government reports. **G**

2. Red tape makers receive $100,000 in additional income. On average, they save 40% of the increase ($40,000) and spend the remaining $60,000 on consumer goods like new cars.

3. Car makers receive $60,000 in additional income. They save 40% ($24,000) and spend the rest on beer.

4. Beer makers receive $36,000 in additional income. They save 40% of this ($14,400) and spend the rest on Big Macs.

5. Hamburger makers receive $21,600 additional income. They save 40% and spend the remaining $12,960 on shoes.

6. Shoemakers receive $12,960 in additional income. They save 40% and spend 60% on consumer goods.

Induced consumption effects continue.

FINISH HERE
A total of $150,000 of consumer spending has been generated by the $100,000 in increased government spending. Total increase in spending (aggregate demand) = $250,000.

Multiplier formula: Change in AD $= \dfrac{1}{1 - MPC} \times$ Change in government spending

purchases of this vital commodity. When the government spends $100,000 for red tape, however, what happens to the money? Does it disappear? Does the chain stop here? No. The people who receive increased income from the red tape purchase normally divide the increase among higher consumption spending and increased saving in constant proportion—the idea of the marginal propensity to consume (MPC) discussed in Chapter 6. If the MPC is 60 percent, then, people on average will spend about 60 percent of any increase in income, while the remaining 40 percent is saved (or paid to the government as involuntary "saving"—taxes). The people who received the total of $100,000 in income generated by the red tape sale will spend about an average of $60,000 on consumer goods, like new cars. These purchases are called **induced consumption expenditures** because they have been caused or made possible by the initial government spending.

Induced consumption expenditures: changes in consumption spending caused by changes in government spending, taxes, and so on; part of the multiplier process

When the $60,000 is spent for things like new cars, this will create $60,000 in income for people in the car business. These folks, like the tape producers, will spend about 60 percent of their increased incomes and save

TABLE 8-2

THE MULTIPLIER PROCESS

Round	Expenditure Type	Amount	Total Increase in Spending
1	Government	$100,000.00	$100,000.00
2	Consumption	60,000.00	160,000.00
3	Consumption	36,000.00	196,000.00
4	Consumption	21,600.00	217,600.00
5	Consumption	12,960.00	230,560.00
6	Consumption	7,776.00	238,336.00
7	Consumption	4,665.60	243,001.60
8	Consumption	2,799.36	245,800.96
9	Consumption	1,679.62	247,480.58
10	Consumption	1,007.77	248,488.35
11	Consumption	604.66	249,093.01
12	Consumption	362.80	249,455.81
13	Consumption	217.68	249,673.49
14	Consumption	130.61	249,804.10
15	Consumption	78.36	249,882.46
16	Consumption	47.02	249,929.48
17	Consumption	28.21	249,957.69
18	Consumption	16.93	249,974.62
19	Consumption	10.15	249,984.77
20	Consumption	6.09	249,990.86
.	.	.	.
.	.	.	.
.	.	.	.
End		0	$250,000.00

the rest. This will generate a total of about $36,000 in further consumption spending.

This spending/income/spending/income/spending cycle will continue, with the amounts getting a little smaller each round because of the leakage from the spending stream into savings and tax accounts. The first twenty steps in this multiplier process are shown in Table 8-2. In the end, a total of $150,000 in increased consumption spending will be generated by the initial $100,000 increase in government spending, causing aggregate demand to increase by a total of $250,000! If this seems unreasonable, the disbelieving reader is invited to check the result with a calculator. It works!

THE MULTIPLIER

Fortunately, we need not attack each change in government spending with a pocket calculator in order to see what the total impact on the economy will be. This type of series is well known to math students, and the total change in spending can be found by applying the following formula:

$$\text{Change in AD} = \frac{1}{1 - \text{MPC}} \times \text{Change in government spending}$$

Spending multiplier: the multiple impact of a change in a spending component on AD

The term $\dfrac{1}{1 - \text{MPC}}$ is called the **spending multiplier**. It allows us to compute the total change in aggregate demand caused by *any* change in total spending. Changes in investment, consumer, or net export spending would have the same multiple impact on aggregate demand and so would be computed using the same formula.

In the example just discussed, the total change in spending is

$$\text{Change in AD} = \frac{1}{1 - 0.6} \times \$100,000$$

$$= \frac{1}{0.4} \times \$100,000$$

$$= 2.5 \times \$100,000$$
$$= \$250,000$$

It is obvious that government spending is a very powerful tool, capable of leaping tall buildings in a single bound and moving the aggregate demand curve faster than a speeding bullet. For the record, the same type of multiplier result holds if government spending is decreased. A $100,000 *cut* in the level of governmental purchases will cause aggregate demand to *fall*

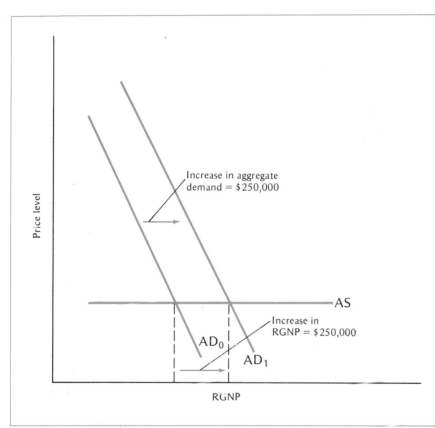

FIGURE 8-1: FISCAL POLICY IN A DEPRESSION
A $100,000 increase in government spending causes a multiplier increase in aggregate demand of $250,000. Because there are large stocks of unemployed resources, this spending becomes production with no increase in prices. All of the increased spending becomes increased RGNP.

by about $250,000 as the cut in government expenditures causes others around the economy to cut back their spending levels as well.

A $100,000 increase in investment spending would also cause an eventual increase in aggregate demand of $250,000—investment spending is just as "powerful" as government spending, although investment spending will generally go to purchase different types of goods and services than government spending. The induced consumption affects are the same in each case.

What affect does the change in government spending have on the economy? As you might guess, it depends upon the state of the economy. If we are faced with a depression economy, as shown in Figure 8-1, a $100,000 increase in government spending will have full impact on the economy and cause real GNP to rise by the full multiplier amount of $250,000. Since prices do not rise, none of the increased spending is used to pay higher prices, so all of it goes to buy new production. The full impact of the multiplier goes to increase production and therefore to decrease unemployment. This makes government spending a very useful tool when the problem facing the nation is high unemployment.

FIGURE 8-2: FISCAL POLICY WITH FULL
EMPLOYMENT
*Since all resources are as fully utilized
as they can be in the short run, the
increased spending cannot induce
greater production. All of the $250,000
spending goes to pay for higher prices.*

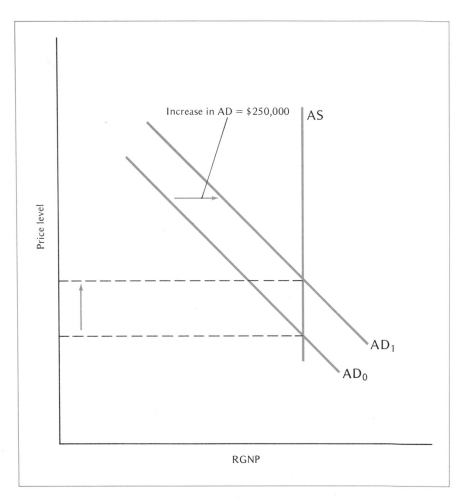

If, however, we are facing a full-employment economy, as illustrated in
Figure 8-2, the impact of government spending is quite different. Here
employment is already high and the economy is running at or near its
capacity—its ability to increase production in response to an increase in
demand is severely limited. As a result, the $250,000 government-induced
increase in aggregate demand is highly inflationary. As the $250,000 is
spent, the increase in demand goes not for new goods (since increasing
production is difficult here) but instead to pay for higher prices on existing
goods. The result is little or no increase in RGNP (a natural consequence of
the "vertical" AS curve) and a *very* large increase in the price level. All of
the $250,000 increase in AD is in fact absorbed in higher prices!
Government spending may be an effective way to fight unemployment in
the "depression" situation, but it is a very good way to *cause* inflation at full
employment.

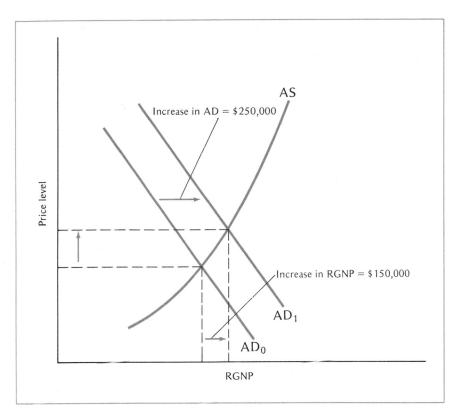

FIGURE 8-3: FISCAL POLICY IN A BOTTLENECK ECONOMY
The $100,000 increase in government spending here causes a $250,000 total increase in aggregate demand. As total spending increases, some of the spending goes for increased production but, because prices are bid up in the process, production does not rise by the full $250,000.

Finally, if the economy is in the "bottleneck" state shown in Figure 8-3, the impact of an increase in government spending will be divided between RGNP and inflation. A $100,000 increase in government spending will cause a $250,000 increase in aggregate demand—the multiplier still works—but here some of the increase in spending will go for higher prices and some of it will go to purchase additional production. The result will be a moderate increase in RGNP—say, $150,000—and a moderate amount of inflation as well.

In the real world the size of the multiplier impact depends on more than just the shape of the aggregate supply curve. A number of other factors will influence what happens here. The first is the time span under consideration. The multiplier formula gives the sum of an infinite series of spending/income steps. How long does it take for this series to take place? This may vary according to the type of expenditure and the plans of the people who receive the income. In the short run, we can't count on the full multiplier impact reaching the economy. A multiplier of 2 or less (compared to the

THE MULTIPLIER IN THE REAL WORLD

theoretical 2.5 with an MPC of 60 percent) may be as much as can be expected.

Tax policies will also influence the final tally. If state and local governments are increasing taxes at the same time that the federal government is increasing spending, then a smaller amount will be respent at each step along the way. State, local, and federal economic policies are not always aimed in the same direction, so the net impact of any one sector's activities may be lessened by what the rest of the governments are doing.

Finally, it is important to note that, since the multiplier impact is different when the MPC is different, not all countries have the same government spending leverage. The greater the MPC, the greater the multiplier impact that the government can have on the aggregate demand. To see this point, suppose that we are comparing three countries facing high unemployment rates caused by insufficient aggregate demand. Assume that the United States has an MPC of 60 percent while the other two countries—Japan and West Germany—have hypothetical marginal propensities to consume of 40 percent and 80 percent respectively.

If all three countries try to stimulate aggregate demand by increasing spending by $5 million, the impacts on aggregate demand will be much different. In the United States, as we have already noted, the spending multiplier will be 2.5, and so a $5 million increase in government spending will cause aggregate demand to rise by a total of $12.5 million. In West Germany the government spending will be even more powerful. With an MPC of 80 percent, the spending multiplier is 5.0, so a total of $25 million will be added to aggregate demand. Unemployment in these two countries should begin to fall.

In Japan, however, the situation would be much different. With an MPC of just 40 percent, a $5 million increase in government spending would cause aggregate demand to rise by only $8.3 million. There is little impact here other than the initial government spending.

Countries with low marginal propensities to consume—like Japan—find that fiscal policy is of little use in influencing aggregate demand. They must resort to the monetary policies described in Part III of this text or the international policies discussed in Part IV.

TAXES

Taxes are the other side of the fiscal coin. We generally think of taxes as being necessary in order to finance government spending, but this is not their only function. Taxation has become more and more a tool of fiscal policy in its own right. Taxes are raised or lowered in response to changes in the level of government spending, but just as often (especially at the national level) they are used as a tool of stabilization policy—lowered to stimulate the economy or raised to decrease aggregate demand independently of other fiscal tools.

The main difference between taxes and government spending, insofar as they affect the economy, is that government spending has a direct impact on aggregate demand, while taxes have only an indirect impact. When the government spends more, this causes a direct increase in total spending. But when taxes are changed, this action has its direct impact on people's **disposable income**. Total spending only changes when people change the amount that they spend. So tax policy attempts to induce consumers to

Disposable income: income actually available for spending (gross income minus direct taxes)

TABLE 8-3

THE MULTIPLIER GAME: TAXES
(MPC = 60%)

START HERE:

1. Government gives $100,000 in tax rebates to consumers (change in taxes) = −$100,000).

2. Consumers receive $100,000 in tax rebate checks. They save (on average) 40% of the total ($40,000) and spend the remaining $60,000 on economics books.

3. Bookmakers receive $60,000 increase in income. They save 40% and spend the remaining $36,000 on furniture.

4. Furniture makers receive $36,000 in increased income. They save 40% of the increase and spend the remaining $21,600 on toilet paper.

5. Paper makers receive $21,600 in additional income. They save 40% and spend the rest on stereo records.

6. Record makers receive $12,960 in additional income. They save 40% and spend the rest on consumer goods.

Induced consumption effects continue.

FINISH HERE

The entire increase in aggregate demand has been in increased consumption spending = $150,000

Multiplier formula: Change in AD = $\dfrac{-\text{MPC}}{1 - \text{MPC}} \times$ Change in taxes

change their spending habits by changing the amount of disposable income at their command.

As was the case with government spending, the impact of a change in taxes on the economy is large. Table 8-3 shows a typical example of a change in the level of taxes—a tax rebate of $100,000.

When the government cuts taxes, this, in and of itself, does nothing to change the level of total spending and therefore nothing to affect aggregate demand. However, assuming an MPC of 60 percent, it can be predicted that, when taxes are cut by $100,000, the beneficiaries of the lower taxes will use their increased disposable incomes to increase spending by about $60,000. This $60,000 in new spending will create new income for people around the economy. They will, on average, save 40 percent of this new income and spend the remaining $36,000. The spending/income/spending/ income process will continue just as before. The total change in spending is $150,000.

Because we are dealing with the same type of mathematical series, there is also a formula which can be used to predict this change in aggregate demand. The formula for the taxation multiplier effect is

$$\text{Change in AD} = \frac{-\text{MPC}}{1 - \text{MPC}} \times \text{Change in taxes}$$

This multiplier is smaller than the government spending multiplier because taxes have a smaller, indirect impact on spending. When taxes are cut by $100,000, this causes total spending to rise initially by only $60,000 because 40 percent of the tax cut is saved by the consumers who receive it. The multiplier contains a minus sign because there is an inverse relationship between changes in taxes and changes in aggregate demand. If taxes are increased (+), aggregate demand falls (−), and a tax cut (−) brings about increased AD (+). As with government spending, tax policies will have different impacts on RGNP and the price level depending on the type of aggregate supply curve that the economy faces.

The multiplier formula gives us a good approximation of the impact of a change in the tax system on aggregate demand, but it makes one implicit assumption that may not always be true. The tax multiplier assumes that people will treat an increase in disposable income caused by a tax cut the same as an increase in disposable income caused by, say, an increase in government spending (i.e., they will spend 60 percent of the tax cut and save 40 percent of it). This need not always be true. Recent studies suggest that people behave differently when they think that tax cuts are temporary (like tax rebates) than when they view them as permanent tax cuts and therefore permanent increases in disposable income. When the tax cuts are thought to be permanent, people seem to behave according to the standard multiplier model. But when the tax cut is thought to be temporary, people seem to treat this transitory increase in their disposable income differently and often save a very high proportion of it. If more is saved, less is spent and the multiplier impact of tax cuts in this case can be very small.

This kind of behavior makes sense. If you thought you were receiving a $10 per month permanent tax cut, you might use this gain in income to, say, purchase a previously unaffordable new car with higher monthly payments. But if you felt that the tax cut would only last a few weeks, you might decide to resist the new car and save the tax windfall until you either had enough to make a larger down payment (and so reduce the monthly expense) or until the tax cut had gone on long enough for you to consider it permanent.

If people behave this way, this suggests two things concerning tax policies. First, one-shot tax cuts (like the tax rebates mailed out under President Ford) probably have only a very small multiplier impact on aggregate demand because a relatively high proportion of the rebate may be saved. Second, tax cuts may be slow in having an impact on aggregate demand because people may wait to see if the tax cuts will be permanent before adjusting their spending plans and increasing aggregate demand.

THE BALANCED-BUDGET MULTIPLIER

One result of the different multipliers for taxation and government spending is that a balanced governmental budget (where taxes equal spending), which is often thought to be "neutral" with respect to its impact on the economy, really does exert a force on aggregate demand. For example, suppose that Congress decides to increase government spending by $15 billion and to finance this increased spending by raising taxes also by $15 billion. What is the net impact on aggregate demand? Assuming an MPC of 60 percent, the increase in government spending will have a multiplier impact on AD of $25 billion. The increase in taxes will tend to make aggregate demand fall by a multiplier total of $15 billion. On net, AD will still rise by $10 billion! This is a surprising result. It suggests that, given a typical bottleneck state of the economy, an increase in government spending will tend to cause some inflation, *even if it is fully funded by higher taxes*!

The same type of analysis works going the other way, too. Many so-called fiscal conservatives have suggested that taxes are too high and that the appropriate action to take is to cut taxes and government spending together, thereby lowering the tax burden and reducing the size of government at the same time. These may be desirable goals, but what impact would such an action have on the national economy? Suppose that both taxes and government spending were cut by $8 billion. The tax cut would cause aggregate demand to grow—by a multiplier total of $12 billion, if the MPC is again 60 percent. But the cut in government spending would cause aggregate demand to fall by about $20 billion. The net result would be a decrease in aggregate demand equal to $8 billion, with the fall in RGNP and increase in unemployment that goes with this.

If the fiscal conservatives want to lessen the size of government in this way, they will need to be willing to live with higher unemployment rates in the future. In order to cut government spending by $8 billion *without* lowering aggregate demand, taxes would need to be cut by more than $8 billion—in fact, they would have to fall by $13.3 billion (work this out for yourself). Sadly, if taxes are cut more than spending is decreased, this forces an increase in government borrowing—and an increase in the national debt—to make up the difference. And this isn't a policy that conservatives are likely to favor.

Balanced-budget multiplier: the multiple impact on AD of equal changes in government spending and taxation; generally equal to 1

The **balanced-budget multiplier** is always 1—equal changes in spending and taxes cause aggregate demand to change by the amount of the initial change in government spending. This is assuming, of course, that the tax changes are treated as "permanent" by taxpayers. If they are not, then the total change can be much larger, since government spending affects outweigh the counteracting impacts of the tax changes.

DIFFERENT TYPES OF TAXES

Up to now, we have been talking about tax increases and cuts as if all taxes were the same. This is not the case, for two reasons. First of all, while tax changes all affect aggregate demand in fairly predictable ways, some of them have side effects which are important. A cut in business taxes, for example, would increase aggregate demand (through the multiplier process just discussed) but could also increase aggregate supply by reducing production costs. It is important not to overlook the impacts that taxes (generally designed to influence aggregate demand) can have indirectly on aggregate supply.

It is also important to realize that taxes can have different impacts because different taxes are paid by different groups. Certain taxes impose heavier burdens on the poor, while others "soak" the rich.

Tax burden: the proportion of income that goes to pay a tax or taxes; tax payment divided by total income

For the purpose of discussion here, let us define a family's **tax burden** to be the proportion of their income which goes to pay taxes. So, for example, a family which has an annual income of $10,000 and pays $2000 in taxes would have a tax burden of $2000/$10,000 = .20 or 20 percent. Given this definition of the tax burden, there are basically three types of taxes: progressive, regressive, and proportional taxes.

1. PROGRESSIVE TAXES.

Progressive taxes are taxes which tend to impose higher tax burdens on people with higher incomes. For example, a tax which takes $1000 from a family with an income of $10,000 (tax burden = 10 percent), but takes $3000 from families with incomes of $20,000 (tax burden = 15 percent) would be a progressive tax.

Progressive tax: a tax that imposes higher tax burdens on groups with higher incomes

2. REGRESSIVE TAXES.

A **regressive tax** is one which imposes higher tax burdens on families with lower incomes. A tax which took $1500 from families which earn $10,000 per year (15 percent), but took $2000 from families with incomes of $20,000 (10 percent) would be regressive. Note that the richer family actually pays a greater tax ($2000 vs. $1500). But their burden is less because a smaller proportion of their income goes to pay the tax.

Regressive tax: a tax which imposes higher tax burdens on groups with lower incomes

3. PROPORTIONAL TAXES.

A **proportional tax** is one which imposes the same burden on all families, regardless of income. A proportional tax, then, would tax $700 from the family with the income of $10,000 (7 percent), and $1400 from the family with income equal to $20,000 (7 percent again).

Proportional tax: a tax which imposes equal tax burdens on all groups

Five basic taxes account for the bulk of governmental revenue: personal and corporate income taxes, Social Security tax, and sales and property taxes. Let's take a look at each of these taxes and see where they fit in this classification scheme.

1. PERSONAL INCOME TAX.

The federal **personal income tax** is certainly the most noticeable tree in our fiscal forest, and every April 15, millions of Americans sit and curse their form 1040. To understand the **incidence** or distribution of the tax burden of the income tax, we first need to know a little about how it is calculated. This discussion won't qualify you for a job at H & R Block, but it is almost enough. Let's take a family of four earning $10,000 and see how their taxes are arrived at.

Personal income tax: the federal income tax collected in the United States every April 15

Incidence: the actual distribution of the burden of a tax.

We start with their income of $10,000. If it is all wage and salary income, it will all be taxed. Certain types of income, like the income from stocks and bonds, may be taxed differently. Our typical family doesn't pay tax on the entire $10,000. They are allowed a number of deductions. First, they may subtract $750 for each person in the family (a family of four can, then, deduct 4 × $750 = $3000). This brings the income subject to tax down to $7000. Next, they are allowed to subtract a fixed amount of income as a "standard deduction" (alternatively, they could "itemize deductions" and subtract interest payments, state and local taxes, charitable contributions, etc.). This deduction (about $3200 for married taxpayers) brings their taxable income down to $7000 − $3200 = $4800. Finally, they apply a sliding scale of tax rates which run from 14 percent on the first $1000 of taxable income up to 70 percent of the taxable income of very-high-income groups. For our "typical" family, the application of these rates leaves them with a tax liability of about $750 or an income tax burden of 7.5 percent. (Congress changes the income tax rates and deductions every few years, so check with the IRS before filing your income tax using the figures in this example.)

In general, the income tax is a progressive tax for two reasons. First, low-income groups pay virtually no tax at all (tax burden = 0) because their deductions ($750 personal exemption plus standard deduction) are larger than their incomes. They owe no taxes, so the poorest part of the population is untouched by the income tax.

For other groups, the progressive tax rates, which rise as income rises, assures that the tax burden is progressive. On the whole, the income tax is progressive, taking about 20 percent of the income of American families.

Social Security tax: the payroll tax which finances the Social Security program

2. THE SOCIAL SECURITY TAX. A lot of people have the wrong idea about the **Social Security tax**. They think that the Social Security tax isn't really a tax at all. It's more like an insurance contribution. The government takes money directly out of your paycheck, invests it for you in high-quality securities, and then pays you back, with interest, when you retire.

The most interesting thing about this description of the Social Security program is that, while many people would find no fault with this statement, it is nevertheless *completely wrong*! The Social Security program is almost nothing like the "insurance" program that most people believe in. So what is the Social Security program really like?

First of all, the Social Security tax is a tax, not an insurance contribution. Your "contributions" are not saved and invested for you; instead, your tax dollars go to Washington, D.C., where they are immediately used to pay Social Security benefits for those already retired. You pay taxes to finance your grandparents' retirement, and your children and grandchildren will be the ones who provide for your Social Security payments.

Payroll tax: a tax which is collected directly from pay checks

The Social Security tax is a **payroll tax**, that is, it is subtracted directly from your paycheck. It is imposed at a flat rate against all wage and salary income up to a predetermined cutoff point. Since the tax must raise enough money to pay current Social Security benefits, the tax rate and the cutoff point are subject to change every year. In 1978, for example, the tax was 6.05 percent of the first $17,700 of earned income. Current estimates suggest that by 1987 the tax will rise to at least 7.15 percent of the first $42,600 of a person's income.

One of the peculiarities of the Social Security tax is that the employer must match the employee's "contribution." So, in 1978, employers also paid a tax of 6.05 percent of the first $17,700 of each worker's wages. Economists have determined that the employer's share of the tax has been passed on to workers over the years in the form of lower wages. So, in effect, the full 12.1 percent tax falls on the employee—part in direct taxes and part indirectly in lower wages.

The Social Security tax is a regressive tax for two reasons. First, individuals who earn incomes above the limit don't have to pay tax on the part of their income above the tax ceiling. So a person who earns $10,000 will pay Social Security tax equal to $605 (6.05 percent burden), while someone who makes $20,000 per year will pay $1070 (5.3 percent burden). All of this assumes a tax rate of 6.05 percent and a ceiling of $17,700 as applied in 1978.

The second cause of the regressivity of the Social Security tax is that the tax applies *only* to earned (wage and salary) income. Income derived from investments is not subject to Social Security taxation. So, if someone earned all of their income—say, $20,000—from stock dividends, they would pay no Social Security tax at all (but they may not qualify for Social Security benefits, either). These higher-income groups escape Social Security taxation, making the tax regressive.

These days the Social Security program is in a lot of trouble. The "pay as you go" system (as opposed to an "insurance-type" pension program) requires large numbers of workers to pay taxes for those retirees who receive benefits. When Social Security benefits were lower—and the number of retired families collecting those benefits smaller as well—it was not difficult to raise enough taxes to pay for Social Security benefits. In the beginning, for example, the Social Security tax took only 1 percent of the first $3000 of a worker's pay (a maximum tax of just $30). The tax is much higher now, and the problem will get worse. Social Security benefits, although not particularly high, have increased over the years. This has forced the tax rates up.

Workers today are living longer, but having fewer children. This means that, when today's college students retire, their children and grandchildren will bear a tremendous burden in Social Security taxes. Today there are six or seven workers paying Social Security taxes for every beneficiary of the program. In a few years, however, this ratio will drop to only about three to one. Tax rates must necessarily soar—Social Security taxes could amount to over 25 percent of income when today's students retire.

Will future generations be willing to bear such high tax burdens? It doesn't seem likely. Therefore, some compromise will eventually need to be reached. Taxes can be kept down if benefit levels are lowered, for example, but current benefits do not support an extravagant standard of living by any means. Funding could be shifted from the payroll to the income tax in order to make the burden of the Social Security program less regressive, but this is just taking out of one pocket to fill another. The high taxes will still have to be collected.

One possible solution which will have to be examined carefully calls for the imposition of a "means" test for Social Security beneficiaries. Currently, the Social Security program is set up to pay roughly the same benefits to people who are poor and need every cent of the payments as to people who have saved or invested for their retirement and don't need Social Security payments as much. This policy exists so that the program will be viewed more as a "pension program" (where all who contribute receive benefits) than as a "welfare program" (where only the needy receive help). A means test could lower the costs of the program by giving benefits to only those who need them. Tax rates could be reduced if this were done, but the broad support for the program might also be lost since people who currently pay the taxes willingly might balk at "contributing" to a system that is unlikely to pay them benefits.

Other solutions designed to cut costs have also been suggested. Social Security benefits paid to orphans, the disabled, and other eligible groups will probably be brought under close scrutiny. There is no easy solution here. Someone will be hurt by whatever decisions are made. Since today's students have much to gain and lose from this decision making, they should pay especially close attention to the discussions that take place and the decisions that are made.

3. THE CORPORATE INCOME TAX.
Businesses also pay income taxes, but not all businesses pay the same type of tax. Corporations are subject to the federal **corporate income tax**, while partnerships and other forms of business organizations pay taxes through the personal income tax.

Corporate income tax: a federal tax levied against the profits of corporations

This is really a corporate profits tax. Corporations are allowed to deduct necessary business expenses and then pay a tax on the remaining profit. The tax rates are relatively simple. The first $25,000 is taxed at a flat rate of 20 percent, the second $25,000 bears a 22 percent tax rate, and all corporate profits above $50,000 are taxed at a 48 percent rate. Small businesses, then, pay only about 20 percent corporate profits taxes, while larger firms pay the full 48 percent on most of their profits. Businesses which are not chartered as corporations, however, pay different rates under the personal income tax.

Who bears the burden of the corporate income tax? There is little agreement within the economics profession here. Arguments have been made that the tax is passed on to consumers in terms of higher prices, passed on to workers in terms of lower wages, or borne by the owners of capital (stockholders) in the form of lower returns on investment. All three theories are probably at least partially true, and we will not enter into the debate here.

The corporate income tax is very controversial. Many economists feel that it discourages investment activities because of the "double taxation" of corporate profits. When a corporation earns a profit, it is normal for at least some of those earnings to be passed on to shareholders of the firm in the form of dividends. These dividends are taxed two times, however. They are taxed at the business level by the corporate income tax, and then again at the personal level by the individual income tax. This double taxation, the argument goes, reduces the incentive to invest in business and so discourages the investment which is necessary to the growth of aggregate demand.

4. SALES TAXES. The general **sales tax** seems like it should be an example of a proportional tax—after all, everyone pays the same sales tax rate, right? It is true that the same sales tax rate applies to everyone in a given state, but that does not mean everyone bears the same tax burden. An example is useful here.

Sales tax: taxes levied on the value of consumer purchases

Let's look at two families; the Ericksons and the Larsons. The Ericksons have an annual disposable income of $10,000 and, since $10,000 doesn't go very far these days, they spend almost all of it on consumer goods. If they spend $9000 on goods and services, then they would pay sales taxes amounting to $450 (assume the sales tax rate is 5 percent). The Larsons have a higher disposable income—$20,000—and are able to save $5000 of it. They pay $750 sales tax on the $15,000 that they spend on goods and services.

Notice the distribution of the tax burden. The poorer Ericksons bear a burden of $450/$10,000 = 4.5 percent. The richer Larsons pay taxes to $750/$20,000 = 3.75 percent of their income. The sales tax is regressive. Since the rich are better able to save, they may "avoid" or delay paying the sales tax by purchasing nontaxable savings accounts instead of other, taxable items. The poor, however, must spend all of their incomes, and so are taxed on all of their income. The result is a regressive tax, which tends to hit the poor the hardest.

In practice, the sales tax tends to be less regressive than our example shows, however. Most states which impose a general sales tax now exempt certain classes of goods—food, prescription drugs, and so on—from the tax. When food is taken out of the tax base, the sales tax tends toward proportionality instead of being regressive.

Property tax: a tax collected by state and local governments based on the value of the property that people and firms own

5. PROPERTY TAXES. The **property tax** is an example of an **ad valorem tax**. Like the sales tax, the property tax is levied against the *value* of a certain

Ad valorem taxation: taxation according to the value of an item (e.g., sales and property taxes)

good—in this case, property and structures. Like the sales tax, the property tax seems as if it should be proportional since the same rate is paid by all. But this is not the case because the property tax is collected based upon the value of a household's property, not the size of its current income.

The property tax on residential housing is probably regressive for two reasons. First, a significant part of the property tax base is owned by retired people. These families have low incomes, but property with high value and therefore subject to high taxes. As a result, they often bear a very large tax burden.

The second reason for the regressivity of the property tax is based on the general behavior of households with respect to their purchase of housing services. Here again, an example is in order. Our friends the Ericksons make $10,000 per year and, if they are average, own a house worth about $30,000. The average property tax rate these days is about 2.5 percent of the property value, so the Ericksons pay about $750 yearly property tax, for a tax burden of 7.5 percent. The Larsons have twice as much income ($20,000), but, if they are typical, they may own a house that is not twice as costly as the Erickson's. Their home may be worth, say, $50,000. They pay the same 2.5 percent property tax rate, so their tax is $1250, for a tax burden of about 6 percent (less than the 7 percent burden of the Ericksons). The relationship between income and property value that the Ericksons and the Larsons display here is fairly typical in today's world, and the regressivity of the property tax is the result of these spending habits.

How are the property tax rates set? The property tax is interesting because the tax rates depend almost entirely upon how much the government wishes to spend and the amount of property available from which to collect taxes.

Suppose, for example, that you live in Noah County and that the Noah County school district raises all of the money for schools through the property tax (in reality, much of it would come from aid from federal and state governments). Let's suppose, in addition, that there is property valued at $100 million in Noah County. If the school board votes to spend $2.5 million this year, then the tax rate will be $2.5 million divided by $100 million or 2.5 percent of property value.

The property tax rate can rise in two ways. The tax rate will go up if the school board votes to spend more money or if the value of the property in Noah County declines. Tax rates can fall if the schools spend less money or if the value of the property in the county rises because of new construction, economic development, or some other reason. This is why many local government officials are so interested in seeing industries locate in their area. It expands the tax base, making higher revenues possible without higher tax rates (think about it).

For an individual, the property tax on a home or business will rise if either the tax rate rises (for one of the reasons discussed above) or if the value of the property in question rises due to changing market conditions or inflation. People in many parts of the country are finding that the combination of inflation plus the high demand for single-family houses is causing property values (and therefore, property taxes) to rise much faster than their incomes are rising, creating a larger and larger tax burden for them.

THE TOTAL TAX BURDEN

Since all of these various taxes are imposed by different levels of government, no one part of the government really has direct control over the total tax burden. Joseph Peckman and Benjamin Okner of the Brookings Institution have studied the impact of all taxes and they concluded that, in total, the tax burden is roughly proportional.

The exact results vary depending upon what shifting assumptions are used and which taxes are counted, but overall the total tax burden is roughly proportional at about 25 percent of income.

When the effect of government programs are included (which tend to benefit the poor somewhat more than the rich), we are led to the conclusion that the government sector as a whole is mildly progressive, taking from upper-income groups and giving to lower-income families.

TAX EXPENDITURES

Taxes serve four functions in our fiscal system. They raise revenues to finance purchases of government goods and services. They are used to influence the distribution of income. They are a major part of stabilization policy. They also are used as a substitute tool for government spending. Instead of the government directly performing some task, selective tax breaks are often used to induce private individuals to perform the actions that the government wishes to encourage.

Tax breaks that are designed to motivate desirable private activities are often called **tax expenditures**. They are currently a very important part of our fiscal system.

Tax expenditures: tax reductions or loopholes designed to encourage certain types of private sector activities

As Table 8-4 indicates, the federal government gave up over $124 billion in tax collections in fiscal year 1978 in order to induce private actions or otherwise affect the economy. Many of these loopholes resulted in lower taxes for businesses and rich people, but some of the largest tax breaks benefited middle-income families.

The deduction of interest payments, for example, is one of the greatest benefits to those who have a great deal of debt relative to their incomes. Middle-income homeowners fit this category, and this tax expenditure made

FISCAL POLICY

TABLE 8-4

MAJOR TAX EXPENDITURES, FEDERAL GOVERNMENT FISCAL YEAR 1978

Tax Expenditure	Value to Individuals ($ millions)	Value to Corporations ($ millions)	Total ($ millions)
Deduction of charitable contributions	5,830	730	6,560
Deduction of mortgage interest and interest on consumer credit	7,105	—	7,105
Investment tax credit	2,390	10,735	13,125
Preferential treatment of capital gains	17,020	775	17,795
Total of all tax expenditures (includes those not listed above)	92,600	31,815	124,415

Source: *Special Analyses, Budget of the United States Government, Fiscal Year 1979.*

it significantly easier for people in this group to buy and keep their homes. In fact, home ownership is one of the activities that this tax expenditure is designed to promote.

The government also encourages contributions to charitable organizations by not taxing these donations. In fiscal 1978 these foregone taxes amounted to over $6 billion.

A substantial amount of tax expenditures go toward promoting private investment expenditures. The reduced taxes on capital gains plus the investment tax credit (total tax expenditure over $30 billion) are designed to encourage investment spending by increasing the after-tax profits of these investments. This investment is desirable because of the positive impact that it has on the growth of aggregate supply.

Tax expenditures are a substitute for direct government spending. They are good in the sense that they keep the government out of areas where its actions may not be appropriate, but they are costly because they impose an additional burden on the economy. The existence of these tax loopholes means that people will spend time not trying to produce goods and services, but merely attempting to meet the provisions of some specific loophole in the tax laws. As well, inequitable tax advantages are sometimes lost in the mass of tax items that form the tax expenditures. Good or bad, however, the tax expenditures are a major feature of our tax system, and one that is likely to grow, not shrink, in the future.

Transfer payments are the third tool of fiscal policy. Transfer payments are governmental "gifts" like Social Security payments, unemployment benefits, welfare payments, and the like. They are like gifts in the sense that the giver—the government—expects nothing in return for the payment.

Because transfer payments appear to be just another form of government spending, one would think that they would affect the economy in basically the same way that government spending does. But there may be differences between the total impacts on the economy of transfer payments and government spending. The multiplier impacts of transfer payments depends upon the behavior of the transfer recipients.

First, suppose that transfer payments recipients (retired families or unemployed persons, for example) behave about the same way that the rest of the population does. In this case, assuming an MPC of 60 percent, if transfer payments increase by $100,000, the transfer recipients will save about $40,000 and spend the remaining $60,000. This will start in motion a spending/income/spending/income multiplier cycle just as in the previous cases. The total impact on the economy will be an increase in aggregate demand of $150,000—the same as for a $100,000 tax cut. In fact, in this instance, transfers are just like negative taxes insofar as their final impact on aggregate demand is concerned. The multiplier formula here is

$$\text{Change in AD} = \frac{\text{MPC}}{1 - \text{MPC}} \times \text{Change in transfer payments}$$

If, however, transfer recipients spend all of any increase in income (MPC = 1), then government spending and transfer spending have equal impact on aggregate demand. The formula for the government-spending multiplier would be used. In this case, a $100,000 transfer payment would cause a $100,000 increase in spending by transfer recipients and generate a total $250,000 increase in AD.

TRANSFER PAYMENTS

Transfer payments: payments from one group to another with no payment of goods or services in return

---

Congress and the president can use the tools of taxes, transfers, and government spending to try to regulate the economy so as to achieve our economic goals. But this same system also has features that automatically compensate for changes in the economic weather. These **automatic stabilizer** features tend to slow down the growth in aggregate demand during inflationary periods and dampen falling income during periods of economic distress.

The transfer payments system is part of the automatic stabilizer scheme.

AUTOMATIC STABILIZERS

Automatic stabilizers: government spending, taxation, and transfer programs which automatically (i.e., without legislative action) act to increase AD during economic downturns and decrease AD during periods of prosperity

During periods of recession, transfer payments such as unemployment benefits and welfare payments increase automatically. This props up aggregate demand, keeping spending and income higher than would otherwise be the case. During periods of high employment, transfer payments automatically fall, lowering aggregate demand and so lowering the threat of inflation.

The tax system works as an automatic stabilizer, too. Because unemployed people fall into lower tax brackets, and because transfer payments are generally not taxable, tax collections fall more than proportionally when income falls. Thus, after-tax or disposable income does not fall as fast as gross income. This sounds complicated, but it really just means that the tax bite is reduced during recessions so that more income is left over to spend and so to increase aggregate demand.

Government spending also automatically rises and falls with changes in the unemployment rate. The federal government allocates countercyclical aid to state and local governments on the basis of their unemployment rates. Local governments in areas with especially high unemployment get more federal dollars so that they can put the unemployed back to work on the public payroll. This system works automatically to reduce unemployment during recessions and to slow the growth in aggregate demand in times of prosperity.

ADVANTAGES AND DISADVANTAGES OF FISCAL POLICIES

Each of the tools of fiscal policy has advantages and disadvantages. For this reason there is often argument not only concerning what should be done (increase aggregate demand? increase aggregate supply?) but also which tools to use to accomplish these ends.

Government spending is useful because it is the most powerful of the fiscal policies. Its multiplier impact is larger, so the impact on the economy is larger, too. Government spending is also useful because it can be "targeted" to particularly needy parts of the economy. If the aerospace industry is at the heart of the unemployment problem, for example, government purchases can be tailored to affect this area directly, with the indirect multiplier effects benefiting the rest of the economy.

A principal disadvantage of government spending, however, is that it often takes too long to implement a change in expenditures (the other tools of fiscal policy also suffer from this problem of lags). First, there is a **legislative lag**—it takes months and sometimes years between the moment

Legislative lag: a lag in fiscal policy equal to the time it takes legislative bodies to decide the proper governmental actions

that a bill is introduced in Congress affecting fiscal policy and the time that it is finally enacted into law. There follows the **implementation lag**—which may be particularly long in the case of spending policies. Rules and regulations, contracts and bids, and miles of red tape all must be followed to their end before the money which Congress has appropriated can finally be spent. Finally, there is the **impact lag**—the time it takes for the change in spending to make its multiplier impact on aggregate demand.

The combination of these three delays can be detrimental to the economy. Programs designed to reduce unemployment may not hit the economy until full employment has already been achieved by other means. At this point, the spending programs can become inflationary. The problem of lags is one reason for our current heavy dependence on the automatic stabilizers for a great deal of stabilization policy.

Tax policies can escape one of these lags, and so are preferable when quick action is called for. Once a tax change has been passed into law, it takes only a few weeks to work out the details and then taxes are cut (or raised). It all can happen very fast. When President Ford called for tax rebates in 1975, for example, it took Congress about three months to decide how much should be distributed, and then just a month more for the checks to arrive and begin stimulating demand. (In this case, however, the impact lag was apparently very long, as people did *not* immediately run out and spend this windfall gain.)

Taxes are also a useful tool because they affect almost every part of the population, so they can be used as a general stimulus or depressant for aggregate demand (as opposed to government spending which affects some sectors more than others). The complexity of the tax laws, however, reduces their usefulness. The Tax Reform Bill of 1969 was popularly known as the "Accountants' and Lawyers' Full-employment Bill" because of its complicated nature. Working fiscal policy using the tax codes can be dangerous because of the temptation this gives Congress to fiddle with tax laws. Often the result here is a double tax: one which is collected by the government and another that we pay to H & R Block and other tax preparers, advisors, and accountants.

Transfer payments suffer all of the lag problems of other fiscal policies and one more: the **identification lag**. Transfer payments are most often designed to help especially needy groups. But first these groups must be identified. The rules and regulations by which this search is carried out may be lengthy, and the time span long as well.

Transfer payments may, in certain cases, be as powerful as government spending programs, and they have the additional advantage that they directly affect the neediest groups within the economy, while providing general stimulus through the multiplier process.

Implementation lag: the lag in fiscal policy equal to the time it takes for implementing a decision to change spending transfers or taxes

Impact lag: the lag in fiscal policy equal to the time it takes a change in spending transfers or taxes to have its full impact on the economy

Identification lag: a problem in fiscal policies involving transfer payments caused by the time which must be spent identifying the proper transfer recipient groups

DEFICIT SPENDING AND THE NATIONAL DEBT

Deficit spending: spending in excess of tax revenues

Deficit spending isn't really spending at all; it is borrowing. Like the rest of us, the government often spends more than it takes in. When government spending exceeds tax collections, we say that the government is undertaking deficit spending, but this just means that it is going into debt. Like the rest of us, the government must borrow money when it spends more than it has, and it is this deficit spending which creates the national debt (the total amount that the government owes).

Who does the government borrow from? From a lot of people, actually, probably including you or your family. United States savings bonds are really debt instruments of the federal government. When you buy a U.S. savings bond, you are really lending the government money to finance deficit spending. Instead of a "piece of the rock," however, you merely have a chunk of the national debt.

These days the federal government is running huge deficits—about $50 billion toward the end of the 1970s—in an attempt to stimulate aggregate demand and halt the rise in unemployment. These deficits have boosted the national debt: the total amount of federal government debt was about $720 billion dollars in 1977, or 40 percent of GNP.

Is the national debt a problem? The answer to this sticky question is no . . . and yes. Some folks claim that we shouldn't worry about the national debt because "we owe it to ourselves." As silly as this sounds, it is at least partially true. Since the government has the power to coerce—to force you and I to pay taxes—it is a very good credit risk. As a result, the national debt need never actually be paid off. When the government needs to pay back the loan from Mr. A, the Treasury can raise the money necessary by borrowing from Mr. B. The national debt will never "come due"—and no one will ever foreclose on the White House—so long as the government remains a good credit risk. Since deficit spending can be financed forever, the national debt is not harmful, so long as the deficits finance worthwhile government activities. Much of the current national debt was produced by government spending for wars and to fight unemployment.

On the other hand, the national debt does have a dark side. Since the government is borrowing so much money from individuals, banks, and others, this leaves just that much less money available for private businesses to borrow to finance investment opportunities. We say that governmental borrowing tends to crowd out private-sector borrowing. We will see how this works, and what impact it has on the economy, in Part III when we look at money, credit, and debt.

There is also the matter of the interest payments on the national debt. The government, like any other borrower, must pay interest if it is to get anyone to lend it money. When you buy the U.S. savings bond for $18.75 and cash it in for $25.00 several years later, the $6.25 difference represents the accumulated interest that the government owes you on your loan.

The interest on the national debt currently is almost $40 billion per year—an extremely large amount almost equal to the total current deficit. It is, in fact, reasonable to conclude that nearly all of this year's increase in government borrowing goes just to pay the interest on previous borrowing. This creates something of a drag on the government sector. In general, taxes are higher, and spending on necessary government programs is lower, because a significant part of the government's budget (about 10 percent) must go to these interest payments. In this sense, the national debt *is* a problem, and a problem which is not likely to disappear in a few years or even decades.

SUMMARY

1. Fiscal policies are governmental activities involving spending, taxation, and transfer payments.

2. Government spending affects aggregate demand directly (by increasing total spending) and generates high induced consumption spending. The total impact of a change in government spending is given by the spending multiplier. Taxation and transfer payments affect the economy indirectly. These policies affect disposable income with the effect of altering consumption spending. They also have multiplier impacts on aggregate demand.

3. A number of factors influence the effectiveness of fiscal policies. The type of aggregate supply curve that the economy faces is one such variable. Depending upon the state of aggregate supply, a given increase in government spending can have a large affect on RGNP (the depression AS case), cause large increases in the price level (with a full-employment AS) or be divided between higher prices and increased production (in a bottleneck AS situation). Other factors are also important. Tax policies can succeed or fail depending upon whether they are viewed as "permanent" or not by taxpayers. Timing is also important in fiscal policies since governmental actions suffer from a variety of lags which can delay the final impact of these policies for months or even years.

4. All taxes are not the same. All taxes affect aggregate demand (through their impact on disposable income), but some have side effects on aggregate supply and all are paid by different groups. Progressive taxes impose higher burdens on high-income groups. Regressive taxes fall heaviest on low-income groups, and proportional taxes are borne in equal proportion by all.

5. The income tax is a progressive

tax because of the progressive rate structure and the various deductions that benefit low-income groups. The Social Security tax is regressive because of the ceiling on tax payments and the fact that it taxes only wage and salary incomes. Property taxes are also probably regressive with respect to their burden on residential housing. The sales tax is regressive when it falls on all consumer items, but may be roughly proportional when food and drugs are excluded from taxation. The incidence of the corporate income tax is uncertain. The total tax burden is roughly proportional.

6. Deficit spending is spending in excess of tax revenues. Deficits are most common at the federal government level and produce the national debt.

7. The national debt is not a problem, insofar as "we owe it to ourselves." Yet the fact that governmental borrowing may "crowd out" private borrowing and the burden that interest payments impose force us to be concerned about the size of the government's debt.

DISCUSSION QUESTIONS

1. Suppose that government spending increases by $17 billion. What will be the initial impact on income? What will be the eventual impact on aggregate demand? Would the total impact be different if the MPC were 50 percent?

2. Suppose that the government increases taxes by $12 billion. What are the initial and eventual impacts of this action on aggregate demand? Would the eventual impact be different if the MPC were 90 percent?

3. Suppose that the government cut both taxes and government spending by $25 billion. What would happen to the economy?

4. Suppose that the government increased Social Security benefits by $35 billion, and also raised Social Security taxes by $35 billion to pay for the increased benefits. What would be the impact of this action on the economy? Would the distribution of income within the economy change?

5. The corporate income tax is a tax on businesses. Do you think that it is progressive, regressive, or proportional? Defend your choice.

6. Should *all* taxes be progressive? Regressive? Proportional? What is your opinion of your state's tax system—is it progressive, regressive, or proportional? Is it about the same as those of neighboring states?

7. Who *owes* the national debt? Is

there any justification for the government going into debt when they can always raise the money they need by increasing taxes?

8. Suppose that it has been decided that aggregate demand should be increased, through some sort of fiscal policy, by $40 billion in total. This can be done either by purchasing new military aircraft, cutting income taxes, or increasing welfare benefits. Assuming an MPC of 60 percent, how big would each of these actions have to be to raise AD by the desired amount? What affect would these different actions have upon the distribution of income in the United States?

9. Suppose that Congress has decided that it is desirable to increase aggregate supply by giving a tax break to people and firms who invest to raise the capacity of the economy. What impact would this have on the distribution of income? Is it likely to be popular? Who would this action benefit in the short run? Who would it benefit in the long-run?

TEST YOURSELF

Indicate whether each of the following statements is *true* or *false*. Be able to defend your choice.

1. A $100 billion increase in government spending would increase RGNP by $250 billion (assuming MPC = 60 percent).

2. An increase in government spending by $50 billion would cause consumption spending to rise by a total of $125 billion (MPC = 60 percent).

3. An increase in taxes of $50 billion would cause consumption spending to fall by $75 billion (MPC = 60 percent).

4. Suppose that both taxes and government spending are cut by $45 billion. The impact on the economy would be greater if MPC = 75 percent than if MPC = 60 percent.

5. A $50 billion increase in transfer payments combined with a $50 billion increase in taxes would cause AD to rise by $50 billion (MPC = 60 percent).

6. An increase in the Social Security tax might cause a decrease in aggregate supply.

7. Suppose that everyone received a 10 percent cut in income taxes. This would benefit the poor relatively more than the rich.

8. An individual family's property taxes rise whenever their income rises.

9. An increase in tax expenditures would increase deficit spending.

10. One-shot tax rebates are less effective in altering AD than permanent tax cuts.

ECONOMIC CONTROVERSIES IV: IS THERE TOO MUCH GOVERNMENT?

One of the most important trends in the United States has been the rapid increase in the size of government since the Great Depression. In 1933 combined federal-state-local government expenditures totaled just $10.7 billion. By 1977 this total had increased sixty-fold to over $600 billion. In *real* terms (adjusting for inflation) total government spending grew by 74 percent during the decade of the 1950s, by 72 percent during the 1960s, and by 28 percent between 1970 and 1977.

Is this rapid increase in the size of government justified? Is it desirable? Is government too big? These are questions that are important in today's world and about which economists hold differing points of view.

TOO MUCH GOVERNMENT!

Government has grown too big in the United States. This growth has had a number of undesirable results. The first and most apparent impact of public sector growth has been on the individual tax burden. The average tax burden now has reached the point where an open tax revolt is entirely possible. People feel, quite rightly, that they are paying too much taxes and not getting their money's worth. They demand not more services, but lower taxes. They demand the right to spend their dollars for what they want and need—not what some government bureaucrat thinks is necessary.

We can also see the dangerous growth in government's size in the degree to which government regulations have come to dominate our lives. Our cars, homes, appliances, hiring practices, educational services—nearly every aspect of one's life is now a subject for governmental rules, regulations, and controls. Many of these rules and regulations are not even written by our elected representatives. They are, instead, promogulated by hired bureaucrats.

Fiscal policies (designed to stabilize the economy) have contributed to the unfortunate growth in government. Slowly fiscal policy matters have come to dominate the scene in Congress and elsewhere. Important matters of law and government have been set aside so that tax cuts or fiscal stimulus packages could be constructed. More often than not, the more important law and government matters have ended up being decided within the vast bureaucracy where they have contributed to our current array of regulations and acted to increase the size of the bureaucracy itself.

Government has gotten so big that it cannot be adequately supervised. Its inefficiency is legendary. When President Carter called in 1977 for a reorganization of the federal government, he found that even reorganizing the relatively small Office of the President was time-consuming, inefficient, and resulted in very little change.

Why has government grown so large? We can lay the blame at two doorsteps: inflation and politics. Inflation has caused government to grow so rapidly because it has increased the size of the government's wallet. Inflation and the income tax have produced increases in governmental revenues without any legislative increase in tax rates. Government has taken a free ride on these inflation tax dollars, and the easy money has not been wisely spent. The result is what we see today: waste, inefficiency, and a government sector which is a drag on the economy.

The politics of government spending have also played a part in the growth of government. One of the problems with government spending is that the benefits from any particular government program are usually concentrated—reaped by a relatively small group—while the costs are diffused and borne by all taxpayers. The group that will receive most of the benefits but pay only a little of the cost of a particular government program will obviously lobby very hard to get their bill enacted. Because Congress is overburdened with bills, laws, and committees, senators and congressmen cannot fully understand all of what they are voting on. It takes just a few highly motivated pressure groups, therefore, to push a bill through Congress. This, together with "vote swapping" (whereby congressmen see that advantageous programs are spread out over most states and congressional districts) results in an oversupply of government services.

Government is too big and, as we have seen, its very size makes it difficult to control and so likely to grow bigger.

GOVERNMENT SIZE NOT A PROBLEM

Those who complain so loudly about the growth in government simply do not understand the reasons for this growth. The world has grown, too, and the increased size of government simply reflects that growth. A larger population has caused increases in school, fire, and police protection expenditures. An increased concern for the quality of these services has boosted the cost of expenditures in these areas. As the world has become more complicated, government policies have had to grow to deal with the new and complex problems we face.

The foes of government also fail to see how the role of government has changed over the years. At the turn of the century the government was primarily a defender (army, navy, marines) and a law giver (criminal and civil law and enforcement). It did not take very much government to perform these tasks.

As the economy has grown and the standard of living improved, voters have come to demand more services from the government. As a result, the role of government has expanded greatly. Now government is not only defender and lawgiver, but also equalizer (responsible for helping the old, the poor, and the disadvantaged) and the chief supplier of such basic services as education, health care, and environmental protection. The role of stabilizer did not really exist until the 1930s. It is clear, however, that this is a part that needs playing in today's world. The economy is strong, but it cannot manage itself. A guiding hand is necessary to turn the wheel and avoid disaster.

The role of equalizer had traditionally been performed by the private (nongovernment) part of the economy. The old and poor of the past were taken care of by their families or by private charities. This, in many cases, meant that the old, poor, and disadvantaged were left to suffer or bear economic hardship. As we grew richer, the public demanded that the government step in to assume a greater role in this area.

The same is true in the areas of education and health care. As family incomes increased, the demand for these public services increased as well. The growth in government spending here comes as a logical response to the increased demand for these services. A market would have responded in the same way, although perhaps less efficiently. Environmental protection activities of the government also come in response to increased demand. As we have accumulated more material wealth, we have become more aware that having cars and boats is of little utility if the air and water are polluted.

We have been conditioned over the years to think that we have too much government and not enough private goods. It is easy to see how this conclusion could be reached. We face a barrage of advertising designed to make us want more and more private goods (and, implicitly, fewer and fewer public goods). When we pay for private goods, we immediately get the pleasure of acquiring those goods—and we need not share them with anyone. The pain of paying is quickly offset by the pleasure of consuming the goods and services involved.

This is not the case with public goods. We pay our taxes at one time and often receive the benefits of the services (which must be shared with others) that the tax dollars buy at much different times. We do not normally make the connection between the pain that taxation causes and the pleasure that government services bring. Indeed, we are not even aware of many of the public goods and services that our tax dollars buy. Many government services are "invisibles"— they remain unseen while they are at work. The police department, for example, discourages crime in many different ways, yet we normally think of the police not when a crime has been avoided or discouraged (good news is no news) but only when the protection has failed. Hence, we do not consciously consider the benefits of such government services when we pay the taxes that support them.

Because we receive direct benefit from private expenditures, but only indirect benefits from public goods, it is easy to think that we are not getting out our money's worth and that government is too big. Some government programs may be wasteful or unnecessary, but for the most part government has grown in response to an increased demand for its services. The growth of government, then, is fully justified and we should not be overly concerned about the size of government today.

DISCUSSION QUESTIONS

1. Which side of this argument do you agree with? Can you find flaws in the logic that either side presents? Is government too big?

2. Evaluate the argument that, because small groups can reap many benefits but bear few costs of a particular government program, this has led these groups to promote "special-interest" legislation which has increased the size of government.

3. Evaluate the argument that the separation between the pleasure of receiving benefits from government programs and the pain of paying taxes has caused us to undervalue the benefits of government services.

Part 3
Money, Credit, and the Economy

9
Money and Banking

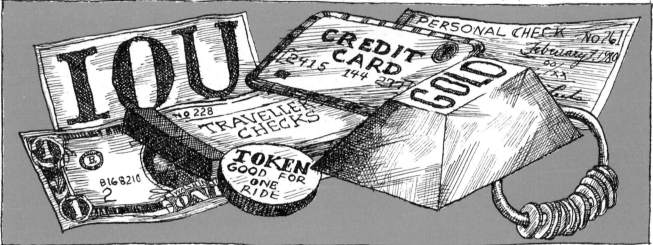

This chapter begins the study of some of the factors behind the aggregate demand and supply curves. Money and credit are discussed and the basic tools of monetary policy presented. This chapter will answer a wide variety of questions, including the following:

What is money?

What factors determine the interest rate?

How do modern banks work?

How can banks "create" money?

What role does the Federal Reserve System play in the economy?

Money: anything which is generally accepted in exchange for goods and services and in payment of debt

What is **money?** Well, you might say, money is money—greenbacks, dollar bills, those pieces of paper that you carry around in your wallet or purse. You know . . . *money!*

This definition of money may be good enough to get by at the grocery store, but it wouldn't come close to describing the money used by the bulk of the world's population for most of history. Paper money—currency—is really a relatively recent development in money. Your great-grandfather probably wouldn't have accepted your "money." Most of your monetary "roots" are buried in "real money"—money with intrinsic value. Gold and silver.

Many things have served as money around the world. In the United States, before paper money was used, money meant precious metal coinage, and before that, a variety of items, including tobacco (you could either spend it, save it . . . or smoke it!). Seashells have acted as money in some parts of the world. Beer has also served this purpose (money with a head!—but be careful or it'll go flat).

Barter: a system where goods and services are exchanged for one another without the use of money

On one Polynesian island, stones served as money. It all got started when people on the island discovered that **barter** was not a very useful way to exchange goods and services. In a barter system, if one person wants coconuts and has pineapples, then he or she has to hunt for someone who wants to exchange coconuts for pineapples, or alternatively, trade the pineapples for something that the coconut person does want. Exchange is very complicated, time-consuming, and inefficient in this type of system. The Polynesian islanders soon discovered that they could pick one item—stones, for example—and value everything in terms of its worth in stones. Stones might have been picked because of their scarcity, durability, and the ease with which change can be made (two little stones = one large one).

In any case, the natives of this island quickly found the advantages of a monetary system of exchange. When someone wanted a haircut he simply acquired the proper amount of stones and bought it. He didn't have to worry about first getting something that the barber would trade for a haircut. The barber could buy whatever he liked with the stones. People put their money in the bank and earned pebbles on it. It really worked a lot like our system does now, with one or two exceptions.

One of these exceptions is instructive. Situated on a cliff overlooking the sea stood a massive boulder—the largest rock on the island. The rock was so big that it was impossible to move. This mass of wealth, therefore, couldn't actually be spent. This should have created problems for fellows that owned the rock—the Rockerfellows—but it didn't. Since everyone knew the value of this huge rock, and since everyone knew who owned it, the Rockerfellows found that all the merchants on the island were willing to take their

IOUs in exchange for goods and services. They were willing to take this paper money because they knew that it was backed up by the value of the boulder. Each IOU represented a "piece of the rock."

This system rolled on for some time until the local volcano erupted, dumping the boulder into the sea. This should have wiped out the Rockerfellows and upset the economy of the island, but it didn't. In fact, nothing changed. Everyone knew where the big rock was, even if they couldn't see or touch it. Everyone knew who owned it. And the IOUs still circulated as currency because they were backed up by a rock which existed, even if it wasn't anywhere to be seen.

It is interesting to compare the islanders' monetary system with our own. Like the islanders' currency, our money is backed up with a precious good—gold. Right? Well, actually, it isn't. There is a little gold left in Fort Knox, but it doesn't back up the dollar bills in your pocket. Your five-dollar bill cannot be exchanged for gold; it is worth only five one-dollar bills. Our money, technically, is worth its weight in paper or pennies. But that's about it.

If the dollar isn't backed up by gold, then where does its value come from? Well, it is issued by the federal government, so the Great White Fathers in Washington, D.C. must guarantee its value with the backing of the government. Right? Wrong again. The federal government doesn't even issue the dollar bills you have. Take a good look at your money. Sure, the Secretary of the Treasury has signed your currency, but who issued it? The **Federal Reserve System** did, which is why these are called Federal Reserve Notes.

Federal Reserve System (FRS): national bank regulatory organization which has principal responsibility for monetary policy

Well, the Federal Reserve is part of the federal government, isn't it? Sorry, but while some of the leaders of the Federal Reserve System (FRS) are appointed by the president, the FRS itself is a private institution owned and operated by the banking industry, and the FRS doesn't back up the notes with anything in particular.

If this is all true, then money doesn't have any inherent value in the United States. Why, then, do we value it so highly? It is like the Rockerfellows' IOUs on the island. Their currency was valued because people trusted that it had value (even though they couldn't see or touch the basis for this value) and would accept it in exchange for goods and services. Likewise, our Federal Reserve Notes have value only because we think that they do. Trust, it turns out, is the basis of our monetary system, too.

Obviously, there are lots of things that act as money. To narrow the range, we define money to be anything which is generally accepted in exchange for goods and services and in payment of debt. What fits this definition in

THE MONEY SUPPLY

Demand deposits: deposits in checking accounts in commercial banks

Commercial banks: banks which issue demand deposits

Money supply: the amount of money available in an economy (depends on the exact definition of money used)

M1: one level of the money supply; currency plus demand deposit balances

M2: currency and demand deposit balances plus time deposits held by commercial banks

Time deposit: savings account balances

M3: currency and demand deposits plus time deposit balances held at both commercial and savings banks

today's economy? There are two types of "money" according to this rule: currency (including coins) and **demand deposits.** Demand deposits are checking account balances held in **commercial banks.** Economists call them demand deposits because they can be removed "on demand" from the banks and are spent just like currency in most cases.

These two forms of money make up the **money supply.** This money supply in 1977 amounted to $335 billion in the United States. About 26 percent of the money supply is made up of coins and currency, while the remaining 74 percent is demand deposits. Clearly, demand deposits are the most important form of money in today's economy, and most transactions today take place with checks, not bills or coins.

When economists talk about the "money supply" they are generally using this narrow definition of money: currency plus demand deposits. But the definition of money is arbitrary since there are other things in the economy which act very much like money at times. Economists recognize this and so they have developed a whole series of money supply measures. The definition developed above—currency plus demand deposits—is called **M1** and is the measure of the money supply that we will use in this text.

A broader measure of the money supply is called **M2.** M2 looks at all of M1—currency and demand deposit balances—but also adds **time deposit** balances (savings accounts) held in commercial banks. Since these time deposits are very near to being money, it is reasonable to include them in this measure. And since both demand and time deposits form the basis for commercial bank lending, the M2 gives us a pretty good idea of what is happening to the availability of commercial bank credit.

M3 takes us one step further. M3 includes everything in M2 and adds time deposits held outside of commercial banks—at savings banks and savings-and-loan associations. This broad measure is really a measure of the availability of credit, since M3 includes the deposits which back up most bank lending activities in the United States. Since M2 and M3 include more deposits, they are obviously larger amounts than M1. At the end of 1977, for example, M1 was about $335 billion, while M2 (M1 + commercial bank time deposits) amounted to about $800 billion, and M3 (M2 + savings bank time deposits) was $1365 billion. M3 is about four times the size of M1.

Economists keep track of M1, M2, and M3 (as well as other M's), in an attempt to better understand just what is happening to the economy. M1 looks at narrowly defined money—money that can be spent quickly and easily. M2 looks at bank deposits which form the basis for commercial bank loans. Because M3 includes savings banks (which account for a lot of real estate loans), M3 is a very broad and very good measure of the availability of credit in the economy.

Which M is the best? This isn't a question that has an unambiguous answer. Each of the money supply definitions is designed to measure a different thing for a different purpose. They all give a general idea of what is happening to the availability of money and credit in the economy. The M2 measure—perhaps because it is a middle ground between the narrowly defined M1 and the very broad M3—seems to be gaining acceptance as the most useful single measure of the money supply, since it looks at both money and credit availability.

MONEY SUBSTITUTES

Near-money: assets such as time deposits which have money-like properties or can act as money substitutes

So far our look at money has concentrated on currency and bank accounts. There are, however, other types of assets which sometimes act like money but don't satisfy our definition of money. We call these things **near-money.** Examples of near-monies are not hard to find. Bus tokens and food stamps, for example, are used like money in certain instances, although they would never be mistaken for money in most cases.

Two money substitutes are particularly interesting: credit cards and traveler's checks. These two items cannot be called money in a strict sense. Credit cards are only useful in limited areas. You might be able to pay for a restaurant dinner with a credit card, for example, but it would be hard to pay off a debt to your roommate using one. Traveler's checks are good only for the person who purchases them and, once transferred to a merchant, must be returned to the issuing company for redemption. They act like money, but can't be used in all of the ways that currency or checks can.

Let's look at how credit cards and traveler's checks work. With a credit card, you purchase items and are billed for the sum of these purchases at the end of the month. If you don't pay the total promptly, you are billed for interest or service charges at rates up to 18 percent per year, depending upon local interest rate regulations. Most people assume that credit card companies make their profits from these interest charges. While these loans may be profitable, credit cards actually earn profits in two other, more interesting ways.

First of all, the merchant who takes payment by credit card pays a premium—usually about 3 to 5 percent of credit card sales—to the credit card issuer. So, for example, if you purchase a $100 coat using a credit card, the merchant will actually receive only about $95 payment. The credit card company keeps the difference. Some of the merchant's loss, of course, is eventually passed on to his customers in the form of higher prices.

Why should the merchant agree to pay the credit card company this 5 percent premium? Mostly because sellers count on the availability of credit to lure customers away from stores which demand cash payment and to

Float: occurs when two or more individuals temporarily own the same asset

promote impulse buying. If they can sell more at higher prices, then the credit card fees will be worth their cost to the merchant.

The second way that credit card companies make profits, aside from consumer interest charges, is through management of the payments' **float.** Economists use the term *float* to describe what happens when there is a distance between the buyer and seller in a transaction. If the buyer pays a middleman (the credit card company) before the middleman has to pay the seller, then the intermediary can invest the temporary cash holding—the float—and earn interest on someone else's money.

The credit card companies work in the middle here. You pay your bill, say, on the thirtieth of every month. If the credit card company pays the merchant on the thirtieth of the following month, then it has the interest-free use of the merchant's money for one month until this debt is paid. When enough money is involved (and it is) and the flows are predictable (and they are), then this float can amount to literally billions of dollars which credit card companies invest and earn interest on during the period that the funds are floating from buyer to seller.

Traveler's check companies also use the idea of the float. Most folks think that the traveler's check companies make their profits from the 2 percent fee that buyers typically pay for these checks. Most of this issuance fee, however, goes to the institution which markets the checks. The traveler's check company makes its money on the float.

Here's the way the traveler's check float works. Suppose that you buy $500 in traveler's checks on July 1 because you are going on vacation. During the next month, you spend all $500 by giving them to merchants in exchange for goods and services. The merchants redeem your traveler's checks to a representative of the issuing company and will get paid about, say, September 1 (depending upon the time it takes to process the checks).

Notice the float here. You gave the traveler's check people $500 on July 1 and they didn't have to pay out anything until September. They have had interest-free use of that $500 for two months. In that time the money was invested and earned a considerable return. These investments can be of a long-term nature, too, since new traveler's checks are always being sold to replace old ones that are redeemed. The average float here is very large and very profitable. The float makes the simple conversion of a near money into a "real" money an interesting and profitable affair. Money orders work much the same way.

THE INTEREST RATE

Money, besides being something that is spent, is also a good which is exchanged. More specifically, money's services are exchanged when borrowing and lending takes place. Money exchanged in this way is called

credit. The interest rate is the price of credit. When I borrow money (obtain the use of someone else's money for a period of time) the interest rate is the price that I pay for the use of that money for the period of the loan.

Why must borrowers pay an interest rate? Why should money increase in value just because the borrower and the lender exchange it? The answer is that it is not just the money that is exchanged, but the command over resources that money represents. The borrower gains the power to purchase goods and services now (instead of waiting until an equal amount was saved). The lender gives up this ability. Lenders trade the power to purchase goods now for the right to purchase those things, instead, some time in the future when the loan is repaid. Because the borrower prefers to have consumption now (by borrowing) instead of later (by saving), he or she is willing to "bribe" lenders to give up money now. That "bribe" is the interest rate. On the other side, lenders, too, prefer present consumption to future consumption. They will only give up money now if they can be sure of trading it for even more consumption items in the future. Hence they must be bribed in order to delay consumption and make the loan.

All of this falls into what economists call **time preference.** People who want to have things now will be willing to pay something extra (the interest rate) in order to increase current consumption. Lenders are happy to delay consumption so long as they receive enough extra payment (interest, again) to make it worth their while to do so.

The interest rate, then, is the price of credit, and credit has a price because of people's preference for present consumption over future consumption. This gives us the idea of an interest rate, but it doesn't go far in explaining why there are different interest rates for different types of credit, or why interest rates can change over time. While time preference forms the basis for interest rates, it is not the only determinant of the interest rate. There are, in general, five factors which, added together make up the interest rate.

1. TIME PREFERENCE.

As we have discussed, time preference is the elementary particle in the calculus of interest rates. Time preference changes little over time. Economists estimate the interest rate stemming from time preference to be very low—maybe 2 percent. The other four factors will act to make different types of interest rates and different levels of interest rates over time.

2. RISK PREMIUM.

Loans are risky propositions. There is always a chance that the loan will not be repaid and that the lender will have to resort to legal means to gain repayment. A **risk premium,** then, is automatically added into interest rates as a kind of insurance to protect the lender from the

Credit: the temporary exchange of money among individuals, as when loans are made

Time preference: a component of the interest rate which results from simple preference for present over future consumption

Risk premium: a component of the interest rate which depends upon the relative risk of different forms of credit

default of the loan. This explains why some types of loans are more expensive than others. A credit card "loan," for example, is very costly (12–18 percent, depending on the laws of the state) because there is a high likelihood of default on the loan. The typical credit card loan is not secured by **collateral.** If you don't pay your credit card bill, it is very difficult for the bank to collect. They can't just come in and repossess your car or house or wallet. Therefore, the chance of nonpayment is high for credit card loans, and the high risk premium on these loans reflects this.

Housing loans, on the other hand, are less risky and therefore subject to lower risk premiums and lower interest rates. If you don't pay your mortgage, the bank *can* seize your house in lieu of payment. Because the loan is backed with this kind of collateral, the bank is assured of payment in some form. The risk is lower, and so is the interest rate.

Loans on new and used cars fall somewhere in between. While auto loans are secured by collateral (the car), there is more risk here because the car may be damaged or driven away. As a result, car loans carry a higher risk premium than home loans, but lower than credit card loans.

The reputation and economic status of the borrower also contribute to the risk premium. When General Motors needs to borrow money, for example, their risk premium is practically nil since their financial status and borrowing record indicates that payment will be forthcoming in almost any event (except, perhaps, intergalactic nuclear war). The very poor who may need money the most find that they, on the other hand, are considered a bad risk and must therefore pay "loan shark" interest rates for even small loans.

Since many loans are used to undertake investment projects, the profitability of the investment also enters into the determination of the risk premium. The risk premium on a loan to finance a new McDonald's Hamburger store is likely to be lower, for example, than one which will be used to bet on horses. You get the idea. The risk premium is one of the main reasons for different interest rates on different loans.

3. INFLATION PREMIUM. If the risk premium causes interest rate differentials at any point in time, inflation causes the general level of interest rates to change over time. We talked about this concept in Chapter 4. Because inflation effectively lowers the real value of loan repayments, it tends to distort the borrower/lender relationship. As a result, the expected rate of inflation over the term of a loan tends to get "built into" the interest rate on a loan. For example, if a bank were willing to lend you $1000 at 5 percent interest for one year if they expected no inflation, then they would probably want at least 10 percent interest if they expected prices to rise by 5 percent during the year. This relationship is shown in Figure 9-1. Higher

Collateral: assets which are held as security for a loan and may be seized if repayment is not made

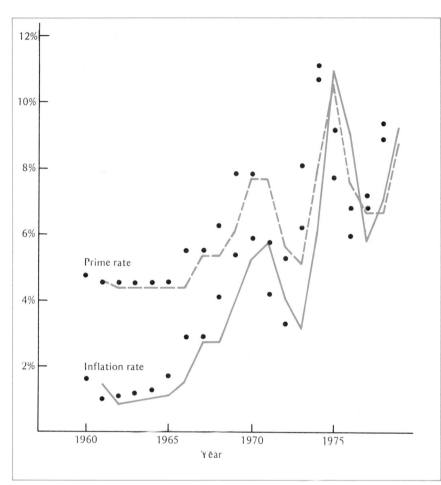

FIGURE 9-1: INFLATION AND INTEREST RATES
The effect of the inflation premium is seen here. The prime interest rate has risen and declined pretty much in step with changes in the inflation rate. Note that in the high-inflation years of the 1970s, the inflation rate exceeded the interest rate—giving a negative real interest rate!

inflation rates tend to cause higher interest rates, and interest rates come down as the inflation rate falls.

This is the reason why many people in business fear inflation more than unemployment. When inflation occurs, it tends to bid up interest rates. This affects businesses which must borrow to expand factories and buy equipment, and it also affects consumers who must borrow to buy the goods and services that these factories produce. Because inflation causes higher interest rates, it tends to discourage borrowing and therefore to lessen aggregate demand.

This **inflation premium** explains much of the variance in interest rates over the years. Why were interest rates on home loans over ten percent in the late 1970s, whereas they were about 5 percent only a few years before? The answer is that the expected inflation rate was much higher, so the inflation premium boosted up interest rates.

Inflation premium: a component of the interest rate resulting from changing anticipated inflation rates

4. ADMINISTRATIVE COSTS.

It costs something to process a loan, and the lender usually passes this cost on to the borrower. Some loans are very cheap to administer. With a home loan, for example, there is some paperwork when the loan is made, but then very little need be done for the next ten or twenty years. This is a relatively cheap loan to administer, so the cost premium (**administrative cost**) is low, causing the interest rate to be low.

A credit card loan, on the other hand, is very costly to handle. Paper must pass through many hands on a credit card transaction, and expensive computer time must also enter the picture every month to keep track of payments and debts and mail the monthly bill. None of this is cheap, and it contributes to the high cost of the credit card loan.

5. SCARCITY PREMIUM.

Sometimes money and credit are relatively more scarce than at other times. When this happens, the interest rates tend to rise to reflect this scarcity as banks and other financial institutions ration the scarce funds by lending to those who are willing to pay the most for the money's services. You've probably heard of this phenomenon called by the name *tight money*. When money is tight, this **scarcity premium** adds to the interest rate, causing the general level of interest rates to rise in the economy. The opposite of tight money is "easy money," and when this happens, interest rates tend to fall to reflect the general availability of money, credit, and loans in the economy.

The actual interest rate which is charged on any loan is the sum of these five costs: basic time preference plus the risk, inflation, and scarcity premiums, plus the administrative cost. Or at least this is what the interest rate usually is. Often the government intervenes into the money market to try to "protect" the borrower, lenders, or others. States set maximum interest rates that financial institutions may charge on loans. These **usury laws** prevent lenders from charging very high interest rates, even when cost, inflation, and risk make high interest rates necessary. Usury laws often actually end up hurting those who need to borrow money at very high interest rates. These groups are forced to borrow from illegal loan sharks who, because they are few in number and powerful, can extract even higher interest rates.

There is an interest rate which we hear a lot about in the news. It is called the **prime rate.** This isn't some kind of official government economic indicator, or even a kind of beef steak. The prime rate is set by individual banks. It is the lowest interest rate that the bank will offer, usually on loans to their best customers for short periods of time. The reason that we pay attention to the prime interest rate is that it serves as a general indicator of the level of interest rates in the economy. When the prime rate rises, for

Administrative costs: a component of the interest rate which depends on the cost of setting up and administering credit transactions

Scarcity premium: a component of the interest rate which depends upon the relative scarcity of credit at different times

Usury laws: state laws which set maximum legal interest rates on credit

Prime rate: the lowest interest rate that a bank charges on short-term loans example, this usually indicates that interest rates on all types of loans throughout the economy are rising. It tells us that tight money prevails. Likewise, cuts in the prime rate foretell a general lowering of interest rates on all kinds of loans throughout the economy.

The history of the prime rate is interesting. It came about during the Great Depression, when interest rates were going very low—as low as 2 percent. How could interest rates go so low? Think about it. During the Depression deflation was occurring—falling price levels. In a situation like this, there is a negative inflation premium built into the interest rates, causing them to fall with the price level. The banking industry got very concerned at the low level of interest rates—it is hard for a bank to make any money when interest rates are so low—so they developed the prime rate as a kind of floor to interest rates. They used the prime rate to hold the line on interest rate reductions. Since then, the prime rate has become another financial statistic—although an important one—which is useful in telling us what is going on in the financial part of the economy. We will learn more about how interest rates are determined in Chapter 10 when the credit market is examined.

MONEY AND BANKS

Since banks are such an important part of our system of money and credit, it is important that we learn how they work. Banks did not always exist. In days when all money was made of precious metals (gold, silver, etc.) the closest thing to a bank was a gold warehouse. In those days holding money (gold coins) was a risky business. You had to be on the constant lookout for thieves and protecting your money was very difficult (Robin Hood took advantage of this to promote his socialist schemes for redistribution of national income in Sherwood Forest). Since goldsmiths were well equipped to protect their gold, many people would pay the local goldsmith a small fee to store gold in his vault. They put their coins in the vault and received, in exchange, a receipt that could be redeemed at some later date for the stored gold.

This system of gold warehouses worked better than being robbed, but it was still inconvenient, since people had to go to the warehouse before they could spend their money. This took time, was expensive, and was still risky, since thieves might station themselves near the goldsmith shops. To get around these problems, two solutions were applied. The first was a system where the goldsmith gave not one receipt for a bag of gold, but a number of receipts—each worth a certain amount of gold—which would be paid to the bearer by the goldsmith on demand. These bearer receipts were the first currency. If the Sheriff of Nottingham, for example, wanted to pay his troops, he didn't have to go to the goldsmith, he had only to give his men receipts that were honored by the goldsmith. The workers could then either collect the gold themselves, or they could pass the receipts on to merchants in exchange for goods and services. The bearer receipts circulated in place of the gold and so, like our currency, acted as money.

The second solution was even simpler. Instead of issuing bearer receipts in exchange for gold, the goldsmith merely agreed to pay the gold to third parties on written instructions from the depositor. Therefore, when the Sheriff of Nottingham wanted to pay his troops, he simply gave to each of them a small note that said:

Dear Goldsmith:
Please pay to the order of Sir Gawain: 10 pieces of gold.
          Sincerely,
          Sheriff of Nottingham

This was, as you can see, the first checking account. In fact, the checks that you and I write even today take the form of a note to the bank (although now the note is read mostly by computers).

Currency and bank check innovations made transactions much easier to conclude and so speeded economic development. While these money substitutes were created for the convenience of the goldsmith's customers, they created an interesting situation for the goldsmith. Every day some people would come with bearer receipts or checks and withdraw gold from the smith's vault. But other people would show up with new gold to deposit (taken from other goldsmiths' vaults). On the average, this gold inflow was just balanced by the gold outflow. Most of the gold in the vault collected dust and never was used. Only a small fraction of the goldsmiths' gold was needed to back up the large amounts of deposit claims outstanding.

Fractional-reserve banking: the modern system of bank operation where only a fraction of deposits are held on reserve by the banking system while remaining funds are invested or loaned

Clever goldsmiths discovered that they could loan out most of these "excess reserves" and no one would be the wiser, since this spare gold was hardly ever called for because of the day-to-day balancing of deposits and withdrawals. This discovery lead to the creation of our current system of **fractional-reserve banks.**

FRACTIONAL-RESERVE BANKING

Today's banks operate much like the goldsmith warehouses. We deposit money into the bank and trust that it will be there when we call for it. The bank then loans out much of these funds at interest to generate profits for the bank and to pay interest on our deposits. When someone calls on the bank to collect a deposit (or cashes a check), the bank will have enough money to pay off that debt because of offsetting deposits by other customers and because it keeps a reserve of money on hand to handle situations when normal deposits aren't large enough to handle withdrawals.

What would happen if all of the bank's customers came for their money at once? The bank wouldn't be able to pay, since most of its funds have been loaned to people in the community. The bank would shut down in response to this "run" and depositors would lose all or some of their money, unless bank deposits were insured by a federal agency (most banks now carry this insurance).

As long as its customers trust the bank, however, this run never needs to happen. If we all act as if our money were safely in the vault, then each of us individually can, in fact, draw out whatever funds we need. If, on the other hand, we all mistrust the bank and so run to take our money out, the bank will fold and our deposits will disappear. The fractional-reserve bank, then, depends upon trust for its very existence.

The Federal Reserve System regulates the amount of money that banks must keep on reserve. The **reserve requirement** for money put in demand deposits is currently about 15 percent. This means that 15 percent of any new demand deposit must be kept on hand by the bank (in the bank's vault or, more often, in a special account at the local Federal Reserve Bank). The remaining 85 percent of demand deposit balances are called **excess reserves** and may be invested, kept in the vault, or as is usually the case, lent out at interest. For time deposits the reserve requirements are a little different. Because there are fewer withdrawals from time deposits, banks are only required to keep 5 percent as required reserves, and may lend out up to 95 percent of time deposit balances.

Figure 9-2 shows what actually happens to a new demand deposit as it enters a commercial bank. If a new demand deposit of $100,000 enters the banking system, about 15 percent will be transferred to the required reserve account at the Federal Reserve. This 15 percent will act to "back up" the new deposit. Any sudden withdrawals from the bank can generally be paid from this large reserve of funds. The remaining $85,000 then becomes excess reserves. Banks may keep some excess reserves on hand as vault cash. They may also invest part of these excess reserves in safe financial instruments like U.S. government bonds and Treasury bills. The bulk of it, however, is sent to the loan office where it is used to make loans for individuals and businesses.

Not surprisingly, the chain does not end here. When the bank loans out the $85,000 in excess reserves, this money does not just disappear. The persons who got the loans did not acquire this money only to let it sit in the bank. They took out the loans because they wanted to buy things with the

Reserve requirement: the proportion of total deposits that a bank must hold on reserve; determined by the FRS or by state law (for non-FRS banks)

Excess reserves: bank's holdings of reserves in excess of those required by law or FRS regulation

FIGURE 9-2: FRACTIONAL-RESERVE
BANKING

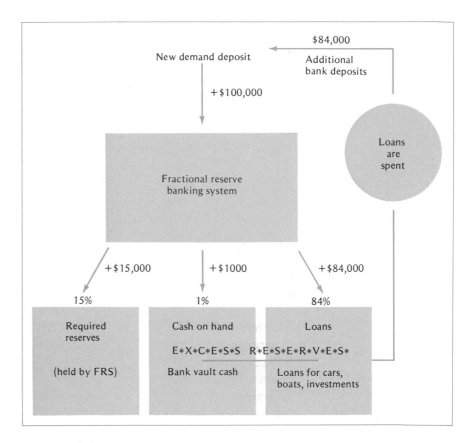

money. When they make their purchases, the money will go to the seller who, if he or she is typical, will then deposit these new funds right back into the banking system (although probably in a different bank). So a new loan tends to be recycled right back into the banking system in the form of additional new deposits.

HOW BANKS "CREATE" MONEY

The truth is that when banks make loans, they actually create money. Think about it. When a loan is made, the money is spent and whoever ends up with it generally deposits it in his or her bank. Suddenly, there are two bank deposits where before there was only one. In the previous example, the bank that ended up with the $85,000 loan money had $85,000 more than existed before the loan was made! Loans actually tend to increase the total amount of money in the banking system and in the economy.

This loan/deposit money creation process can go on for some time, much like the government-spending multiplier process in Chapter 8. To see how it

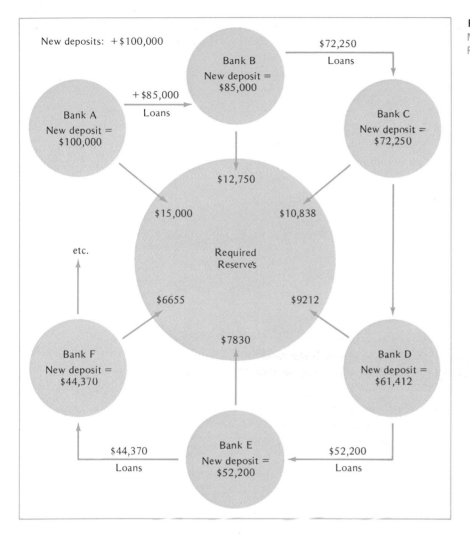

New deposits: +$100,000

Bank B
New deposit =
$85,000

Bank A
New deposit =
$100,000

+$85,000
Loans

$72,250
Loans

Bank C
New deposit =
$72,250

$12,750

$15,000 $10,838

Required
Reserves

etc.

$6655 $9212

$7830

Bank F
New deposit =
$44,370

Bank D
New deposit =
$61,412

$44,370
Loans

Bank E
New deposit =
$52,200

$52,200
Loans

FIGURE 9-3: HOW BANKS CREATE MONEY: THE DEPOSIT-EXPANSION PROCESS

works, examine Figure 9-3. Suppose that, again, a new deposit of $100,000 enters the banking system (we'll discuss where such a new deposit can come from in a moment). Fifteen percent of the new deposit will normally be put in the required reserve cache, while the remaining $85,000 will go to loans. These loans will then be spent, and the final recipients of the fund will deposit them in another bank (Bank B in the picture). Bank B will treat this new deposit just as Bank A dealt with the original $100,000. Again, 15 percent of the deposit will be sent to the Federal Reserve System as required reserves, while 85 percent ($72,250) will be loaned to customers of the bank. These borrowers will spend their loans, and whoever ends up with the money as a result of this spending will deposit it in another bank—Bank

C—where the process will repeat itself. Again, 15 percent of the deposit will be sent to the required reserve vault, while 85 percent ($61,412) will go to make new loans and create new money.

This loan/deposit/loan/deposit sequence will happen again and again until eventually all of the original money injection has leaked into required reserves. In the meantime, however, many many loans have been made using this original $100,000 deposit. It is a simple exercise (with a pocket calculator) to calculate the total amount of loans that have been made. Fortunately, there is a simple formula which will help us. If a new deposit enters the banking system, then the money supply will increase according to the following formula:

$$\text{Change in money supply} = \frac{1}{\text{Reserve requirement}} \times \text{Initial deposit}$$

Therefore, a $100,000 increase in initial deposits will cause the money supply to rise by a total of $666,667. Most of this increase—$566,667—is money which the banking system has "created" through the loan process. The remaining $100,000 is the initial deposit itself.

Deposit-expansion process: the process by which banks create money by loaning out funds acquired through deposits

This is called the **deposit-expansion process** and it is made possible by the fractional-reserve banking system. Even a relatively small injection into the banking system will be continuously recycled by the banks and create huge amounts of new credit and loans.

The formula just given actually overestimates the ultimate impact of an initial deposit on the banking system. Our formula assumes that all loans are eventually deposited into other banks (they may not be, some money may be held as cash or buried in tin cans), and it also assumes that banks lend out all their excess reserves, which is not always the case. Because some deposits do not go directly into demand deposits and all excess reserves are not loaned out, it follows that the real money multiplier is less than the 6.67 given here. In fact, some estimates are that a $1 new deposit may generate only a total of about $2 or $3 of total increase in the money supply. All of this depends, of course, upon what definition of money is used and the length of the time period counted.

The money multiplier tends to work best during periods when banks have few excess reserves on hand. At these times, any change in bank reserves is pretty quickly translated into changes in loan accounts. When banks have accumulated lots of excess reserves, however, the money creation process slows up significantly.

Where does a "new deposit" into the banking system come from? Actually, it can come from a variety of sources, but the most common source is—you guessed it—the Federal Reserve System.

The Federal Reserve System (the FRS for short, or simply the Fed to its friends and neighbors) was created in the early 1900s as a "Supreme Court" of banking. The Fed is a quasipublic corporation. That is, the Fed is a body owned and operated by banks which are members of the Federal Reserve System. For these members, the Fed performs a variety of useful services such as providing check-clearing services and making loans. The Fed also is involved in regulating its member banks. But the Fed has a public policy aspect, too. The Board of Governors of the Federal Reserve are appointed by the president, and they are involved in making national economic policy. Once the president appoints the FRS chiefs, however, they cannot easily be removed. Hence the Fed cannot be "controlled" by the president or the Congress the way other government agencies can. This is why it has been called the Supreme Court of banking. The Fed may form the fourth house of government.

Why is the Fed so important? As we have seen, the banking system can create money, credit, and loans which are necessary to the economic health of the nation. The FRS is the "banker's bank" and can control the total money and credit flows for the economy. The FRS uses three tools to control the supply of money and credit: open market operations, reserve requirement changes, and the discount rate.

THE FED

Open market operations are actions which the FRS takes to purchase or sell U.S. government securities (bonds) on the "open market." Over the years, the FRS has purchased literally billions of dollars of government bonds. They have purchased these bonds by "printing money" to pay for them (not literally, but the FRS does have the power to create money whenever it sees fit). The FRS uses open market sales and purchases of bonds to inject funds into the bank money-creation process. An example here will help.

Suppose that the FRS goes into the bond market and buys $10 million worth of U.S. government bonds from a private bond trader (a bank or an insurance company, for example). As a result of the bond market transaction the FRS has $10 million additional bonds in its vault, and the bond seller has a check for $10 million from the FRS. When the bond seller deposits this check in his bank, this represents a "new deposit" into the banking system and the bank will find an additional $10 million in its FRS account. The banking system, as we have seen, will take this new deposit and subject it to the loan/deposit/loan/deposit cycle of money creation. As a result, the FRS's

OPEN MARKET OPERATIONS

Open market operations: FRS sales and purchases of bonds designed to affect the money supply

$10 million open market purchase will cause the money supply to rise initially by $10 million, and eventually by as much as $66.7 million, as the deposit-expansion process takes its course.

Where does the FRS get the money to buy these bonds? It could, if necessary, actually have the cash printed up to make the purchase. Normally, however, a simpler accounting method is used. The FRS credits the bond-seller's bank with additional reserves equal to the amount of the open market purchase. Because the bank has more reserves, the economy has more money and the loan/deposit process is started.

An open market sale works in just the opposite direction. When the FRS sells a bond on the open market, they give up the bond, but they get money in return. This money then leaves the money supply—since it is in the FRS vault, it is no longer available for use by banks or individuals, so the money supply falls. Therefore, a $10 million open market sale will make the money supply fall, initially, by $10 million. It is possible that, once the initial $10 million has left the money supply, another multiplier effect will take place so as to make the money supply fall by more than $10 million. While this is possible in theory, it seldom happens. An open market sale lowers the money supply initially, and in the process lowers the amounts of excess reserves in the banking system. This restricts the amount of loans that banks can make in the future, and therefore slows the natural money-creation process.

To summarize open market operations, a $10 million open market purchase will inject $10 million into the money supply, and the banking system will take this new deposit and, through the deposit-expansion process, create additional funds so that the total increase in the money supply will be as much as $66.7 million. An open market sale, on the other hand, would remove $10 million from the money supply and lower the amount of reserves left in the banking system for future loans.

The open market operation is the main FRS tool for regulating the supply of money and credit in the economy. Every week the FRS enters the bond market to buy or sell (or sometimes buy *and* sell) government securities. Since this tool is used so often—and since the exact amounts bought and sold are not released for several weeks—open market operations can be effective without being disruptive to the financial sector of the economy. Open market operations are used as the main tool of FRS policy because they are so very powerful. The only disadvantage to open market operations is that FRS open market policies are kept secret (in order to prevent insiders from gaining from advance knowledge of FRS actions), so that it is difficult for bankers and others to immediately tell what the Fed is up to. These days, however, the FRS is making it a policy to tell the economy what their general plans are, so this disadvantage is becoming less of a problem.

The Federal Reserve can also affect the supply of money and credit by making changes in the reserve requirement. The Fed has broad latitude in setting the reserve requirements on demand and time deposits for member banks, and this tool can have a large impact on the money supply.

RESERVE REQUIREMENT POLICY

Suppose that the FRS were to lower the reserve requirement on demand deposits from about 15 percent to about 10 percent. What impact would this have on banks? Well, since banks now have lower reserve requirements, this suggests that some of the funds that had previously been tied up in required reserves on deposit at the Fed can now be removed from the FRS vaults and used to make loans. These loans (created money) will be recycled throughout the banking system, causing the money supply to rise dramatically. A lowered reserve requirement, then, frees some of the required reserves and allows banks to expand loans all around the economy.

If the FRS were to raise the reserve requirement, just the opposite effect would prevail. With a higher reserve requirement, banks would have to allocate even more funds to the FRS required reserve accounts. This would leave them with less money available for loans, and so the money creation process would slow and, in an extreme case, the money supply could even fall.

Lower reserve requirements, then, tend to create excess reserves which are used to make additional loans and so expand the money supply. Higher reserve requirements tend to destroy excess reserves (since they become, instead, required reserves) and so restrict the ability of the banking system to make loans and create money.

The principal advantage of reserve requirement policy is that it is very powerful. A small cut in the reserve requirement, because it will affect huge total amounts of required reserves, can make the money supply rise very quickly or, if the reserve requirement is increased, create a "tight money" situation with equal speed. While this power is a great advantage, it is also a great disadvantage. Such large swings in the amount of required reserves necessary are not popular among bankers. They would prefer that the money supply be manipulated through less disruptive means—like open market operations. As a result, the reserve requirement is changed infrequently, generally only when the FRS wants to make the directions of its actions very clear.

Discount rate: the interest rate charged by the FRS on short-term loans to member banks

The **discount rate** is an interest rate. When FRS member banks fall below the average reserve requirement for a time, the FRS will lend them the funds necessary to meet the required level, and the discount rate is the interest rate charged on these loans. The discount rate, then, is the interest rate on FRS

DISCOUNT RATE POLICY

loans to member banks. The discount rate is seldom used—because banks don't very often borrow from the FRS—yet it is still a key economic variable. How can this be?

First of all, banks don't borrow money from the FRS very much because the Fed tends to view this as a sign that the bank is being unnecessarily reckless in its operations. If a bank borrows from the FRS very much, they will likely get audited and checked over more frequently, and this is a pain. As a result most banks, if they have trouble getting up enough required reserves, will borrow from other commercial banks (who have some excess reserves sitting around) instead of the FRS. If this is the case, then why does it make a difference what the discount rate is?

The discount rate is used by the FRS as a signaling device. When the Fed lowers the discount rate, this is meant to signal the banking community that the FRS wants them to be liberal in making loans and expanding the money supply. The Fed is saying, in effect, "Make lots of loans, and if you get in trouble, you can borrow from us for cheap." The banks buy this line of reasoning largely because the discount rate is generally used together with other tools, like open market operations. So when the Fed lowers the discount rate, banks immediately begin to expand loans and, pretty soon, the FRS injects more money into the system to help finance these loans.

When the Fed raises the discount rate, this signals the banking system that the Fed wishes them to be more conservative in their loan practices. They should make fewer loans and slow the money-creation process. Very often the Fed will accompany an increase in the discount rate with other actions, like open market sales, designed to further restrict the money supply.

Because the discount rate acts as a signal telling the economy what the FRS intends to do, it is a very important item to keep track of. Any change in the discount rate will make news, appearing prominently on the front page of the *Wall Street Journal,* making headlines in the financial section of daily newspapers, and even showing up on TV news programs. Because the discount rate is so visible, the FRS will change it when they want to make clear to the economy the direction that they are heading.

These three tools of FRS policy are used to expand, restrict, and sometimes contract the money supply in the economy. Obviously, these actions have great impact on banks and other financial institutions, but they also are important to other parts of the economy since these funds, through loans, finance business investments and consumer purchases. This makes the Federal Reserve an extremely powerful force within the economy. As Senator Hubert Humphrey once said, "The guy who controls the money supply, he's in charge, and the rest of us are just playing ring-around-the-rosy." This perhaps overstates the impact of money on the economy, but not by much. In the next chapter we will investigate the total impact of changes in the money supply on the economy and explore further the tools of monetary policy.

SUMMARY

1. Money is anything which is generally accepted in exchange for goods and services and in payment of debt. Many things have served as money throughout history. Today we generally define money as currency and demand deposit balances, although many forms of "near-money" exist which can act like money under certain circumstances.

2. Interest rates are, in the end, determined by the credit market (which will be discussed in Chapter 10). In general, the interest rate which prevails on any type of credit is made up of a time preference factor plus risk and inflation premiums and components reflecting administrative costs and the relative scarcity of credit.

3. Modern banks are fractional-reserve banks. When a deposit is made, only a small fraction of these funds are held on reserve, with the larger part invested or loaned at interest. This seemingly reckless behavior is sound because of normally offsetting deposits and withdrawals and by the existence of government insurance programs.

4. Banks create money by making loans. Even a relatively small injection into the banking system can create a large increase in the supply of money and credit through the deposit-expansion process.

5. The Federal Reserve System acts to regulate member banks. The FRS controls the amounts of money and credit available through the tools of open market operations, reserve requirement policy, and changes in the discount rate.

DISCUSSION QUESTIONS

1. Suppose that you are a Peace Corps worker in primitive New Guinea. The tribe that you are working with trades using the barter system. The tribe is prosperous and growing. Convince the chief of the tribe of the advantages of using a money system instead of barter.

2. Who or what "backs up" the money in your pocket? Does it make a difference to you? Explain.

3. Which would likely have the higher interest rate: a car loan in 1965 or a house loan in 1977? Explain.

4. Under what circumstances would a negative interest rate make sense? Is this likely to happen today?

5. What is the prime interest rate today? Does this level of interest rate make sense in terms of the determinants of interest rates discussed in the text? Justify your answer.

6. Modern banks are fractional-reserve banks. What does that mean? How can you possibly put your trust in a bank (and also put your money there) when they behave the way that a fractional-reserve bank does?

7. Define the following terms:

☐ Required reserves
☐ Excess reserves
☐ Open market sale
☐ Open market purchase
☐ Discount rate

8. Suppose that the FRS buys $50 million in bonds on the open market. Trace the impact of this action on the banking system, the money supply, and the amount of loans in the economy. What will be the total impact of this action on the money supply? What factors could make the total impact less than the total suggested by the deposit expansion formula?

9. Bus tokens are an example of a near-money. Bus tokens are sometimes sold at a discount when large quantities are purchased. Use the concept of the "float" to explain why these discount sales make sense.

TEST YOURSELF

Indicate whether each of the following statements is *true* or *false*. Be able to defend your choice.

1. Checking accounts are not counted as "money" because checks are not accepted everywhere in payment for goods and services.

2. The "float" occurs when a middleman collects from one party before paying to another and has interest-free use of the money during the interval.

3. It doesn't make any difference in terms of the deposit-expansion formula what type of bank or bank account that funds are deposited in. All banks create money equally.

4. Suppose that the reserve requirement is 10 percent and that the FRS undertakes an open market purchase of $50 million. This will cause the total amount of loans in the economy to rise by $450 million.

5. Suppose that the reserve requirement is 10 percent and that the FRS undertakes an open market sale of $50 million. This will cause the money supply to fall by $500 million.

6. Excess reserves are bank money holdings over and above the amounts required by the FRS.

7. The discount rate affects the money supply by signaling FRS intentions to financial intermediaries.

8. Interest rates are higher these days because of the relatively high inflation premiums.

9. The interest rate on government bonds is lower than the interest rate on car loans because the government has a relatively lower inflation premium.

10. An increase in the reserve requirement would increase total loans.

10
Money, Credit, and the Economy

This chapter describes how the financial sector works and how it affects aggregate demand and the economy. Some of the questions that this chapter will answer include the following:

What is the difference between the stock market and the credit market?

What factors affect the demand for credit?

How are interest rates set?

What is disintermediation and what causes it?

How is the "inflation premium" built into interest rates?

How do changes in the interest rate affect aggregate demand?

How can the FRS act to increase or decrease aggregate demand?

Now that we know how banks work and how credit can be created by the Federal Reserve and banking system, it is important for us to understand how all of this affects the economy. In order to do this, we will discuss two important concepts. The first is the **credit market.** The credit market sets interest rates in the economy and determines the amount and kinds of loans that are made.

Credit market: the financial market where loanable funds are exchanged; made up of borrowers and lenders

Events in the credit market affect the economy through the **monetary transmission mechanism**—the link between the credit market and aggregate supply and demand. We will examine this link and see how it can be used to induce actions in the private sector through manipulation of interest rates.

Monetary transmission mechanism: the process whereby monetary policies affect AD and AS through their impact on interest rates and investment spending

Finally, we will briefly examine **monetary policy**—FRS actions designed to guide the economy through the control of forces in the credit market.

Monetary policy: policies designed to affect the economy by regulating the availability of money and credit

If all of this sounds complicated, it isn't. An understanding of the credit markets and the monetary transmission mechanism requires only a basic understanding of the forces of supply and demand and aggregate supply and demand. The chain reactions are logical, consistent, and predictable.

THE CREDIT MARKET

The credit market, like any other market, is made up of buyers and sellers. The interesting thing about this market is, of course, the item that is bought and sold: money's services. The demanders of credit wish to secure loans. The sellers of credit—banks, savings institutions, insurance companies, and private individuals—wish to make loans. Credit demanders (loan seekers) wish to acquire credit at the lowest possible price. The price of credit is the interest rate. Credit sellers, on the other hand, want to hold out for the highest interest rate available. Both sides are affected by the conflict and competition inherent in any market. In the end, the interest rate will be used to ration the scarce credit to those who are most willing and able to pay for it.

The credit market in the real world is divided into many submarkets with characteristics of their own. The **federal funds market,** for example, deals with short-term credit of a specific nature. Banks borrow from or lend to other banks on the federal funds market for the purpose of meeting weekly legal reserve requirement averages. The interest rate in this market reflects the anticipated inflation rate and credit scarcity in the short term. The federal funds market is relatively centralized, and efficiently responds to market forces.

Federal funds market: the financial market where banks lend excess reserves to each other

The **mortgage credit market,** on the other hand, is less centralized and really has many submarkets of its own. Since mortgage loans are normally written for twenty- or thirty-year periods, this credit market deals with the

Mortgage credit market: the financial market where loans are made for homes, buildings, and so on

long-term use of funds. The credit suppliers here are savings institutions, insurance and mortgage companies, and, to a certain extent, the federal government. The government, through a variety of credit supply and guaranteed loan programs, has considerable influence in this long-term credit market.

For short-term and long-term credit, borrowers and lenders often participate in the various **bond markets.** A bond is just an IOU issued by a government or private corporation. It is a promise to pay a certain amount at some specified time in the future (plus in many cases, periodic interest payments as well). When a government or corporation sells a bond, they are, in fact, borrowing money, and the bond represents their promise to repay the loan to whomever owns the bond certificate when the loan comes due. Because these bonds are transferable, the buyers of bonds (lenders of credit) can resell their certificates at any time in the future when they, too, need money. This creates a competitive market for the bonds that are issued and that already exist.

Bond market: the financial market where bonds (i.e., IOUs issued by governments, businesses, and others) are exchanged

Here's how a typical bond transaction might work. Suppose that the Noah County School Board wants to raise money to pay for a new gymnasium. They would normally do this by "floating" a bond issue. You might, then, be able to purchase a Noah County bond certificate which represents a promise to pay $1000 in one year (a one-year loan). Would you pay $1000 for this promise? Clearly not. There is no profit in paying $1000 for the right to receive $1000 in one year. Therefore, Noah County will have to **discount** the bond in order to get their money. By discounting we mean that they will sell the $1000 bond for *less than* $1000. The difference between the selling price and the face value of the bond ($1000) represents the interest that Noah County pays for the loan.

Discount: the difference between the face value and the selling price of a bond; the interest rate on a bond

Suppose that you pay $900 for the $1000 Noah County bond. This means that you are receiving $100 interest on a $900 investment for an implicit interest rate of $100/$900 = 11 percent. This is basically how interest is paid on bonds. The lower the price of the bond, the higher is the interest rate (if you had purchased the bond for $850, for example, the return would have been $150/$850 = 17.6 percent). Similarly, high bond prices mean low interest rates (a $1000 one-year bond which sells for $950 earns just $50/$950 = 5.3 percent interest). Once a bond is sold by the issuer (the initial loan is made) it can be sold and resold again and again as bondholders seek money and bond purchasers attempt to gain high-interest earnings.

There are markets for long-term, short-term, corporate, and state and local government bonds (interest income from state and local bonds is not taxed by the federal government, which makes this market attractive to households in high tax brackets). One good way to get a feel for what is happening to interest rates around the economy is to watch bond prices, remembering that bond prices and interest rates are inversely related.

The credit market is made up of many separate and distinct parts. In general, however, these different parts all yield to the same pressures. While there are instances where it is important to distinguish among the several submarkets, in general we can talk about a single credit market and our conclusions will be accurate when applied to the separate credit submarkets as well.

THE STOCK MARKET

Stock market: markets like the New York Stock Exchange where shares representing ownership of corporations are bought and sold

Equity: ownership of an asset

Dividends: corporation profits which are paid to stockholders

Appreciation: a gain in value of any asset (e.g., stock, bond, house, or currency)

Before we go on to examine the operation of the credit market, let's take a moment to look at another, related market: the **stock market.** Whereas the credit market deals with the buying and selling of debt, the stock market is interested in transactions involving **equity** or ownership of assets. Stock certificates are symbols of ownership in a firm. If you own one share of Mike's Livestock, Inc. (which buys sheep and sells deer) and there are a total of 1000 shares outstanding, then you own 1/1000 of the company and are entitled to 1/1000 of any profits that the company may generate.

Stocks have value because they can generate income in two ways. First, when a company is profitable, some or all of its earnings are normally distributed to the owners of the firm (the shareholders) in the form of **dividends.** Stock certificates have value because they represent the right to receive the dividends of a profitable company. (Not all of a company's profits are paid out in dividends, however; some part is often retained for investment.)

If other people would like to own a piece of Mike's Livestock, Inc., they may be willing to pay more for your share than you paid for it originally. This is the second way to gain from stock ownership—**appreciation** of the stock. Of course, the value of the stock can fall as well as rise, so there is no guarantee of profits here. And dividends can dry up during hard times. So stock ownership contains some element of risk.

Where do these stock certificates come from in the first place? Stocks are issued by companies that wish to raise money by selling part or all of themselves to the public—"going public" is the Wall Street term. They could, of course, raise the money by issuing bonds instead, but the issuance of stock carries with it no promise of future payment (the shareholders hope to see dividends, but they are not assured of actually receiving them), whereas bonds normally are paid off eventually.

Who owns stock? Many of us have pictures of rich stock speculators being the prime movers on the stock market. This picture is wrong. Many middle-income families have stock holdings, and a lot of people have a stake in the stock market through their participation in life insurance or pension plans. These institutional investors (insurance companies, pension funds, mutual funds, etc.) account for a large proportion of the stocks which are bought and sold.

The stock market and the credit market are closely related because financial investors, in general, have their choice of earning profits either through the ownership of stock shares or by lending their funds on the credit market. Because stocks and bonds are in many ways substitutes for one another, the prices of stocks and interest rate on credit are inversely related. When interest rates are high, for example, many financial investors will sell their stocks in order to gain the higher yields available on the credit market. This will, of course, bid down the price of stock shares. High interest rates, therefore, often produce low stock market prices. When interest rates are low, on the other hand, lenders will be tempted to purchase stock shares. So they will take their money out of lending institutions and buy stocks instead. This will have the tendency to bid up the price of the stocks. Low interest rates, then, often produce higher stock prices.

There is more to the stock market than this, of course. Stock prices can rise and fall because of the profitability of individual companies, the prospects for national economic growth, and investor expectations concerning future events. But the interest rate effects are clearly important to stock marketeers, and Wall Street analysts keep one eye closely fixed on developments in the credit market.

DEMAND FOR CREDIT

Many people are involved in the demand side of the credit market. It is useful, however, to pare the list down and look at the behavior of three basic groups that have normal need of credit: households, businesses and governments.

Households have need of credit in order to purchase goods and services. Cars, boats, houses, and educations are all often purchased using borrowed funds. The credit market allows consumers to have goods and services now and pay for them a little at a time over a period of years. Credit makes life easier and more convenient; providing consumer credit is one of the important functions of the credit market.

Consumer loans for cars, recreational vehicles, and the like are taken for relatively short periods of time (normally, less than four years) and in relatively small amounts. These loans (plus credit card loans) are generally obtained from commercial banks or credit unions. Mortgage loans (used to purchase real estate), on the other hand, are long-term in nature (up to thirty years) and involve many thousands of dollars. Most of this credit is obtained from savings institutions (savings-and-loan associations, mutual savings banks) and mortgage companies.

Businesses also need credit for many different purposes. Businesses need long-term loans in order to undertake investment opportunities. Plants, equipment, and assembly lines are costly and are normally financed with large loans which are paid off over the life of the equipment purchased. Businesses also need short-term loans for use in purchasing inventories. A farmer, for example, may borrow in the spring to purchase seed and fertilizer and repay the loan in the fall when the harvest comes in. But he will also need to undertake long-term loans to finance new equipment or the purchase of farmland.

Since investment spending is important to both aggregate demand and aggregate supply, the effect of changes in the credit market on business borrowing will be of central concern to us.

Governments also need credit. Federal, state, and local governments all borrow money, but for different reasons. The federal government borrows funds (deficit spending) generally as a part of fiscal policies designed to fight inflation or unemployment, and during periods of national emergency, as during wartime. State and local governments also borrow money, but this is done in order to finance capital expenditures—the building of roads, schools, bridges, and dams, for example. Since some of these capital expenditures can increase the productive ability of the economy (i.e., a new hydroelectric plant increases the supply of electricity for industry), some of this state and local borrowing can act to increase aggregate supply for the economy.

The total demand for credit is influenced by a variety of things. Business confidence, consumer desires, government deficits, school enrollments—all of these and more can cause the demand for credit to change. In general, however, four main demand determinants are important:

1. INTEREST RATES. The quantity of credit demanded is most directly influenced by the general level of interest rates. As interest rates fall, credit becomes cheaper and more of it is demanded. Higher interest rates, on the other hand, discourage borrowing.

In looking at interest rates, however, it is important to distinguish between the **nominal interest rate** and the **real interest rate** (this distinction was made earlier in Chapter 4). The nominal interest rate is the rate of interest that is actually paid or received on the credit market. The real interest rate is the rate that prevails after the effects of inflation are taken into account. The difference is important.

Suppose that you can borrow money to purchase a car from your bank at

Nominal interest rate: the interest rate unadjusted for inflation

Real interest rate: the interest rate adjusted for inflation

10 percent interest for three years. Is this a good interest rate or a bad one? The answer to this question depends, of course, on what the competition is offering and on what the inflation rate will be over the life of the loan. If the inflation rate averages only 3 percent, for example, then a loan with a nominal interest rate of 10 percent will have a real interest rate of 7 percent. That is, after inflation is accounted for, the borrower has paid back 7 percent more purchasing power than was initially borrowed.

If the inflation rate is 8 percent over this period, however, then the real interest rate is just 2 percent. The loan is relatively cheap in this case. If you had saved up for the car instead of borrowing in order to pay for it, each saved dollar would have lost 8 percent per year in value. Since you would have "paid" 8 percent to inflation anyway, the car loan only cost you 2 percent additional. This is the logic of the real interest rate.

One reason that we pay attention to the real interest rate is that people make many decisions based upon the real rather than the nominal interest rate. Thus, people who expect prices (and wages) to rise swiftly in the future are willing to pay high nominal interest rates for loans, betting that the high inflation will lower the real interest burden for them. This brings us to the second determinant of credit demand:

2. INFLATION AND INFLATION EXPECTATIONS. Besides affecting the real interest rate, inflation also affects the quantity of credit demanded in other ways. As prices rise, the amount and size of loans that consumers and businesses demand tends to rise, too. This occurs for two reasons. First, some households will attempt to increase their debt as a hedge against expected inflation. Since most recent inflations have been "surprise" inflation (i.e., higher-than-expected inflation rates), borrowers have tended to gain. Households that borrow now and purchase goods and services at today's lower prices can sometimes beat inflation.

The quantity of credit demanded will also rise because inflation boosts the prices of the things that households and businesses want to purchase. If houses, cars, trucks, and machines have higher prices, then the size of the loans necessary to purchase them will rise as well. Inflation, therefore, increases the demand for credit.

3. INCOME. The demand for credit will also rise as the national income rises. As households attain higher standards of living, they can afford to purchase better houses, more expensive cars and luxuries like boats, motor homes, or vacation properties.

Rising incomes, then, allow people to expand their consumption by expanding their debt. Falling incomes, on the other hand, cause people to cut back on expenditures and often to use less credit. The relationship between income and credit use is really just an extension of the link between income and consumption. Credit is a way of extending the time frame over which consumption goods are purchased.

4. FISCAL POLICIES. Finally, the demand for credit is very much affected by the policies undertaken by federal, state, and local governments. In 1977, for example, the federal government owed over $700 billion to a variety of creditors, including the Federal Reserve and other governments. Whenever governments spend more than they take in through taxation, the resulting deficits must be financed by borrowing. This adds to the demand for credit and affects interest rates, as we shall see later.

THE CREDIT DEMAND CURVE

The easiest way to model the workings of the credit market is through the use of supply-and-demand analysis. The credit demand curve (CD) is shown in Figure 10-1. This curve shows the relationship between the quantity of credit that households, businesses, and governments demand and the nominal interest rate (given fixed incomes, fiscal policies, and inflation expectations). This curve is labelled CD (instead of just D for demand) to denote that it is a very specific demand—the demand for credit.

The credit demand curve is downward-sloping to indicate the inverse relationship between the interest rate and the amount of credit demanded. As the price of credit falls, more of it is demanded.

The demand curve for credit will shift whenever any one of the basic

FIGURE 10-1: THE DEMAND FOR CREDIT

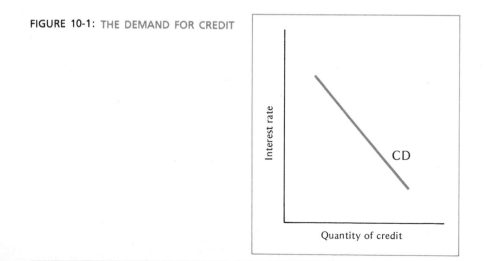

determinants of credit demand is altered. Credit demand will *increase,* for example, if

☐ Higher inflation rates are expected;

☐ National income rises;

☐ Local governments borrow more for school and road construction;

☐ The federal government borrows as part of fiscal policy; or

☐ Businesses expect high profits in the future and so increase investment spending now.

An increase in credit demand is shown in Figure 10-2 as a rightward shift in the CD curve.

The total demand for credit will fall (shift to the left, as shown in Figure 10-3) if events occur which reduce the need for credit and loans. The demand for credit would fall, then, if the following situations occurred:

☐ Falling expectations of inflation, which reduce the amount of hedging which takes place through borrowing.

☐ A fall in national income, which reduces the amount that households wish to borrow.

☐ A change in the corporate income tax, which discourages business investment spending and so reduces borrowing for this purpose.

☐ A fall in governmental borrowing because of changing national economic priorities.

FIGURE 10-2: INCREASE IN CREDIT DEMAND **FIGURE 10-3:** DECREASE IN CREDIT DEMAND

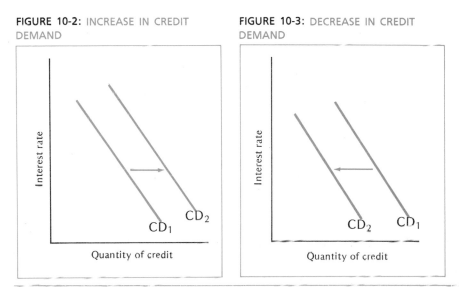

THE SUPPLY OF CREDIT

The other side of the market is made up of lenders—those who are involved in supplying credit. The supply side of this market is made up of a large number of different types of lending organizations. Banks, both commercial and savings, are obviously suppliers of credit. So are other firms and households who have more money than they desire at some time. Pension systems, insurance companies, and credit unions are all part of the supply of credit.

A principal participant in the credit supply is the Federal Reserve System. The FRS can control the amount of credit available through its member banks directly and can influence the amount of credit available elsewhere as well. The FRS, then, is a major determinant of the supply of credit in the economy.

A typical credit supply curve is shown in Figure 10-4. The credit supply curve (denoted CS to distinguish it from other supplies) is upward-sloping to show a direct relationship between the interest rate and the quantity of credit supplied. As interest rates rise, a number of forces act to increase the amount of credit available. Households, for example, will respond to higher interest rates by holding less of their money as checking account balances and put more into interest-earning savings accounts. Since savings accounts have lower reserve requirements than demand deposits, more loans can be made and the amount of credit rises.

Banks and savings institutions respond to higher interest rates by holding even fewer excess reserves. With more loans being made, the money multiplier will generate more credit. At high enough interest rates, banks may even borrow from the FRS in order to loan the money to customers. At

FIGURE 10-4: SUPPLY OF CREDIT

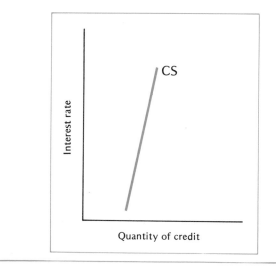

high interest rates, too, financial investors will shift from stocks into bonds and savings certificates and so further increase credit availability. Falling interest rates will reverse all of these movements and result in smaller quantities of credit supplied.

The supply curve of credit will shift whenever something happens to change the amount of credit available at any interest rate. The supply of credit will *increase*, for example, when

- ☐ The FRS undertakes an open market purchase;
- ☐ The FRS lowers the reserve requirement;
- ☐ The FRS lowers the discount rate;
- ☐ Bankers decide to hold fewer excess reserves;
- ☐ Banks which are not part of the FRS succeed in having their reserve requirements lowered; or
- ☐ Loanable funds enter the country from abroad.

Any of these activities would cause a shift to the right in the CS curve, which signifies an increase in credit supply.

A decrease in the supply of credit (shown by a shift to the left in the CS curve) could be caused by anything which lowered the amount of loanable funds available in the economy. A *decrease* in credit supply will be brought about if

- ☐ The FRS undertakes an open market sale;
- ☐ The FRS increases the reserve requirement;
- ☐ The FRS increases the discount rate;
- ☐ Insurance companies decide to invest their funds in the stock market instead of loans; or
- ☐ International banks decide to supply funds to countries other than the United States.

In looking at the supply of credit, we will be principally interested in changes which are brought about as a result of FRS actions affecting the reserve requirement and discount rate and through open market operations. The FRS attempts to influence the course of the economy by affecting the supply of credit. How do they do this? To understand, we need to put together the credit market.

THE CREDIT MARKET AT WORK

Borrowers and lenders meet in the credit market to wheel, deal, and determine interest rates. Lenders make up the credit supply curve shown in Figure 10-5, and borrowers form the credit demand curve. In this hypothetical credit market, equilibrium occurs at an interest rate of 6 percent. At 6 percent, the quantity of credit that borrowers wish to acquire (measured in dollars) is equal to the amount of credit that lenders wish to extend.

The credit market is stable in the sense that, whenever the interest rate differs from the equilibrium, market forces are at work to bring borrowers and lenders back into line. Suppose, for example, that the interest rate were temporarily shifted to 8 percent. At an 8 percent interest rate, as illustrated in Figure 10-5, there would be a surplus of credit. At the high interest rate, the supply of credit would be very large. This would be the case because banks

FIGURE 10-5: THE CREDIT MARKET
The credit market determines the equilibrium rate of interest for the economy (here 6 percent). At any interest rate different from 6 percent, market forces exist which will move interest rates back toward equilibrium.

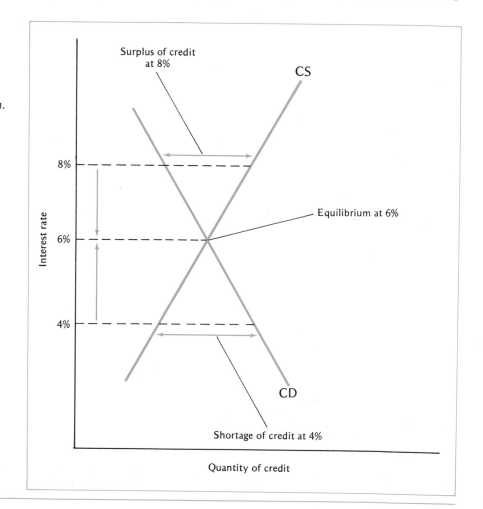

and other lending institutions would increase loans (and lower holdings of excess reserves) at these high interest rates. In addition, some financial investors would shift their holdings from the stock market to the credit market. They would want to lend out the proceeds of their stock sales at these relatively high returns.

The quantity of credit demanded, on the other hand, is relatively low at 8 percent interest. Borrowers are deterred by high interest rates. Businesses find that their investments are not profitable when funded at this high cost. The demand for credit, therefore, is low and the surplus prevails. Lenders will see that the surplus exists because they will find themselves with unintended inventory accumulations of money! Banks, loaded with excess reserves, will have trouble making loans. Some banks will begin to advertise their excess funds in an attempt to increase loans. A more effective strategy, however, would be to put money "on sale." In response to the surplus of loanable funds, the interest rate will begin to fall as lenders decide that they would rather earn a lower interest rate than not lend their funds at all. Falling interest rates lower the quantity of credit supplied, but increase the quantity demanded. The result is an eventual fall to a 6 percent interest rate and equilibrium.

Suppose, on the other hand, that interest rates should, for some reason, be below the equilibrium interest rate as, for example, the 4 percent interest rate illustrated in Figure 10-5. At low interest rates the supply of credit declines. Lending institutions may decide to hold larger quantities of excess reserves during low-interest periods. Financial investors, as well, may choose to hold more stocks and less debt when interest rates are low. The quantity of credit supplied will be smaller, although perhaps not greatly so, than at the 6 percent equilibrium.

The demand for credit, of course, will be high at this relatively low interest rate. Borrowers will view credit as a bargain and desire to acquire large amounts for investing, homebuying, and other reasons. This will result in a shortage of credit—tight money. Lending institutions will discover unintended inventory reductions in money—more people will ask for loans than there are excess reserves available. Faced with a shortage of credit, lenders will begin to ration the tight money by lending to those who will pay the most. Borrowers act to bid up the interest rates. As the interest rates rise, the forces of supply and demand creep back into balance and equilibrium is restored again at the market's 6 percent solution.

The equilibrium will prevail until something happens to alter the desires of either borrowers or lenders. Such a change is shown in Figure 10-6. Here, an increase in national income has increased the demand for credit. Since households have greater incomes, they wish to purchase newer cars, better houses, and the like and so desire larger quantities of credit in order to make

FIGURE 10-6: INCREASE IN CREDIT
DEMAND
*An increase in income causes a rising
credit demand which bids up interest
rates.*

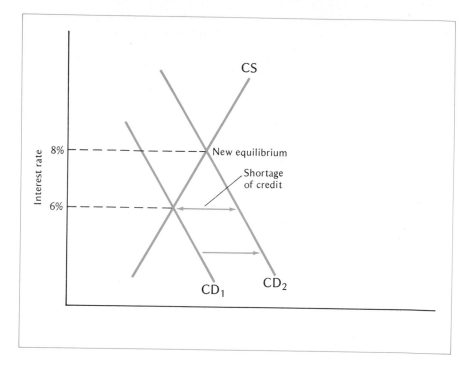

these purchases. This increase in credit demand throws the market out of equilibrium. The market was in equilibrium at 6 percent interest. Now, with the larger credit demand, a shortage of credit prevails at this interest rate. Lending institutions find that they haven't enough excess reserves to go around, and so begin to tighten credit and increase interest rates. With credit scarce, only those who are willing to pay the most will receive loans. The interest rate is bid up and equilibrium is eventually restored at a higher interest rate of 8 percent.

The Federal Reserve can also influence interest rates through money market actions. Let's suppose that we are back at the 6 percent initial equilibrium shown in Figure 10-7. Now assume that the FRS acts to increase the money supply through an open market purchase. As we saw in Chapter 9, an open market purchase increases the amount of money and credit in the financial system. As the deposit-expansion process takes place, the supply of credit is increased, since all of the money that banks "create" is produced through the creation of loans and credit.

The FRS action here produces a surplus of credit at the initial equilibrium. The credit market was in equilibrium, but the FRS has increased bank reserves. Lending institutions find themselves with an unintended inventory accumulation of money. They respond by increasing their loans through the best way available: cutting the interest rate. Lenders will bid down the

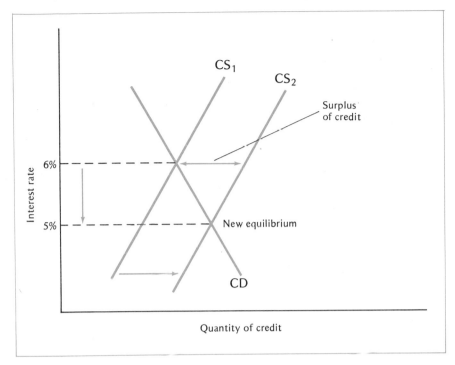

FIGURE 10-7: INCREASE IN CREDIT SUPPLY
An increase in the credit supply drives down interest rates.

interest rate and, as interest rates fall, the market will regain the equilibrium, this time at a 5 percent rate of interest.

It is interesting to note that this fall in interest rates occurs while the deposit-expansion process is taking place. The FRS pumps reserves into the banking system. In order to profitably use those reserves, lenders must cut interest rates. As interest rates fall, loans are made and the next round in the money and credit expansion process takes place.

When the FRS acts to contract the money supply, on the other hand, they reduce bank reserves and so force lending to be curtailed and interest rates to rise. By manipulating the supply of money and credit, the FRS can have great influence on the credit market.

THE INFLATION PREMIUM

In Chapter 4 we noted that interest rates tend to rise and fall with anticipated inflation rates, and we called this the inflation premium interest rate component. But how does the expected inflation rate come to be built into the interest rate? It is the result of market forces.

Let us assume that, to begin with, both borrowers and lenders expect inflation to average 5 percent during the relevant time period for the credit market shown in Figure 10-8. As a result of these expectations, combined

FIGURE 10-8: THE INFLATION PREMIUM
A change in the expected inflation rate affects both borrowers and lenders. Here a change in the anticipated inflation rate from 5 to 7 percent causes the nominal inflation rate to increase from 8 to 10 percent. In this example the real inflation rate is constant if the expected inflation occurs.

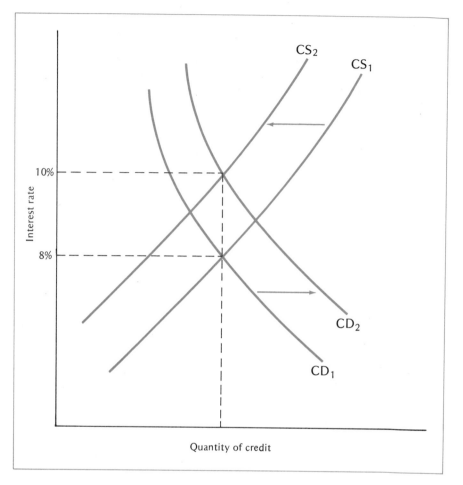

with the usual other influences such as scarcity, risk, and income, assume that the market equilibrium rate of interest is 8 percent. Borrowers and lenders expect to pay an 8 percent nominal interest rate, and a 3 percent real rate of interest since they anticipate a 5 percent increase in prices.

Now suppose that economic events make borrowers and lenders doubt the accuracy of their expectations. Higher-than-anticipated increases in the Wholesale Price Index or large rises in the prices of some basic goods could increase the expected inflation rate to 7 percent (to simplify this example, we assume that all borrowers and lenders have the same inflationary expectations). This change in expectations will affect both sides of the credit market.

Borrowers, first of all, will wish to increase their indebtedness. Since they expect inflation rates to rise, they foresee a temporary decrease in the real interest rate. An 8 percent loan bears a real interest rate of only 1 percent if prices actually increase at the anticipated 7 percent rate. Credit is cheap, in real terms, so the demand for it will be high.

What will they do with this larger quantity of credit? If prices are going to rise in the future, households and businesses will stand to benefit by purchasing high-inflation goods now at current prices instead of waiting while both prices and interest rates rise.

Buying now and borrowing to do so makes a lot of sense when inflation rates are on the rise. Suppose that someone were planning on purchasing a house, for example, and needed a $50,000 loan to do so. Borrowing $50,000 at 8 percent interest for thirty years results in a $366.88 monthly mortgage payment. If the prospective home buyer waited a year, however, the price of the home might rise at the expected 7 percent rate and the interest rate might rise by 2 percentage points (reflecting the higher inflation rate) to 10 percent. The same house would now be financed by a $53,500 loan at 10 percent interest for thirty years. The monthly payment here would be $469.50! An increase in the inflation rate from 5 to 7 percent, if it is felt in both the price of the house and the mortgage interest rate, would result in a 28 percent increase in the monthly mortgage payment! It is no surprise that smart buyers would rush to beat the inflation since even a small increase in price or interest rate can cause a large rise in monthly loan payments. The demand for credit, then, will soar.

The change in expectations will also affect the supply side of the credit market. With inflation rates expected to rise, lenders will be less willing to part with their money. Financial investors, for example, will be aware that the real interest rate is declining on the credit market and will be tempted to shift their funds to the stock market. Lending institutions as well will begin to make fewer loans since they do not wish to be the loser in the inflation game. Holdings of excess reserves may rise.

These combined forces—larger credit demand combined with a reduction in the supply of credit—produces a shortage of money and credit. At the initial 8 percent rate of interest, borrowers outnumber lenders. Borrowers, anxious to beat the inflation crunch, will offer to pay higher interest rates in order to secure loans now. This will induce a somewhat larger supply of loanable funds and slowly bring the market into equilibrium.

In the end, if borrower and lender expectations are identical, a new equilibrium like the one shown in Figure 10-8 will be achieved. Here, because both borrowers and lenders have the same expectations, both demand and supply of credit have shifted equally. The new interest rate—10 percent—fully reflects the 2 percent increase in inflation rates that was initially anticipated. The same amount of credit is exchanged here since the real interest rate—the nominal rate (10 percent) minus the anticipated inflation rate (7 percent)—is now equal to 3 percent, the same as it was at the start of our example.

If borrowers and lenders have guessed correctly, neither group will gain or lose on account of the inflation. If, however, the inflation rate differs from that which was expected, or if borrowers and lenders have different expectations of inflation, then the winners and losers discussed in Chapter 4 will be created.

DISINTERMEDIATION

When interest rates rise, as we saw in the last example, this does not affect all parts of the credit market equally. Some segments of the market—like the bond market—are relatively free from government interference and here, interest rates and bond yields will adjust, as our model suggests, to changing market conditions. But other parts of the market are tightly regulated, and strange things result.

Commercial and savings banks are often called financial intermediaries because they act as a middleman or intermediary between the ultimate lenders in the economy (mostly households) and the ultimate borrowers (governments, businesses, and, again, households). These lending institutions borrow from households in order to relend the funds to the ultimate borrowers. They provide a useful service in efficiently connecting borrowers and lenders and earn a profit from this activity. But in order to be able to make loans, they must attract deposits. During periods of high interest rates, their ability to do this is severely hampered because of FRS regulations which set a ceiling on the interest rates that they can pay their depositors. In 1977, for example, about the highest interest rate that a savings institution could pay in order to attract funds was 8 percent, and this yield could only be achieved if the funds were held for a period of up to ten years.

As interest rates rise, savings institutions and commercial banks find that the interest rate regulations keep them from being competitive with substitute financial investments like stocks and bonds. Big savers, then, shift their money out of these savings institutions and into assets that will yield a higher, noncontrolled, return. This process of funds leaving financial intermediaries in search of greater returns is called **disintermediation.**

Disintermediation: the process whereby savers take funds out of financial intermediaries and invest directly in credit markets in order to achieve higher returns

The housing market is particularly hurt when disintermediation occurs. A large proportion of houses are financed through savings institutions. Disintermediation results in a particularly low quantity of credit being available for mortgage loans. This causes interest rates for these loans to be especially high, and, as a result of the interest rate ceiling, a continuing shortage of these funds is likely to occur.

This lack of mortgage money is a serious problem. The housing industry is one of the most important parts of our economy. When new houses are built, this brings about purchases of labor, building materials, plumbing supplies, electrical goods, and eventually leads to increased spending on furniture, appliances, and other items when the house is inhabited. Housing construction, then, brings about a great deal of income, creates many jobs, and is important to the aggregate level of economic activity. Housing starts (the number of new houses that begin construction in some time period) is another leading indicator of economic activity. When mortgage credit dries up due to disintermediation, this can have a big impact on the economy through its effect on the housing industry, even if the credit eventually reappears in a different part of the credit market to finance other activities.

In the 1970s the FRS acted to try to hold down disintermediation. Interest rate ceilings were slowly lifted, and new gimmicks were tried in order to keep funds in savings institutions. One such plan, for example, now allows savers to receive roughly the same return from savings institutions that they could receive if they invested in short-term bonds. By keeping the savings institutions competitive, these programs may prevent the damaging segmentation of the credit market that results when high inflation rates, tight money, or high loan demand causes disintermediation of financial markets.

THE REAL INTEREST RATE

Throughout this discussion we have noted the difference between the nominal interest rate and the real interest rate. A question which needs to be answered is; Do people respond to changes in the real interest rate or to changes in the nominal interest rate when making decisions? This is a question which does not have an easy answer.

The evidence can lead us either way. Savers, for example, have seemingly showed little concern for the real interest rate. In the 1970s, for example, people with savings in commercial banks received an average of about 5 percent nominal interest on their funds, while inflation rates averaged about 7 percent. The real interest rate computes to a *negative* 2 percent return. Money stored in commercial bank savings accounts shrunk most years, even with the positive affects of compound interest growth. People with accounts in savings institutions fared better, but still probably received a negative real return on their funds.

Why this apparent disregard for real interest rates? Several explanations can be given. For many, especially small savers, the only alternatives to low-interest savings accounts are probably spending the money instead of saving it (and most people consider savings desirable as a financial backstop in case of emergencies) or storing it, instead, in checking accounts which earn no interest at all. Given these alternatives, savings accounts that yield low interest rates may still be desirable.

Why not put the money, instead, into the stock or bond markets where the return is not limited by government regulation? Intelligent participation in these markets requires more information than many people feel they have, and often also involves the payment of fees which can reduce the rate of return from these financial investments, especially if the amounts involved are small. As well, many of these better-paying alternatives require fairly substantial initial investments (some mutual funds, for example, demand at least $2500 to start with) and lack the convenience of savings accounts.

Borrowers seem clearly aware of the difference between real and nominal interest rates. When interest rates are high because of high inflation rates, for example, the demand for credit does not greatly falter. In 1978, for example, the interest rate on mortgage loans often exceeded 10 percent. Borrowers, however, noted rising inflation rates and willingly agreed to the relatively high nominal loan rates in anticipation of inflation reducing the real interest rate to acceptable levels.

The real interest rate, then, probably is the more important determinant of borrowing and lending activities, although, as we have noted before, governmental rules and regulations with respect to interest rates are often set in nominal form, complicating the actions of the credit market.

INVESTMENT AND THE CREDIT MARKET

Opportunity cost: the cost of an economic action as determined by the value of the opportunities foregone

Activities in the credit market affect the economy in many ways. Obviously, the relative availability of credit will affect consumer, business, and governmental spending. The most direct impact is on business investment expenditures.

To the business investor planning expenditures for new factories, equipment, or inventories, the interest rate represents a dual cost. First, it is a direct cost of investing. Most investments are taken with borrowed funds. Higher interest rates, like higher costs of any sort, reduce the profits that can be expected from investment projects. The interest rate is also an **opportunity cost** to the firm since retained business earnings can always be placed in the credit market and earn the going rate of return. A firm which chooses to invest using its own funds, therefore, is giving up the return that could have been achieved in the credit market.

Because interest rates are, directly or indirectly, a cost of investment, businesses must weigh them carefully in making investment decisions. In general, businesses will follow the following rule:

Undertake *all investment opportunities that have an expected rate of return* greater than or equal to *the interest rate*. Reject *all investments which have an expected rate of return* less than *the interest rate*.

This **investment rule** makes sense in that it simply says to make all investments which are profitable once the interest cost is taken into consideration, and to pass up all unprofitable investments. Since business investors by and large obey this investment rule, changes in the interest rate can have a very large impact on investment spending, aggregate demand, and aggregate supply.

Investment rule: tendency of firms to invest in opportunities whenever the anticipated return on investment exceeds the interest rate

Suppose that the interest rate is 8 percent. Then we can be pretty sure that all investment opportunities that have an expected rate of return of 8 percent or more will be undertaken simply because it is profitable to do so (of course, the investments with the largest potential profits are made first, with the last investments earning the lowest return). What would happen if the interest rate were to suddenly rise to 9 percent? Assuming that nothing has happened to affect the profitability of business investments, the rising interest rate will lower investment spending. Previously, all investments yielding 8 percent return or more were profitable. With a rising interest rate, however, investments which only earn, say, 8½ percent and which were profitable at an 8 percent interest rate are losing propositions at a 9 percent interest rate. These marginal investments will be dropped and investment spending will fall, as only the profitable investment activities are pursued.

Using the same type of logic, a fall in interest rates (again assuming no change in investment returns) will tend to increase investment spending. If the interest rate were to fall to 7 percent, this would make previously unprofitable activities money-makers. Investment spending would rise because more machines, stores, and factories would be profitable due to the lower investment cost.

Investment spending, then, tends to rise and fall with the cost of investing—the interest rate. Since investment spending (which is important to aggregate demand and supply) is so directly affected by the interest rate (which is determined by the credit market), it forms a link between the financial sector and the rest of the economy. We call the interest rate–investment relationship the monetary transmission mechanism. Investment spending is the power line that links monetary policy actions to the rest of the economy.

MONETARY POLICY

Expansionary monetary policy: FRS actions designed to increase the supplies of money and credit

Federal Reserve actions which directly affect the credit market will indirectly affect the rest of the economy through their effect on interest rates and investment spending. We will look at monetary policies in greater detail in the next chapter, but, for now, let's note their basic form.

An **expansionary monetary policy** is designed to stimulate the economy by increasing the supplies of money and credit in the economy. If the FRS were to undertake an open market purchase, for example, this would tend to increase bank reserves and increase credit and loans. This will increase the supply of credit, as shown in Figure 10-9, and cause the interest rate to be bid down. Falling interest rates, all else being equal, will stimulate investment spending. In the short run this will tend to increase aggregate demand (in the longer run aggregate supply may also rise).

We can summarize this process as follows:

Open market purchase → ↑CS → ↓i → ↑I → ↑AD
Expansionary Monetary Policy

---

where 'i' indicates the interest rate, I denotes investment spending and the other symbols are as defined previously in the text.

FIGURE 10-9: INCREASE IN THE CREDIT SUPPLY
An increase in the credit supply drives down the interest rate, thereby stimulating investment spending and therefore causing an increase in aggregate demand.

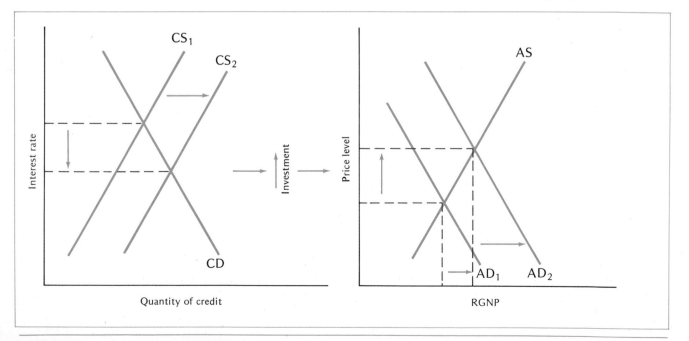

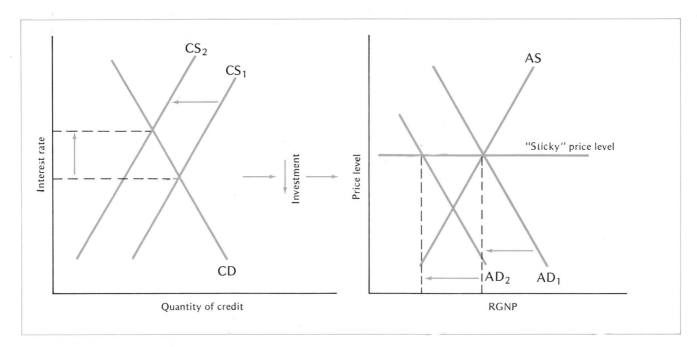

FIGURE 10-10: CONTRACTIONARY MONETARY POLICY
When the FRS contracts the credit supply, this forces interest up, investment spending down, and aggregate demand falls as a result.

Contractionary monetary policy, on the other hand, is designed to reduce aggregate demand by reducing the amount of investment spending in the economy and therefore to reduce total spending because of the multiplier process. The FRS can undertake contractionary policy by making an open market sale, raising the reserve requirement, or raising the discount rate. Let's suppose that they raise the reserve requirement for the purposes of this example (illustrated in Figure 10-10 for an economy with bottleneck AS and sticky prices).

As the reserve requirement rises, banks find that they have fewer excess reserves available (some of their excess reserves must now be sent to the FRS to meet the new higher reserve requirement). The supply of credit falls as a result. This tends to bid up the interest rate, discouraging investment spending. As investment spending falls, aggregate demand falls in the short run and aggregate supply may fall, as well, in the long run as the reduced investment spending lowers the productive capacity of the economy.

We can summarize this chain-reaction process as follows:

Increase reserve requirement → ↓ CS → ↑ i → ↓↓ I → ↓ AD
Contractionary Monetary Policy

Contractionary monetary policy: FRS actions designed to decrease the supplies of money and credit in the economy

By affecting the credit market, the FRS can cause either a balanced growth in aggregate demand and supply through expansionary monetary policies or a reduction in AD and AS. But these results can also be obtained through manipulation of taxes and government spending. Which way is better? This question is answered in the next chapter.

SUMMARY

1. In general, money can be raised either through the sale of debt (the credit market) or through the sale of equity (as in the stock market). Shares of stock represent partial ownership in a firm and have value because they carry with them the right to receive dividends. Bonds and other debt instruments, issued by both firms and governments, represent a promise of future repayment.

2. The demand for credit is affected by the level of the interest rate, income, inflation rates, inflation expectations, and governmental policies that affect borrowing.

3. Interest rates are set through the interaction of borrowers and lenders on the credit market. Factors which cause a change in either the supply of credit or the demand for it will change the interest rate.

4. Disintermediation occurs when interest rates rise above the legal maximums that financial intermediaries may pay. Money is then withdrawn from these financial institutions and invested directly in credit markets, resulting in an increase in credit availability there, but a reduction in credit available through banks and the financial institutions.

5. When expected inflation rates rise, the demand for credit rises and the supply of credit is reduced. This tends to bid up interest rates, resulting in the "inflation premium" discussed in Chapter 9.

6. Changes in financial markets affect aggregate demand and supply through the impact of interest rates on investment spending. As interest rates fall, investment spending is encouraged, causing aggregate demand to rise (in the short run) and inducing long-run rises in aggregate supply. Higher interest rates discourage investment spending and so reduce aggregate demand.

7. The FRS acts to affect the economy through monetary policy. By changing the supplies of money and credit, the FRS can cause increases or decreases in the interest rate which, through their impact on investment spending, will alter aggregate demand and supply.

DISCUSSION QUESTIONS

1. High interest rates induce holders of stock certificates to sell those stocks and put funds in the credit market instead of the stock market. Low interest rates cause an opposite flow of funds. What, then, is the relationship between interest rates and prices on the stock market? If you thought that interest rates were going to rise, would you expect stock prices to rise, fall, or stay the same? What effect will this have on interest rates? Why?

2. Graphically show how interest rate ceilings in one segment of the credit market can cause disintermediation.

3. When would a business investor be interested in the real interest rate and when would he or she pay attention to the nominal rate of interest? Does it make a difference to our analysis?

4. The FRS is nearly always working to increase the money supply. Why, then, are not interest rates constantly falling?

5. Suppose that the FRS undertakes a $10 billion open market purchase and that banks have a reserve requirement of 10 percent. What will happen to the money supply, credit supply, interest rates, aggregate demand, and RGNP? Can you tell exactly how much RGNP will change? Why or why not?

TEST YOURSELF

Indicate whether each of the following statements is *true* or *false*. Be able to defend your choice.

1. Bond prices generally rise when interest rates rise.

2. Stock prices often fall when interest rates rise.

3. The FRS determines the inflation premium component of the interest rate.

4. Borrowers in recent years have apparently responded to the real, rather than the nominal, interest rate.

5. All things being equal, increases in national income result in rising interest rates only if the money supply increases at the same time.

6. Falling interest rates tend to increase total investment spending.

7. Disintermediation occurs because of government floors on interest rates.

8. Disintermediation tends to occur during periods of high inflation rates.

9. Investment spending would increase if either interest rates fall or the expected return on investments rises.

10. Contractionary monetary policy tends to drive up interest rates, drive down investment spending, and so reduce aggregate demand.

ECONOMIC CONTROVERSIES V: CREDIT MARKET CONTROLS?

The credit market in general and the banking industry in particular is one of the most highly controlled and regulated sectors of the economy. Virtually every aspect of a bank's operation is subject to rules and regulations determined by national or state governments and organizations.

Some of the most important regulations of banks and credit market activities are issued by the Federal Reserve System in their famous Regulation Q and elsewhere. In these regulations, the FRS determines who can issue checking accounts (generally just commercial banks), the interest rate that can be paid on these demand deposit balances (zero), and the maximum interest rates that banks can pay on customer deposits (around 5 percent for commercial banks, slightly higher for savings banks, and up to around 8 percent for certificates of deposit). Interest rates paid by banks are set mostly by regulation; market forces have relatively little impact. Market forces do, however, tend to set the interest rates that banks receive on the loans that they make with customer deposits.

The regulations on this aspect of the credit market tend to reduce the return on consumer deposits (zero percent on demand deposits and only modest returns on savings) while having little influence on the rates that the banks can charge when they loan this money to others. These regulations seem, at first glance, to be designed to insure high bank profits. Are the credit market controls necessary?

Are they desirable? Let's look at both sides of the debate.

CREDIT REGULATIONS NEEDED

The banking sector is too important to take chances with. One of the most frightening economic events is a run on a bank. It is in the public's interest to preserve and protect the banking industry so that it will continue to be a stable, strong, and useful cornerstone of the economy.

Banking regulations are especially necessary because, while banks are crucial to economic activity, they can also be abused for individual gain. During the "state" banking period of the nineteenth century (when banking was only loosely regulated by state governments) we saw many instances of fly-by-night banks opening for business, rapidly "creating money" for the profit of bank directors, and then just as quickly vanishing, sometimes leaving depositors penniless. Because of the interdependence of the banking system, these weak banks often pulled down legitimate banks with them. This is what can happen when banks are poorly regulated. We cannot risk the kind of bank panics that were caused in the past.

Bank regulations on interest rates may seem to be designed to line the bankers' pockets, but the intention (and, indeed, the result) is much different. Bank deposit interest rules are designed to prevent *destructive competition* among banks. If banks were allowed to compete on the basis of interest rates, we might well see an increase in bank failures. Banks, remember, make loans for long periods of time—home loans are made for thirty years, for example. Deposits, however, can be withdrawn in short order. If interest rates were not limited by law, depositors might "shop around" constantly for the best rate. In the process, they could swing funds from one bank to another, creating a real crisis each time withdrawals exceeded deposits. Basically sound banks might be forced to close their doors because of a short-term liquidity crunch. Those banks that remained would be very careful about making further loans (and would probably demand higher interest rates) because of the risks of competition from other banks "raiding" the deposits.

The interest rate regulations, by limiting this destructive competition, actually increase the availability of bank services and may even make credit available to consumers at a lower cost than would otherwise be the case. True, the regulations mean that depositors receive a little less on savings and checking accounts than they otherwise would, but this is a small price to pay for the preservation of a dynamic, stable banking system.

DEREGULATE THE CREDIT MARKET

Interest rate regulations are costly and inefficient. They surely create more problems than they solve and should be done away with, for the most part, as quickly as possible.

Interest rate controls discriminate against consumers. Consumers, who have only small bank accounts and not many assets in general, cannot take advantage of investments (like Treasury bills) or bank services (like large-denomination certificates of deposits) that would earn a high return. They must put their money into regulated institutions where they earn little or no real interest on their deposits. They lose every time inflation creeps up above 2 or 3 percent. What use is saving if inflation wipes out time deposit balances? Consumers face the unhappy choice of being wiped out by inflation when they save or creating more inflation if they choose to spend their funds instead. This isn't much of a choice.

When they go to the banks to borrow, however, they find relatively few regulations on their side to keep interest rates low on loans. Here they must compete with corporations and governments in a relatively competitive market for loanable funds. Competition for funds ought to work both ways.

The regulations cause some major problems in the credit market. When high inflation rates prevail, disintermediation (discussed in Chapter 10) takes place. This really leaves the consumer in the lurch. While his or her savings are being wiped out by inflation, the average householder finds that large depositors have taken their money out of the banks and invested directly in the credit market. Thus there are few loans available from the banks, and these are likely to carry hefty interest rate premiums. There's no way to win in this kind of situation.

The rationale for these interest rate regulations is that they prevent destructive competition and so preserve the banking system. Destructive competition? The proponents of these regulations must think that bankers and loan officers are exceptionally foolish businessmen who would drive themselves out of business in no time flat. Or else they must be crooks who would quickly find shady ways to profit from the lack of regulations at the expense of saving the public.

This picture is inaccurate. Most bankers are solid, stable, responsible businessmen who are not likely to go on interest rate binges if the rules of the game are loosened. Competition among a group like this is not likely to be destabilizing. The equilibrium interest rates on loans and deposits would be quickly found and would adjust slowly over time to changes in the supply and demand forces within the economy.

Bank failures? This seems hardly likely. The current regulations assure that most banks now operating are strong and would be strong even in a competitive world. If a bank did fail, however, the deposit insurance programs already in effect would protect depositors from the kinds of problems that were apparent in the past.

DISCUSSION QUESTIONS

1. Which side of this debate do you agree with? Can you find flaws in any of the arguments presented? Should interest rate regulations be done away with?

2. Should interest rates be paid on checking account balances? Are they in any way different from savings account balances? Explain.

3. Evaluate the argument that low interest rates on deposits tend to guarantee consumers low interest rates on loans.

11
Monetary versus Fiscal Policy

This chapter looks at some of the options available in making economic policy and notes the problems that our economic leaders must face as they attempt to achieve prosperity. Some of the questions which this chapter will answer include the following:

What is the difference between monetary and fiscal policies?

Which policy is better?

Are monetary and fiscal policies equally inflationary?

Does it make any difference how government spending programs are financed?

Do monetary and fiscal policies always work together?

One of the uncomfortable realities of the American economic system is that the controls of the machines of monetary and fiscal policies are controlled by entirely different people. Fiscal policy is managed by a cooperative lead by the president and his Council of Economic Advisors, but also controlled by Congress and, to a lesser extent, by the many state and local governments which undertake spending and taxing activities.

The Federal Reserve System, however, is often not greatly influenced by the makers of fiscal policy. Although appointed by the president, the chairman of the Board of Governors of the FRS cannot be removed by him and serves for a longer term than the president. The FRS undertakes the formulation of monetary economic policy on its own initiative. Sometimes it pays attention to the actions of Congress and the president, and at other times it attempts to offset what it thinks are undesirable fiscal policies.

The separation between the makers of monetary and fiscal policies can be very great. They may have different political persuasions (the FRS is thought to be conservative, while Congress is more liberal). They may believe in different economic models (congressmen may be Keynesians, believing in the extensive use of government spending to control the economy, while FRS decision makers subscribe to the monetarist point of view). They are even separated geographically—Congress meets on Capitol Hill in Washington, D.C., while the FRS holds court at the other end of town near the Washington Monument and actually implements many of its policies in the financial capital of New York City.

Since there is very often great disagreement concerning what should be done and how it should be accomplished, let us begin with a comparison of monetary and fiscal policies.

EXPANSIONARY MONETARY POLICIES

To start this comparison of policy tools, suppose that the economy is experiencing a high level of unemployment and that policy makers have decided—and agreed—that it is necessary to stimulate aggregate demand in order to increase production and so cause employment to rise. This can be accomplished through either expansionary monetary policies or through fiscal policy actions. We examine the monetary option first.

FRS policies that increase the supply of money and credit will tend to cause aggregate demand to expand. The FRS can do this by using either open market purchases or by cutting the reserve requirement (or lowering the discount rate coupled with either of the above) to cause the supply of money and credit to expand. Let's suppose that the open market purchase

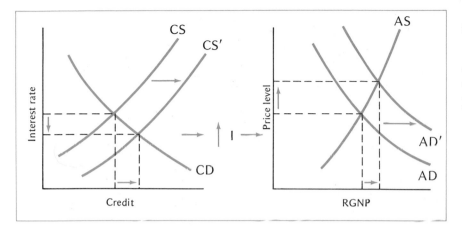

FIGURE 11-1: EXPANSIONARY MONETARY POLICY
Federal Reserve System actions increase the supplies of money and credit, causing the interest rate to be bid down. Lower interest rates induce higher private investment spending, which increases aggregate demand.

option is used and trace its effects through the economy. The impact of this policy is shown graphically in Figure 11-1.

When the FRS undertakes an open market purchase, it buys bonds on the open market. It pays for them by issuing a check against itself which is a "new" injection of money into the financial system. This new deposit is made and the money multiplier takes over, causing the money supply and the supply of credit to rise as deposits become loans which become deposits again.

The increase in the supply of credit creates a surplus of loanable funds on the credit market. Commercial banks, savings institutions, and others find themselves with an unintended accumulation of money and so cut interest rates in order to make loans. The falling interest rates induce a greater amount of investment spending, which causes aggregate demand to rise. If the economy is at neither full employment nor in a deep recession (i.e., if the "bottleneck AS curve," as in Figure 11-1, applies), then this increase in aggregate demand will cause an increase in RGNP (the desired result of the policy action) and also an increase in the price level, however measured, as greater production brings about higher prices.

It is convenient to summarize this chain reaction as follows:

Open market purchase → ↑CS → ↓i → ↑I → ↑AD → ↑RGNP → Inflation
Expansionary Monetary Policy

Note that this expansionary monetary policy works through the investment sector of the economy. By lowering interest rates and increasing investment spending by businesses, the FRS expects to cause a multiplier increase in aggregate demand to produce the desired result of increasing RGNP and lowering the unemployment rate.

EXPANSIONARY FISCAL POLICIES

The increase in aggregate demand which the FRS brought about through an open market purchase could also be achieved through fiscal policy actions. By increasing government spending, cutting taxes, or increasing transfer payments by varying amounts, the Congress and the president could achieve the same end. Let's examine how this would work in the easiest case—an increase in government spending. This policy is shown in Figure 11-2.

As the government spends more on, say, public employment projects, this causes spending to rise directly in the economy. The beneficiaries of the government spending programs will then go on to respend these funds and so cause a larger multiplier total increase in aggregate demand. As the spending/income cycle repeats, production will rise and, assuming again the bottleneck AS curve, inflation will take place. The desired goal of lowering the unemployment rate will be achieved, albeit with higher prices in the bargain.

This chain-reaction can be summarized as follows:

Increased government spending → ↑ AD → ↑ RGNP → Inflation
Expansionary Fiscal Policies—First-order Impact

First order impact: the initial changes in the economy brought on by monetary or fiscal policies

We call this chain the **first-order impact** of expansionary fiscal policy because, while these are the principal effects of the increase in government spending, the shock waves of this policy action do not end here. Since prices and income have been increased (and, perhaps, inflationary expectations altered), there will also be an impact on the credit market.

The government hasn't increased the supply of credit (it has little control over that), but its actions have a significant impact on the demand side of this market. Since both prices and incomes are higher, households and

FIGURE 11-2: EXPANSIONARY FISCAL POLICY

An increase in government spending causes aggregate demand to increase from AD$_0$ to AD$_1$. Rising incomes and prices, however, affect the credit market, causing the demand for credit to rise. This forces interest rates up, which reduces private investment spending and so causes aggregate demand to fall back from AD$_1$ to AD$_2$.

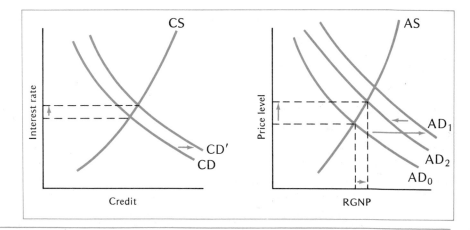

businesses will have need of more credit. Higher prices boost the cost of the things that people borrow to purchase, and rising incomes mean that people can now afford loans for bigger houses and newer cars. In all, this will increase the demand for credit. As credit demand (CD) rises, with no accompanying increase in credit supply, interest rates rise around the economy. Banks find themselves with an unintended inventory reduction of money and so boost interest rates in order to ration the scarce credit. As interest rates rise, previously planned investment projects will be found to be unprofitable and will be abandoned. Investment spending will fall, with a multiplier effect on aggregate demand. The chain-reaction process here is as follows:

$\uparrow$ RGNP and Inflation $\rightarrow$ $\uparrow$ CD $\rightarrow$ $\uparrow$ i $\rightarrow$ $\downarrow$ I $\rightarrow$ $\downarrow$ AD $\rightarrow$ $\downarrow$ RGNP

Expansionary Fiscal Policies—Secondary Impacts

Falling investment spending will offset part of the initial increase in aggregate demand. Monetary policies also have these secondary impacts; they do not reverse the first-order effects, however, but merely reduce their final magnitudes.

PUBLIC VERSUS PRIVATE SECTOR GROWTH

A key difference between monetary and fiscal policies lies in the part of the economy where the rise in spending initially occurs. Both policies cause consumption expenditures to rise indirectly through the multiplier process, but the primary expenditures are often different.

Expansionary fiscal policies which cause government purchases to rise tend to make private investment spending fall. This kind of fiscal policy therefore tends to substitute public sector growth for private sector growth. Since public goods must ultimately be supported by tax dollars (whereas private investment expenditures are paid for through business profits), this type of policy eventually results in increased tax burdens.

There is also a question of public choice. When monetary policies are used, the private sector chooses which goods and services are to be produced through the market process. When fiscal policies are implemented, government decision makers do the choosing. Are their choices better, in the long run, than the choices that households and businesses would make themselves?

When fiscal policies are implemented through tax cuts, however, the results are somewhat different. A tax cut would increase spending by households but still cause investment spending to fall. Here consumption spending (spending for today's wants) replaces investment spending (spending to provide for tomorrow's needs). Private choice, however, is preserved as consumers, not government officials, determine which goods and services are produced.

INFLATION IN THE LONG RUN

A second difference between monetary and fiscal policies concerns their long-run impacts on aggregate supply. Monetary policy, by causing investment spending to rise, tends to build the base for long-run increases in the aggregate supply. Fiscal policy, however, discourages investment spending and so limits the AS growth. Why is this important? In Chapter 7 we saw that our economic goals of low unemployment and stable prices can best be achieved through a balanced growth in aggregate supply and aggregate demand. Monetary policy tends to cause this kind of economic growth; fiscal policy does not. This phenomenon is illustrated in Figure 11-3.

FIGURE 11-3: LONG-RUN DIFFERENCES BETWEEN MONETARY AND FISCAL POLICIES
Both monetary and fiscal policies shown here act to stimulate aggregate demand and so cause economic growth and inflation in the short run. Fiscal policy, however, discourages investment spending and so discourages the long-term growth in aggregate supply. Monetary policy stimulates investment and therefore causes a larger long-run increase in aggregate supply. The result is that, over the long haul, monetary policy is less inflationary than fiscal policy.

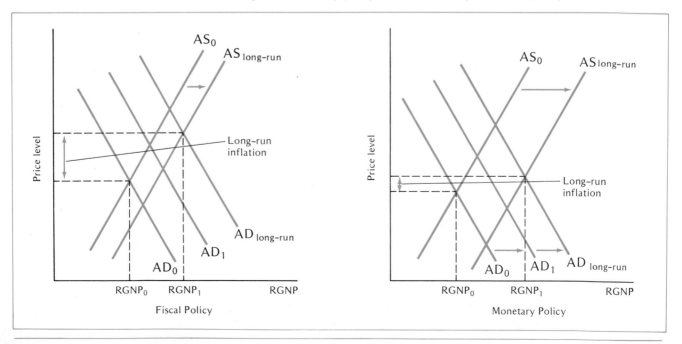

Fiscal policy causes aggregate demand to rise directly, but has the undesirable side effect of discouraging investment. Because investment falls, the natural growth of aggregate supply is reduced in Figure 11-3. As a result, production rises, in the long run, to only $RGNP_1$ and the price level also tends to rise. Monetary policy, on the other hand, increases aggregate demand through investment spending and therefore brings about increased long-term growth in aggregate supply. In Figure 11-3, AS increases from AS_0 to AS_1, causing production in the long run to rise to $RGNP_2$ without an increase in the long-term price level.

Monetary policy, then, tends to promote the kind of balanced economy necessary for long-run economic growth without inflation. This, plus the fact that it puts the decision of what the increased production should go for (guns or butter?) into the hands of the private sector instead of those of Congress (or the government bureaucracy) makes FRS actions a very appealing way to stimulate economic growth.

Monetary policy, then, is obviously the best way to stimulate the economy. Or is it?

ADVANTAGES AND DISADVANTAGES

Despite its obvious advantages, monetary policy is not always used to stimulate economic activity. And despite its obvious disadvantages, fiscal policy is often pursued. Are economic policy makers blind? Or are there other factors which we have not yet discovered? The latter case prevails.

In spite of their other problems, fiscal policies have one important virtue: they are relatively certain. When we undertake government spending or taxation policies, we can be relatively sure of both the total effects of the policies and the time frame during which those effects will take place. This certainty is appealing. When actions are taken to increase aggregate demand, it is likely that the increased demand will take effect soon enough to be beneficial to the economy.

This advantage of fiscal policy is moderated, however, by the existence of the various lags in fiscal policy discussed in Chapter 8. Legislative, implementation, and impact lags can slow the reactions of fiscal policy measures. But once the policies have been carried out, their impact on the economy is relatively certain.

Fiscal policies can also be designed to minimize the side effects of reduced investment spending and slowed growth in aggregate supply. Tax cuts, for example, are often implemented so that business taxes are reduced along with levies on households. In recent years business taxes have been reduced through **investment tax credits.** These tax credits reduce the tax bite for businesses which undertake new investment projects. This tends to

Investment tax credits: tax programs which lower tax rates on new investments and so encourage investment spending by increasing after tax returns increase the profitability of those investments and so acts to promote increased private investment spending. This tax break tends to promote investment spending while the interest rate effects of expansionary fiscal policy discourage it. The two impacts may cancel out or, if the tax credit is large enough, actually result in increased investment spending.

By undertaking the right kind of fiscal policy, then, the government can bring about rising aggregate demand while minimizing the investment spending problems that slow future growth in aggregate supply. All of this can be accomplished with relative certainty.

Monetary policy is less predictable. Undertaking expansionary monetary policy yields less certain results for a number of reasons. The first problem is the uncertainty of the monetary transmission mechanism itself.

By increasing the supply of credit, the FRS can normally lower the interest rate, and the lower interest rate will normally cause investment spending to rise—as predicted—*eventually*. The last word—*eventually*—is important. How quickly will investors respond to the lower interest rates? Will they react immediately and so begin their investment projects? Will they wait to see if interest rates go still lower? Will they hold out for a tax cut before committing their funds to a project? Will inflation cause them to cancel their plans altogether? All of these questions enter into the investment decision process. Sometimes investment spending quickly follows monetary policy. But sometimes there is a lag—the **variable lag** of monetary policy—between policy actions and results. This variable lag makes monetary policy risky. The nature of this risk is shown in Figure 11-4.

Variable lag: the lag between the implementation of monetary policy and the time when its impact is felt in the economy, a lag that can vary from a few months to several years

Suppose that the economy is in a deep recession at production level $RGNP_0$ in Figure 11-4. Now assume that the FRS undertakes a large open market purchase in an attempt to lower unemployment. If the policy is immediately effective, aggregate demand would increase and production would rise dramatically to $RGNP_1$. Much of the unemployment would go away with little or no resulting inflation.

But suppose there is a lag of two years between the FRS action and the investment rise. Suppose, further, that during this period fiscal policies are successful in increasing aggregate demand to such an extent that the economy is operating at or near full employment. In this setting, the sudden increase in investment spending would still cause aggregate demand to rise, but since the economy is already operating at full capacity, the only result is rapid inflation. The variable lag in monetary policy has caused inflation, and has not contributed to the solution of the unemployment problem.

The existence of this variable lag makes using monetary policy something like driving a car with a variable-lag steering mechanism. When you turn the steering wheel you will also turn the car—eventually. Somewhere in the next mile the car will turn, but where? Obviously, this uncertainty can be

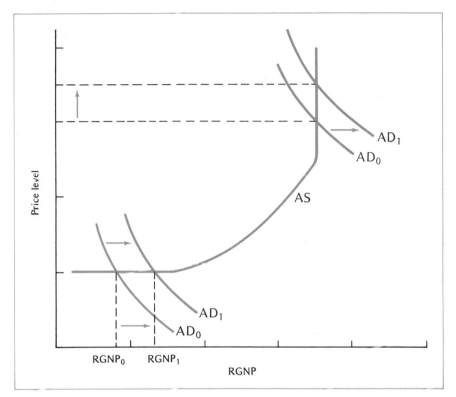

FIGURE 11-4: PROBLEMS OF THE VARIABLE LAG IN MONETARY POLICY
The effectiveness of monetary policy depends very much upon when it finally takes effect—how long the variable lag takes. If expansionary policy is undertaken during a depression and takes hold quickly, then growth from $RGNP_0$ to $RGNP_1$ without inflation is possible. If the monetary actions do not take effect until the economy has already been moved to the full-employment range by other factors, however, the money supply actions cause nothing but inflation.

very dangerous to the car so equipped and to the economy so managed. As a result, monetary policy is a risky business. The lag between implementation and impact of monetary policy can vary from a few months to several years. The economy and its needs can change drastically in that period of time. The lags in fiscal policy can cause these types of problems, too. But the fiscal lags may be more predictable, more visible, and easier to deal with.

Another problem with monetary policy is that the FRS may be slowly losing control of the supply of credit. In recent years more and more banks and savings institutions have left the FRS. FRS member banks receive a variety of useful services from the Fed, but they are subject to banking regulations which are often more severe than those which apply to non-FRS banks. Banks which are not members of the FRS often have lower legal reserve requirements (which makes banking for them more profitable, since they can lend out more money with a given amount of reserves) and are subject to looser regulation in other areas, too. More and more, banks have decided that the advantages of FRS membership are no longer worth the cost. As the number of member banks decreases, the FRS's ability to carry out monetary policy could be hurt. Although the FRS can still apply a lot of leverage to the credit market, it must now take larger actions just to compensate for the actions of the nonmember institutions.

For these reasons, the advantages of monetary policy must be discounted when picking a national economic policy. The correctly chosen fiscal policy may, in the end, be the best choice. Neither type of policy, however, is clearly superior.

CONTRACTIONARY POLICIES

Now that we have examined expansionary monetary and fiscal policies it is useful to look at what happens when actions are taken to reduce aggregate demand in order to reduce demand-pull inflation pressures. Let's look first at contractionary monetary policy.

The FRS can reduce aggregate demand indirectly by contracting the supplies of money and credit in the economy. They do this by either increasing the reserve requirement or undertaking open market sales.

When the FRS cuts the supplies of money and credit this has the effect of reducing bank reserves. With fewer excess reserves, financial institutions find themselves in the midst of a credit shortage. Their ability to make loans is reduced, while the demand for credit remains high. Interest rates rise in reaction to this credit squeeze.

Rising interest rates eventually discourage investment spending (the variable lag may also apply to contractionary actions). When investment spending falls, aggregate demand will fall as well, causing a reduction in RGNP.

The chain-reaction here is given by

$$\downarrow CS \rightarrow \uparrow i \rightarrow \downarrow I \rightarrow \downarrow AD \rightarrow \downarrow RGNP$$
Contractionary monetary policies

Real GNP is reduced in the short run, and inflationary pressure may subside if the rising prices had been caused by demand-pull forces. Notice, however, that investment spending has fallen. This suggests that aggregate supply may also fall in the future, causing cost-push inflation which creates both rising prices and rising unemployment.

In this setting, contractionary monetary policy, with the disadvantages of the variable lag still with us, has an even darker side. By raising interest rates and discouraging investment spending, this kind of policy trades demand-pull inflation for cost-push inflation. This is not a desirable trade-off.

Contractionary fiscal policy can also be used to reduce an excess aggregate demand, but with different side effects. Suppose that government spending is reduced. This will directly reduce aggregate demand and, as aggregate demand falls, production levels will fall, too. The chain reaction is

---

Decreased government spending → ↓AD → ↓RGNP
Contractionary Fiscal Policy—First-order Impact

The secondary impacts of this policy are worth noting. As income falls due to the contractionary fiscal policy, the demand for credit is reduced as well. Since people have less income, they will be less able to undertake loan obligations. With credit demand falling, interest rates should fall, too. This stimulates investment spending and so in the short run (assuming no large lag here) acts to offset part of the initial cut in government spending. The chain is

---

↓RGNP → ↓CD → ↓i → ↑I → ↑AD
Contractionary Fiscal Policy—Secondary Impacts

This policy is not as contractionary as it first seems, since private investment spending rises to replace some of the fallen government spending. It also has the advantage that, since investment spending is rising, aggregate supply should grow in the long run. Thus, contractionary fiscal policy, while reducing demand-pull inflation pressures in the short run, can set up the growth of aggregate supply which is beneficial to the economy in the long run.

Whereas monetary policy may be the best way to expand the economy—providing that it works when you want it to—fiscal policies which cut government spending or raise taxes may be better ways to restrict aggregate demand.

FINANCING GOVERNMENT SPENDING

Increasing government spending is not really as easy as we have suggested so far. When government spending is increased, money must come from somewhere to finance the purchases that the government makes. There are only three sources for these funds: they can come from increased tax collections; they can be borrowed from the public by selling them new issues of government bonds; or they can be borrowed from the FRS by selling the bonds to the Fed. Each of these methods has distinctly different impacts on the economy in the short run and the long run.

Let's look at the tax-financed method first. This case is illustrated in Figure 11-5. As government spending rises, this directly increases aggregate demand, with all of the secondary impacts that we have discussed

FIGURE 11-5: TAX-FINANCED
GOVERNMENT SPENDING
*Tax-financed increases in government
spending are not very stimulative since
the increases in spending and taxes
tend to work in opposite directions on
aggregate demand.*

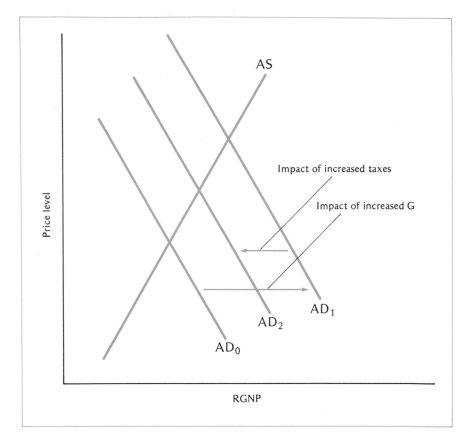

previously. The tax increase, on the other hand, reduces disposable income and so causes aggregate demand to fall, but by less than the government-spending increase, because of the difference in the two multipliers discussed in Chapter 8. The dual chain reactions are

$$\uparrow G \rightarrow \ \uparrow AD \rightarrow \ \uparrow RGNP \rightarrow \ \uparrow CD \rightarrow \ \uparrow i \rightarrow \ \downarrow I$$
$$\uparrow TAX \rightarrow \ \downarrow AD \rightarrow \ \downarrow RGNP \rightarrow \ \downarrow CD \rightarrow \ \downarrow i \rightarrow \ \uparrow I$$
Tax-Financed Government Spending

In the end, the tax increase will largely offset the impacts of the initial increase in government spending. On net, RGNP should rise a little, a little inflation will be created, and interest rates should rise and investment spending fall by relatively small amounts. The result here is slow economic growth (higher government spending has a greater impact on the economy than the tax increase). In the long run, economic growth may be even less and inflation even more because of investment-spending reductions induced by the somewhat higher interest rates.

If the president and the Congress do not want to increase taxes in order to finance higher government spending, they can instead increase spending and finance the resulting deficit by selling bonds to the public. They do not tax away the public's money, but merely borrow it and increase the national debt.

When the government borrows from the public, this produces an increase in the demand for credit. The government, along with everyone else, competes for the scarce credit supply. The impact of this borrowing on the economy depends on conditions in the credit market. Figure 11-6 tells the story.

There are three possible cases here. If there are very large amounts of excess reserves in the financial system (as shown in Figure 11-6a), then government borrowing of, say, $10 billion can be financed with no increase in interest rates. Since interest rates do not rise, investment spending is not affected and so aggregate demand rises by a large multiplier amount. Such large amounts of excess reserves, however, are probably not often available.

If the financial system is completely loaned out (as illustrated in Figure 11-6c), then we have a large increase in interest rates as government borrowing increases credit demand, and the phenomenon of **complete crowding out.** We say that the government crowds out private sector

BORROWING FROM THE PUBLIC

Complete crowding out: an increase in government borrowing causing an equal decrease in private sector borrowing due to fixed credit supplies

FIGURE 11-6: CROWDING OUT
An increase in government borrowing tends to ''crowd out'' private borrowing to a greater or lesser extent depending on conditions in the credit market. Here we assume that a $10 billion increase in government borrowing takes place. When there are many excess reserves available (a), no crowding out takes place. When the supply of credit is completely fixed (c), private borrowing falls by the same amount that public borrowing increases. In the intermediate case (b), the $10 billion government borrowing results in higher interest rates (which make $5 billion more credit available) so that private borrowing falls by $5 billion.

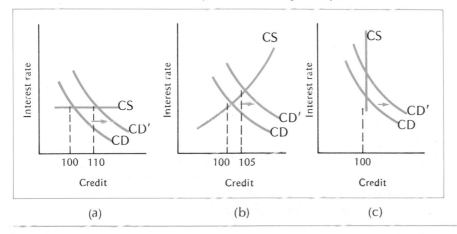

borrowing when the increase in government debt results in fewer funds available for private borrowing. This is clearly the case in Figure 11-6c. Here, because the financial system has no excess reserves, there is a fixed amount—$100 billion—of loanable funds available. If the government borrows $10 billion of this total—and if there are no additional funds created by the FRS or elsewhere—then it follows that there are only $90 billion left for private investment spending.

In the case of complete crowding out, the increase in government spending has no impact on the economy. As government spending rises by $10 billion, the credit market crowding out forces private investment spending to *fall* by $10 billion. With a finite limit of credit, an increase in government borrowing means a decrease for everyone else. On net, no increase in debt-financed spending is possible. The limited credit is simply shifted from one user to another.

Partial crowding out: increased government borrowing resulting in reduced private sector borrowing

The most "normal" case occurs when there is **partial crowding out** as illustrated in Figure 11-6b. Here, additional credit will be created, to a certain extent, as interest rates rise. When the government borrows $10 billion here, its action drives up the interest rate. The total credit supply rises to a total of $105 billion at the new, higher interest rate. Before, private borrowing amounted to $100 billion. After the government action, $105 billion of credit is supplied, but only $95 billion is available for private use with the remaining $10 billion going to the government; $5 billion has been crowded out.

Partial crowding out causes the kind of total impact illustrated in Figure 11-7. The increase in government spending causes aggregate demand to rise, but the increase in total spending is partially offset by falling private investment spending. The chain-reaction impacts are

---

$$\uparrow G \rightarrow \ \uparrow AD \rightarrow \ \uparrow RGNP \rightarrow \ \uparrow CD \rightarrow \ \uparrow i \rightarrow \ \downarrow I$$
Borrowing from the public $\rightarrow \ \uparrow CD \rightarrow \ \uparrow i \rightarrow \ \downarrow I \rightarrow \ \downarrow AD \rightarrow \ \downarrow RGNP$
Borrowing from the Public

This policy tends to have little impact in the short run, and some very detrimental impacts over the longer haul. Both of these actions—spending and borrowing from the public—tend to increase demand on the credit market. Interest rates will go very high and investment spending will likely tumble when these actions are taken. In the long run, cost-push inflation can result from this kind of policy.

President Ford attempted to fight unemployment by increasing government spending and financing the deficit through public borrowing in 1975–1976. This had, as suggested above, little impact on unemployment in the short run, and could be at least partially to blame for the rising inflation rates which plagued the nation later in the decade.

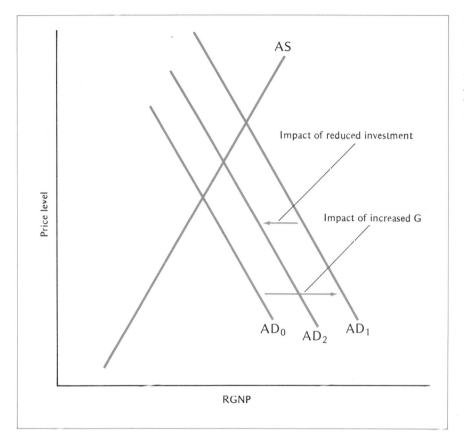

FIGURE 11-7: BORROWING FROM THE PUBLIC
Increases in government spending financed by borrowing from the public are not very stimulative since the government borrowing tends to "crowd out" private-sector borrowing and so reduce real investment expenditures.

BORROWING FROM THE FRS

If the governors of the Federal Reserve wish, they can purchase new issues of government bonds and so finance any government deficit by creating money. This causes fiscal policies to be very expansionary.

When the deficit is financed by borrowing from the FRS, both sides of the credit market are affected. The demand for credit rises because of the government borrowing, but at the same time the FRS increases the supply of credit to make the government action possible. Because of the money multiplier, the supply of credit grows by more than the demand for credit. To see this, suppose that the government wants to borrow $10 billion, so the FRS buys $10 billion worth of government bonds from the Treasury. This affects the money supply just like any other $10 billion open market purchase. Indeed, it is exactly an open market purchase with the exception that the FRS is buying the bonds from the Treasury instead of a bank, corporation, or individual. When the $10 billion that the FRS has created is spent, it will be deposited into the financial system and start the loan/deposit process which results in more than $10 billion in additional credit.

FIGURE 11-8: BORROWING FROM THE FRS

Increases in government spending which are financed by borrowing from the FRS tend to be very stimulative since the Fed increases the money supply in order to lend to the government. Large increases in real GNP can be expected here. Alas, high inflation rates may also result in the short run.

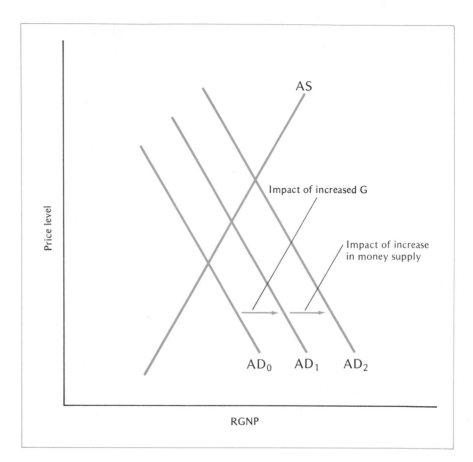

In the end, if credit supply expands by more than credit demand rises, interest rates will fall and investment spending rise. The result is illustrated in Figure 11-8. Aggregate demand rises due to the increase in government spending, and then rises again as the increase in investment spending is felt. The result is a very large increase in aggregate demand and, depending on the state of AS, in large increases in RGNP or the price level or both.

The chain reaction for this policy option has three parts: government spending, government borrowing, and, because of the FRS action, money creation:

$$\uparrow G \rightarrow \uparrow AD \rightarrow \uparrow RGNP \rightarrow \uparrow CD \rightarrow \uparrow i \rightarrow \downarrow I$$
$$\text{Government borrowing} \rightarrow \uparrow CD \rightarrow \uparrow i \rightarrow \downarrow I \rightarrow \downarrow AD \rightarrow \downarrow RGNP$$
$$\text{FRS lending} \rightarrow \uparrow CS \rightarrow \downarrow i \rightarrow \uparrow I \rightarrow \uparrow AD \rightarrow \uparrow RGNP$$
$$\text{Borrowing from the FRS}$$

This is the kind of economic policy that was used during much of the 1960s when the FRS and the fiscal policy makers worked together. The result then was, as it is in Figure 11-8, substantial demand-pull inflation.

The choice of which type of government finance to use depends, obviously, on many factors. Tax finance may be unpopular. Borrowing from the public causes crowding out. And borrowing from the FRS is possible only if the FRS wishes to cooperate. There are political and economic trade-offs apparent here.

ACCOMMODATING MONETARY POLICY

Since the Congress and the Federal Reserve are populated by different people who often have different political and economic philosophies, it is not always the case that the two groups agree concerning what actions must be taken in order to achieve our economic goals. When they do agree, we say that the FRS is undertaking **accommodating monetary policy.**

Accommodating monetary policy: FRS actions which are chosen to complement fiscal policies

An example of accommodating monetary policy is when the FRS acts to finance a government deficit by lending to the government. By increasing the money supply, the FRS makes the fiscal policy easier to implement and more effective. As we saw in Figure 11-8, this accommodating policy can cause a very large increase in aggregate demand—much larger than through any of the other forms of government finance.

So long as the FRS is working in the same direction as the fiscal policy makers, this accommodating policy will make the fiscal policies more effective. Suppose, for example, that Congress wants to fight unemployment through a tax-cut program. If the FRS moves in the same direction, pursuing expansionary monetary policy, aggregate demand will grow significantly. The chain-reactions are as follows:

Tax cut $\rightarrow$ $\uparrow$ AD $\rightarrow$ $\uparrow$ RGNP $\rightarrow$ $\uparrow$ CD $\rightarrow$ $\uparrow$ i $\rightarrow$ $\downarrow$ I
Open market purchase $\rightarrow$ $\uparrow$ CS $\rightarrow$ $\downarrow$ i $\rightarrow$ $\uparrow$ I $\rightarrow$ $\uparrow$ RGNP
Accommodating Monetary Policy

Here fiscal policy causes an expansion of aggregate demand, but has the undesirable side effect of bidding up the interest rate as the credit demand increases. The FRS, however, accommodates the government action by increasing credit supply thus keeping interest rates low and offsetting any investment impact that the fiscal policy might cause. By increasing the money supply sufficiently, the FRS can keep fiscal policy operating at its fullest.

CONFLICTING MONETARY POLICY

Conflicting policies: monetary and fiscal policies that work in opposite directions, often with undesirable side effects

This cooperation between monetary and fiscal policy makers is not always the case, however. Often they will disagree about the nature of our economic problems and the proper goals of economic policy. The result of this disagreement can be **conflicting policies**—monetary and fiscal policies which act to cancel out each other or, worse, combine to create new economic problems.

This conflict of policies is not intentional. Different people can view the same economic situation and see different priorities. This was the case in 1978, for example. The Federal Reserve's Board of Governors saw an economy with both high rates of inflation and high levels of unemployment and decided that inflation was the more serious economic problem. Because they viewed inflation as a particular threat—and a threat that the president and the Congress were not likely to do very much about, the governors of the FRS decided to fight higher prices by tightening the money supply. They raised the discount rate and engaged in open market sales to a greater extent than before. The money supply increased at a slower rate than before and at times even fell. By limiting the supplies of money and credit, the FRS intended to cut aggregate demand and slow the demand-pull inflation which was then apparent.

The president and the Congress viewed the problem differently. President Carter relied on a voluntary inflation program and proposed to fight unemployment with a tax cut. The tax cut was designed to stimulate aggregate demand and so move the economy to higher levels of production and lower levels of unemployment.

Let's examine the chain-reaction process that these two policies set in motion:

$$\text{Tax cut} \rightarrow \uparrow AD \rightarrow \uparrow RGNP \rightarrow \uparrow CD \rightarrow \uparrow i \rightarrow \downarrow I$$
$$\text{FRS actions} \rightarrow \downarrow CS \rightarrow \uparrow i \rightarrow \downarrow I \rightarrow \downarrow AD \rightarrow \downarrow RGNP$$
$$\text{Conflicting Policies}$$

These two policies tend to offset one another in terms of their impact on aggregate demand. The tax cut causes spending to rise, but higher interest rates reduce total spending. In the short run not very much was likely to happen. Neither policy can work.

In the longer run, much more is at stake. Both of these policies tend to bid up interest rates. Interest rates rise steeply, especially since the tax cut has to be financed (the foregone tax dollars replaced) by borrowing from the public (the missing dollars cannot come from higher taxes and will not come from the FRS). Investment spending is severely discouraged, with the result of a long-run decrease in aggregate supply with the cost-push inflation that follows such a shift.

When the FRS attempts to fight inflation and the Congress battles unemployment, as shown above, the result is little impact in the short run and cost-push inflation in the long run. Both policies are ineffective, and our economic problems worsen.

It is interesting to note, however, that conflicting policies do not always have to have such dismal consequences. Suppose that the FRS were more concerned about unemployment and the Congress worried most about inflation. This role reversal changes the results of the conflict significantly.

Since the FRS is now worried about fighting unemployment, they will engage in open market purchases and act to increase the supplies of money and credit. This will tend to lower the interest rate on the credit market and so encourage investment spending.

If congress, on the other hand, is concerned about inflation, they might increase taxes in an attempt to diminish demand-pull inflation pressures. The twin chain reactions here are as follows:

FRS actions → ↑CS→ ↓i → ↑I → ↑RGNP

Tax increase → ↓AD → ↓RGNP → ↓CD → ↓i → ↑I

Conflicting Policies

Here, again, the policies tend to cancel each other in the short run. But look at the impacts on investment spending. Since both policies lower interest rates and encourage investment spending, it follows that aggregate supply should grow in the future, causing economic growth without higher prices. Here we have just the opposite of the cost-push inflation that resulted from the first set of conflicting policies.

This description of monetary and fiscal policies is complicated, but realistic. It highlights the many trade-offs which must be made as a part of any comprehensive economic policy. Which is more important, the long run or the short run? Certainty or uncertainty? Politics or economics? National economic policy is not an easy game to play, and the game gets very much more complicated because there are two teams playing, each with their own priorities and their own rules. They may not intentionally work in opposite directions, but that result is always possible.

1. Monetary and fiscal policies affect the economy in very different ways, although they can be chosen so as to have roughly similar impacts on aggregate demand. Fiscal policies affect the economy directly, but often cause problems in credit markets. Expansionary fiscal policies, for example, tend to drive up interest rates and cause reduction in investment spending. Expansionary monetary policy, on the other hand, only works if it can force down interest rates and increase investment.

2. It is probably impossible to say which economic policy is better all of the time. Monetary policies often have desirable long-run impacts on aggregate supply, but are subject to variable lags which reduce their dependability. Fiscal policies may be more politically acceptable because of their visibility and greater certainty, but sometimes cause long-run problems.

3. In the short run, both kinds of policies can be equally inflationary. In the long run, however, whichever policy brings about the greatest increase in investment spending (all else being equal) should be less inflationary.

4. Government spending can be financed by taxation, borrowing from the public, or borrowing from the FRS. The effectiveness of fiscal policy is largely determined by the way that it is financed. Borrowing from the public is a particularly poor policy when the problem of crowding out exists.

5. Monetary and fiscal policies can be designed to work together or in different directions. In recent years, conflicting monetary and fiscal policies have often been the case. When conflicting policies are pursued, neither policy is very effective and a variety of side effects are possible.

DISCUSSION QUESTIONS

1. What is the "best" policy for the government or the FRS to undertake if the economy is faced with the problem of unemployment?

2. What is the best policy if the goal of economic policy is to "cool off" aggregate demand?

3. What effect does the existence of a variable lag in monetary policy have on your answers to the preceding two questions?

4. Suppose that the government wished to implement a tax cut. They will need to find additional funds to replace the revenues lost from taxes. What are the options? What are the effects on the economy? If the economy is in a deep depression, which is the best alternative?

5. Are government and Federal Reserve policies currently working together or working in opposite directions? How can you tell?

TEST YOURSELF

Indicate whether each of the following statements is *true* or *false*. Be able to defend your choice.

1. Monetary and fiscal policies tend to bring about opposite changes in interest rates and investment spending even when they have similar impacts on aggregate demand.

2. The secondary impacts of fiscal policies act to increase its effectiveness.

3. Tax reductions tend to substi-

tute public priorities for private ones.

4. Expansionary monetary and fiscal policies are equally inflationary in the short run.

5. Expansionary monetary and fiscal policies are equally inflationary in the long run.

6. Contractionary fiscal policies tend to induce higher levels of investment spending.

7. The existence of lags is a problem in monetary policy, but not in fiscal policies.

8. Fiscal policies can be designed to increase both aggregate demand and aggregate supply by changing the appropriate tax laws.

9. Monetary and fiscal policies always work together.

10. A tax cut accompanied by an increase in the reserve requirement would be an example of accommodating monetary policy.

12
The
Monetarists

This chapter presents a different view of the way the national economy works—that of the monetarists. Some of the questions that this chapter will answer include the following:

Who are the monetarists?

Why do monetarists hold a different view of the economy?

How does the monetarist model of economic policy differ from traditional Keynesian theory?

What should be the proper role of monetary and fiscal policies?

Who is correct—the monetarists or the nonmonetarists?

What is the role of money in the economy? How important is monetary policy? How much do changes in the money supply contribute to inflation and unemployment?

The preceding two chapters have answered these questions from a traditional Keynesian viewpoint. Money is important because it is the basis for credit. Monetary policy affects the economy by increasing or decreasing the supply of credit and so altering the interest rate. Increases in the money supply can cause inflation only indirectly because expansionary monetary policies bid down interest rates, induce increased investment spending, and so contribute to demand-pull inflation.

This traditional view of money's impact on a modern economy is held by many but not all economists. This chapter will examine an alternative point of view: that of the **monetarists.** Monetarists are subscribers to a school of economic thought that holds that money is *more* important to the economy than the traditionalists believe, but that, paradoxically, monetary policy should be *less* important and *less* used in our quest for high employment with stable prices. The monetarist family has deep roots. Today's best-known economist, Milton Friedman, is also today's most respected monetarist.

Because monetarists have a different view of the economy, they also have much different policy prescriptions for today's problems. In this chapter we will briefly describe a much simplified model of the monetarist economy and then examine the principal differences between the monetarist and traditional Keynesian views concerning the function of money and the role of economic policy.

Monetarists: members of a school of economics that hold that money is the most important factor in macroeconomic analysis

THE EQUATION OF EXCHANGE

To get a feel for the increased importance that the monetarists assign to money in the economy, let's begin this discussion by looking at one of the earliest statements of the monetarist viewpoint: the **equation of exchange.** This equation presents a relatively simple accounting identity and then draws some interesting conclusions from it.

There are many ways to measure the amount of economic activity that takes place in an economy in a year. We can, for example, measure the amount of money that is spent on final goods and services. In the past we have written this as GNP, but there are other ways to define total spending. Since there is only a limited amount of money available at any time, large amounts of total spending must be accomplished by spending and respending each dollar several times during the year. In 1975, for example, a total of $1528.8 billion was spent using a total money supply (M1 = currency plus demand deposit balances) of just $294.8 billion. This

Equation of exchange: an accounting identity associated with the monetarists; the equation of exchange states that $M \times V = P \times Q$ (where M is the money supply, V is the velocity of money, P is the price level, and Q is the level of real output)

suggests, mathematically, that each dollar of the money supply was spent an average of 5.2 times in order for the smaller quantity of money to purchase the larger amount of goods.

If we call the average number of times that a dollar is spent in a year the **velocity of money** (the speed with which money changes hands), then it is possible to write the following formula:

$$\text{Total spending} = M \times V$$

where M is the money supply and V is the velocity of money and total spending is defined to be total purchases of final goods (GNP).

This is not the only way to measure economic activity, however. We could equally as well choose to measure the total value of final goods produced in the economy. **Total production** would be a measure of the amount of goods produced and the prices paid for those goods. Mathematically, this can be stated as

$$\text{Total production} = P \times Q$$

where Q is the amount of final goods produced (RGNP for our purposes) and P is a measure of the average price paid for those goods (a price index like the GNP Implicit Price Deflator Index). Again taking 1975 as an example, total production (money GNP) was $1528.2 billion. This is equal to the quantity produced (RGNP of $1202.1 billion in 1972 dollars) times the average price of those goods (1.272 where the base year 1972 is arbitrarily set equal to 1.000).

So far, all of this is simply writing the concepts of total final sales and production in different mathematical ways. The equation of exchange now makes the logical statement that, from a GNP standpoint, total spending on final goods in a year equals total production of final goods. Since

$$\text{Total spending} = \text{Total production}$$

it follows that

$$M \times V = P \times Q$$
The Equation of Exchange

Since this is merely an accounting identity, it is always true, and therefore this relationship among M, V, P, and Q must always hold. The equation of exchange says that the amount that people pay for final goods and services (M × V) is equal to the amount that producers receive for these goods (P × Q), nothing more nor less.

Because this identity always holds, it gives us an interesting insight into the role that money must play in the economy. Suppose that the FRS suddenly acts to increase the money supply M. In order for the equation to

Velocity of money: the average number of times that the money supply is exchanged (spent) in a period of time

Total production: a measure of amount of goods produced and the prices paid for those goods

remain in balance, one of the following conditions (or some combination of them) must result:

☐ *Q rises*—the increase in the money supply directly causes an increase in the amount of final goods and services produced.

☐ *P rises*—more money results in higher prices for the current level of production.

☐ *V falls*—people respond to the larger supply of money by slowing their rate of spending. By holding cash balances longer, each dollar is made to circulate fewer times, reducing the velocity of the money supply.

For a long time economists believed that Q and V (output and money velocity) were unlikely to change in the short run. If this assumption holds, then it follows mathematically that changes in the money supply directly cause changes in only the price level. More money means simply more inflation. If V and Q are fixed, monetary policy is ineffective in combatting unemployment and can only be used to manipulate the price level!

The assumptions that lead these economic thinkers to conclude that monetary policy was ineffective are not always true, as can be seen by examining Table 12-1 (which gives values for the variables of the equation of exchange for selected years 1960–1975). During this period, all of the variables, M, V, P and Q, rose, and they rose at different rates.

The equation of exchange, aside from its mathematical form, is interesting in that it highlights an important fact about economic activity—the concept of exchange. Transactions involve exchange—money is exchanged for goods and services. To fully understand how the economy works, the monetarists hold, we must better understand the nature of that exchange. To begin this task, let's look at an economy in which exchange is more clearly seen: a pure barter economy.

TABLE 12-1

THE EQUATION OF EXCHANGE

YEAR	GNP Current $ (billions)	M M1 $ billions	V GNP/M1	P Implicit Price Index (1972=1.00)	Q RGNP, 1972 $ (billions)
1960	506.0	144.2	3.51	0.687	736.8
1965	688.1	171.3	4.02	0.743	925.9
1970	982.4	219.6	4.47	0.914	1075.3
1975	1528.8	294.8	5.18	1.272	1202.1

Source: *Economic Report of the President, 1978.*

In a barter economy, money as such does not exist. Goods are traded for other goods, and prices are given in terms of an **exchange rate.** To make this model as simple as possible, let's look at a very primitive but famous barter economy. Suppose that our "economy" is a desert island (complete with sandy beaches, active volcano, and hidden lagoon, but missing the usual scantily clad natives). The only two residents of this island economy are Robinson Crusoe and his faithful companion Friday.

As luck would have it, the shipwreck that stranded Robinson Crusoe also washed several obscure economics texts onto the island. Following the teachings of Adam Smith (the father of economics), Robinson Crusoe and Friday have undertaken division of labor and specialization of production. Robinson Crusoe now works exclusively in the production of goat cheese that he makes by trapping native goats and processing their milk until it gets thick and smells funny. He eats much of this concoction himself, and trades the rest to Friday. Friday, for his part, is a skilled fisherman. He casts his net in the hidden lagoon and brings forth a variety of succulent fish which he consumes himself and trades with Robinson Crusoe for goat cheese.

THE BARTER ECONOMY

Exchange rate: the ratio at which commodities can be traded for one another

FIGURE 12-1: ROBINSON CRUSOE'S BARTER BEHAVIOR
Robinson Crusoe is the supplier of cheese in this simple barter economy. His supply of cheese, however, also indicates the amount of fish that he would like to swap his cheese for. We can therefore interpret his behavior as either supplying cheese or demanding fish. Both the supply curve for cheese and the corresponding demand curve for fish are shown.

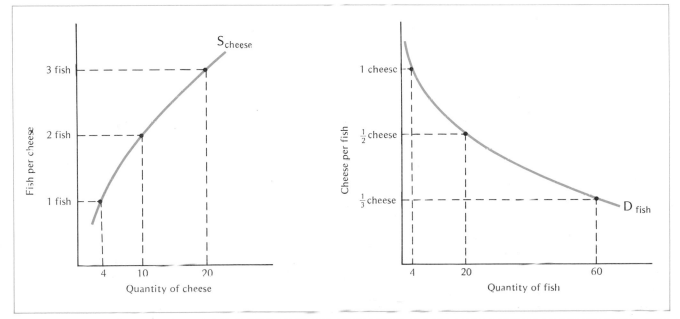

Robinson Crusoe, having carefully weighed the costs of production of goat cheese and his desire for cheese, fish, and leisure time, has determined the amounts of cheese that he will supply in return for fish. Not surprisingly, the amount of cheese that he is willing to produce and sell depends on the exchange rate for cheese—the number of fishes that he will get in exchange for the cheese. His supply curve is shown in Figure 12-1. At an exchange rate of 1 fish per cheese, he will sell Friday only 4 cheeses. At 2 fish per cheese he is willing to produce and sell 10 cheeses, and at 3 fish per cheese he is willing to devote a lot of time to catching goats and so will produce and sell 20 cheeses to Friday.

Robinson Crusoe's supply curve for cheese also tells us about his demand for fish, since it is the fish that he is receiving in return. When the exchange rate is 1 fish per cheese (or, as Friday views it, 1 cheese per fish) Robinson Crusoe wants to obtain 4 fish by paying 4 cheeses. At an exchange rate of 2 fish per cheese (½ cheese per fish), he wants to trade a total of 10 cheeses for a total of 20 fish. He therefore demands 20 fish. Finally, at the exchange rate of 3 fish per cheese (⅓ cheese per fish) Crusoe wants to sell 20 cheeses, meaning that he wants to receive (demands) a total of 60 fish. Crusoe's supply of cheese determines this demand for Friday's fish.

Friday also balances his desires for cheese, fish, and leisure time. His behavior is shown in Figure 12-2. The amount of fish that he is willing to catch and sell depends upon the amount of cheese that he receives for them. At ⅓ cheese per fish, for example, he will sell only 15 fish (and receive, in return, 5 cheeses). If the exchange rate is ½ cheese per fish, Friday would like to trade 20 fish for a total of 10 cheeses. And if the exchange rate is 1 cheese per fish, he will exchange 30 fish for 30 cheeses.

Friday's supply of fish also represents his demand for Crusoe's cheese. As cheese becomes more expensive (fish buys less cheese) Friday is less willing to trade for cheeses. Check Figure 12-2 to see that, at equivalent exchange rates, the supply behavior for fish translates into the demand curve for cheese shown.

We can summarize these supply and demand relationships as shown in Table 12-2. The equilibrium here occurs at the exchange rate of 2 fish per cheese (½ cheese per fish). At this exchange rate the quantity of fish supplied equals the quantity demanded (20 fish) and, as well, the amount of cheese supplied equals the amount demanded (10 cheeses). As can be seen by examining the table and Figure 12-3, at any other exchange rate both goods markets will be out of equilibrium. At the exchange rate of 1 fish for 1 cheese, too many fish and not enough cheese will be offered for trade. At the exchange rate of 3 fish per cheese (⅓ cheese per fish) too much cheese and not enough fish are offered in exchange. The normal market forces of surplus and shortage act to bring the exchange rate into equilibrium.

FIGURE 12-2: FRIDAY'S BARTER BEHAVIOR

Friday is a supplier of fish, but in a barter economy his behavior can also be viewed as demanding cheese. His fish supply curve and the corresponding cheese demand curve are shown here.

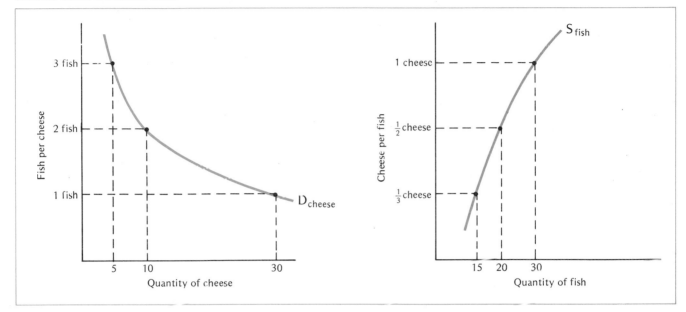

What would happen to this barter economy if, say, Friday were to come up with a technological improvement (a net with smaller holes) that increased the supply of fish available for exchange? This case is shown in Figure 12-4. Friday now catches more fish and he will attempt to trade each of them for ½ cheese at the going exchange rate. But Robinson Crusoe is unwilling to accept so many fish in exchange. Friday finds that, at the going exchange rate, he has too many fish. He can either offer to take less cheese in exchange for them (pay more fish per cheese), eat them himself, or watch them rot. He chooses to cut the price of his abundant fish.

TABLE 12-2

EXCHANGE IN A SIMPLE ECONOMY

Exchange Rate	Trader	Supplies	Demands
1 fish per cheese	Crusoe	4 cheeses	4 fish
1 cheese per fish	Friday	15 fish	15 cheeses
2 fish per cheese	Crusoe	10 cheeses	20 fish
½ cheese per fish	Friday	20 fish	10 cheeses
3 fish per cheese	Crusoe	20 cheeses	60 fish
⅓ cheese per fish	Friday	15 fish	5 cheeses

FIGURE 12-3: A BARTER ECONOMY AT WORK
The barter economy determines the equilibrium exchange rate between cheese and fish—here the equilibrium occurs at 2 fish per cheese (or ½ cheese per fish). At any other exchange rate surpluses and shortages prevail.

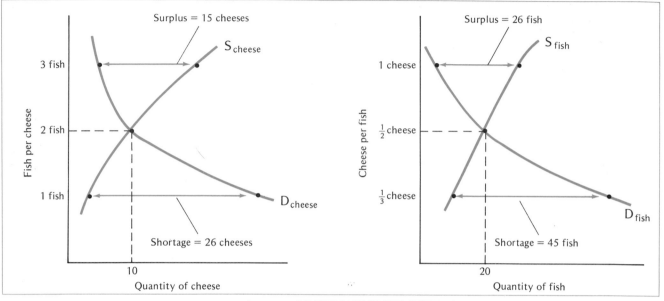

FIGURE 12-4: AN INCREASE IN THE SUPPLY OF FISH
An increase in the supply of fish affects both goods markets. The larger number of fish that Friday catches causes a surplus of fish, with the result that the price of fish falls. Robinson Crusoe views Friday's behavior as an increase in the demand for cheese. This creates a shortage of cheese and its price rises. A new equilibrium is found at an exchange rate of 3 fish per cheese (⅓ cheese per fish).

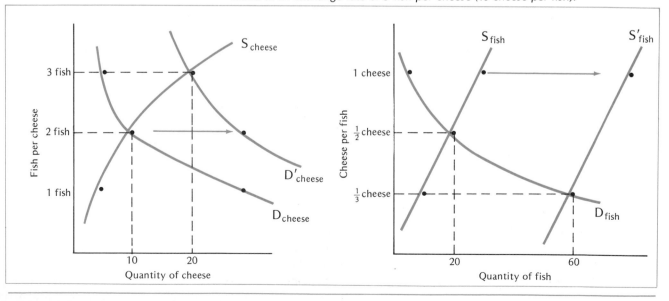

The surplus of fish tends to bid down the price of fish in Figure 12-4 from ½ cheese per fish to ⅓ cheese per fish. At the same time, this apparent increase in Friday's demand for cheese (as Crusoe views it) has the result of bidding up the price of cheese from 2 fish per cheese to 3 fish per cheese. At this new exchange rate, the dual markets are again in equilibrium; both more fish *and* more cheese are traded, and the amounts supplied and demanded are again in balance.

The effect of the increase in the supply of fish has been to lower the value of the fish and increase the price of the goods (cheese) that fish are used to purchase.

Looking at fish and goat cheese is interesting, but what has all of this to do with monetarists? The monetarists view money not as something special, but as just another commodity that is used in exchange. To see this, let's alter our example a bit.

In Chapter 9 we learned that money need not be just dollar bills or checks—anything that can be exchanged for goods and services and used to pay debts and is generally accepted for these purposes can be thought of as money. Indeed, many things have performed this task: rocks, beer, and tobacco among them. Since anything can be money, Robinson Crusoe and Friday can easily convert their barter economy to an economy with money. They could use seashells or something of that nature as money, but why should they complicate matters? Suppose that we simply give the fish a new name. Call them "dollars" instead of fish. If we denominate all prices in terms of these "dollars," and they are used in payment for goods, then the renamed fish are definitionally money and should be viewed as such.

Robinson Crusoe, seen in this light, is a supplier of cheese and a demander of dollars. He produces goods and services so that he can acquire money through exchange. Friday, on the other hand, is a holder of dollars. He acquires dollars so that he can trade them for goods and services.

This is very important to the monetarist model. *Producers sell goods and services in order to acquire money* (Robinson Crusoe supplies cheese and demands money, as seen in Figure 12-5) and *buyers want to trade money for goods* (Friday supplies dollars and demands cheese).

We can rewrite the demand and supply relationships as shown in Table 12-3. Only at the exchange rate of $2 per cheese (a dollar buys ½ cheese) do the supplies and demands for money and cheese balance. When the price of cheese is higher (the value of money less) there is a surplus of cheese and a shortage of dollars. When the price of cheese is below equilibrium

MONEY AS A COMMODITY

FIGURE 12-5: A BARTER ECONOMY WITH MONEY
*By declaring fish to be money, these barter markets begin to look more familiar.
The market for cheese determines the price of cheese in dollars and, at the same
time, the demand and supply of money determines its values. The supply of
money arises from the demand for goods and the supply of goods arises from the
demand for money. Compare this figure with Figure 12-3.*

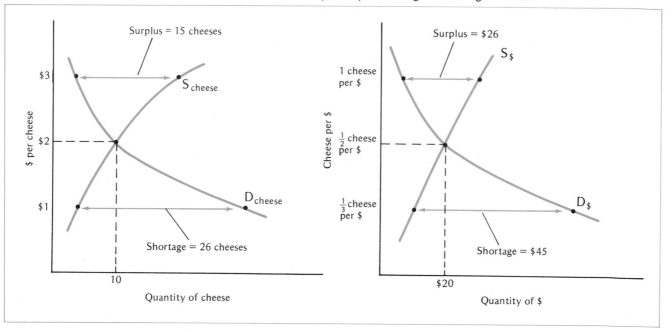

(the value of the dollar higher) there prevails a shortage of cheese and a
surplus of dollars.

The money market (market for dollars) and the goods market (market for
cheese) form a dual equilibrium. The price of goods and the value or
purchasing power of the money are determined jointly.

TABLE 12-3

EXCHANGE WITH MONEY

Exchange Rate	Trader	Supplies	Demands
$1 per cheese 1 cheese per $1	Crusoe Friday	4 cheeses $15	$4 15 cheeses
$2 per cheese ½ cheese per $1	Crusoe Friday	10 cheeses $20	$20 10 cheeses
$3 per cheese ⅓ cheese per $1	Crusoe Friday	20 cheeses $15	$60 5 cheeses

Let's now leave our simple island economy and move to a more complicated economic system. There are many more goods and services being bought and sold, but the basic motivations are much the same. In previous chapters we have divided the economy neatly into the components of aggregate demand (total spending) and aggregate supply (total production). The monetarist also sees this separation but interprets it differently.

Aggregate demand represents people attempting to exchange money for goods. The amount that they spend is determined by the supply of money that they have. Aggregate demand increases when the money supply increases. Given an equilibrium, an increase in the supply of dollars will cause people to attempt to exchange the excess dollars for goods, causing total spending to rise. The only other case is that aggregate demand can rise if people choose to hold fewer dollars on average and so spend the dollars that they receive more quickly. This would be an increase in the velocity of money. Given a fixed velocity, aggregate demand depends only on the stock of money available for spending.

Aggregate supply represents producers wishing to exchange goods and services in order to get money. Producers may view themselves as selling goods, but monetarists interpret their actions as demanding money. Aggregate supply, therefore, represents the demand for money in the economy while aggregate demand forms the supply of money. This dual market, shown in Figure 12-6, jointly determines the price level for goods and the value or purchasing power of money (goods per dollar—the inverse of the price level).

It is important to see the direction of causation here. Aggregate demand is determined, in the monetarist view, by the supply of money and will rise and fall with increases and decreases in the money supply (it will also change with variations in money velocity, but velocity is thought to be invariant for short periods of time). If we give people money, they will attempt to exchange it for goods at the going price level and so they create aggregate demand.

The demand for money, on the other hand, results from the production process (people make and sell things, like Crusoe, in order to acquire money). The demand for money is very stable in the short run because the factors which can change the money demand are the same things that alter aggregate supply. Aggregate supply changes only slowly in response to changes in population, labor force, or capital stock. Factors which affect aggregate supply will bring about changes in money demand. Since aggregate supply cannot change much in the short run, this also holds for money demand.

If aggregate supply is fixed in the short run, then the only way to affect production is through aggregate demand. But following the monetarist

MONEY
AND
THE
ECONOMY

FIGURE 12-6: THE MONETARIST MODEL OF THE ECONOMY
Aggregate demand arises from the supply of money. Aggregate supply determines the demand for money. Together, these dual markets determine the price level in the economy and the purchasing power of money (defined to be the inverse of the price level).

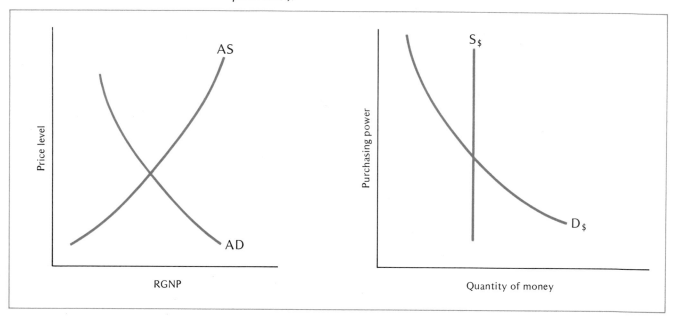

logic, if velocity is fixed, then aggregate demand will change only if the supply of money changes.

It is easy to see how the monetarists conclude that money is, if not the only thing, at least the most important thing in economic policy.

To get a better feel for how the monetarist model works, let's examine expansionary monetary and fiscal policy through the eyes of a monetarist.

MONETARY POLICY: THE MONETARIST VIEW

Before examining the monetarist view of expansionary monetary policy, let's first review the traditional analysis. An increase in the money supply is important because it causes an increase in the supply of credit. As the credit supply rises, the interest rate falls, inducing increased levels of business investment spending. It is this interest rate–induced increase in investment spending which has the desired effect of increasing aggregate demand.

The monetarist sees this process much differently. When the FRS increases the money supply, this disrupts the balance between the supply and demand for money, as shown in Figure 12-7. The demand for money, you should recall, derives from the production of goods and services

FIGURE 12-7: EXPANSIONARY MONETARY POLICY—THE MONETARIST VIEW
An increase in the money supply causes an increase in aggregate demand. This bids up the price level (reducing the purchasing power of money) and increases RGNP.

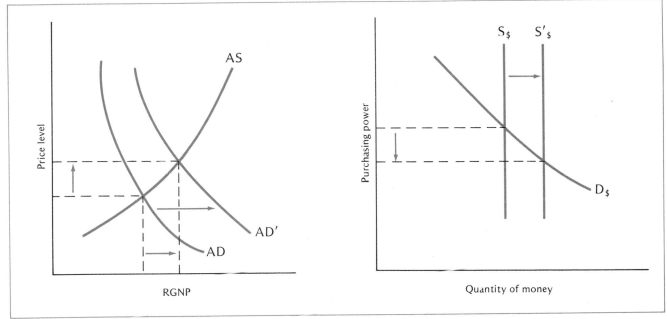

(aggregate supply). The mere fact of an increase in the money supply does nothing to alter the quantity of money that people wish to acquire because it does not affect the amount produced. The number of factories and machines, the amount of coal available, the number of skilled workers for hire—none of these important determinants of aggregate supply (and the demand for money) are affected by the monetary policy.

The increase in the money supply will therefore create a surplus of money. Consumers and other money holders will attempt to spend their cash balances, but will find that the supply of dollars exceeds the demand for them. In order to get someone to take their money, cash holders will be forced to "sell" them for less. This has the effect of bidding down the purchasing power of money and bidding up the price level of goods and services. If aggregate supply responds to the increased price level (as shown in Figure 12-7 by the upward-sloping AS curve), then the increase in the price level will cause some increase in RGNP. If, however, total production is fixed in the short run (because, say, the economy is operating at full employment), then the result of the increased money supply will be pure inflation.

The results here may *seem* the same as the traditional view of the economy. In both the traditional and monetarist models an increase in the money supply results in rising aggregate demand, but the transmission mechanism is completely different. The traditional view holds that, when people get money, they deposit it into the financial sector where it is transformed into investment spending. The monetarist argument suggests that when people get money over and above their equilibrium holdings, they get rid of the surplus by trading the money for goods and services and so increasing aggregate demand directly.

To see how big this difference is, let us now examine the two views of expansionary fiscal policy.

FISCAL POLICY: THE MONETARIST VIEW

The traditional view of fiscal policy is that, by increasing government spending, fiscal policy makers can cause total spending to rise directly and so increase aggregate demand and RGNP. Because it does not depend on the weak link of investment spending, fiscal policy is seen, in the traditional view, as being more reliable than monetary policy.

Monetarists, on the other hand, hold that fiscal policy is, at best, a poor way to increase aggregate demand and probably completely ineffective in affecting total spending. Here is the monetarist logic: Since an increase in government spending (or a cut in taxes) does nothing to affect the total supply of money, it can have no impact on aggregate demand. People buy things because they have money that they wish to exchange for goods and services. All that fiscal policy does is affect who spends this money, not how much is spent. Where does the money come from for a government spending increase? Since it must come from somewhere (taxes or borrowing), it follows that consumer and business spending falls (by an equal amount) when government spending increases because the government is taking money from these sectors of the economy and spending it instead of them.

Fiscal policy, then, has no impact in the aggregate (except when it is financed by the FRS increasing the money supply). Government spending merely replaces private spending. Different things are purchased, to be sure, but there is no change in the aggregate. The only possible impact might be an increase in the velocity of money which could increase aggregate demand—if the government spends money fast enough to cause the velocity to rise. This increase in velocity is temporary, however, since the rate of money turnover returns to normal once consumers and businesses receive back the dollars that the government took from them.

This view of fiscal policy leads monetarists to be very cynical concerning government policies. When the government spends money, they argue, individual consumers lose the power to decide how scarce resources should be used. Private priorities are replaced by government priorities. Since these policies have no impact on the economy, they say, why not let the private sector keep control over this spending and reduce the size of government to the minimum amount necessary to provide necessary public services.

MONETARIST POLICY RECOMMENDATIONS

Given the monetarist views on economic theory, what policies should be followed? Because aggregate supply is viewed as pretty much fixed in the short run, most monetarist policies concentrate on growth in long-run aggregate supply as the solution to the unemployment problem. Expansionary policies tend to expand prices, not production, in the short run. Once the economy has adjusted to the higher prices, little increase in employment will be experienced. As a result, unemployment can only be dealt with through long-term expansion of the supply side of the economy.

Inflation, in the monetarist view, is caused by too rapid an expansion of the money supply. If the supply of money grows faster than the demand for it, it follows that a surplus of money will follow and the value of money will fall as the price level rises. Since the demand for money (resulting from aggregate supply) expands only very slowly, anything but a slow, steady increase in the supply of money is bound to be inflationary.

CRITICISMS OF MONETARY POLICIES

In the past, monetary policy has concentrated on increasing and decreasing the money supply in order to affect interest rates and investment spending. In the process, the monetarists claim, it has created more recessions and caused more inflations than it has cured. The reason for this, they suggest, is that the makers of monetary policy do not recognize the difference between value and price.

The interest rate is the price of credit. Most monetary policies over the years have attempted to affect this price. But the economy responds not to the price of this form of money, but to its value—the purchasing power of money. Monetarists note that the interest rate has been relatively stable over the past hundred years, but the value of money has declined significantly.

Because they look at interest rates, FRS policy makers miss the point of money. They should look instead at the value of money and so, since value is proportional to supply, concentrate on attaining the optimal supply of money, not the best level of interest rates.

Traditional monetary policy has ignored the importance of the supply of money by looking myopically at interest rates. This has caused the money supply to vary widely, producing broad ups and downs in the economy.

FRIEDMAN'S POLICY OF RULES

Recognizing the fact that the FRS is likely to continue to pay attention to interest rates instead of watching the money supply itself, Milton Friedman has suggested that discretionary monetary policy be done away with. If policy makers are going to cause recessions and high inflation because they don't understand the true role of money, he suggests, FRS policy should be replaced by a simple rule: The money supply should be automatically increased at a constant average rate—say, 5 percent per year. This is roughly the increase in aggregate supply that we might expect, so this rate of increase should cause a noninflationary "balanced growth" of aggregate demand and supply.

If the money supply is increased at this steady rate, monetary policy cannot, obviously, be used as a tool of stabilization policy to fight inflation or unemployment. But, the monetarists insist, monetary policy cannot be unwittingly used to *cause* inflation or unemployment, either.

Rules policy: a policy whereby the money supply is constantly expanded at a uniform rate according to a 'rule' or formula

This **rules policy** would essentially take the government out of the economic policy business, in the monetarist's view. If monetary policy is not used in dealing with inflation or unemployment, and if fiscal policy cannot be used to affect these problems (as the monetarists hold), then the economy must operate on its own. This laissez-faire policy, the monetarists suggest, will result in more stable long-run growth, with fewer booms and busts in the short run as well. Monetarists hold that the economy, left to its own means, is really very stable anyway, and little needs the help that government policies provide. The policy of rules would take advantage of this natural stability.

WHO'S RIGHT, HERE?

At one time the separation between monetarists and traditional Keynesian economists was very great. Recently, however, the gap has narrowed as each side has seen virtue in the other's camp.

While the point is certainly arguable, it is likely that neither side of this issue is completely correct. Traditionalists who insist that when people are faced with an increase in the money supply they will run out and buy bonds are probably wrong in the same way that monetarists are who insist that all of any increased money supply will be immediately spent. The truth probably lies somewhere in the middle, with both traditional Keynesian and monetarist analyses holding to a certain extent.

A true test of the monetarist model may be difficult to achieve, however. So long as the policy makers at the FRS and the president and leaders of Congress have substantially different views of the economy, they will probably attempt to offset one another's actions by actively using monetary and fiscal policies. If this is the case, then the effectiveness of either viewpoint will be unclear.

To complicate matters, the international economy is of increasing importance in any discussion of national economic problems. This complicates our analysis of monetary and fiscal policies. Part IV of this text is devoted to the discussion of international economics.

SUMMARY

1. Monetarists belong to a school of economic thought which analyzes economic activity in terms of exchange. Money, as the medium of exchange, occupies a central position in the monetarist model of the economy. Monetarists see control of the money supply as the most important aspect of economic policy.

2. The traditional view of the economy (as presented in the preceding two chapters) holds money to be important because of its role in credit creation. Investment spending rises and falls when interest rates change. Money is important because it affects these interest rates. Monetarists theorize that total spending depends on the amount of money available. Aggregate supply (sellers) are money demanders, and aggregate demand (buyers) are the suppliers of money. Aggregate demand and supply, then, are determined by the supply and demand for money.

3. Monetarists view all economic policy as being dependent upon changes in the money supply. Monetary policy, then, can directly affect aggregate demand. Fiscal policy is ineffective (since it cannot alter the supply of money) unless monetary policy is also used.

4. Monetarists suggest that fiscal policies should be minimized (since they are ineffective). Monetary policy should not be used either, since sudden rises and falls in the money supply designed to fight inflation or unemployment will instead cause economic ills. The monetarist prescription for "balanced growth" of aggregate demand and supply calls for a slow, steady expansion of the money supply (and therefore aggregate demand) at about the same rate as the historical expansion of

money demand (aggregate supply). Monetarists call for this policy of rules rather than discretionary actions.

5. The true model of the economy may well lie between the monetarist and traditional Keynesian

extremes. In the meantime, however, political priorities often prevail, and the need for short-term solutions to long-term problems makes economic policy hard to understand and difficult to implement.

DISCUSSION QUESTIONS

1. Suppose that the economy is experiencing high levels of unemployment. What would be the traditional Keynesian policy recommendation to deal with this problem? What would the monetarists suggest? If the monetarists are correct, what would traditional policies do to the economy? If the traditional view is correct, what would the monetarist policies accomplish?

2. Answer the questions in Question 1 in the case when the economy is experiencing high levels of inflation.

3. How does the monetarist view of fiscal policy differ from the traditional Keynesian view? Where does the key difference lie?

4. Would you favor Friedman's rules policy for money supply growth if you subscribed to the traditional view of the economy? Why or why not?

TEST YOURSELF

Indicate whether each of the following statements is *true* or *false*. Be able to defend your choice.

1. Monetarists believe that money is important because it serves as a basis for credit transactions.

2. Monetarists believe that the FRS should undertake actions designed to stabilize interest rates through a policy of "rules."

3. The equation of exchange is a simple statement of monetarism. If the money supply and total output are fixed in the short run, then an increase in the velocity of money can only cause the price level to fall.

4. In the monetarist view, the only impact that government spending can have on the economy is to alter the velocity of money for short periods.

5. Aggregate demand represents the supply of money, since purchasers supply dollars in exchange for goods and services.

6. Aggregate supply represents the demand for money, since producers demand dollars in exchange for goods and services.

7. An increase in the money supply causes an equal and opposite decrease in the aggregate supply.

8. In the monetarist view, an increase in government spending accompanied by an increase in taxes of the same amount will cause aggregate demand to rise because of the difference in the multiplier impacts of spending and taxation.

9. In the monetarist model, an increase in government spending can only expand the economy if it is financed by borrowing from the FRS.

10. The monetarist policy of rules is designed to expand aggregate demand and aggregate supply at the same rate so as to provide economic growth without inflation.

The Federal Reserve System was created by the Congress in 1913. Congress took great pains to see that the administrators of the FRS would be isolated from political and popular pressures. The FRS was to be the "Supreme Court of Banking." The important officers of the FRS are appointed by the president, but they serve for fourteen years (while the presidential tenure is only four years). Once appointed, they are responsible to neither the Congress nor the president. The FRS does not even depend on Congress for annual funding. The FRS earns so much interest on its holdings of government securities that it can pay all of its bills and still show a yearly surplus (which is given back to the Treasury).

Although the FRS was created by legislative, not constitutional, initiative, it has seemingly become the fourth branch of government (along with the executive, legislative, and judicial branches). When the independence of the FRS was established in the early part of this century, the economic policy importance of the FRS was much less than it is today. Since, as we have seen, the FRS can reinforce fiscal policies or act to counteract them, the question arises: Should the FRS be an independent branch of government? Or should this independence be terminated?

The debate over the independence of the FRS has raged for some years. Discussion is hottest when the Board of Governors of the FRS hold different political or economic views from those of the president and the Congress. Let's look at some of the arguments on each side of this debate.

ECONOMIC CONTROVERSIES VI: INDEPENDENCE OF THE FEDERAL RESERVE SYSTEM

END THE FRS' INDEPENDENCE

The Federal Reserve System should be made responsible to and controllable by the Congress. The current situation is dangerous to the economy and to democracy. One of the fundamental principles of democracy is that the people ought to have a say in the making of government policy. The makers of fiscal policy have to face the voters periodically and account for the decisions that they and their administrators have made. If they pass a tax law or fail to adequately deal with economic events, the people can throw them out. This is not the case with the governors of the FRS. They can impose a tax on money—inflation—or create high levels of unemployment without facing the public and accounting for their actions.

Public policy ought to be carried out by elected government representatives. The FRS policy makers are not now accountable to the public's elected representatives—the Congress and the President.

Under the current structure, the Federal Reserve does not take adequate care in coordinating its activities with the Congress's fiscal policies. In fact, the FRS often makes fiscal policy harder to carry out. In 1977–1978, for example, the Congress and the President enacted budgets that had large deficits. The purpose of this borrowing was to cut taxes, increase spending, and so increase aggregate demand and help the unemployed.

The leaders of the FRS, however, were working to accomplish other goals. Their restrictive monetary policies bid up interest rates, making it harder for the government to borrow and making the deficit more expensive to finance. More importantly, perhaps, the high interest rates that the FRS caused acted to offset some of the impact of the fiscal policies.

Federal reserve policies are sometimes irresponsible in that they move in the opposite direction from fiscal policies. If the FRS were made responsible to the Congress, then accommodating monetary policy would be assured. Monetary and fiscal policies would be more effective operating together than they are today operating apart.

KEEP THE FRS INDEPENDENT

One of the reasons for the independence of the FRS was, from the start, to insulate monetary policy from the cold winds of politics. The money, credit, and banking system is too important to our overall economic health to be entrusted to politicians who do not understand how it works and what its powers are. The FRS should remain in the hands of responsible people who understand what money can and cannot do and who will act sensibly to cope with our economic problems.

There are great advantages in having monetary and fiscal policies determined by separate groups. This minimizes the probability of another great depression or a period of very high inflation.

Economic policy makers know that their actions take time to work. They must look to the future and guess what will be happening when their policies take effect. If there is just one economic policy agent, then these policies will be either right or wrong. The ups and downs in economic trends will be very large. Boom and bust will prevail.

If, however, there are two groups making policy, the chances for disaster are reduced. Suppose that each group has a 50 percent chance of being right about policy needs. Then it follows that there is only a 25 percent chance that they will both be wrong at the same time and cause either high inflation, unemployment, or both. There is also a 25 percent chance that they will both be right and we will get, perhaps, too much of a good thing. And there is a 50 percent chance that each will guess differently and they will effectively cancel each other's actions out, leaving the economy to manage by itself. A strong economy may actually be better off in this situation.

Since the leaders of monetary and fiscal policies are reasonably intelligent, they ought to be able to guess right more than 50 percent of the time, so our chances of having both policies lean the wrong way at any time are much reduced. The countervailing forces act to promote economic growth and development.

Monetarists argue that politicians are too likely to tinker with the money supply needlessly and so bring on economic woes. A system of steady monetary policy is probably only possible under an independent FRS, and so the status quo should be maintained.

DISCUSSION QUESTIONS

1. Can you think of other government agencies which have an independence similar to that of the FRS?

2. How would a monetarist view the impact of a monetary policy that always accommodates fiscal actions? Would this be desirable or detrimental to the economy?

3. Evaluate the "probabilities" argument in favor of FRS independence.

Part 4
International Economics

13
International Trade

This chapter begins a discussion of international economics with an analysis of foreign trade and payments. International trade is becoming an increasingly controversial part of the economy. This chapter will answer a number of important questions, including the following:

Why do nations trade?

What determines a nation's imports and exports?

What are tariffs and quotas?

Who bears the burden of tariffs and quotas?

Are tariffs good or bad?

What are the balance of payments and balance of trade?

Should we be concerned if the United States has a deficit in the balance of payments or balance of trade?

Closed economy: an economy that has no economic interaction with the rest of the world

Open economy: an economy which has free economic interaction with the rest of the world

Thus far we have developed a fairly sophisticated and descriptive model of the way the national economy works. We have analyzed some of the causes of and solutions to inflation and unemployment and looked at the form and substance of monetary and fiscal policies. Through it all, we have neglected only one significant area: the rest of the world!

Our analysis has concentrated on the workings of a **closed economy.** A closed economy is one that doesn't trade or otherwise interact with any other economy. Such closed economies do not now exist and probably haven't since feudal times. We live in **open economies**—economic systems that are open to international trade and exert economic influence across national borders.

Open economies face two economic facts of life: scarcity and interdependence. Resources are scarce in the world, and so the competition for and control of those resources is important to all nations. Interdependence results from the fact that no nation can—or should—produce all of the things that it wants. Given the scarce nature of resources, the efficient use of those resources demands the cooperative step of international trade. Trade, as we shall see, serves as an allocator of scarce resources and helps assure that resources are used as efficiently as possible, which is advantageous to us all.

Free trade is beneficial to all parties involved (why else would they trade?), but it also presents problems in our modern economic setting. Flows of goods and services across national borders (imports and exports) generate jobs in the exporting countries but may lead to unemployment in the importing nations. Money flows must accompany imports and exports. These currency movements further serve to complicate the international scene. International investment activities add to the complications as well.

Part IV of this text explains why nations trade and indicates some of the consequences of that trade on exchange rates, international payments, and economic policy. This chapter deals with questions relating to international trade. Chapter 14 develops a useful model of foreign exchange markets. Finally, Chapters 15 and 16 tie together all that we have learned by building models of open economies and an interdependent world.

WHY DO NATIONS TRADE?

Why *do* nations trade? The obvious answer to this question is that nations trade in order to acquire goods, services, and resources that they cannot produce at home. The obvious answer, however, explains only a small part of international trade flows.

Goods which are physically unavailable, such as natural resources or agricultural goods which require unusual climatic conditions, account for only a small (but important) fraction of all traded goods. In the United States, for example, we *must* trade in order to get coffee, tea, and chromium because these goods cannot be produced given our climate (in the case of coffee and tea) or are not found within our geographical borders (chromium). But most traded goods do not fall into either of these categories.

Most of the things that we import are readily available within our nation or could be produced here if we wished to do so. Think for a moment of the things which we import from abroad. Oil, autos, cameras, chemicals, textiles, electronic items, steel, musical instruments—the list is long and made up primarily of items which could be produced at home. Why do we purchase these foreign goods? Because they are cheaper? But why are they cheaper? The answer here is not so clear. Autos in Europe and Japan are not produced in factories substantially different from those in Detroit. Where does the difference lie?

The question is not a new one. It was first posed in the nineteenth century by the English economist David Ricardo. Ricardo observed a great deal of trade taking place between Great Britain and Portugal. Great Britain exported cloth to Portugal and imported wine. Either country, however, could produce both goods, so there was no obvious reason why this particular trade pattern should exist. It was just as possible, on the face of it, that Portugal should export cloth and Britain export wine, or that no trade would take place and each country could satisfy its own needs. How did the cloth-wine trade pattern come about? Ricardo decided to find out.

Ricardo first sought the answer by looking at the productivity of resources in both countries. Perhaps there was some technological reason for the trade pattern. To find out, Ricardo defined a basic "resource unit" (composed of set amounts of labor, land, and capital) and studied the produuctivity of resource units in each country.

In Great Britain, Ricardo discovered that a hypothetical resource bundle could be put to work in the mills and would produce four yards of cloth. If the same resources were devoted to the production of wine in Great Britain, the yield would be six bottles.

In Portugal the story was different. If a resource bundle were put to work producing textiles, it would be able to make five yards of cloth. And if used in the wine industry, the resource bundle would make fifteen bottles of wine.

Here was clearly a paradox! The same resources in Portugal could produce more wine than in Great Britain (as you might expect), but they could also produce more cloth! Ricardo said that Portugal had an **absolute advantage** in the production of both goods, meaning that the Portuguese were more efficient in production—could produce more with the same resources.

This lead to a new question: Why should Portugal import cloth from

Absolute advantage: the advantage enjoyed by a country which is more efficient in production of a particular good

Great Britain when they can produce it more efficiently themselves? Portugal should have no incentive to trade with Great Britain, since they have the absolute advantage in the production of both goods. But the wine-cloth trade did exist, so there must be something else going on. To understand the rationale for international trade Ricardo introduced one additional concept: scarcity.

Portugal is the more efficient producer in this example, but its ability to produce is limited by a finite supply of scarce resources. There are physical limits to the amounts of land, labor, and capital available in the short run to each country for use in production. Because resources are finite, there are trade-offs in production. Whenever the Portuguese decide to produce more wine they are implicitly choosing, because resources are finite, to produce less of cloth and other things. Additional resources used to produce good A necessarily means that there is less available to produce good B. When we choose to produce more wine, we are, in fact, giving up the cloth that those same resources could have produced instead. These foregone goods represent an *opportunity cost* of production.

Ricardo decided to analyze his trade problem in terms of the opportunity costs of production in each country. With finite resources, for example, the last resource bundle in Great Britain could be used to produce *either* 4 yards of cloth *or* 6 bottles of wine. Therefore, if a yard of cloth is produced, on average the British are *giving up* the 1½ bottles of wine which could have been produced instead.

Likewise, if a bottle of wine is produced in Great Britain, an average ⅔ of a yard of cloth must be foregone. The opportunity costs of production in Britain, then, are as follows:

1 yard cloth = 1½ bottles of wine
1 bottle of wine = ⅔ yard of cloth

The production trade-offs are different in Portugal. With the last resource unit in Portugal *either* 5 yards of cloth *or* 15 bottles of wine may be produced. It follows, then, that the opportunity costs of production are

1 yard of cloth = 3 bottles of wine
1 bottle of wine = ⅓ yard of cloth

Now a reason for the trade pattern starts to become clear. Why should Great Britain import wine? If they produce wine at home, because they are not very efficient at producing wine it will take the resource equivalent of ⅔ yards of cloth to do so. So they must give up ⅔ yard of cloth in order to make wine. But the Portugese need give up only ⅓ yard of cloth to produce a bottle of wine. The opportunity cost of producing wine is less in Portugal. The Portugese have a **comparative advantage** in producing wine. Since they

Comparative advantage: the advantage enjoyed by a country which can produce a particular good at lower opportunity cost

give up fewer other goods when they produce wine, Ricardo concluded, Portugal should (and did!) export the good in which they had a comparative advantage.

Why should Portugal, who is the more efficient producer of cloth as well, choose to import that commodity? The answer, again, lies in the opportunity costs. When Portugal produces a yard of cloth, they must give up the equivalent of 3 bottles of wine. But in Great Britain, a yard of cloth can be produced with the loss of only 1½ bottles of wine. Great Britain has the comparative advantage in the production of cloth, since they give up fewer other goods when they produce cloth.

GAINS FROM TRADE

When trade takes place according to the laws of comparative advantage, with each country exporting the good in which it holds the comparative advantage, both nations will gain. How can both gain? Well, suppose that some mutually agreeable trading scheme were proposed. For example, suppose that a trading ratio of 1 yard of cloth = 2 bottles of wine (or, put another way, 1 bottle of wine = ½ yard of cloth) were proposed. Both countries could purchase goods cheaper than they could make them at home. In Britain, for example, they could acquire wine by trading ½ yard of cloth for each bottle. If they made the wine at home, it would cost them the equivalent of ⅔ yard of cloth which would have to be given up. It is therefore cheaper to buy wine from Portugal than to make it at home for the British.

Would the Portuguese be willing to sell wine at this price? Of course! They can sell wine to the British (who would be happy to buy it) for ½ yard of cloth, but it costs them only the equivalent of ⅓ yard of cloth to produce a bottle of wine. Therefore, if the Portuguese specialize in producing wine, they can sell it to Britain and receive in return more cloth than they could produce with the same resources at home. The British gain from this trade because they buy wine for less than it would cost to make it, and the Portuguese gain because they receive in payment more cloth than they could make themselves with a similar amount of resources.

The Portuguese are likewise happy to purchase cloth from Britain. It costs them 3 bottles of wine to produce a yard of cloth at home, but they can buy the cloth from the British (at our hypothetical trading ratio) for only 2 bottles of wine. So imported cloth is cheaper, in terms of wine, than domestic cloth.

The British, for their part, are happy to sell the cloth. They receive the wine equivalent of 2 bottles of wine for each yard of cloth that they export,

FIGURE 13-1: GAINS FROM TRADE BETWEEN GREAT BRITAIN AND PORTUGAL
These production possibilities curves show the limitations of the economies of Great Britain and Portugal. Without trade, Great Britain can have only 150 units of wine if they choose to consume 300 units of cloth. Through specialization and trade, however, more wine may be obtained without giving up any cloth consumption. The same idea holds true in Portugal. Hence mutually beneficial trade is possible.

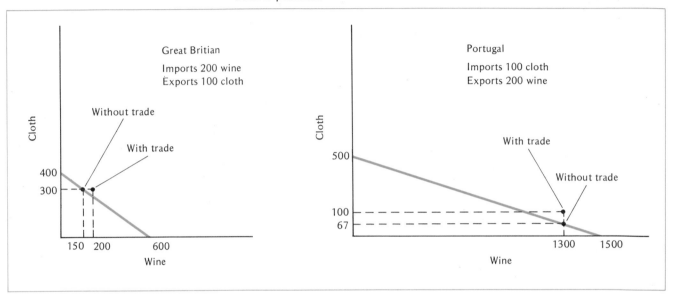

Production possibility curve (PPC): a graph showing the different possible combinations of two goods which can be produced with limited resources

but that cloth costs only 1½ bottles of wine worth of resources to produce. Both countries are better off from this trade.

We can see the gains from trade another way using the **production possibility curves** shown in Figure 13-1. A production possibility curve shows the amounts of different goods that a country can produce with its scarce resources.

Let us suppose, for example, that both Great Britain and Portugal have 100 resource bundles to use in producing either cloth or wine, and that all resource bundles are equally productive in both uses. In Britain, then, these scarce resources can be used to produce *either* 400 yards of cloth *or* 600 bottles of wine, or any of the combinations of cloth and wine given by the production possibilities curve (PPC) in Figure 13-1. All combinations on or below the PPC line in Figure 13-1 are attainable. All combinations outside the PPC are impossible for Britain to attain by itself. For instance, if the British choose to produce 300 yards of cloth, they can produce only 150 bottles of wine with the remaining resources. It is impossible for them to produce both more cloth and more wine than this.

In Portugal a like situation prevails. With their 100 resource bundles, the

Portuguese can have either 1500 bottles of wine or 500 yards of cloth or any combination of wine and cloth given by their production possibility curve. As a result, if they choose to produce 1300 bottles of wine, the remaining resources will make only 67 yards of cloth.

Now, suppose that both countries specialize in the production of the good in which they hold the comparative advantage. In Britain, this means that they devote all of their resources to the production of 400 yards of cloth. But at the trading ratio of 1 yard of cloth = 2 bottles of wine, they can keep 300 yards of cloth and trade the remaining 100 yards for 200 bottles of wine—a combination which they were unable to produce on their own. International trade, in this case, allows the British to have as much cloth as before, and even more wine! Obviously, the British gain from this transaction.

But the Protuguese gain as well. If they specialize and produce 1500 bottles of wine using all of their resources for this purpose, they can drink 1300 bottles and trade the remaining 200 bottles for 100 yards of cloth. Without trade, they were capable of producing only 67 yards of cloth when they made 1300 bottles of wine. Now, with trade, they can produce 1500 bottles of wine, keep 1300 bottles, and trade the remaining 200 bottles for 100 yards of cloth. They gain the equivalent of 33 yards of cloth through trade!

Both countries can attain consumption combinations which were previously impossible and thereby escape the bounds of their production possibilities curves. Each country is better off in that they are able to consume more goods and services through trade than they could produce without trade. The world gains, as well, since there is more total production taking place with the use of the same amounts of limited resources, as can be seen in the following:

	Production without Trade			Production with Trade	
	Wine	Cloth		Wine	Cloth
England	150	300	England	0.	400
Portugal	1300	67	Portugal	1500	0
Total	1450	367	Total	1500	400

Two gains from trade are apparent here. First, there is an increase in the amount of goods which each country has available for consumption when trade takes place. Further, there is a production gain in that the total of 200 resource bundles are able to produce both more total cloth and more total wine when each country specializes along the lines of comparative advantage.

International trade, then, is mutually advantageous. This is the result that Ricardo was searching for. Since each country can gain materially by specializing according to comparative advantage, international trade makes sense and the pattern of trade he observed was both natural and profitable for all concerned.

COMPARATIVE ADVANTAGE IN THE REAL WORLD

All of this looks nice on paper and may have even made sense in Ricardo's world, but does it work in today's real world? The answer, surprisingly enough, is yes!

We need not look very far for an example to bear this conclusion out. The United States imports oil from the OPEC nations and tends to export to them agricultural goods. It is obvious that both trading partners could satisfy their needs at home without international trade. That is, the United States could produce all of its own oil and OPEC could produce their own agricultural goods, but what would this involve?

If the United States were to decide to produce all its own oil, this could be accomplished in a relatively short period of time, but at what cost? Billions of dollars of resources would have to be diverted from other uses in order to increase oil production (the Alaska pipeline, which alone cost nearly $10 billion, is a good example of the costs necessary). More oil would be produced, of course, but the process would drain our production of other goods dramatically. The opportunity cost of producing all this additional oil would be very, very high.

Likewise, the OPEC nations could produce all the foodstuffs they require, but this would involve turning the deserts into farms. Expensive dams would need to be built, soils and technologies imported, and billions and billions of dollars of resources would need to be diverted from other uses. Here, again, the opportunity costs are high.

However, in the United States, the opportunity cost of producing agricultural goods is low, because of the abundance of good farmland. And in the OPEC countries, the opportunity cost of producing oil is similarly low because of its abundance and ease of extraction.

It follows, then, that it is cheaper for the United States to buy oil from OPEC rather than increasing production at home, and it is cheaper for the OPEC nations to buy foodstuffs rather than increase their domestic production of these commodities. This is the law of comparative advantage at work, and it assures effective and efficient use of resources around the world. This is a happy case where what is profitable for businesses and nations also conserves (or prevents waste of) scarce resources around the world. In short, Ricardo was right.

Even though free trade among nations carries with it all of these very desirable results, there are still many barriers to international trade which are erected by individual countries. These trade barriers take two main forms: tariffs and quotas.

A **tariff** is a tax on imports levied at the national level. Tariffs may be charged in two ways. An **ad valorem tariff** is a tariff calculated according to the value of the imported good involved. Such a tariff might be, for example, 10 percent of the wholesale value of an imported car. With a **unit tariff,** on the other hand, a fixed tax is charged for each unit of a commodity imported, regardless of its value. A tariff of 20¢ per pound of tea is an example of a unit tariff.

The whole idea of the tariff is to discourage consumption of imported goods by raising their price. Tariffs can be very effective in doing this, as shown in Figure 13-2. Before the tariff is imposed, this imported item sells for a price P_0 and an amount Q_0 is imported. When the tariff is imposed, however, this increases the importer's cost of selling imported goods. Since the government is increasing their cost of doing business, the importers react by passing the higher costs along to consumers. This causes the shift in the

TRADE RESTRICTIONS

Tariff: a tax on imports

Ad valorem tariff: a tariff levied according to the value of an imported item

Unit tariff: a tariff levied according to the number of units of an item imported

FIGURE 13-2: THE EFFECTS OF A TARIFF
The tariff increases the cost of selling the imported good, and so acts to decrease the supply of the import. The tariff causes price to rise, and so the equilibrium amount purchased falls.

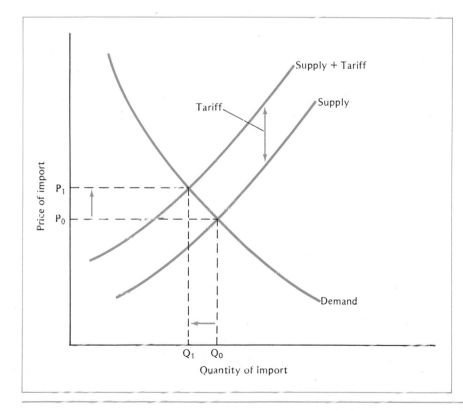

supply curve shown in Figure 13-2, forcing the price up to P_1. At the higher price, of course, there is a smaller demand for the imported goods, and as a result the amount of imports falls from Q_0 to Q_1. This is the result that the government wished to induce. Tariffs are a way to raise revenue for the government, but their true purpose is to discourage imports.

Tariffs do not always work this way, however. In 1971 President Nixon imposed a special tariff on imported cars in an attempt to raise their price so that car buyers would shift their purchases to Detroit products. It didn't work because some of the foreign producers—especially the Japanese car-makers—did something unexpected. When the higher tariff was imposed on them, they *didn't* try to pass it onto the consumers. Instead, they bore the full burden of the tariffs themselves (so the supply curve did not shift) and kept their prices low, even though it meant losing money. They did this because they felt that the special tariff would be short-lived and that it would be worthwhile to take losses for a while in order to keep their foot in the door. A glance at recent car sales figures indicates that this was a pretty good idea.

Since a tariff does not always accomplish its goals, people who want to limit imports sometimes resort to a more direct means: a **quota.**

Quota: the physical limitation on the amount of a good that can be imported

A quota is a physical limitation on an import. For example, instead of putting a tax on imported liquor, a quota would simply set a maximum amount of booze that could enter the country. Once the quota is filled, all other import shipments are turned away at the border. This restriction is administered by the use of special quota allocations. If a good is subject to a quota, then any importation must be accompanied by a special voucher which the importer has usually purchased from the government. Because only a limited number of these vouchers or import licenses are available, only a limited number of the goods may come into the country.

A quota accomplishes the same end as a tariff in a different way. In Figure 13-3, the imported goods shown would sell for a price P_0 if no tariff or quota were in force, and imports would total an amount Q_0. The quota arbitrarily restricts the imported supply. As a result, the limited supply creates a shortage of the good and only those who are willing to pay a great deal for it will receive it. The market rations the quota supply to the highest bidders and the price rises to P_1. The quota is completely effective in reducing imports.

Economists generally dislike both tariffs and quotas because they undermine the beneficial effects of international trade, but of the two the quota is singled out for particular criticism. With a quota, once the limit is reached, additional imported goods cannot be bought no matter how much people want them or how badly they are needed. With a tariff, additional imports can always be had, so long as consumers are willing to pay the high

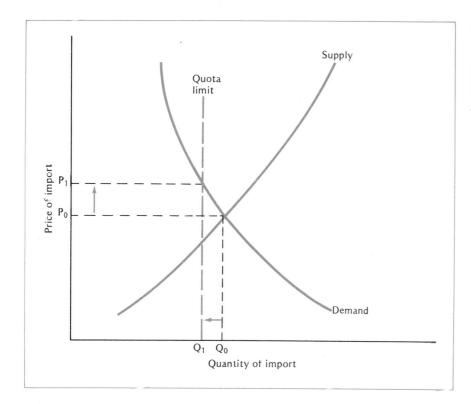

FIGURE 13-3: THE EFFECTS OF A QUOTA
The quota sets a physical limit on the amount of an import which may enter the country. This limitation directly reduces imports and also creates a shortage which leads to higher prices.

import price. So if an imported item like coffee is in great demand, people who want it enough can induce more imports by agreeing to pay a high price. With a quota this just isn't possible.

When a tariff is imposed, who bears the burden of the import tax? Politicians might suspect that, since the foreign producer actually writes the check to pay the tax, the burden falls on the maker of the imported good. Consumers, however, suspect that they pay for the tariff in higher prices at the market. In reality, both views hold to some extent. The burden of the tariff is normally split between consumer and foreign producers. The division of the burden depends upon the type of good involved.

To see this, let's divide all imports into two classes. In the first group we will put imported items which are necessities or have few close substitutes (imported coffee, tea, or oil, for example). Because people cannot or will not switch in the short run to substitute products when the price of these necessary goods rise, the amount purchased is unlikely to change very much when the price changes. We say that this demand is unresponsive to

WHO PAYS THE TARIFF?

FIGURE 13-4: TARIFF ON A GOOD WITH INELASTIC DEMAND
A tariff on a good with an inelastic demand is paid mostly by the consumer. Here a $1.00 tax on imported oil ends up with a 75¢ increase in price and a 25¢ producer burden.

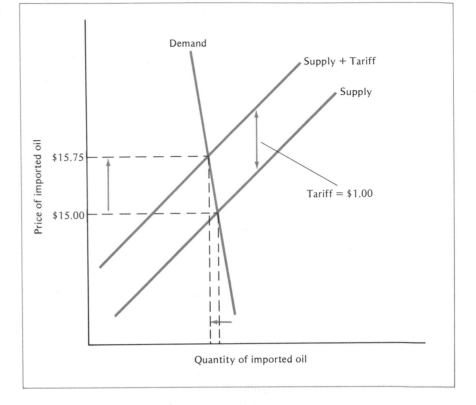

Inelastic demand: the property of a product when quantity demanded does not change very much relative to price changes, e.g., necessity items or goods with few close substitutes

Elastic demand: the property of a product when the quantity demanded changes substantially when price changes, e.g., goods which have close substitutes or are luxury items

price—or, to use the economist's term, that the good has an **inelastic demand.**

Other types of goods, however, have many close substitutes or are essentially luxury items. When the price of these goods changes, the quantity demanded changes, too, by a large amount. We say that these goods have responsive demands—or, in the economists' jargon, have **elastic demands.** A small change in price generates a relatively large change in quantity demanded because of the wide variety of options available.

Let's see how the burden of the tariff is divided in each of these demand cases. First let's look at a hypothetical tariff on a good with an inelastic demand. Suppose that the market for imported oil in the United States looks like that picture in Figure 13-4. Here the equilibrium price for imported oil is assumed to be $15.00 per barrel. The demand curve for oil is drawn very steeply here to suggest that the quantity of oil demanded does not change much in the short run even when price changes are large.

Now, let's impose a $1.00-per-barrel tariff on oil imports. Because the tariff is imposed on the importer of oil, it increases the cost of importing oil by $1.00 per barrel. Oil importers will attempt to pass this cost increase on to their customers (the supply curve shifts) and will temporarily raise the price of oil to $16.00 per barrel.

At the post-tariff price of $16.00, there is a surplus of imported oil. Most people continue to buy the oil even at the higher price because their options, in the short run, are very limited. In the long run, users of oil products may insulate their homes, buy more economical cars, or shift to alternative energy sources in order to avoid the higher oil prices. In the short run, however, they can only turn down their thermostats and drive fewer miles. As a result, the quantity of oil demanded falls only a little bit in the face of the price increase. Even this small surplus, however, will have some effect on the market. Oil importers will find that they have unintended inventory accumulations of petroleum and will cut the price in order to sell off the excess. The equilibrium price occurs here at $15.75 per barrel.

Who has paid the tariff? Two groups must bear higher costs. Consumers pay 75¢ more per barrel. This represents the **consumers' burden** of the tariff. Because they have few options in the short run, consumers have little choice but to bear the bulk of the $1.00 tariff. The producer bears a small (25¢) burden. The producer pays $1.00 per barrel to the government, but receives only an additional 75¢ from consumers. The producer pays part of the tariff in lower effective price. Before the tariff the producer received $15.00 per barrel for the oil. Now, he receives $15.75, but must pay $1.00 to the government as a tariff. The net price is only $14.75. The 25¢ difference is the **producers' burden.** The consumer bears the bulk of the burden of a tariff imposed on a good with an inelastic demand.

Consumer's burden: the proportion of a tariff that is passed along to consumers in terms of higher import prices

Producer's burden: the reduction in net selling price caused by the imposition of a tariff

What has happened to the quantity of imports (the equilibrium quantity of this market)? It has fallen (as tariff theory suggests it ought), but not by very much. Because oil has an inelastic demand, the tariff is not very effective in the short run in limiting imports. It mostly raises price to consumers.

This is not the case when the tariffed good has an elastic (responsive) demand. Figure 13-5, for example, shows the impact of a tariff on a good which has many close domestically produced substitutes: imported wine. Here we assume that the preimport equilibrium occurs at a price of $4.00 per bottle for a certain type of French wine (Chateau Nuef du Charles de Gaulle). Again, a $1.00-per-bottle tariff is imposed. What happens?

As the $1.00 tariff is imposed, wine importers react by passing the entire tariff on to their customers—raising the price temporarily to $5.00 per bottle and shifting the supply curve back by the $1.00 amount of the tax. At $5.00 per bottle, however, a large surplus of wine is created. People who were willing to purchase imported wine at $4.00 a bottle will readily shift to substitutes like California wines when the price of French wine rises. The quantity demanded falls off substantially when the price hits $5.00.

Wine importers need to sell wine in order to survive, and the tariff has

FIGURE 13-5: A TARIFF ON A GOOD
WITH AN ELASTIC DEMAND
*The demand for imported wine is here
assumed to be elastic. When a
$1.00-per-bottle tariff on imported
wine is imposed, only 25¢ of the tariff
is paid by the consumer in higher
prices. The remaining 75¢ burden falls
on producers. Note how much greater
the fall in quantity imported is in this
case compared with the inelastic-good
example.*

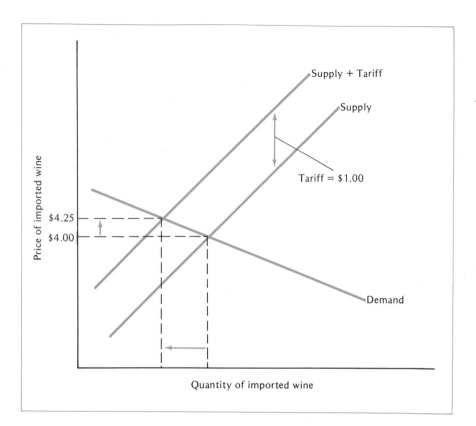

Quantity of imported wine

made them uncompetitive with domestic wine producers. In order to regain
their market, they will cut price, putting their wine on sale. As price falls, the
quantity demanded increases until equilibrium is finally restored at a price
of $4.25 per bottle.

Consumers bear only a small part of the burden of the tariff in this case.
The tariff is $1.00 per bottle, but the price of the wine has risen by only 25¢
because of the many close substitutes for imported wine. Consumers'
burden is small when a good with an elastic demand is tariffed. The
producer or importer bears most of the burden of the tariff in this case. The
seller now receives a higher price ($4.25), but must pay $1.00 more in
taxes, leaving a net price of just $3.25. The seller, then, receives 75¢ less
than before the tariff. This is the producers' burden.

Note, as well, the effect on quantity in this case. Because there are many
alternative domestic suppliers of wine, even the small increase in the price
of imported wine has caused the amount of wine imports to fall substantially. Sales of domestically produced wines rise by a large amount in response
to the tariff as foreign sales decline. The tariff shifts sales from foreign to
domestic suppliers and so serves to protect home-country firms from foreign

competitors. In the case of a good with an inelastic demand, the protection is less successful.

Finally, we can look at the amount of taxes that the government collects in each case. The tariff on the good with the inelastic demand (oil) generated lots of revenue, since the $1.00 tax was paid on almost as many barrels of oil as were imported before the tariff. The tariff on the good with an elastic demand (wine), however, yields few tax dollars because a great deal less of the taxed good now comes into the country.

This may suggest why the British imposed a tariff on tea in the American colonies when they wanted to raise money (producing high revenues to the Crown, placing most of the burden on the colonists and provoking the Boston Tea Party) and why tariffs today are imposed very largely on goods that are also manufactured at home (where protection is the motive for the tariff and revenue considerations are of lesser importance).

Who bears the burden of a quota? In this case, all of the burden falls on the consumer (unless the right to import the fixed quantity is sold by the government). When these import licenses are auctioned, a part of the burden falls on the producer as well.

We have talked about how beneficial free trade is to all involved, so why are trade barriers erected which slow or halt this trade? Most economists agree that there are not many instances where tariffs make much sense to the economy. But still, tariffs and quotas are not set by economists but by Congress, and the Congress isn't bound to make decisions which are economically appealing. Some of the rationale for trade barriers are discussed below.

THE RATIONALE OF BARRIERS TO TRADE

1. PROTECTIVE TARIFF. Many trade restrictions are designed to protect domestic industries from "unfair" (that is, cheaper) foreign competitors. A tariff or quota in this case is designed to raise the price of the imported good so that the home-country product can be produced and sold at a profit. Japanese steelmakers, for example, apparently can make steel in the Far East, ship it across the Pacific Ocean, and still sell for less than many American steel producers. The reason for this is clear: most steel producers in the United States are working with ancient factories and old technology, while the Japanese have newer plants and have taken advantage of technological improvements in steel manufacture. As a result, they can sell for less.

Many American steelmakers have lobbied for a quota on imported steel to protect their companies from this "unfair" competition. To economists, however, this argument does not make sense. If the Japanese are able to produce steel more cheaply, it must be because they have a comparative advantage in this industry (and, indeed, with their modern equipment, they do). Logic suggests that the United States buy as much of this imported steel as possible, and shift their production to areas where the United States has a comparative advantage—agriculture and high-technology goods such as computers. But there are costs in the short run here which many feel may outweigh the long-term benefits. It is probable that the Japanese competition would put some American workers and companies out of business. This would result in unemployment, at least temporarily, among steelworkers. But if a tariff or quota is erected to "protect" these jobs, the economist is quick to point out, all users of steel and steel products (i.e., all of us) will be paying higher prices for these goods because of the trade barriers in order to protect the jobs of a few workers in a particular industry. This doesn't make a lot of sense.

2. INFANT-INDUSTRY ARGUMENT. A slightly better argument for tariffs and quotas is to provide protection to certain types of industries called "infant" industries. The argument here is as follows. Suppose there exists a ready market for a certain good in a country. A healthy and competitive industry could be built up around this demand except for one problem. At the start, because of high initial expenses, the industry will have to sell its goods for a very high price. Because short-run costs are so high, foreign competition will prevent the industry from getting off the ground. If a temporary tariff barrier were erected, however, the business could get started and in a short time be running full-blast so that a tariff protection could be lifted and the international competition met head-on successfully.

This argument makes some sense. In Japan following the Second World War, for example, there was a large potential market for new cars. But because of the high costs of starting up auto factories, it did not appear that Japanese carmakers could compete with foreign imports. To remedy this, the Japanese virtually stopped importation of foreign cars. The "infant" car industry sprang up to fill the demand, and the rest is history.

The problem with this infant-industry argument is that trade restrictions, once on the books, are seldom lifted. As a result, the "temporary" protective tariff becomes, instead, a permanent burdensome tariff which keeps domestic prices high and keeps cheaper imported goods out of the home market.

3. THE NATIONAL DEFENSE ARGUMENT. A final argument for trade barriers involves the controversial matter of national defense. To take an outlandish example, let us suppose that the Japanese became extremely

good at making steel. So good, in fact, that if left alone they would quickly put U.S. Steel out of business. In this case, an argument for a tariff on national defense grounds might run along these lines: Suppose that we got in a war. Also suppose that we weren't all killed in an initial ICBM blast. In that case, we would need steel in order to build tanks, guns, and fallout shelters. But if all our steel came from Japan, then we probably couldn't get any and, as a result, we would lose the war.

So, the argument goes, we should protect the steel industry just so that we will have it around if we need it.

You have to make a lot of assumptions in order to make this argument work, so the whole thing is very iffy. Basically, the national defense argument asks us to protect an unprofitable industry—and to therefore pay higher prices for a long time on account of the tariff or quota protection— so that we all won't be killed in a war, if one ever happens. If you think that all of this is likely, then the trade restrictions make sense. If not, then they don't.

As you can see, there are only a few instances where tariffs and quotas make very much economic sense. Yet these restrictions apply, to a greater or lesser extent, to most things which come across our borders. Why should tariffs be charged against French wines and Scotch whiskey, for example? Clearly, tariffs and quotas are tools of dubious value which act to help the few at the expense of the many.

THE BALANCE OF PAYMENTS

Flows of goods and services across national borders are of concern to businesses, policy makers, and economists. It is useful to be able to measure these flows in order to determine the extent and nature of international trade and to see how economic policies affect our trade relations with other countries. There are two basic measures of these international flows: the **balance of payments,** which looks at all international payments, and the **balance of trade,** which measures only payments resulting from trades involving goods and services.

The balance of payments is the broadest measure of a nation's international economic standing. The balance of payments looks at all inflows (payments directed into a country from trading partners) and outflows (payments to the residents of other countries). There are basically three types of inflows and outflows that need concern us here. Money can flow into a country as a result of exports, investment inflows, and transfer payments. Exports generate an inflow because, although goods or services leave the country, a payment for those goods enters from the foreign buyer. Investment inflows are loan or investment funds which cross borders. When a Saudi Arabian firm invests in a U.S. hotel chain, for example, funds enter

Balance of payments: an accounting of total inflows and outflows (including imports and exports, investment flows, and transfer payments) of an economy

Balance of trade: an accounting of the imports and exports of an economy

the United States from Saudi Arabia. This is a capital inflow. Finally, the governments or residents of other nations may give money to governments, businesses, or individuals in this country. These gifts represent transfer inflows.

The outflows are very much of the same nature. Outflows are generated by imports (we get the goods, but must make payment to a foreign firm), investment outflows (when a U.S. firm invests abroad), and transfer outflows (foreign aid and CARE packages).

Balance of payments surplus: a country's total money inflows exceed its total money outflows

We say that a nation experiences a **balance-of-payments surplus** when inflows exceed outflows. This simply means that the country is receiving more in payment for exports, investment from abroad, and transfers from others than it is paying out for imports, investments in foreign countries, and in gifts to other lands. A **balance-of-payments deficit,** on the other hand, means that total outflows exceed total inflows.

Balance of payments deficit: a country's total money outflows exceed its total money inflows

Which is better—surplus or deficit? Most would guess that surplus is to be preferred, since a surplus here indicates that you are taking in more than you are paying out and therefore earning a national "profit" instead of a loss. In truth, however, it depends upon what the funds are purchasing, how much you have to start with, and how long either of the conditions continues.

The United States, for example, has tended to run a deficit in the balance of payments for several years. This has made American policy makers and citizens very nervous about the balance-of-payments figures. The deficit became so upsetting a few years ago, in fact, that the government decided to quit officially announcing balance-of-payments figures. Why did they do this? Was it to cover up a major problem? No. The change was made because there is good reason to believe that the United States will run a balance-of-payments deficit for many years in the future and that, in fact, the United States actually *should* be a deficit nation because of the stage of development that the United States is in.

STAGES OF BALANCE OF PAYMENTS

The United States has passed through four different growth stages with respect to its balance-of-payments status, and other nations may pass through these steps as well. The stages of growth are as follows:

1. IMMATURE DEBTOR.

A developing country (like the United States in colonial days) has many undeveloped natural resources, but often lacks the means to exploit these riches. The nation therefore imports many goods and services (particularly manufactured goods) and also accepts investment funds from abroad (investment inflows) as well as transfer payments. The large imports give the nation a balance-of-payments deficit (makes it an **immature debtor nation**), but this condition is only temporary.

Immature debtor nation: a less-developed country which has a deficit balance of payments resulting from imports of goods and services and high investment and transfer inflows

2. IMMATURE CREDITOR. Once the basic natural resources are developed (in the United States this meant agricultural production), a nation tends to export raw materials and agricultural goods and import the manufactured goods that it needs. Large exports of timber, minerals, and foodstuffs can give the nation a balance-of-payments surplus (**immature creditor** status). The United States held this status in the early 1800s, and Saudi Arabia is probably an immature creditor now, selling oil and buying manufactured goods.

Immature creditor nation: a nation which has a surplus balance of payments resulting from high exports of raw materials

3. MATURE CREDITOR. Next comes the **mature-creditor** stage. The nation here develops the natural resources that it had been exporting and uses them, instead, to produce finished goods which are exported. The mature-creditor nation is an industrial producer and exporter. This is likely to be the next state for Saudi Arabia. The OPEC nations seem likely to reduce their exports of petroleum in the future and develop petrochemical industries within their borders in order to export, instead, the more valuable finished products. The United States was a mature-creditor country from about the 1880s until World War II.

Mature creditor nation: a nation which has a balance-of-payments surplus resulting from exports of finished goods

4. MATURE DEBTOR. The final stage of development occurs when the mature-creditor nation begins to export credit as well as goods and services (**mature debtor** status). It becomes a source of investment funds and so helps finance the other stages of development in other nations. These investment outflows are part of the reason for the continuing balance-of-payments deficits which lead to the end of the balance-of-payments calculations. United States investment abroad, however, is a natural and healthy occurrence. It does, however, tend to obscure the meaning of the balance of payments.

Mature debtor nation: a country which has a balance-of-payments deficit resulting from high investment and transfer outflows

Our other major indicator of international economic health, the balance of trade, is still being officially calculated. The balance of trade shows net inflows and outflows due to imports and exports. A surplus on the balance of trade, therefore, means that we are selling more to the rest of the world than we are buying from them. A deficit, on the other hand, indicates that we buy more than we sell abroad.

While the United States has good reason to run a balance of payments deficit, there is no reason to believe that the balance of trade should be in either surplus or deficit. Historically, surpluses have been the case,

THE BALANCE OF TRADE

FIGURE 13-6: THE BALANCE OF TRADE, 1960–1977.

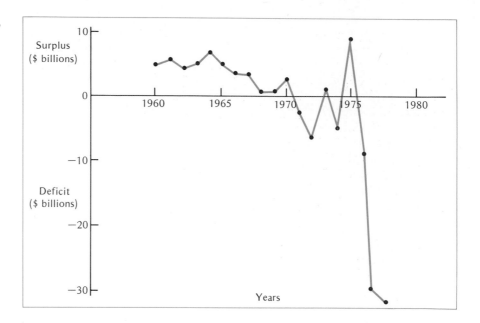

however, until the 1970s. The balance-of-trade figures for 1960–1977 are shown in Figure 13-6. Large outflows to pay for high-price petroleum imports have pushed the balance-of-trade accounts into deficit in the 1970s.

The balance of trade is important because of its relationship to aggregate demand. A surplus in the balance of trade indicates that the United States has positive net exports. On net, foreign purchasers are adding to our aggregate demand, causing RGNP to grow in our economy and creating jobs here. A deficit in the balance of trade, however, means that we have negative net exports. Aggregate demand leaves our country to stimulate the economies of other nations. Their economies grow, our aggregate demand declines.

What has caused this change? Huge imports of oil may be at the root of the change, to be sure, but there are other factors as well. Changes in the exchange rate (to be discussed in the next chapter) have altered trade patterns. As well, comparative advantages seem to be shifting. Goods which the United States has traditionally had a comparative advantage in producing are now being exported by other lands. Japan produces steel. Lightbulbs are imported from Hungary. Television production is shifting from the United States to the Far East. The United States is having trouble adjusting to this changing world, and the balance-of-trade figures show the extent of this problem.

SUMMARY

1. Nations trade because trade is mutually advantageous—both parties to an exchange are better off. Most trade takes place in goods and services that either trading partner could produce. Trade which takes place according to comparative advantage is beneficial for all countries involved, increases total production, and tends to conserve scarce natural resources.

2. Trade is restricted through the use of tariffs and quotas. Tariffs are taxes on imports; quotas are physical limitations on the amounts of imports. Both reduce the amounts of imported goods. The costs of tariffs are shared to a varying degree by consumers and producers, depending on the characteristics of the demand for imported goods.

3. Most economists think that tariffs and quotas are detrimental to the economy because they disrupt the mutually beneficial trade flows. Tariffs and quotas tend to benefit certain groups in the economy at the expense of consumers in general and foreign producers.

4. The balance of payments is an accounting of the net total inflows (exports, investment, and transfer payment inflows) minus outflows (resulting from imports and investment and transfer payments abroad). The balance of trade is simply the value of exports minus imports.

5. There are many reasons for the United States to have its current balance-of-payments deficit. There is no particular reason for the United States to import more than it exports, however. This is a problem for the nation if the deficits are persistent.

DISCUSSION QUESTIONS

1. Bill and Jill are two students who are considering trading services. If Bill works one hour, he can clean and gap four sparkplugs or he can type two pages of notes. If Jill works one hour, she can type three pages of notes or she can clean and gap eight sparkplugs. Use the theory of comparative advantage to determine who should be the typist and why.

2. Suppose that a $10-per-car tariff were imposed on imported cars. Who would bear the burden of this additional tax —the consumer, the importer, or both? Explain.

3. Suppose that a country had a continuing balance-of-trade deficit. What kinds of problems could this cause for the economy?

4. Suppose that a tariff were imposed on imported shoes. Who would gain from this action? Who would lose? Is the gain worth the loss?

5. What impact does the existence of transportation costs have on the theory of comparative advantage?

TEST YOURSELF

Indicate whether each of the following statements is *true* or *false*. Be able to defend your choice.

1. If two nations do not trade, then it must be because there is no difference in opportunity costs between them.

2. If a country has the absolute advantage in the production of a good, then it does not have the absolute advantage.

3. The theory of comparative advantage explains much of the trade in the real world.

4. A tariff on imported cars would be borne mostly by consumers.

5. A tariff on imported cheese would be borne mostly by producers.

6. Tariffs tend to cause inflation.

7. If a country has a balance-of-trade deficit, then it has a balance-of-payments deficit.

8. If a country has a balance-of-payments surplus, then imports exceed exports.

9. The United States has historically had balance-of-trade surpluses.

10. An "immature-creditor country" exports large amounts of raw materials and imports manufactured goods.

14
The Foreign Exchange Market

News reports these days are filled with references to the changing values of the dollar on foreign exchange markets. What does it all mean? This chapter will answer some basic questions about exchange rates and how they work, including the following:

What is an exchange rate?

Why are foreign currencies demanded?

Why are foreign currencies supplied?

What causes an exchange rate to change?

Can governments control the exchange rate?

If money is important to the national economy, as we saw in Part III of this text, it is also important to the functioning of the international economy. Money is constantly flowing across international borders—money to pay for imports, to invest in foreign economies, and as gifts from prosperous to less-developed lands.

These money flows are important, but they also create some peculiar problems for the nations involved. In this chapter we will attempt to understand the basis for the international money market and explore monetary relations among nations.

THE EXCHANGE RATE

Our analysis is complicated from the start because there is no one universal currency used in international trade. Rather, every nation has its own kind of money. In the United States it is the dollar, and all of our prices are denominated in dollars and fractions thereof. In Great Britain, however, the unit of value is the pound, in France the franc, in West Germany the mark, and in Japan the yen. The Russians have their ruble, the Spanish the peseta, the Saudis the riyal, the Italians the lira, and in Venezuela it's the bolivar. The list goes on and on.

Each of these currencies is designed to measure value. Imagine, for a second, that value can be measured like length. There are some currencies which measure large chunks of value—like a meter measures length. Other currencies measure short lengths of value—like an inch. And some measure tiny lengths. The British pound is an example of a "long measure" of value. A pound in the late 1970s measured about the same amount of value as 2 U.S. dollars. A franc is a smaller measure, equivalent to about $.25. And the Japanese yen measures tiny increments in value—about $.006 in 1978.

The important thing to note here is that the unit of measure doesn't really make any difference. Is the meter inherently "better" than the inch, just because it measures more length at a time? Obviously not. Just so, the pound is not inherently "better" than the yen just because it is a larger unit of monetary measure. The size of the unit of value in any country says nothing about the health of the economy or the economic status of the country involved. All currencies are just arbitrary measures of value and have no qualitative meaning over and above this.

One currency may be "as good" as another in the sense that all merely mark off values, but since these different sets of measures exist, we must have a conversion ratio to use in changing from one measure of value to another. We are all skilled in using certain types of conversions. Suppose that two bottles of ketchup sell for the same price in the grocery store, but one contains 18 ounces and the other label reads "1 pint." Which is the better buy! You answer quickly that the first is larger because you are familiar with the conversion ratio 16 ounces = 1 pint. Likewise, if two roads went to the same place, but the sign said that one route was 100 miles long, while the other was 100 kilometers, you would choose the latter, knowing that 1 kilometer = 0.56 mile, so 100 kilometers is just 56 miles and represents the shortcut.

The exchange rate is the conversion ratio between different currencies. If you read in the paper that the exchange rate between Norway and the United States is 1 krone = 20¢, this means that one piece of Norweigian currency measures the same value as $.20 or, conversely, that 5 kroner measure the same value as 1 dollar.

The exchange rate, then, is just a conversion ratio to allow us to convert one measure of value to another. But the exchange rate is also a price. It tells us the cost of purchasing a foreign currency in terms of a home currency. Therefore, if the exchange rate between the United States (the dollar) and Great Britain (the pound) were $2 = £1, this would tell us that it takes two dollar bills to purchase one pound note or, viewed from the other side of the Atlantic, the British would have to pay £.5 to buy one dollar bill.

The exchange rate, in this sense, is a dual price. It tells us how much of our currency it takes to buy someone else's, and it tells them how much of their money it takes to purchase ours. The exchange rate is the price of **foreign exchange** (foreign money) on the international money market. Like any other price, the exchange rate is determined through the interaction of supply and demand for these currencies on the foreign exchange market.

Foreign exchange: foreign currencies

Why would someone want to buy foreign currencies? There are lots of reasons, actually. You could purchase foreign money in order to look at it, for example. If you buy British money you get a picture of the queen, which might excite you. Foreign currencies have interesting pictures, bright colors, and strange writing on them. So you could collect it, which might be fun. You could also buy foreign currencies in order to smoke them, which might be a new high. Or you could buy some to paper your wall or use as toilet paper. There are really lots of uses for other people's money.

There is one main reason why people purchase foreign exchange, however: to spend it. And where would you spend it? In other countries, of course!

The problem here is, you see, that when you import something from a foreign country, the seller in that country will normally ask to be paid in his or her native currency. Therefore, when someone in the United States wants

THE FOREIGN EXCHANGE MARKET

Derived demand: a property of a good that is desired because of the demand for a complimentary good

to import, say, wool sweaters from Norway, he or she must first buy the Norwegian currency in order to buy the foreign goods. The demand for foreign exchange, then, is what economists call **derived demand.** We only want foreign currencies because we want foreign goods. But our demand for foreign goods depends on the exchange rate.

An example will make this idea clearer. Suppose that we are looking at the American demand for the French franc. To make life very simple, let's suppose that the reason that people want to purchase French money is that they all want to purchase a particular French good—say, French wine (Chateau Neuf de Charles de Gaulle) which sells in France for 20 francs (f20).

The amount of the French wine that we wish to purchase will depend on its price, and the price will depend on the exchange rate between the dollar and the franc. For example, if the exchange rate is $.10 = f1, then a f20 bottle of wine would cost just $2.00 in the United States (ignoring transportation costs, taxes, and other such costs). When the franc is cheap (only costs a dime) this makes French goods cheap. As a result, we tend to buy lots of French goods and we therefore need lots of French money to use in making the purchases. Therefore, when the franc is cheap, there is a large demand for it—because there is a large demand for imported goods from France.

Let's see how this would work at other exchange rates. If, for example, the exchange rate were to change to $.20 = f1, the demand for French goods and currency would be much different. When a currency becomes more expensive (here, the franc has risen in price from 10¢ to 20¢) we say that it has appreciated or gained in value (become a ''longer'' measure of value compared to other currencies). If the franc has increased in price from $.10 to $.20, then the price of a f20 bottle of imported wine will rise from $2.00 (at an exchange rate of $.10 = f1) to $4.00. At $4.00 a bottle, the French wine isn't nearly as good a deal as it was at the old exchange rate, so the demand for French wine will fall and, therefore, the demand for French currency will also fall.

When a foreign currency becomes more expensive, this means that foreign imports are costlier as well. At the higher price, we tend to purchase fewer of the imported goods and, therefore, demand less of the foreign currency.

Now suppose that the franc were to further appreciate to $.25 = f1. Since the franc is even more expensive, French goods will cost more, too. The f20 bottle of French wine will now cost $5.00. At this higher price, very little of the French wine will be purchased, so very few pieces of French currency will be demanded for this purpose.

We can see all of this at work in Figure 14-1. The demand curve for francs

FIGURE 14-1: THE DERIVED DEMAND FOR FRANCS
The demand for the French franc is derived from the demand for French goods. As the franc becomes cheaper, French goods become less expensive, too, and so there is a high demand for the goods and a high demand for the French currency necessary to import the goods. As the franc becomes more expensive, French goods become more expensive as well, resulting in a reduced demand for both the goods and the currency. The result is the demand for francs curve (D_f) shown.

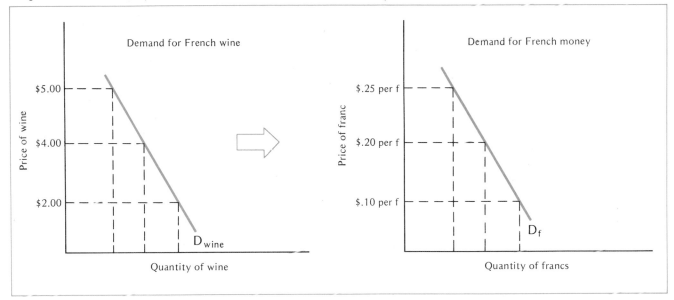

(D_f) depends on the demand for French imports. And the price of these French goods depends on the exchange rate.

This is only one side of the foreign exchange market, and for a look at the other side we will have to travel to France. So let's hop aboard a Concorde SST, don berets, wax our moustaches, and sip a little champagne. Soon we are in gay Paris, home of the Eiffel Tower, the Louvre, and French postcards!

Here, the French are involved in the foreign exchange market, too, only they are not interested in purchasing francs (they already have lots of them). Instead, they are interested in buying American imports, and as a result they want to buy American dollars. Again, to make life easier, let's assume that they all want to buy a single American good—say, American blue jeans, which sell in the United States for $20.

The price that the French have to pay for these jeans will depend on the exchange rate between the dollar and the franc. Let us begin, as we did on the other side of the Atlantic, with the hypothetical exchange rate of $.10 = f1. At a dime a franc, the franc proved to be very cheap to American buyers. However, the French view this price differently. They see the exchange rate as f10 = $1. Since it takes 10 francs to buy a dollar (a high price for a dollar), it will take f200 to purchase a pair of jeans. This is a lot of money for pants (after all, a bottle of wine costs just f20!), so chances are good that there will be only a very small demand for the imported American blue jeans and, therefore, only a small demand for the American dollar.

Suppose now that the exchange rate were to change from $.10 = f1 to $.20 = f1. Before, we said that the franc has appreciated, or gained in value. But the French will view this change differently. They will note that the price of a dollar has *fallen* from f10 = $1 to f5 = $1. The dollar has depreciated or fallen in value relative to the franc.

Because the dollar is now cheaper, American imports will be cheaper, too. A $20 pair of blue jeans will now cost the French just f100. At this lower price, there will be a higher demand for American blue jeans and, therefore, a higher demand for American dollars to use in importing goods from the United States.

Now suppose that the dollar were to further depreciate to f4 = $1 (an exchange rate, viewed from the American perspective, of $.25 = f1). Now American blue jeans would cost but f80 per pair. At this lowest price, there would be a large demand for blue jeans and, therefore, a very large demand for American dollars.

FIGURE 14-2: THE DERIVED DEMAND FOR DOLLARS
The demand for American currency is derived from the foreign demand for American goods. A cheaper dollar means cheaper American imports to people in France. So there is a large demand for cheap dollars (i.e., dollars that cost only 4 or 5 francs) but only a very small demand for expensive (f10) dollars.

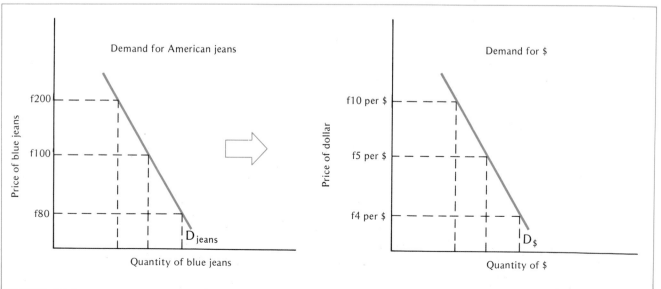

Figure 14-2 shows the French demand for dollars ($D_\$$) and its relationship to the demand for American goods. As the dollar becomes cheaper in France, American goods become cheaper as well. So more American goods are imported, and the French demand larger quantities of dollars for use in paying the American jeans producers.

We now have the demand curve for the dollar ($D_\$$) in Paris and for the franc (D_f) in the United States. We could begin to look at the foreign exchange market if only we could come up with the appropriate supply curves. But where are they? Nowhere to be seen! Has there been some mistake?

Nope. The supply curves necessary for the operation of a market are already there, we just haven't been looking in the right place for them. To see the supply curves for dollars ($S_\$$) and francs (S_f) we will have to view these proceedings from a different perspective.

We have seen the demand for francs: it is made up of people in the United States who are trying to purchase French currency in order to purchase French goods. We in America see ourselves as demanders of

FIGURE 14-3: EXCHANGING DOLLARS AND FRANCS
The U.S. demand for foreign currency provides the supply of dollars to the rest of the world. In our attempts to secure francs, we implicitly offer dollars for sale. As the franc becomes cheaper, we demand more francs, flooding the market with dollars (at the exchange rate $.10 per f or f10 per $). When the franc is expensive ($.25 per f or f4 per $) we demand fewer francs and so supply fewer $.

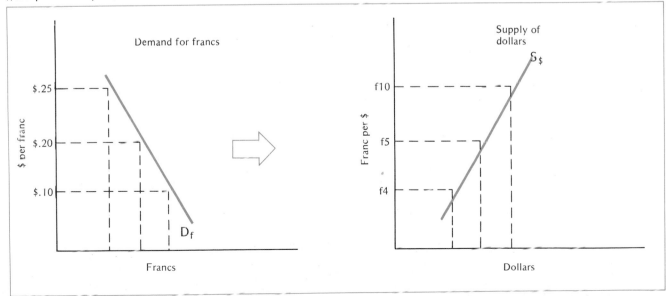

francs, but the French (in their typical Continental fashion) see us differently. To folks in Paris, these sunny-looking Americans are not demanding francs, they are *supplying dollars!* That is, Americans are trying to exchange their dollars for French francs. This exchange can be viewed differently on different sides of the Atlantic. We think that we are acquiring francs—but the French think we are merely disposing of dollars (and accepting francs in exchange).

The demand for francs, then, represents the *supply* of dollars on the French foreign exchange market. How does this supply behave? For an answer to this question, glance at Figure 14-3. Recall that, when the exchange rate was $.25 per franc, French currency and goods were expensive, so our demand for francs was small. From the French perspective, this means that, at the equivalent exchange rate of f4 per dollar, Americans do not wish to exchange very many dollars for francs, so the supply of dollars is small at f4 per dollar.

When the franc is cheap—say, $.10 per franc—Americans are willing to purchase lots of francs, and so the French see this as a situation where the United States is willing to exchange lots of dollars in exchange for lots of francs. As a result, the French perceive that, at the equivalent exchange rate of f10 per dollar, there is a very large supply of dollars!

Since the U.S. demand for francs is also the French supply of dollars, it follows that any increase (or decrease) in our demand for French goods or currency will translate directly in an increase (or decrease) in the supply of dollars available on the foreign exchange markets.

If the U.S. demand for francs represents the supply of dollars in foreign exchange, then it follows that the French *demand* for dollars is the *supply* of francs. This relationship can be seen in Figure 14-4.

When the dollar is cheap (f4 per dollar), the French will want to purchase lots of American goods, lots of American dollars, and so will be willing to exchange (supply us with) lots of French currency. At the equivalent exchange rate of $.25 per franc, then, the supply of francs is high. As the dollar appreciates to, say, f10 per dollar, the demand for dollars declines because American imports are more expensive when the dollar is expensive. We perceive this as a lower supply of francs at the exchange rate of 10 cents per franc. This gives us the supply of francs curve (S_f) shown in Figure 14-4. Any increase (or decrease) in the French demand for dollars will be felt in the United States as an increase (or decrease) in the supply of francs.

Now that we have a full complement of supply and demand curves we are ready to explore the foreign exchange market. A hypothetical foreign exchange market is shown in Figure 14-5. Here the equilibrium exchange rate is shown to be $.20 per franc (f4 per dollar). At this exchange rate, the dual foreign exchange markets become clear: the supply of dollars and its

FIGURE 14-4. DEMANDING DOLLARS MEANS SUPPLYING FRANCS
The French demand for dollars represents the supply of francs in the foreign exchange market. As the French rush to purchase foreign currencies, they offer in exchange their own currency, creating the supply curve (S$_f$) shown.

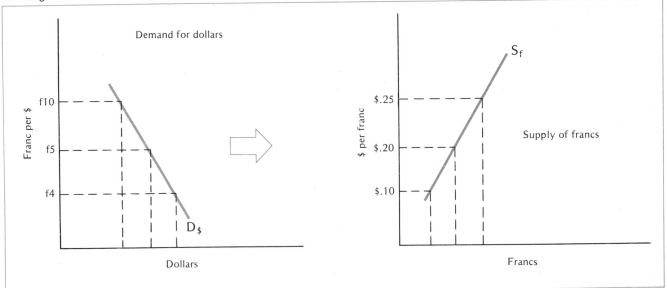

FIGURE 14-5: EXCHANGE MARKET EQUILIBRIUM
The foreign exchange market reaches an equilibrium, here at f5 = $1 (20 cents per f). Since this is really just one market viewed from two perspectives, the equilibrium exchange rate will always be the same in both markets. At equilibrium, there is a balancing of both the demand and supply for francs, and the demand and supply for dollars.

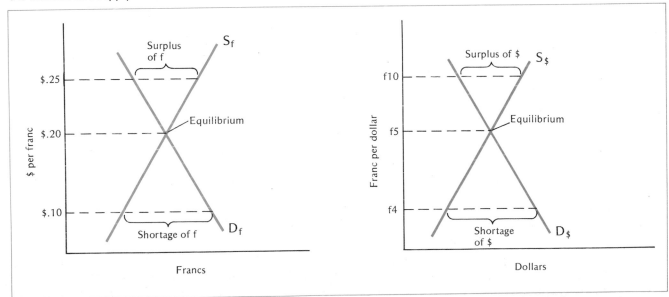

demand balance, while the same situation prevails in the market for francs. The exchange rate will hold to this price until something happens to affect one of the currency demand relationships.

This market, like others we have seen, is self-adjusting. Suppose, for example, that the exchange rate were temporarily set at $.10 = f1 (f10 = $1). In the United States, we would say that, in this instance, the franc is **undervalued** (selling below equilibrium price). At this cheap price for francs, there would be a large demand for francs, creating a shortage. Americans who find themselves a victim of this shortage would offer to pay a higher price for francs, and so would drive the price of French currency (and therefore the exchange rate) back toward the $.20-per-franc equilibrium level.

In France, this same exchange-rate adjustment process would be occurring, but the French would view it in different terms. An exchange rate of 10¢ per franc translates, to the Frenchman, to a price of f10 per dollar. This is a pretty expensive dollar. To the French, the dollar is **overvalued** (selling for more than the equilibrium price). At this high price, there will be a very small demand for dollars, creating a surplus of them. Americans who wish to sell their dollars will have to put them "on sale" for a little less. The surplus tends to drive down the price of the dollar and so move the exchange rate toward its equilibrium position.

Since these two markets are really one and the same, just viewed from different perspectives, we can be sure that they will arrive at the same exchange rate. However, since exchange markets are often many thousands of miles apart, sometimes the dual exchange rates will be a fraction of a cent out of kilter. In these instances, the great equalizers of the foreign exchange world come into action: the foreign exchange **arbitrage** dealers.

These folks work mostly for large banks and they search the international markets for even small exchange rate differentials. They can make lots of money in the following way: Suppose that an arbitragist notices that the franc is selling for $.19 in New York and for the equivalent of $.21 in Paris. These folks will then buy millions of dollars worth of francs in New York at the cheaper price (this increase in demand causing the price of the franc to rise from $.19 to $.20) and then turn around and sell this currency in Paris at the higher price (the increase in supply in Paris causing the price to drop from the equivalent of $.21 per franc to $.20). This force tends to equate the two exchange rates, and can make lots of cash for the arbitrage artist, since he or she has made a cool 2¢ on each franc bought and sold. This is a very profitable business to be in but, unfortunately, only is economic if one has millions and millions of dollars to use in the buying and selling. As a result, only large banks get much of this action. It makes money for them, and assures a dual market equilibrium for us.

Undervalued: a currency which trades at an exchange rate below the market equilibrium

Overvalued: a currency which trades at an exchange rate above the market equilibrium

Arbitrage: the practice of buying currencies on one market and reselling them on another for profit which tends to stabilize exchange rates

We are now ready to use the foreign exchange market to determine the impact that economic actions will have on the dollar and vice versa. In discussing these applications, we will look at just one side of the foreign exchange market at a time (i.e., we will view the market from just one country at a time). This will simplify the graphics a bit, but won't affect our conclusions at all.

THE FOREIGN EXCHANGE MARKET AT WORK

1. A TARIFF ON IMPORTED GOODS. In the preceding chapter, we discussed the impacts of tariffs and quotas when used as tools to restrict imports. We learned that a tariff will raise the price of imported goods and lower the amount of foreign goods brought into the country. But it will also have an impact on the exchange rate.

When a tariff is imposed, this generally forces the price of imports up, cutting consumption of these goods. Since fewer imports are demanded, and the price that the foreign producers receive has fallen (since they bear part of the burden of the tariff in lower prices) the result is that the demand for foreign currency to pay for these imports will fall as well.

This case is illustrated in Figure 14-6. Here we are looking at the foreign

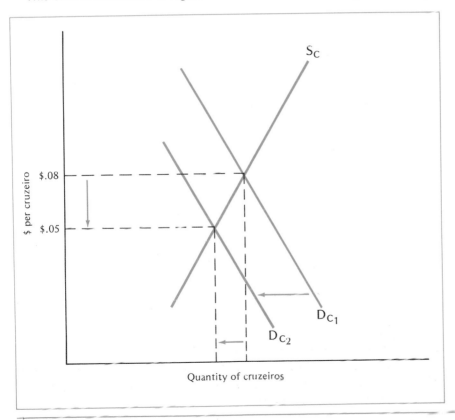

FIGURE 14-6: EXCHANGE RATE EFFECTS OF A TARIFF
A tariff on Brazilian goods causes a reduced demand for the cruzeiro. The cruzeiro depreciates with two results. First, since the cruzeiro is now cheaper, Brazilian imports are cheaper, too, making the tariff less effective. The dollar now costs more in Brazil, however, so fewer American goods will be purchased by Brazilians.

exchange market between the U.S. dollar ($) and the Brazilian cruzeiro (C). Initially, this exchange market is in equilibrium at the prevailing exchange rate of 8¢ = C1 or C12½ = $1. Now suppose that U.S. shoe manufacturers are successful in getting a tariff imposed on Brazilian goods in an attempt to protect the jobs of American shoemakers.

Since fewer Brazilian goods are imported into the United States, the demand for the cruzeiro will fall. This creates a temporary surplus of cruzeiros at the price of 8¢ = C1. Brazilians caught with surplus Brazilian currency will adjust to this phenomenon by offering to sell their currency for fewer cents (or to pay more for American money, which is the same thing). The price of the cruzeiro will fall from 8¢ to 5¢ (and, in Brazil, the price of a dollar will rise from C12½ to C20).

This tariff on Brazilian imports has caused the dollar to appreciate relative to the cruzeiro, and caused the cruzeiro to depreciate relative to the dollar.

It is interesting to note that, because of this exchange rate movement, the tariff will not be as effective as its proponents might think. The tariff will raise the price of Brazilian shoes initially, but as the exchange rate adjusts the price of the cruzeiro falls and, with it, the price of Brazilian imports, including shoes. The fall in import prices due to the exchange rate adjustment will at least partially offset the tariff. So the tariff is not as protective as it seems.

There will also be another unforseen economic event caused by the tariff. As the cruzeiro becomes cheaper to us (5¢ down from 8¢), the dollar becomes more expensive to the Brazilians (C20 up from C12½). As a result, American goods will become more expensive in Brazil, and fewer of them will be purchased. It follows that some U.S. workers who were previously employed in making goods for export to Brazil will lose their jobs. The tariff, it seems, is not very protective at all!

2. INFLATION AND THE EXCHANGE RATE. There are many reasons for exchange rates to change, and one of the most important ones these days is inflation. Inflation, as we have said before, reduces the amount of "value" that a currency "measures." If inflation were to be uniform around the world (so that all currencies were to "shrink" at the same rate), there would be no reason to alter the conversion ratio between national currencies. Inflation is not uniform, however, and as a result, it has a dramatic impact on the foreign exchange market.

To see this, let's look at the foreign exchange market shown in Figure 14-7 between the United States (the $) and the Italian lira (L). The foreign exchange market is here shown in initial equilibrium at an exchange rate of $.02 per lira (equivalent to L50 per dollar). Now let us suppose that both the United States and Italy experience inflation, but inflation of different

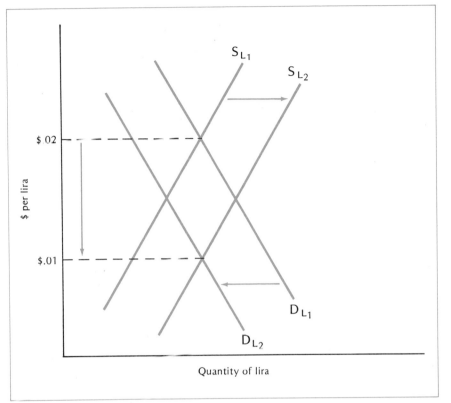

FIGURE 14-7: INFLATION AND THE EXCHANGE RATE
Italy experiences a higher inflation rate than the United States. Since inflation is making Italian goods more expensive, there is small demand for them in the United States, causing the demand for lira to fall. American goods are now bargains in Italy (because of the lower U.S. inflation rate), so the Italian demand for dollars rises. The result, as shown, is a dramatic fall in the value of the lira (and a resulting rise in the dollar's value).

magnitudes. Suppose that in the United States prices rise at a 5 percent rate, while in Italy inflation is 20 percent.

This upsets the foreign exchange market. Because Italy has such a high inflation rate, Italian goods are suddenly very expensive. The high inflation makes Italian cars, wines, shoes, and other exports more expensive than the competition from other countries. As a result, people in the United States import fewer Italian goods and, therefore, need fewer lira. The demand for lira (D_L) falls.

This is not the whole story, however. Let's fly to Rome and view the scene from there.

In Rome, we find that Italian goods are now very expensive, but that imported goods are now cheaper. Because American goods have risen in price at a slower rate, they have actually fallen in price relative to Italian products. As a result, Romans now want to import more American goods and, therefore, need more American dollars. Their demand for dollars increases. We see this in Figure 14-7 as an increase in the amount of lira that the Italians are willing to supply in exchange for dollars.

Predictably, an increase in the supply of lira coupled with a decrease in the demand for it will create a surplus of lira on the foreign exchange markets. The value of the lira will fall (in Figure 14-7 it falls from $.02 to $.01 per lira) until the exchange rate has changed to reflect the new relative values of the dollar and the lira. Italy's high inflation rate has caused the lira to depreciate relative to other currencies.

International inflation rate differentials have been a primary cause of exchange rate movements in recent years. Much of the depreciation of the currencies of the United States, Italy, and Great Britain have been caused by the relatively high inflation rates in these countries compared with nations like West Germany where inflation has been more moderate.

3. BALANCE-OF-PAYMENTS PROBLEMS. One of the advantages of the existence of a well-oiled foreign exchange market is that it can act to minimize a nation's balance-of-payments problems. That is, whenever a country has a balance-of-payments deficit, the foreign exchange market automatically acts to correct it. To see this, let's look at an example.

Figure 14-8 shows the foreign exchange market between the United States and West Germany (the DM—deutsche mark). Suppose that, initially,

FIGURE 14-8: THE BALANCE OF PAYMENTS AND THE EXCHANGE RATES *The United States runs a balance-of-payments deficit. As a result of the deficit, the dollar depreciates (the deutsche mark gains in value), which tends to offset the deficit.*

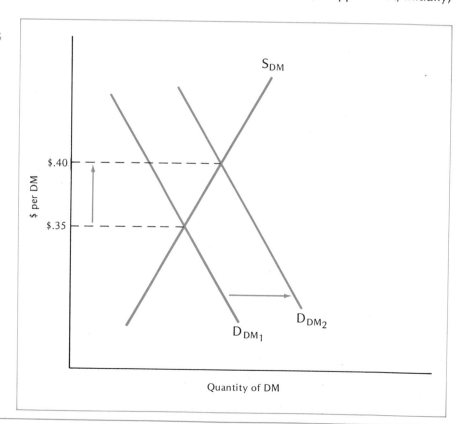

our market is in equilibrium at an exchange rate of $.35 per DM and that, additionally, there is a balance-of-payments equilibrium between the United States and West Germany.

Now let us suppose that the United States starts to run a balance-of-payments deficit with West Germany. This could happen for a number of reasons, but for simplicity let's assume that Americans have become unusually fond of German cars and are now buying Volkswagens, Porsches, and Mercedes-Benzes instead of Fords, Chevys, and Plymouths. This causes a balance-of-payments disequilibrium. Because it is now importing more than it is exporting, the United States has a balance-of-payments deficit, and West Germany, for its part, is running a surplus.

This situation shows up in the foreign exchange market (Figure 14-8) as an increase in the demand for marks. The sudden rise in the demand for German cars causes a shortage of German currency. As car importers compete for the scarce supply of marks, they bid up the exchange rate (from $.35 per DM to $.40). This has an interesting impact on the price of German autos in the United States. At the old exchange rate of $.35 per mark, a Mercedes-Benz costing DM30,000 in Germany would retail for $10,500 in the United States (DM30,000 × $.35 per DM), ignoring taxes and transportation costs. Now, at the new exchange rate, that same car suddenly costs $12,000 (DM30,000 × $.40 per mark). The increased value of the mark has caused the price of German goods to rise. At this higher price, of course, Americans are less willing to purchase Mercedes-Benz cars (they switch, instead, to Ford Granadas). This helps reverse the balance-of-payments deficit problem.

The deficit is also helped another way. Since the mark has appreciated, the dollar must have depreciated or become cheaper in Germany. This will mean that American goods are also cheaper in Europe and that American merchants will likely be able to increase their exports to Germany. The deficit disappears.

To summarize the forces at work here, note that the initial increase in imports caused the exchange rate to change. At the higher exchange rate, German goods were more expensive (and so fewer of them were imported) and U.S. goods became cheaper abroad (and so more of them were exported). This increase in exports and decrease in imports cuts the balance-of-payments deficit and moves the economy back toward equilibrium.

A balance-of-payments deficit, then, is pretty much self-correcting. Why then, do nations continue to have balance-of-payments problems? The answer is that the foreign exchange market is not always free to adjust, as we have indicated in this example. We shall discuss the issue of free versus regulated foreign exchange markets later in this chapter.

4. INTERNATIONAL INVESTMENT FLOWS.

Up to now, we have been talking about the import-derived demand for foreign currency as if this were the only reason that one would seek foreign exchange. This is a very important part of the demand for foreign exchange, but it is not the only one. Also very important is the demand for foreign currencies for financial investment purposes. In this age of world travel and multinational corporations, investors are no longer bound either physically or financially to their home countries. Financial investors (stock and bond investors) will scour the world looking for the highest available return (real interest rate). And in order to invest in foreign stocks or bonds, these financiers need to acquire foreign currency. As a result, there is an investment demand for foreign exchange which depends upon international interest rates.

To see how this works, suppose that we are looking at the exchange market between the United States (the dollar) and Mexico (the peso). We will assume that the exchange rate is initially in equilibrium at a price of 5¢ = P1. Now suppose that the Federal Reserve undertakes a contractionary monetary policy which makes the real interest rate (the interest rate adjusted for inflation) *higher* in the United States than it is in Mexico. Suddenly,

FIGURE 14-9: CAPITAL FLOWS AND THE EXCHANGE RATE

An increase in the U.S. interest rate causes an inflow of funds into the United States. We see this in the foreign exchange market as an increase in the supply of pesos (more pesos are supplied as Mexican investors move to convert pesos to dollars in order to undertake financial investments in the United States). This brings about a depreciation of the peso.

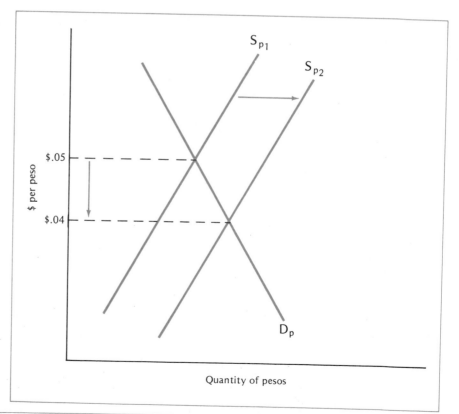

people in Mexico will find that their money will earn a higher return if it is put in banks, savings institutions, and government bonds in the United States than in Mexico. This will cause an increased demand for the dollar, as Mexican investors attempt to move their money across the Rio Grande.

We see this increase in the demand for the dollar in Figure 14-9 as an increased supply of the peso (since more and more Mexicans are offering to exchange pesos for dollars). This creates a surplus of pesos and the price of the peso falls, as a result, from 5¢ to 4¢.

This monetary policy has caused the peso to depreciate (lose value) as the dollar has appreciated (gained in value). Domestic economic policies which alter the interest rate also alter the exchange rate because of international investment flows. We will talk more about the consequences of this fact in Chapter 15.

5. RISING ENERGY PRICES. Another factor which can act to alter the exchange rate is a large change in the price of an important international commodity like oil. Because oil is such a necessary item in a modern economy, when the price of oil rises, oil imports are not likely to fall very

FIGURE 14-10: ENERGY PRICES AND EXCHANGE RATES
As oil prices rise, the United States must acquire more Venezuelan currency to pay for energy. This causes the demand for bolivars to rise, and the dollar to depreciate relative to the bolivar.

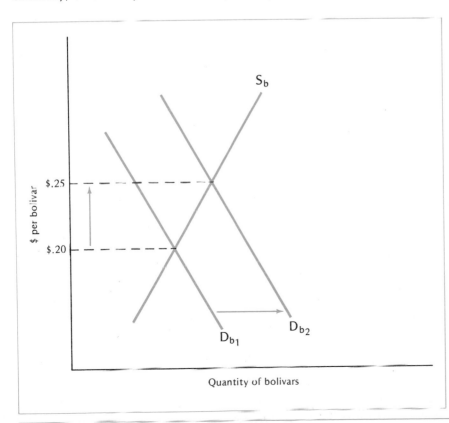

much, at least in the short run (in the longer run people may find substitutes and decrease oil imports). This can have a major impact on the exchange rate.

Figure 14-10 looks at the foreign exchange market between the United States (the dollar) and Venezuela (the bolivar). The initial exchange equilibrium occurs at $.25 = B1. Now suppose that Venezuela (a major oil-exporting country) were to increase the price of its petroleum. Since, in the short run, there are not many substitutes for oil, U.S. importers would be forced to pay the higher prices. As a result, the demand for bolivars would rise, creating a temporary shortage of Venezuelan currency on the foreign exchange markets. American oil importers would respond to this shortage by offering to pay even more for the bolivar. The bolivar would appreciate from $.20 to $.25 (making imported oil even more expensive), and the dollar would depreciate relative to the bolivar (fall in value from B5 to B4).

This is exactly the kind of situation which has been occurring to the United States over the past several years. Since the United States pays so much for foreign oil, the value of the dollar has been in constant decline relative to the currencies of countries which need not import so much expensive energy.

EXCHANGE MARKET INTERVENTION

Flexible exchange rates: a system where exchange rates are set through market forces

Intervention: a situation which prevails when third parties (central banks) enter foreign exchange markets in order to increase or decrease the value of a currency

The foreign exchange system that we have been describing up to now is what is commonly known as **flexible exchange rates**—exchange rates which rise and fall in response to market conditions. But exchange rates do not always go unregulated. Sometimes national governments and their central banks (the FRS is the U.S. central bank) **intervene** in exchange markets in order to influence the value of their currency. Most often, nations intervene in order to "prop up" the value of their currency. There are several reasons for doing this. National pride is one—sometimes people attach undue importance to the exchange rate and see it as a measure of national strength.

In the case of the United States there is another reason for wanting to keep the value of the dollar high (or at least to prevent it from being badly undervalued). Over the years, a lot of dollars have flowed out of the United States in payment for imports, as part of foreign aid, and in the course of international investment. The foreign governments, bankers, and businesses were willing to accept dollars instead of their own currencies in payment because the dollar was valuable and easy to spend (to buy U.S. goods, for example). These people need not hold these dollar balances forever, however. If the dollar were to fall in value, these groups might suddenly get rid of their dollar balances, with detrimental impact on our economy.

Additionally, a depreciating currency tends to be inflationary. When the value of the dollar is falling, this causes import prices to rise. Also, since a falling dollar causes exports to rise, this increase in export demand for U.S. goods could act to bid up these prices, adding to the inflation problems.

When a central bank decides to "defend" its home currency (increase its value), there are two basic options available to it. Both these options are designed to increase the value of the affected currency by increasing the demand for it on international markets.

First, the central bank can attempt to increase the investment demand for its currency by pursuing contractionary monetary policy. This is what the FRS did in January 1978 in its attempt to increase the value of the dollar. Higher U.S. interest rates draw financial investment funds from other countries. Since these investors need to acquire dollars in order to take advantage of the higher U.S. rate of return, the demand for the dollar rises and the value of the dollar improves somewhat. The dollar's value is improved, but at a cost to the economy, since the higher interest rates discourage real investment now (causing AD to fall) and have detrimental impacts on aggregate supply in the long run.

The second way to "defend" a currency is for the central bank to intervene in the foreign exchange market directly and purchase large quantities of its own currency—artificially increasing demand. There are two important problems with this way of defending the dollar. First, this method involves a decrease in the money supply (since FRS dollar purchases on the foreign exchange markets act just like open market sales—both cause dollars to enter the FRS vaults and leave the money supply). The other problem is that you must buy your currency *with* something. When the FRS defends the dollar this way, they often borrow foreign currencies from foreign central banks in what are called "swap agreements" and then use these currencies in purchasing dollars. This method can only last, however, so long as the United States' credit is good. Another method of accomplishing this end would be to purchase the necessary foreign currencies (for use in buying dollars) using something of value, like gold. This process, however, is clearly limited by the amount of gold and similar assets available to the central bank.

Sometimes countries will intervene in foreign exchange markets in order to keep the value of their currency pegged artificially *low!* West Germany has done this several times in the last decade. By buying up other countries' currencies, Germany succeeded in keeping the value of these currencies high and the value of the mark low. Why do this? Since the mark was cheap, German goods (like Volkswagens) were cheap and German workers were kept busy (and employed!) supplying the rest of the world with goods. This intervention idea, then, plainly cuts both ways.

FIXED EXCHANGE RATES

Fixed exchange rates: a system where the relative values of the currencies of different nations are set by international agreement, without the influence of market forces

Special drawing right (SDR): an international form of reserve which acts like gold in terms of transactions involving international central banks; paper gold

Devalue: the lowering of the official value of a currency in a fixed-exchange-rate system

The ultimate form of exchange rate intervention was the system of **fixed exchange rates** which prevailed from 1946 to 1973. During this period, exchange rates were not set by the market at all—they were determined entirely by national governments. Once the exchange rates were set, governments would intervene whenever necessary in order to assure that that value prevailed. When the fixed exchange rate was set "too high"— above the market exchange rate—the central bank of the country with the overvalued currency was forced to repeatedly intervene to keep the exchange rate from falling. This put a lot of strain on the central banks since they were forced to repeatedly borrow from others, sell off gold reserves, or, more recently, sell off **special drawing rights** *(SDRs),* which are international reserves which act like gold and are often called "paper gold."

Sometimes countries found that they could no longer support their overvalued currencies. These countries then **devalued** their currencies— lowered the official value of their currency in international trade. The United States devalued the dollar several times in the early 1970s.

Fixed exchange rates were used in the past because they were convenient (you didn't have to worry about changes in exchange rates very much in making international trade decisions) and because, when fixed exchange rates prevail, things like tariffs and capital flows have little impact on foreign exchange prices.

The problem with fixed exchange rates was that currencies were not able to seek reasonable values on their own and adjust to changing world trade patterns gradually. Instead, exchange rates tended to change infrequently, but dramatically, as crises forced countries to devalue their currencies by large amounts. Most economists today agree that flexible exchange rates are preferable to fixed exchange rates as a form of foreign exchange market organization.

SUMMARY

1. The exchange rate is the conversion ratio between two currencies: it tells the ratio at which they can be evenly traded. It also gives the price of foreign currency.

2. Foreign currencies are demanded because they can be used to buy foreign goods and services. The demand for foreign exchange is called a derived de-mand. Since the price of foreign goods depends on the exchange rate, the quantity of foreign currencies demanded will change with the exchange rate.

3. Foreign currencies are supplied by the residents of other countries. They view themselves as demanding dollars. Since they are willing to exchange their currencies for ours, we view

them as offering to supply us with their money. Because their demand for dollars varies with the exchange rate, we perceive the supply of foreign exchange to depend on the exchange rate as well.

4. Many factors can cause exchange rates to change, including changing tastes and preferences for foreign goods and changing comparative advantage throughout the world. Some of the factors discussed in this chapter include tariffs, dif-

fering inflation rates, rising energy prices, and balance-of-payments problems.

5. Governments can control the exchange rate through foreign exchange market intervention. Between 1946 and 1973 a period of fixed exchange rates prevailed when intervention acted to stabilize exchange rates. Intervention can be difficult, however, and is not necessarily a long-run solution to fluctuating exchange rates.

DISCUSSION QUESTIONS

1. What will be the likely affect on the exchange rate between the United States and West Germany if there is a sudden increase in the demand for Porsche cars in the United States? What will tend to happen to the price of these cars? Why?

2. Suppose that, in the situation in Question 1, the United States imposes a tariff on the German cars. What impact will this action have on the exchange rate?

3. Suppose that a country has a balance-of-payments surplus. What impact does this have on the exchange rate?

4. Suppose that the exchange rate between the United States and Great Britain is $2.00 = £1. Now suppose that the United States has inflation of 10 percent while the British have 20 percent inflation. What will be the likely impact of this on the exchange rate? Explain.

TEST YOURSELF

Indicate whether each of the following statements is *true* or *false*. Be able to defend your choice.

1. If there is an increase in the demand for U.S. goods in Germany, this will cause an increase in the supply of the DM (deutsche mark) on foreign exchange markets.

2. If the dollar appreciates relative to the DM, it will take more dollars to buy a DM.

3. If the exchange rate is $1 = f6, then a franc is worth 33¢.

4. If the dollar appreciates, then the franc appreciates, too.

5. An increase in the value of the dollar will generally cause a reduced demand for U.S. exports.

6. An increase in the value of the dollar will generally cause a larger quantity of imports to be

demanded in the United States.

7. A tariff on a widely imported good could cause the dollar to depreciate.

8. A dollar that rises in value on foreign exchange markets is good for all U.S. workers.

9. A fall in the U.S. interest rate tends to increase the value of the dollar.

10. Under a fixed exchange rate system, if the dollar falls in value, the U.S. central bank must step in and buy up the surplus dollars.

ECONOMIC CONTROVERSIES VII: FLEXIBLE OR FIXED EXCHANGE RATES?

These days foreign exchange transactions are carried out under a system of at least partially flexible exchange rates (governmental intervention keeps them from being truly "floating" rates). The exchange rate system is not God-given, however, it is set cooperatively by national governments based on political and economic considerations. From 1946 until 1973 exchange rates were fixed—set by international agreement and "defended" by national governments. Fixed exchange rates seemed to work pretty well during most of this period, and they might work again. Which system is better? This is an area where economists disagree.

The choice of an exchange rate system makes a difference. Different exchange systems result in different actions when market forces change. To see this, suppose that we are viewing the exchange rate between the dollar and the West German DM (deutsche mark) and suppose further, that the demand for the DM were to suddenly increase.

Under a system of flexible ex-change rates, a sudden rise in the demand for the DM would cause the DM to appreciate—gain in value—and the dollar would depreciate. German imports would become more expensive in the United States, and American goods would fall in price in terms of the German currency. The increased demand for German currency would tend to affect import prices and export sales in both countries.

If fixed exchange rates were in place, however, the result would be much different. The increase in the demand for the DM would be viewed in the United States as an increase in the supply of dollars on the foreign exchange markets. Since this rise in dollar supply tends to reduce the dollar's value, the U.S. central bank would be forced to step in and "defend" the dollar by buying up the excess U.S. currency. How would the dollars be purchased? The simplest method would work as follows. The U.S. central bank (the FRS) would take gold from its reserves and use this asset to purchase marks to buy up the excess dollars, restoring equilibrium at the fixed exchange rate level. By buying up surplus American currency the United States can keep the exchange rate fixed.

The result of the initial increase in the demand for the mark is, in the case of fixed exchange rates, not a change in the exchange rate, but merely a transfer of gold from one country to another and an increase in the German DM supply with a corresponding decrease in the U.S. dollar supply (as the dollars that were purchased leave the money supply). Import and export prices will not change, and the exchange rate will not move, either.

Since there are basic differences between fixed and flexible exchange rates, why is one system chosen over the other? Let's look at both sides of this debate.

FIXED EXCHANGE RATES

The principal advantage of fixed exchange rates is certainty. With the government stepping in to keep foreign exchange markets stable, tourists, businessmen, and bankers do not have to worry about a change in the value of the dollar disrupting their plans. The value of the dollar is determined by the government, so trade is not subject to the uncertainty of changing exchange rates. This tends to promote beneficial free trade among nations.

When exchange rates are fixed, there is little advantage to the kinds of foreign exchange speculation that we see these days. Speculation in currencies (buying one currency in anticipation of appreciation or selling another because of expect-

ed depreciation) tends to destabilize the foreign exchange markets. Exchange rates oscillate back and forth as speculators change their minds. This speculation adds even more uncertainty to international business life and so discourages import and export activities. A stable exchange rate (defended by national governments) leaves little profit for speculators.

The fixed-exchange-rate system is also beneficial because it removes the temptation (always present under flexible exchange rates) to formulate economic policy so as to affect the dollar's value instead of worrying about more important problems like inflation and unemployment. With fixed exchange rates, economic policy can concentrate on our real problems.

A change to a system of fixed exchange rates, then, would lend stability to international business transactions and would also promote stability in domestic monetary and fiscal policies. Exchange rates may have to be changed occasionally even under a fixed-rate system because of large changes in market conditions, but these problems can be handled efficiently and effectively when they take place. Stability, not uncertainty, is the hallmark of fixed exchange rates.

LET EXCHANGE RATES FLOAT

Flexible exchange rates only seem unstable. In fact, they provide greater stability than fixed exchange rates. This is true for two reasons.

First, international business transactions are not, as some would suggest, scared away by the possibility of changing exchange rates. Businessmen can protect themselves from exchange market fluctuations by using the "forward exchange market." The forward market is a "futures" market, just like the futures markets that are found on the Chicago Board of Trade for agricultural commodities. In the forward market, an individual can agree upon a price for foreign exchange delivered in the future (when the currency is needed). Even if the exchange rate changes radically, this futures price will still hold. The forward market, then, allows businessmen to protect themselves from changing exchange rates. The market automatically provides the stability that is needed for international trade.

Flexible exchange rates are also more stable because they tend to change only relatively slowly over time. Currencies do not often halve or double in value overnight. Yet big swings in currency values have often happened under systems or *fixed* exchange rates. With fixed rates, countries do not devalue their currency until they are in a lot of trouble. As a result, devaluation, although infrequent, tends to be by large amounts. This completely disrupts the exchange markets and can hurt businesses and individuals severely.

The fact of devaluation also causes a great deal of currency speculation. Holders of the right currencies tend to gain substantially when devaluation comes. The resulting speculation in these currencies tends to bring on devaluations and cause crisis on the foreign exchange markets.

Speculation with flexible exchange rates tends to move the market toward the true equilibrium, not away from it. Hence speculators in flexible exchange systems actually promote stability in exchange markets.

The final reason for having flexible exchange rates is that only through the market process can the true value of a currency be determined. Flexible exchange rates automatically compensate for changing trade patterns and differences in international inflation rates. By compensating for changing market conditions, the flexible exchange markets keep international trade flowing and promote a stable international community. Flexible exchange rates are desirable and necessary. They should be preserved.

DISCUSSION QUESTIONS

1. With which side do you agree in this debate? Can you find flaws in either side's arguments? Should exchange rates be flexible or fixed?

2. Each side claims that speculators are destabilizing under the alternate exchange rate system. What is the role of international exchange speculators in the

market? Do their actions tend to promote or discourage stable exchange rates? Use supply and demand analysis to determine the answers to these questions.

3. How would the action of limited exchange intervention by national governments be viewed by the proponents of fixed and of flexible exchange rates.

15
International Economics

Making economic policy is a very complex task when all of the international implications of economic actions are considered. This chapter answers questions about the nature of this economic interrelationship, including the following:

How do international credit flows affect economic policy?

Which is more effective, monetary or fiscal policies, when the international impacts are included?

What difference does the type of exchange rate system make?

Does it make any difference if other countries intervene into exchange markets?

Interdependence: mutual dependence

International economic **interdependence** is a fact of life in today's world. The United States relies on foreign producers for much of its energy resources and many essential raw materials. Japan imports about half of the food that its people consume. Most industrialized nations depend on foreign markets for the goods they produce at home. This interdependence can be seen through the two principal ways that economies interact. First, nations engage in trade for goods and services. This international trade affects prices, incomes, and employment in all trading partners. International trading patterns depend, in the long run, on the principle of comparative advantage, but they are very much affected in the short run by changing exchange rates.

Credit markets represent a second point of interaction among open economies. Investment funds flow from nation to nation in search of high returns. National credit markets are thus linked through international credit flows, and changes in any one market will send waves rippling through the rest of the world. National monetary policies, then, can have international consequences.

As funds move from country to country, they have a direct impact on the supply and demand for the currencies involved. Exchange rates change, causing changes in trade patterns. The international system is, indeed, an interdependent one.

In this chapter we will try to understand how this interdependence affects economic policy. We will look at the nature and impacts of international trade and credit flows, and then examine their impact on national monetary and fiscal policies under different exchange rate systems. In the end, we will have a better idea of how the world economy works and why matters of international economics should concern us.

TRADE AND THE ECONOMY

The level of economic activity within a country is directly affected by the extent of its international trade. Exports (sales to foreign buyers) tend to increase aggregate demand directly. Aggregate demand, you will recall, is defined to be the total amount of goods and services that buyers wish to purchase within the economy. It is, therefore, the demand for domestically produced goods. In Chapter 6 this demand was divided into several parts: consumption, investment, government, and net export spending. But we can also divide aggregate demand another way: demand by domestic purchasers and demand by foreign purchasers.

Exports are the foreign demand for our goods and services. When exports rise, aggregate demand rises, too, with the impacts on prices, RGNP, and employment that we have come to expect. Imports (purchases from foreign sellers), on the other hand, are the demand for foreign goods. Rising imports tend to increase aggregate demand abroad, but to decrease aggregate demand at home. Since, in the short run, the level of employment in a country is largely influenced by aggregate demand, anything which increases exports or decreases imports (or, more simply, raises net exports) tends to raise aggregate demand and so increase employment at home. Events which lower net exports (measured by the balance of trade) will tend to lower aggregate demand and employment at home.

Since net exports affect the level of aggregate demand, it follows that aggregate demand is also influenced by the exchange rate. When the dollar gains in value, for example, net exports are reduced and so is aggregate demand. A rising dollar will make U.S. goods more expensive to foreign buyers (causing exports of those goods to fall) but, since a more valuable dollar can purchase more imports, spending on foreign goods tends to rise as they become cheaper in terms of dollars. Appreciation of the dollar, then, reduces exports and increases imports. This lowers net exports and pushes the balance of trade toward deficit. Aggregate demand falls as the dollar appreciates.

Just the opposite impacts will be seen when the dollar falls in value. As the dollar depreciates, foreign buyers find that it takes less of their currency to purchase a dollar and so less, as well, to purchase American goods. Exports tend to rise. At the same time, however, Americans find that it takes more of the less-valuable dollars to purchase foreign currencies and foreign goods. Imports become more expensive and so fewer of them are bought. A falling dollar, then, increases net exports and aggregate demand and moves the balance of trade toward surplus.

International events which affect exchange rates, therefore, will have direct impacts on the economies of the countries involved through the impact of the exchange rate on imports, exports, the balance of trade, and, finally, aggregate demand.

INTERNATIONAL CREDIT MARKETS

National economies are also connected by credit markets. Large banks, corporations, and individuals all have the option of lending money in their home country (as we have thus far assumed they do) or in foreign lands where returns may differ. Where they choose to supply credit will depend on the real interest rates available in each country. When domestic financial conditions change, changing returns can cause credit to move from one country to another.

To see how these international credit movements work, imagine that the major countries of the world are represented by banks lined up on a downtown street. Let's suppose that, at the start of the day, each nation-bank is offering the same real interest rate to its customers (since nations may experience different inflation rates, nominal interest rates may be different, but financiers will tend to pay more attention to the real rates). Now suppose that, because of some internal action, the U.S. bank lowers the real interest rate that it will pay on deposits. What will its depositors (the suppliers of credit) do? Some may do nothing because moving funds among nation-banks is inconvenient and expensive, or because they have long-term agreements with the bank. Other depositors, however, will tend to move some or all of their funds to another bank that offers a relatively higher return.

An interest rate reduction in the United States, then, causes an outflow of loanable funds. These funds must be converted into other currencies before they can be deposited into other nation-banks (loaned to borrowers in other countries), so there will be an impact on the exchange rate. Holders of U.S. funds will attempt to sell dollars and buy foreign currencies as they move those funds from the lower-interest U.S. credit market and into the credit markets of other lands. This higher supply of dollars on the foreign exchange market (and the corresponding increase in the demand for foreign currencies) will cause the dollar to depreciate (lose value) and the foreign currencies to appreciate (gain value). This process was discussed in Chapter 14.

As the supply of credit falls in the United States (due to the exodus of loanable funds abroad), U.S. interest rates will rise (and foreign interest rates fall) until an international real interest rate equilibrium prevails again. Lower U.S. interest rates tend to cause an outflow of loanable funds with the result that the dollar depreciates, producing all of the trade impacts that go with the falling dollar.

Just the opposite effects take place when interest rates rise at home. Suppose that real interest rates were to rise in the U.S. nation-bank because of Federal Reserve action. This would induce depositors in other nation-banks to shift some of their funds to the U.S. bank in order to gain the higher return available there. In order to make these deposits, however, they will have to first purchase dollars, causing the value of the dollar to rise on foreign exchange markets relative to the other currencies involved. The flow of funds into the U.S. bank continues until the rising supply of credit in the United States and the falling supply of credit in the other nation-banks cause international interest rates to fall back into line.

Obviously, nations are not really banks lined up in a row, but to major financial institutions the different national credit markets do represent competing markets for their loanable funds. Credit supplies do actually flow across national borders in response to interest rate differentials.

All of these interactions can be seen graphically in Figure 15-1, which

FIGURE 15-1: INTERNATIONAL CREDIT MOVEMENTS
*As the FRS increases the supply of credit in the United States, the interest rate falls
to 6 percent. Japan's interest rate temporarily remains at 8 percent, so credit funds
flow from the United States (reducing the supply of credit to S''$_{US}$) and increasing
the supply of credit in Japan. These credit flows continue until interest rates are
equalized at 7 percent.*

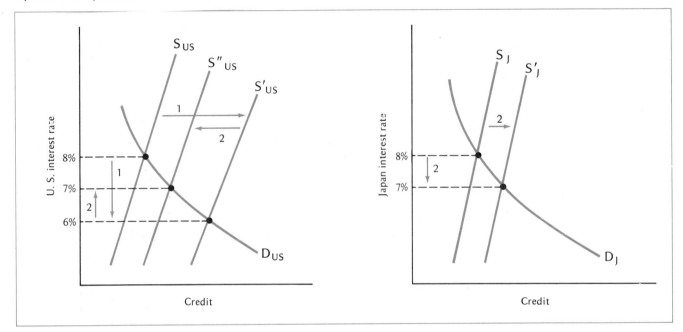

shows credit markets for the United States and Japan. Suppose that the
United States and Japan have the same inflation rates so that their real
interest rates are in equilibrium at the same level (if inflation rates differ, real
interest rates tend to be equal, but nominal rates can differ by the inflation
difference). At the initial equilibrium, both the United States and Japan have
interest rates of 8 percent.

Now suppose that the FRS acts to increase supplies of money and credit
in the United States. The open market purchases that the FRS undertakes act
to increase the supply of credit in the U.S. from S_{US} to S'_{US} and to bid the
interest rate in the United States down to 6 percent.

The falling interest rate in the United States will throw the international
credit markets out of equilibrium. Before, there was no reason to move
credit across national borders, since real returns were equilized worldwide.
Now, however, lenders in the United States can earn higher returns by
shifting their funds to Japan. This credit outflow occurs, increasing the
supply of credit in Japan from S_J to S'_J and reducing the supply of credit in
the United States from S'_{US} to S''_{US}. These credit flows act to equalize

international interest rates. They will also affect the exchange rates as American lenders increase the demand for the yen as they transfer their funds from the United States to Japan.

The international impact here has moderated the increase in the credit supply in the United States and kept interest rates from dropping as far as they might. Note, as well, that Japan's credit supply has increased even though the Japanese have taken no monetary action! In an open economy, the economic policies of one nation tend to be exported to those of its trade and financial market competitors. We will discuss this aspect of international policy at greater length later in this chapter.

EURODOLLARS

Eurodollars: dollar-denominated deposits in foreign banks

Eurodollars are interesting in that they demonstrate just how mobile money is internationally. Eurodollars are simply dollar-denominated bank accounts held in foreign banks. They are created when someone deposits dollars into a foreign bank. Normally, depositors first convert their dollars into the local currency before making a deposit. But because dollars are used so much in international trade, it is possible to instead have the dollars themselves held in the account.

Why would someone deposit dollars abroad? During periods of high inflation or tight money at home, bank interest rates in the United States fall below the international equilibrium interest rate levels because of the ceilings placed on interest rates in U.S. financial institutions. People who have the option are induced to remove their funds from U.S. banks and deposit them abroad, creating the Eurodollars.

When world interest rates fall, on the other hand, these Eurodollar deposits are often returned to the United States, increasing the supplies of money and credit in this country and reducing bank reserves abroad. Eurodollars are a result of international credit movements that occur in response to interest rate differentials.

Because changes in the credit markets of individual countries can have international as well as national impacts, the analysis of economic policy alternatives is much complicated. In many cases, international impacts act to offset the national policies; in other cases, the two types of policies actually reinforce one another. The size of the international impacts relative to the national economic effects depends upon the "openness" of the economy involved. In Japan, for example, the international effects of any

Intranational: within one nation

policy action are perhaps more important than the **intranational** ones, simply because a large part of the Japanese economy is built on foreign trade. In the United States, on the other hand, the international effects are less important than the intranational impacts, because trade makes up a smaller part of our economic activity. All world economies, however, seem to be becoming increasingly "open." As a result, the international consequences on economic policies are important now and will become increasingly important in the future.

We can see the importance of international economics by analyzing domestic monetary and fiscal policies once again in light of the impacts that they will have on international credit flows, exchange rates, imports, and exports. First, we will look at monetary policies.

Suppose that the Federal Reserve were to act to increase the money supply in an attempt to stimulate aggregate demand. Assuming that no "lag" problems occur, what is the impact of this action on the economy? We can divide the effects into national and international components. Ignoring the international side for a moment, we can summarize the impacts of an open market purchase conveniently. An increase in the domestic money supply will cause the supply of credit within the United States to rise. As the supply of credit rises, interest rates are bid down and investment spending increases. All of this results in increased aggregate demand in the short run (with the increases in prices and/or RGNP that this brings) and an increase in aggregate supply over the long haul. This chain reaction is seen in Figure 15-2.

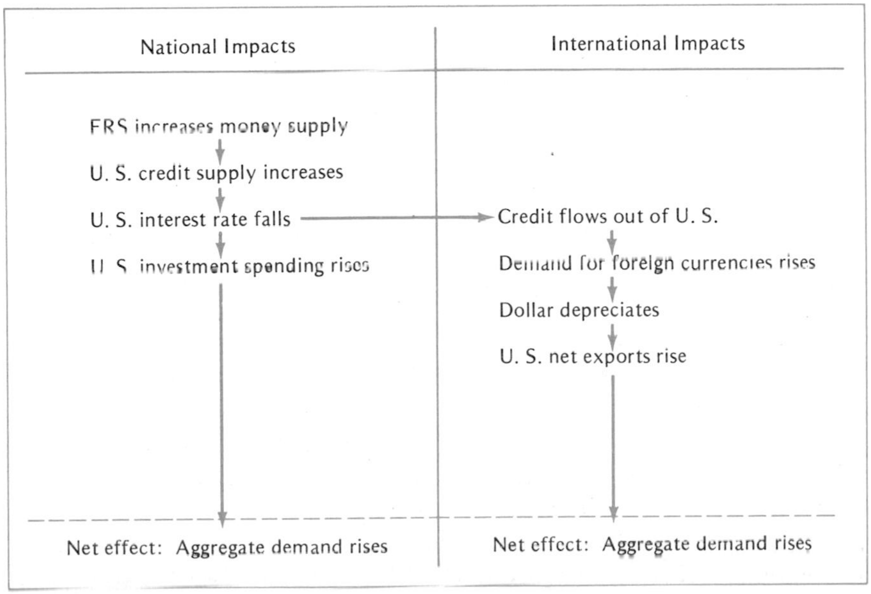

MONETARY POLICY WITH FLEXIBLE EXCHANGE RATES

FIGURE 15-2: EXPANSIONARY MONETARY POLICY WITH FLEXIBLE EXCHANGE RATES

National Impacts	International Impacts
FRS increases money supply	
U. S. credit supply increases	
U. S. interest rate falls	Credit flows out of U. S.
U. S. investment spending rises	Demand for foreign currencies rises
	Dollar depreciates
	U. S. net exports rise
Net effect: Aggregate demand rises	Net effect: Aggregate demand rises

The effects of this policy will not stop here, however, since we now have the rest of the world to cope with. The FRS action has lowered interest rates in the United States. Assuming that the real interest rate has also fallen, this creates a disequilibrium in the international credit markets. The FRS action has caused real returns to be lower in the United States than elsewhere. Lenders in the United States will, therefore, begin to search for higher returns in other countries. Credit will flow out of the economy to foreign lands. The *net* increase in the supply of credit resulting from this FRS action will, then, be less than originally indicated (this was shown in Figure 15-1). The FRS will increase the supply of credit, but some of it will leave the country because of the interest rate response. The supplies of credit and money in the United States will be higher as a result of the FRS action, to be sure, but the increase will not be as great as would have been the case without these international impacts.

The flow of credit out of the United States will also have an impact on the exchange rate. Dollars leaving the United States must eventually be converted to foreign currencies. The increase in the supply of dollars on the foreign exchange markets will tend to bid down the value of the dollar and so bid up the prices of other currencies. The falling dollar will, as we have discussed before, cause exports to rise and imports to fall for the United States as American goods become cheaper to foreign buyers and foreign goods rise in price to American consumers. The international effects of the monetary policy are summarized in Figure 15-2.

Note that the impact of the international effects on aggregate demand is the same as in the closed economy—aggregate demand still rises. In fact, in this case, both national and international effects act to stimulate the economy and actually reinforce one another. Monetary policy still works, but the mechanism is a little different. An expansionary monetary policy will, on net, have the following effects:

☐ Increase the supply of credit.
☐ Lower interest rates.
☐ Stimulate investment spending.
☐ Cause the dollar to depreciate.
☐ Increase net exports.
☐ Stimulate aggregate demand.

The process, which may be a little complicated to read about, is described graphically in Figure 15-2.

If monetary policy works well, even considering the changes that take place when we look at international impacts, does the same hold true for fiscal policy? Here a surprise awaits us: international effects make fiscal policy much less potent than our closed-economy models suggested.

Suppose that the Congress decides to stimulate aggregate demand by increasing government spending (we won't worry here about how this increase in spending is funded). We are already familiar with the national impacts of this action, as shown in Figure 15-3. As aggregate demand rises, prices and/or incomes rise (the desired effect of the action). The secondary impacts of rising credit demand, rising interest rates, and falling investment spending at least partially offset the initial increase in aggregate demand, leaving a small but important net increase in AD to stimulate the economy.

These national effects, however, are further offset by actions in the international arena. As fiscal policy causes domestic interest rates to rise, it will upset the international interest rates that lenders can receive in the credit markets of other nations. Credit will begin to flow into the United States. This is good, of course, in that it acts to somewhat reduce interest rates in the United States and so help keep investment spending from falling. But there is another undesirable impact as well.

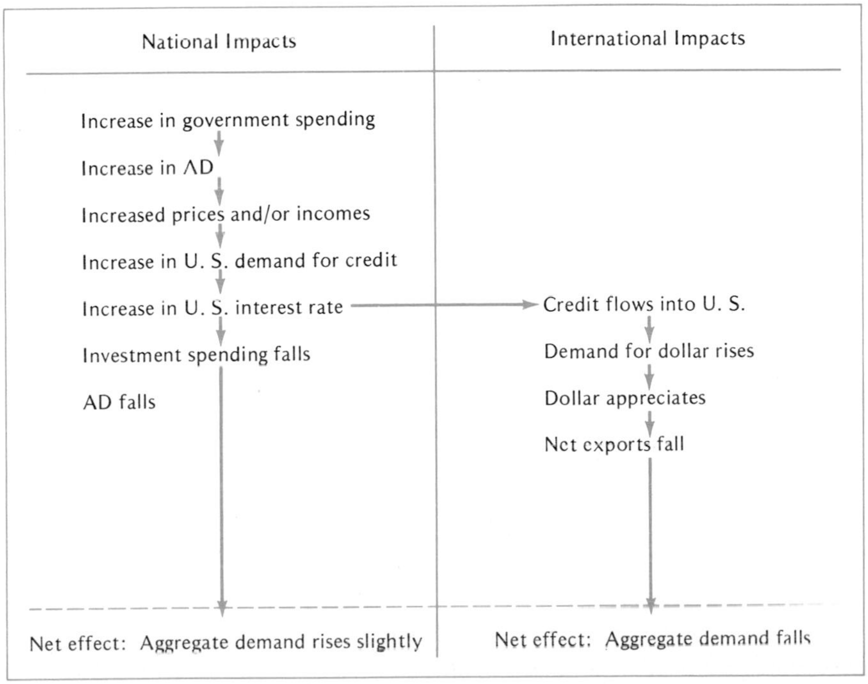

FISCAL POLICY WITH FLEXIBLE EXCHANGE RATES

FIGURE 15-3: EXPANSIONARY FISCAL POLICY WITH FLEXIBLE EXCHANGE RATES

National Impacts	International Impacts
Increase in government spending	
↓	
Increase in AD	
↓	
Increased prices and/or incomes	
↓	
Increase in U. S. demand for credit	
↓	
Increase in U. S. interest rate ⟶	Credit flows into U. S.
	↓
Investment spending falls	Demand for dollar rises
	↓
AD falls	Dollar appreciates
	↓
	Net exports fall
Net effect: Aggregate demand rises slightly	Net effect: Aggregate demand falls

As foreign money holders transfer their loanable funds to the United States, they must purchase dollars. This increased demand for dollars causes the value of the dollar to rise and the prices of foreign currencies to fall. As the dollar becomes more expensive, U.S. goods become more costly to foreign buyers and so fewer of them are purchased. Exports fall when the dollar appreciates. At the same time, however, cheaper foreign currencies have made imports less expensive in the United States, and so import spending rises. The balance of trade (net exports) will move toward deficit, causing aggregate demand to fall.

When both the national and international impacts are taken into consideration, expansionary fiscal policies are less effective than monetary policies. As government spending rises, investment spending falls and export activity falls as well. Aggregate demand may still rise, but only by a relatively small amount.

ECONOMIC POLICY WITH FLEXIBLE EXCHANGE RATES

Monetary policy has grown in importance in the last several years, and the analysis presented above suggests why. Exchange rates became flexible in the early 1970s. In a regime of freely floating exchange rates, monetary policy has greater impact on the economy than does fiscal policy. The recent heavy emphasis on Federal Reserve actions (compared to years past) results from the fact that those actions are now more likely to have an impact on the economy than are fiscal policies.

These international effects also help explain some of the fiscal policy actions of the 1970s. Starting about 1975, the president and Congress have discussed absolutely huge tax cuts and deficits in formulating economic policy. The reason for these large amounts (tax cuts of $10–30 billion and deficits of $40–70 billion) is now clear: when the international effects are considered, it takes a much larger fiscal action to bring about any given increase in aggregate demand. The international effects act to offset part of the fiscal policy activity. The government must therefore push harder than before to bring about the same movement of the economy.

As you can see, the international economy serves to complicate our analysis. Now policy makers must be concerned not only with lags in monetary and fiscal policies, but with offsetting or compounding movements in exchange rates and credit flows. There are other problems, too, which can result from exchange market intervention.

In recent years many different parties have become concerned about the falling value of the dollar. Americans have seen the falling dollar as a cause of inflation since import prices rise as the dollar depreciates. Policy makers in other countries have viewed the declining dollar as a cause of unemployment. As the dollar loses value, foreign goods become more expensive to U.S. buyers, and production of export goods falls in other countries, reducing employment levels in the process.

Because of these problems, the central banks of several countries have intervened in the foreign exchange markets, purchasing dollars in excess of market demand in order to artificially prop up the price of U.S. currency. The central banks of Japan and West Germany have been particularly active in intervention in support of the dollar, and the Federal Reserve has also taken actions designed to "defend" the dollar. Let's see how economic policy works when intervention takes place.

Suppose that the FRS wishes to stimulate aggregate demand by increasing the money supply. The national actions of this policy are familiar to us by now. The increasing supply of credit lowers interest rates and stimulates investment spending. Aggregate demand rises in the short run, and aggregate supply may also rise in the long run.

The international impacts were discussed a few pages ago. Falling interest rates in the United States will cause some of the increased supply of credit to leave the country in search of higher returns abroad. This credit outflow has two effects. First, it lessens the total impact of the expansionary monetary policy by "exporting" some of the increased money supply to other nations. Second, the credit outflow increases the demand for foreign currencies, causing the value of those currencies to rise and the price of the dollar to fall.

So far, nothing different has happened. Now, however, let's assume that the Japanese central bank wishes to keep the value of the dollar high (and the price of the yen low) in order to protect jobs in Japan's export industries. The Japanese central bank will therefore create additional yen and use the yen to buy up the excess supply of dollars on the foreign exchange market. This increased supply of yen and demand for dollars will keep the exchange rate from changing. The mechanics of exchange intervention were discussed in Chapter 14. The effects are shown in Figure 15-4.

Since the exchange rate is not allowed to change, most of the international impacts of the expansionary monetary policy are lost. Exports do not rise and imports do not fall because the exchange rate is held up through intervention (it doesn't matter that it is the Japanese who intervene here—the result would be the same if the FRS were to take these actions instead). Monetary policy will now have only a relatively small impact on

ECONOMIC POLICY WITH INTERVENTION

FIGURE 15-4: MONETARY POLICY WITH
INTERVENTION

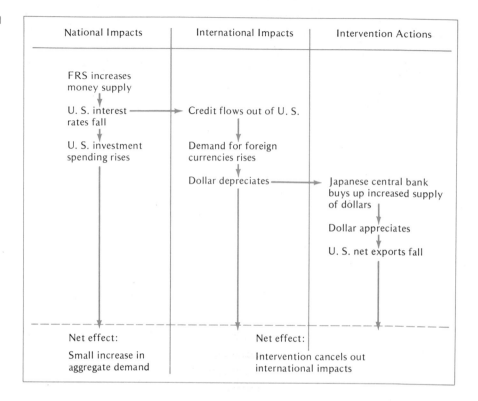

National Impacts	International Impacts	Intervention Actions
FRS increases money supply		
U.S. interest rates fall	Credit flows out of U.S.	
U.S. investment spending rises	Demand for foreign currencies rises	
	Dollar depreciates	Japanese central bank buys up increased supply of dollars
		Dollar appreciates
		U.S. net exports fall
Net effect:	Net effect:	
Small increase in aggregate demand	Intervention cancels out international impacts	

the economy. Some part of the increased money supply will still go to increase credit supplies and stimulate investment spending, but a relatively large proportion of the FRS-created money will leave the country and end up in the vaults of the Japanese central bank, which purchased them to keep the dollar from falling. Monetary policy is not very effective here.

What about fiscal policy when central banks intervene in exchange markets? This case is shown in Figure 15-5. As we concluded before, fiscal policies have only limited effectiveness in an international setting because of offsetting impacts on exchange rates and the balance of trade. These conclusions still hold when intervention takes place. In fact, since the value of the dollar actually rises when expansionary fiscal policies are implemented, there is no need for foreign governments to intervene. The rising dollar value (which reduces U.S. net exports and so reduces the impact of domestic fiscal policy) increases the net exports of foreign countries and acts to increase aggregated demand abroad. This is exactly the result that these foreign governments would like. Exchange market intervention is unnecessary here.

When central banks intervene to "protect" the dollar, neither monetary nor fiscal policies seem to be very effective. Each can accomplish a little,

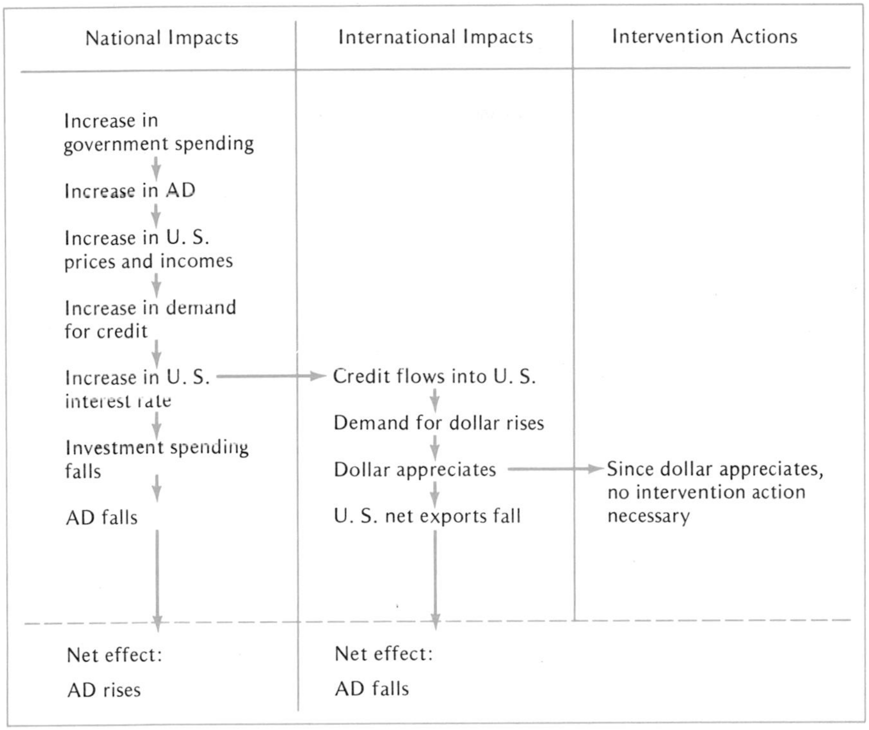

National Impacts	International Impacts	Intervention Actions
Increase in government spending		
↓		
Increase in AD		
↓		
Increase in U. S. prices and incomes		
↓		
Increase in demand for credit		
↓		
Increase in U. S. interest rate	→ Credit flows into U. S.	
↓	↓	
Investment spending falls	Demand for dollar rises	
↓	↓	
	Dollar appreciates ——→	Since dollar appreciates, no intervention action necessary
AD falls	↓	
	U. S. net exports fall	
↓	↓	
Net effect:	Net effect:	
AD rises	AD falls	

FIGURE 15-5: FISCAL POLICY WITH EXCHANGE INTERVENTION

but many of the important impacts of expansionary policy are lost through international actions and reactions. Policy makers must either choose to take very large quantative actions (so that the resulting impacts will be of the desired size) or let the economy find its own equilibrium.

A second problem is that policy actions spill over onto other countries in this situation. When the FRS increased the U.S. money supply, for example, this forced the Japanese central bank to increase the money supply of that country in order to keep the dollar high. Essentially, the Japanese had to print up more yen in order to purchase the dollars that the FRS had printed up earlier. This can create political and economic problems for both countries involved.

FIXED EXCHANGE RATES

Flexible exchange rates are relatively recent phenomenon on the international scene. Fixed exchange rates prevailed during the period from 1946 to about 1973. During this time, each country had to undertake actions designed to keep its currency at a constant value in terms of gold. This meant, roughly, that when the value of the dollar began to drop, the FRS had to buy up the excess supply of dollars using gold or some alternative asset as currency. When the dollar began to rise higher than the agreed-upon value, the FRS was required to print more dollars and flood the exchange markets so as to keep the value of the dollar low. In a fixed-exchange-rate system, then, the money supply must expand and contract so as to stabilize the value of the dollar. This tends to take away some of the power of monetary policies. Let's examine how economic policy worked in this period.

Suppose that the FRS were to undertake an expansionary monetary policy in an attempt to increase aggregate demand and reduce unemployment. The chain reactions are shown in Figure 15-6. As the money supply increases, interest rates fall and investment spending rises, causing aggregate demand to move in the desired direction. Under normal circumstances, reductions in the U.S. interest rate would induce credit to flow out of the country, causing the value of the dollar to fall. The FRS, however, is charged with maintaining the value of the dollar. So as surplus dollars hit the foreign exchange markets, the FRS must purchase them and take them off the market in order to preserve the value of the dollar.

FIGURE 15-6: MONETARY POLICY WITH FIXED EXCHANGE RATES

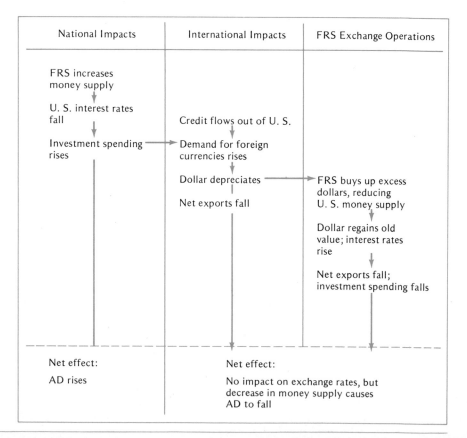

The result is strange, indeed. The FRS increases the supplies of money and credit through open market operations, but must then act to *decrease* these same supplies by buying up dollars on the international markets. In the end, very little happens here. The FRS must work against itself. Domestic policy actions are partially offset by international responsibilities. Monetary policy is therefore not very powerful in this setting. And monetary policy was little used, in fact, during the period of fixed exchange rates. From 1946 to 1951, in fact, the FRS took little or no action of its own and instead merely served as a tool of the Treasury to facilitate the implementation of fiscal policies. Let's see how those fiscal policies worked.

Suppose that the Congress were to increase government spending during a period of fixed exchange rates, as indicated in Figure 15-7. Since we are by now very familiar with the national impacts of this kind of policy, we will concentrate here on the international implications. Expansionary fiscal policies tend to increase interest rates in the United States. This tends, as we

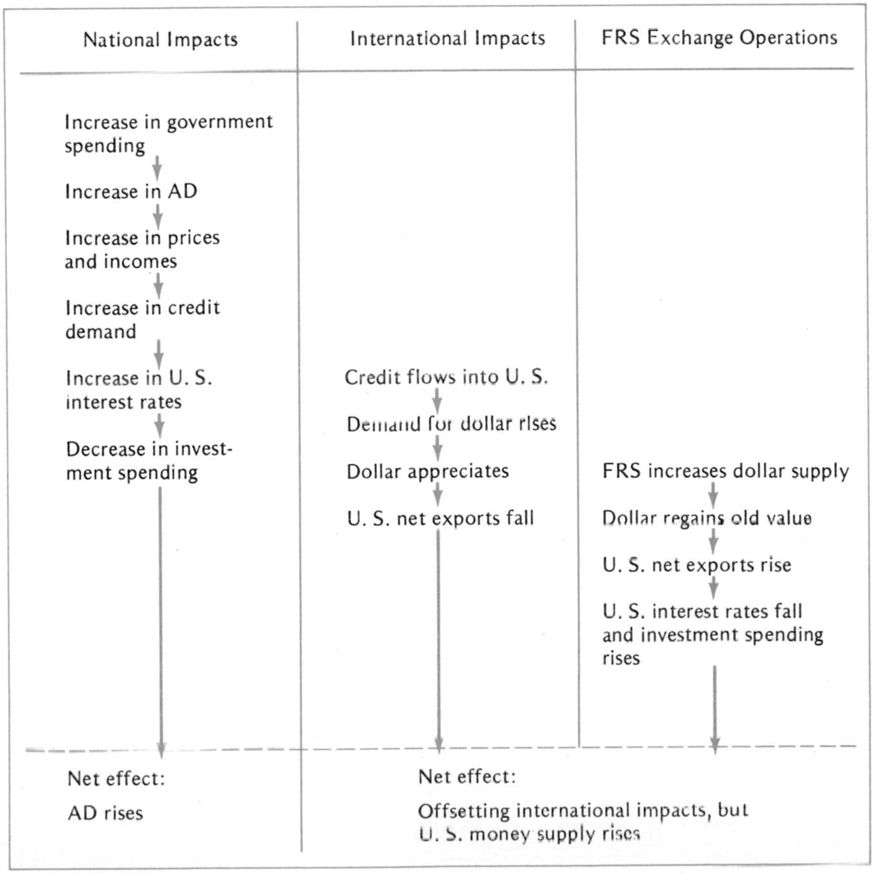

National Impacts	International Impacts	FRS Exchange Operations
Increase in government spending		
↓		
Increase in AD		
↓		
Increase in prices and incomes		
↓		
Increase in credit demand		
↓		
Increase in U. S. interest rates	Credit flows into U. S.	
↓	↓	
Decrease in investment spending	Demand for dollar rises	
	↓	
	Dollar appreciates	FRS increases dollar supply
	↓	↓
	U. S. net exports fall	Dollar regains old value
		↓
		U. S. net exports rise
		↓
		U. S. interest rates fall and investment spending rises
Net effect:	Net effect:	
AD rises	Offsetting international impacts, but U. S. money supply rises	

FIGURE 15-7: FISCAL POLICY WITH FIXED EXCHANGE RATES

have seen, to induce credit movements into the United States, which increase the value of the dollar. The FRS, in this case, must keep the dollar's price fixed at its current level. In order to do this, the FRS will have to satisfy the additional demand for U.S. currency brought on by international credit movements. The FRS will therefore be forced to expand the money supply in order to provide additional dollars to sell on the foreign exchange market. This increase in the supply of dollars will keep the price of the dollar fixed, even in the face of the higher demands brought on by the credit inflows.

The results here are highly stimulative. The FRS has been forced to accommodate fiscal policy. As government spending rises, so does the money supply. Aggregate demand will increase. Fiscal policies are very effective when fixed exchange rates prevail.

Throughout this discussion of fixed exchange rates, we have ignored the impacts of imports and exports. Since the exchange rate does not change under a fixed exchange rate system, imports and exports are not affected by changing currency values. But they will still be affected by economic policies. With exchange rates fixed, the prices of imports and exports will be determined by the inflation rates in the countries involved. Goods from low-inflation countries will sell well abroad. Thus, for example, West Germany benefited during the fixed exchange rates of the 1960s because Germany's relatively low inflations made their goods cheap abroad (the $2000 Volkswagen) and caused German exports to soar. Low-inflation economies prosper with fixed exchange rates.

High-inflation lands, on the other hand, are hurt when fixed exchange rates prevail. Under a flexible-exchange-rate scheme, the exchange rate tends to offset differences in international inflation rates, and so reduces the impact of inflation on exports (we saw this in Chapter 14). With fixed exchange rates, however, goods from high-inflation countries cost more abroad and fewer of them are sold. Unemployment in the high-inflation country is the result.

INTERNATIONAL ECONOMIC POLICIES

It is easy to see why the type of exchange rate system makes a difference to economic policy makers. With flexible exchange rates, monetary policies are very effective, but fiscal policies lack clout. When we had fixed exchange rates, just the opposite was the case, with fiscal actions having great influence over economic events and monetary actions following along. When exchange intervention takes place, neither policy is seen to be very effective. Economic policies must adjust to the realities of the international scene, and what might have been good policy in the past can be very bad policy today, depending upon events elsewhere in the world.

Governments often find that international events serve to tie their hands in making economic policies. Japan, for example, has relatively few policy options in a world of flexible exchange rates. Fiscal policy is relatively ineffective both because of the low multiplier impact (the marginal propensity to consume in Japan is relatively low) and also because of the offsetting exchange impacts. Monetary policy could be effective, but the tools of monetary policy may be tied up, instead, trying to stabilize the dollar and the yen in order to preserve jobs in the Japanese export industries. Since so much of Japan's employment depends upon exports, this is an appropriate action for their central bank.

Japan's money supply, however, is then determined by monetary actions of other countries. When the FRS expands the money supply in the United States, for example, the Japanese central banks must create more yen in order to balance the exchange markets. With fiscal policies ineffective, and monetary policies determined by other governments, how can economic policies be made?

The answer is that, in very open economies like Japan, economic policies tend to be made through nontraditional means. Political pressures are brought to bear upon trading partners—for example, to undertake actions that will benefit both sides. Thus, representatives of the other industrialized nations called, at the economic summit meetings of 1977 and 1978, for the United States to reduce energy consumption in order to improve the value of the dollar.

Other policies are used, as well. Japan, for example, negotiates tariffs and quotas with its trading partners. Instead of having these trade restrictions imposed on them, the Japanese attempt to negotiate the best possible terms so as to preserve as many jobs as possible in their export industries. Export subsidies and import tariffs and quotas are used widely in other countries to regulate trade. In short, the international sector becomes the principal tool of stabilization policy in these open economies.

The international sector of the economy not only complicates the implementation of economic policy, but it also introduces new and uncomfortable trade-offs into the balance. These will be discussed in the next chapter.

SUMMARY

1. International credit flows affect economic policy because credit market activities have international consequences. Lenders seek out the highest real interest rate in world credit markets. Rising real interest rates attract foreign funds, and falling real rates produce outflows of loanable funds. These credit flows

affect interest rates, imports, exports, and aggregate demand.

2. With flexible exchange rates, monetary policy is more effective in stimulating the economy than is fiscal policies. Expansionary monetary policy has the national impacts that were discussed in previous chapters, as well as expansionary international side effects. Expansionary fiscal policies are offset by contractionary international side effects and so are less effective than in the closed-economy models.

3. The type of exchange rate system makes a difference for economic policy. Under a system of flexible exchange rates, monetary policy is more effective than fiscal policies. When fixed exchange rates prevail, however, international impacts act to give fiscal actions greater clout. This helps explain the concentration on fiscal policies during the 1950s and 1960s and the recent increased emphasis on monetary actions.

4. Exchange market intervention frustrates economic policies because foreign governments act to wipe out some international side effects of policy actions. This can create problems for all of the countries involved in making international policy.

DISCUSSION QUESTIONS

1. Compare and contrast the impacts of contractionary monetary and fiscal policies under flexible and fixed exchange rates. Do the different policies work as well for contractionary policy as for the expansionary policies discussed in the text?

2. How would contractionary monetary and fiscal policies work if the Japanese central bank were to intervene whenever the dollar depreciated? Under what conditions would the Japanese bank have to act?

3. How realistic is the assumption that real interest rates are equalized among major nations by international credit movements? What factors might contribute to residual interest rate differences?

4. Suppose that the West German government were to pursue expansionary fiscal policies. What impact would this have on the U.S. economy? What would happen if the Germans were to use monetary policy instead? How would the U.S. economy react in this case?

TEST YOURSELF

Indicate whether each of the following statements is *true* or *false*. Be able to defend your choice.

1. The existence of Eurodollars makes monetary policy easier for the FRS to carry out.

2. Eurodollars are part of the U.S. money supply.

3. An open market purchase tends to drive down interest rates and drive up the value of the dollar.

4. An open market purchase tends to produce an outflow of loanable funds from the United States.

5. Monetary policy is more effective with flexible exchange rates than with fixed exchange rates.

6. Lags in monetary and fiscal policies are not a problem when we are considering the international effects.

7. Economic theory suggests that fiscal policies should have been especially effective during the period 1946–1973.

8. Economic theory suggests that monetary policies should be especially effective since 1973.

9. When foreign governments intervene to hold the value of the dollar up, monetary policies are more effective than fiscal policies.

10. An intervening country must alter its money supply whenever other countries pursue monetary policy.

16
Problems, Goals, and Trade-offs

This chapter looks back at all that we have learned in order to achieve a better perspective on macroeconomic goals, tools, and policies. This discussion will deal with a number of important questions, including the following:

What are the goals of economic policy?
What tools are available in our quest for these goals?
What trade-offs must be made?
Is it necessary to give up a goal?
Are economic goals the only ones we need worry about?

The first fifteen chapters of this text have constructed a relatively simple but very useful model of how the national economy works and how it interacts with the rest of the world. We have learned about economic problems, monetary and fiscal policies, financial markets, and international trade. It is now time to pause and look back over the landscape that we have traversed. How are our various economic problems interrelated? How do economic policy tools work? What are the trade-offs that must be faced in achieving prosperity?

The economic world is a very complicated and interdependent one. Actions taken to affect one goal often have unexpected results in other areas. The choice of economic policy is made difficult, then, when only a few tools must be used to achieve a number of major goals. It is not always possible, as we will see, to solve all of our problems at once. When this happens, the choice is particularly difficult. When an economic goal must be given up, losers are created. A different set of people are affected by each of our major national problems. The choice, in this context, is very basically one of who should gain and who should lose? Economic theory can help us understand the implications of our actions. The best choice, however, is not always clear.

MACROECONOMIC GOALS

Our national macroeconomic goals were first discussed in Chapter 1. There we learned that Congress, in the Employment Act of 1946, set the goals of full employment, stable prices, and economic growth. Let's return to those goals in light of all that we have learned. At the same time, let's look at some new goals that have become important since 1946.

GOAL 1: FULL EMPLOYMENT. Full employment remains one of our most important national goals, but it is a goal that is difficult both to understand and to achieve. What is full employment? As we saw in Chapter 3, there is no pat answer to this question. In 1978 Congress passed the Humphrey-Hawkins Bill which seemed to define full employment as a 4 percent unemployment rate. In any case, that is the unemployment goal that the bill set for the economy. In the meantime, however, other groups push for different goals. On the one hand, many economists and policy makers suggest that 4 percent is an unreasonable unemployment target; the changing size and nature of the labor force has increased frictional employment, they say, so that 5½ or 6 percent unemployment may be the best we can do. A few groups at the opposite end of the spectrum, have called for "true" full employment—zero percent unemployment—claiming that this would be the only true solution to our national problems.

Definitions aside, the goal of full employment involves more than just meeting some unemployment rate benchmark. As we saw in Chapter 3, unemployment is not evenly distributed among groups in the population. People who are young, members of a racial or ethnic minority, or female all suffer unemployment rates greater than the "average." Many of the people in these groups would still be left jobless even in a prosperous economy because the labor market cannot easily assimilate them.

The goal of full employment, then, involves two types of policies. One would attempt to lower the average unemployment rate through stimulating aggregate demand and supply. A second set of policies, however, must be designed to help those groups who are not "average" to successfully enter the working mainstream.

GOAL 2: STABLE PRICES. Truly stable prices—a no-inflation economy—is probably no longer a realistic economic goal. The economy is now harder to fool with inflation. Our sophisticated inflationary expectations, however, tend to bring on the price increases that we fear. Some sort of inflation seems to be built into the economy.

While stable prices may remain as an ideal, a more immediate goal should be to achieve low inflation rates. Recent price increases have created too many winners and losers in our society (discussed in Chapter 4) to be tolerated.

Fighting inflation, however, is no snap. Inflation can be caused in several different ways (as discussed in Chapter 7), and it may not be obvious which type of inflation prevails—demand-pull or cost-push. In fact, both cost and demand forces may be at work at the same time. Yet it is crucial to know which cause is at the root of the current inflation. If the problem is demand-pull, then policies to lower aggregate demand may be justified. If we are experiencing cost-push inflation, however, reducing aggregate demand is less effective in fighting price rises and serves to cause high unemployment rates (see Chapter 7). The fact of inflationary expectations complicates the matter.

Inflation and the policies that we choose to deal with it have a great deal to do with our ability to achieve our other national economic goals. Demand-pull inflation, for example, increases employment, and so can be used to move the economy toward full employment. Cost-push inflation, however, takes us further from both the goals of price stability and high employment. Inflation can influence economic growth, the value of the dollar, and the balance of trade in undesirable ways.

Because inflation is such a widespread problem, it is basic to the

PROBLEMS, GOALS, AND TRADE-OFFS

discussion of any other economic goal. But the solution of the inflation problem requires careful policy application and perhaps a large amount of luck.

GOAL 3: ECONOMIC GROWTH. Achieving economic growth these days means taking actions which stimulate the growth of aggregate supply. Aggregate supply (see Chapter 7) grows in response to increases in the labor force and worker productivity and through business investments which increase the economy's capacity to produce.

In the real world, economic growth seems to have become a less important goal than full employment or price stability. While growth is of obvious importance, few seem to be persuaded that we should bear high inflation or low employment in the short run in order to achieve high growth rates down the road. The economy may be short sighted in this matter, but our impatience gets the better of us. Perhaps the fact that political leaders must face reelection in the short run tends to bias policy toward focusing on short-run problems and solutions.

Economic growth is desirable because it improves the standard of living and makes possible a redistribution of income and wealth without creating losers. With a fixed pie, some must lose if others gain. With a growing pie, winners need not take from losers.

This discussion has concentrated on the fact of economic growth—increases in aggregate supply—but it should be remembered that what is produced and how it is produced are also important factors. Environmental quality is a major concern these days. Economic growth that increases the quantity of material goods while reducing the quality of life is no bargain. Here we must look beyond mere quantitative measures and examine the economic and social consequences of economic growth.

OTHER NATIONAL GOALS. While the Big Three economic goals (low inflation, high employment, economic growth) remain the principal targets of macroeconomic policy at the national level, a number of other goals have become clear in recent years. These secondary goals may be more or less important at different times, but they always enter into the policy decision process.

Balanced federal government budget: total federal government expenditures equal total federal tax collections

One of these goals is a **balanced federal government budget.** Federal government expenditures have grown rapidly over the years, and taxes have risen with them. Many voters have begun to feel that they are not getting their money's worth out of government. Tax cuts to stimulate the economy have produced large budget deficits. Large amounts of governmental borrowing of the 1970s have produced the threat of government "crowding out" of private borrowing (see Chapter 11).

Large, long-term deficit spending may not be good for the economy. In the late 1970s the goal of a balanced budget became a more important one. Deadlines of first 1980 and then 1983 were set for the achievement of balanced spending and taxing. While a balanced budget may be beneficial to the growth of aggregate supply in the long run (because of the absence of crowding out), the short-term impact may be to reduce aggregate demand and cause unemployment (this was discussed in Chapter 8). This goal, then, is an appealing one for political and economic reasons, but has dark aspects since it may increase unemployment as well as create losers depending upon how the budget is brought into balance—by raising taxes or by cutting government programs.

Another national goal is to bring about an **equitable distribution of income.** While income and production are high in the United States compared to the rest of the world (see the international RGNP comparison in Chapter 5), the distribution of that income remains uneven. The richest 1 percent of the population has as much after-tax income as the poorest 20 percent of the population. While numbers alone only suggest that a problem exists (they can be stated differently to make the distribution of income seem more or less even), a goal clearly remains to at least narrow the gap by increasing the incomes of the poorest groups in the economy.

Equitable distribution of income: a more equal distribution of income among groups in the population

INTERNATIONAL ECONOMIC GOALS

When the Employment Act of 1946 was enacted, the United States held a dominant position in the world economy. In the post–World War II world, the dollar reigned almighty and the U.S. economy was busy producing more and more goods to meet demands at home and abroad. The existence of fixed exchange rates made concern over the value of the dollar unnecessary. The international sector of the economy was important, but largely a source of benefits, not problems.

The world has changed much since 1946, and now international economic goals are clearly a part of the scene. In addition to national macroeconomic goals, then, a pair of international concerns must be noted:

1. EXCHANGE RATE GOALS. Exchange rates are now an important part of the economic scene. Since 1973, when exchange rates became more or less flexible, the value of the dollar has been of national concern. A falling dollar creates winners and losers. A stable or rising dollar seems to have become a major economic goal. This is not an easy goal to achieve, however. Direct intervention into exchange markets can create the kinds of pressures that developed during the periods of fixed exchange rates (see Chapter 14). Increasing the value of the dollar through monetary policies, as

noted in Chapter 15, can have detrimental impacts on both aggregate demand and aggregate supply. And a rising dollar, if it should occur, would create additional difficulties by encouraging imports and discouraging exports. This is a problem with no easy solutions.

2. BALANCE-OF-TRADE GOALS.

A second international economic goal is to return the United States to a surplus in the balance of trade. The United States has traditionally been a strong producing economy which exported much of this production to the rest of the world. Today's trade figures (see Chapter 13) indicate that this situation is changed as exports have fallen and spending on the imports of many items, including energy products, have soared.

Improving the balance of trade is important for two reasons. Improving exports tends to increase aggregate demand at home and so help employment prospects. As well, increased exports should increase the demand for the dollar on foreign exchange markets and so help achieve the exchange rate goal. But the goal of a trade surplus is not an easy one to reach. As the world has changed, the pattern of comparative advantage has changed, too. The United States may have to change what it produces and how this production takes place in order to regain a major larger share of world exports. This kind of change, however, is not likely to take place overnight.

POLICY TOOLS

To deal with this long list of economic goals and problems, policy makers have available a menu of tools and methods. We can divide these tools into three main groups: fiscal policies, monetary policies, and international policies.

1. FISCAL TOOLS.

A variety of fiscal policies are available to economic decision makers. Taxes, transfers, and government spending can all be changed in attempts to manipulate aggregate demand, aggregate supply, or both.

A number of "nontraditional" tools are also available if they are determined to be desirable. Wage and price controls (discussed in Chapter 7) have several times been used to control price inflation. Since controls have undesirable side effects (shortages of goods and services), while traditional policies may also be ineffective in fighting inflation, a number of other options are sometimes used in the fiscal fight against inflation. **Jawboning** is one such tool. Presidents and economic leaders have often spoken out against specific price increases ("used the jawbone") in an attempt to mobilize public opinion and induce "voluntary" price controls.

Jawboning: governmental actions designed to hold down wages or prices by pointing out unwarranted increases and applying public pressure to reduce price increases

Guidelines have also been used. Guidelines are norms established by the government for wage and price increases. Guidelines are designed to give workers and producers an idea of what would be considered "reasonable" and unreasonable increases in wages and prices. Jawboning and guidelines may have been useful in specific cases in the past, but their overall impact on inflation has probably been minimal.

New fiscal tools are being developed all of the time. In the 1970s, for example, economists began to discuss the use of **tax-based incomes policy** (TIP) programs. TIP plans, of which there are a number of differing types, generally rely on the use of tax "carrots" and "sticks" to attempt control inflation. Industries that raise wages or prices faster than the "acceptable" rate are punished with higher taxes. Those that help fight inflation by limiting wage and price increase are rewarded with lower tax rates. There are still a lot of bugs to be worked out with TIP programs, and there is no guarantee that they would actually work if implemented. They are, for now, an example of how fiscal tools are being reworked in an attempt to better deal with current problems.

Guidelines: announced governmental standards for wage and price increases designed to induce voluntary reductions in price increases

Tax-based incomes policy (TIP): a program which attempts to use tax incentives to accomplish macroeconomic policies

2. MONETARY TOOLS. Monetary policies are also used in the fight to achieve prosperity. Here the more traditional tools prevail. Open market operations, changes in reserve requirements, and discount rate changes are the basic ways of implementing monetary policy. The making of monetary policy is complicated, however, by the existence of a basic disagreement over what the goals of monetary policy should be. The traditional approach (Chapter 11) holds that monetary policy works by affecting the real interest rate. The monetarists, however, suggest that more attention should be paid to the money stock and long-range money supply targets (see Chapter 12).

3. INTERNATIONAL TOOLS. Economic policies can also be manipulated using monetary and fiscal tools to affect the international side of the economy. Federal Reserve actions can be used to alter the value of the dollar by inducing credit flows. The government can affect imports and exports through decisions involving foreign aid, tariffs, and quotas and laws which regulate international business. As the international economy becomes increasingly important, we can expect to see economic policy used to a greater extent to influence the foreign sector.

The variety of our economic goals and the fact that economic problems are so interrelated that side effects are always produced makes macroeconomic policy a particularly difficult task. Trade-offs between policy goals abound. This fact is illustrated in Table 16-1, which compares the impacts of several

TRADE-OFFS IN ECONOMIC POLICIES

TABLE 16-1

GOALS, POLICIES, AND TRADE-OFFS

		ECONOMIC GOALS				
		Stable Prices				
Policy Options	Full Employment	Short Run	Long Run	Economic Growth	Exchange Rates	Balance of Trade
Increase government spending	+	−	−	−	+	−
Cut consumer taxes	+	−	−	−	+	−
Cut business taxes	+	−	+	+	+	+
Increase transfer payments	+	−	−	−	+	−
Increase money supply	+	−	+	+	−	+
Intervene to defend dollar	−	+	?	?	+	−
Enact trade barriers	?	−	−	?	+	+
Wage and price controls	−	+	?	−	+	?

Key: + Policy helpful in achieving goal; − Policy detrimental to goal; ? Impact on goal uncertain.

possible policies on the national economic goals outlined in the first part of this chapter. Here policies that help achieve a particular goal are marked with a plus sign (+), those that are detrimental to that goal with a minus (−), and those that affect the goal in ambiguous ways with a question mark (?).

The trade-off between inflation and unemployment in the short run is particularly apparent (given the "bottleneck" aggregate supply assumed here). Policies designed to increase employment in the short run also act to increase the price level. Policies such as lower business taxes or increases in the money supply (which act to increase investment spending) may moderate inflation in the long run, but even these policies still are inflationary in the short run.

Another hard trade-off exists between exchange rate goals and a surplus in the balance of trade. In general, those policies which improve the trade balance tend to worsen the exchange rate, and vice versa. Trade restrictions may increase the cost of imports and help achieve both goals (explained in Chapter 14), but only with the cost of higher inflation (as import costs rise) and possible reduced employment (as export-related jobs disappear). Cutting business taxes can also help achieve both international goals. In the short run the tax cut may improve the value of the dollar (see Chapter 15). In the long run, increased business investment may make the United States a more competitive producer in international markets and so move the trade balance into surplus.

ECONOMIC POLICY CHOICES

The trade-offs in macroeconomic policy are best illustrated by examining a specific example. Suppose that it was decided to improve the balance of trade. Let's examine the types of policies and problems that might result. If the balance-of-trade deficits pose a national economic problem, then what are the solutions available to restore trade surplus? At least four types of solutions could be tried: energy policy, exchange rate adjustment, trade restrictions, and monetary and fiscal policy. We will look briefly at each of these policies to see how they would work and the problems that each would cause.

1. ENERGY POLICY. The United States spends billions of dollars every year for imported oil. These high payments may be at the bottom of the trade problem. One way to restore a trade surplus would be to lower oil payments. This is easier said than done, however.

The reason that we buy oil from abroad is clearly that it is cheaper to buy it than to produce it ourselves (comparative advantage at work). The experience with the Alaska oil pipeline is instructive here. The oil pipeline alone cost $9 billion. And the pipeline only brings the oil from the oil fields down to a port where it can then be loaded into tankers for transport (at higher cost) to oil refiners. Just getting the remaining U.S. oil reserves to market is an expensive proposition. Increasing domestic production to meet current demand (if it could be done) would cause energy prices to rise significantly in the short run, and still leave us with long-term difficulties when oil reserves run out.

Conservation is one way to reduce oil imports. Conservation can be either enforced (through energy quotas and allocations) or induced (by raising the price of oil in order to get people to use less of it). Either of these plans is likely to cause major economic problems. Rationing of energy is bound to create equity problems (who deserves to have their oil allocation reduced?) as well as bottlenecks in production due to allocation problems. Some unemployment would surely result.

Raising oil prices (through taxes, for example) poses different problems from the rationing scheme. The demand for oil is thought to be fairly inelastic. That is, a large price increase would be necessary in order to reduce energy consumption significantly. Even if the energy taxes were recycled as transfer payments in order to reduce hardship caused by the tax (as President Carter suggested in 1977), it is still likely that cost-push inflation much like the 1973–1974 experience would result.

A third way of coping with the energy problem is to pass laws which, while not going so far as setting quotas, still strive to enforce conservation. Laws which mandate the insulation of new homes, for example, or that set fuel economy standards for new cars are steps in this direction. The price of oil is not directly affected through these rules, but the cost of the items which use oil are increased.

Energy policies have the desirable side effect of increasing the value of the dollar, but they also probably cause cost-push inflation at home. Other solutions to the trade problems must also be examined.

2. EXCHANGE RATE ADJUSTMENT. A second solution to the balance-of-trade deficit would be to allow the dollar to fall sufficiently to bring trade back into balance. As the dollar falls, exports tend to increase and imports decline. Giving up the goal of a stable dollar, then, could help achieve the goals of a trade surplus. But there are other problems as well.

Much of the pressure to keep the dollar high in recent years has come from abroad. Foreign central banks have worked to keep the dollar in high demand. They have done this in order to keep the price of the dollar high because a valuable dollar preserves jobs in countries which trade with the United States. In order to bring the U.S. trade balance into surplus, these nations would have to give up their exchange market activities in support of the dollar. As the dollar declines and the U.S. trade balance improves, jobs would be transferred from Japan and West Germany, among others, to the United States. These foreign countries are not likely to view this transfer favorably.

As well, consumers in the United States would see import prices rise as the dollar declines. To the extent that people would continue to purchase these higher-priced goods, the dollar's decline would bring about inflation in the United States. While jobs would be created in exporting industries, the cost-push inflation caused by rising import prices could reduce employment in other areas of the economy.

The falling dollar could also cause the OPEC nations to raise oil prices (causing further cost-push inflation) or to change the medium of international oil payment from the dollar to some other currency (further disrupting the foreign exchange markets).

There are many good points to this policy, but undesirable impacts also exist. The United States could not implement this policy alone. It would need the cooperation of its trading partners, who would be the ones most hurt by this action.

3. TARIFFS AND QUOTAS. Many people see the solution to the U.S. trade problem in imposing higher tariff and quota barriers on imports. In this way, it is held, imports can be restricted without affecting exports. The trade deficit, then, would disappear with the appropriate import restrictions.

Trade restrictions have the effect of driving up the prices of imports. Hence, tariffs and quotas would cause import-price inflation and some form of cost-push inflation as well. Jobs would be created in U.S. import-competing industries, but the exchange-rate effects of the trade restrictions (as we saw in Chapter 14) would tend to damage U.S. firms that export goods and services. Trade restrictions would reduce imports and increase the value of the dollar, but at the expense of inflation and unemployment.

The consequences might be even worse. Protection fever tends to be catching. Other nations can be expected to retaliate if the United States erects high trade barriers. Any improvement in the U.S. trade balance, then, may be short-lived as retaliatory trade restrictions act to reduce U.S. exports. All trading partners would lose in such an event.

4. INTERNAL ECONOMIC POLICIES. Domestic monetary and fiscal policies can also be used to alter the position of the trade balance, but the trade-offs are rather severe. Expansionary monetary policy tends to increase net exports, but only if the dollar is allowed to fall. International cooperation here is necessary and may not be forthcoming. Contractionary fiscal policies could also be used to improve the trade balance, but here again the exchange-rate effect is used to increase exports and reduce imports, and other nations may not be willing to allow the dollar to fall.

Other ways can be found to improve the trade balance by reducing imports. If contractionary policies were used to bring on a recession at home, for example, the trade balance would likely improve. Few unemployed people manage to purchase Mercedes-Benz automobiles. Causing a recession in order to achieve the goal of a trade surplus does not make a great deal of sense, however.

None of these four ways of achieving a trade surplus can do so without costs to the economy.

Trade-offs in economic policy are made more complicated by a variety of other problems which policy makers must face. The first such problem, already discussed in Chapters 8 and 11, is the dilemma of lags. Few economic policies can take effect immediately. The lags in monetary and fiscal policies can turn well-intentioned actions into disasters for the economy. Lags cannot be legislated away; they remain one of the uncomfortable "givens" of macroeconomics.

A second policy problem is one of measurement. It is often difficult to tell exactly what the economic problems are. When prices rise, for example, it may be difficult to tell immediately whether the cause is cost-push, demand-pull, or a combination of these forces. When the right solution is applied to the wrong problem (as we saw in Chapter 7), the problem can only be made worse.

A third problem results from disagreements among the various policy-

POLICY PROBLEMS

making bodies in the United States. When the president, the Congress, and the leaders of the Federal Reserve all hold different views as to the most important economic problems or the most appropriate solutions, the results can be a stalemate or, worse, policies which combine, like certain combinations of drugs, to become a deadly potion.

Finally, the international economy adds a number of problems to the practice of making national economic policy. Actions which other nations take can have a profound influence on the domestic policy. Foreign central bank operations can affect the U.S. exchange rate and balance-of-trade situation. Foreign tariff and quota policies (which can be used to retaliate against U.S. tariff changes) affect the levels of imports and exports. Foreign control of scarce resources (oil is just the most obvious example) enters the picture, too.

SETTING NATIONAL PRIORITIES

What is the moral of this long story? The lesson to be learned here may be that we cannot achieve all of our economic goals at once. Living in a complicated world means that fighting one problem can inflame another. In the short run, at least, we may have to choose which problem to live with.

Giving up a goal does not make the problem any easier, however, because we must then decide which problem to live with. Every economic problem creates losers, so which part of the economy should be so punished? Those hurt most by inflation? The victims of unemployment? Export-industry workers? Import-competing workers? Those who would be aided most by economic growth?

These are hard choices to make. The goal of this text has not been to announce how these choices should be made, but rather to increase the reader's understanding of the problems and of the policies that are available.

One further complication must be noted. Not all of our goals and problems are purely "economic" in nature (although they all have their economic aspect). Goals of social welfare, justice, equality, and environmental quality also demand our attention. These goals present additional economic trade-offs, however. A cleaner environment may be one with less economic growth. A world with greater justice and equality might produce fewer goods and services. There are no pat answers here, only hard questions and choices. The economic reality of scarcity and choice prevails.

SUMMARY

1. We can identify many national economic goals. The Employment Act of 1946 specified the national goals of full employment, stable prices, and economic growth. These goals still

remain, although their meanings may have changed over the years. Two international goals seem to have been picked up along the way. We also have new goals concerning the value of the dollar and the balance of trade. Additional goals, such as a balanced federal government budget and a more equal distribution of income, exist as well.

2. Fiscal, monetary, and international tools are available to meet economic problems. The government can use taxes, transfers, and government spending as well as wage and price controls and other less obvious tools. Open market transactions are the principal monetary tool. Exchange rate policies and trade restrictions can be used to affect the international sector of the economy.

3. With all of these tools and problems, trade-offs are hard to avoid. In particular, the short-term trade-offs exist between inflation and unemployment and exchange rates and the balance of trade. Other trade-offs persist as well. Giving up a goal may be necessary, but it still remains to choose which goals are important and which may be foregone. This choice is not an easy one.

4. Economic goals are not the only ones we need consider. Social and environmental concerns are also important, and these problems impose additional economic trade-offs.

DISCUSSION QUESTIONS

1. If both a strong dollar and a trade surplus are not attainable, which goal should be given up? What are the impacts on the economy of choosing one goal over another?

2. Suppose that we make a commitment to fight inflation at all costs. What are the best policies for accomplishing this? What impacts would these policies have on the remaining economic goals?

3. Do other nations have the same economic goals that we do? How do Japan's economic goals compare to ours?

4. Looking at current economic problems and current economic policies, what choices do current policies make? Has a goal been given up? Have the goals changed?

TEST YOURSELF

Indicate whether each of the following statements is *true* or *false*. Be able to defend your choice.

1. Economic goals have changed over the years as the economy has changed.

2. The goal of economic growth can be interpreted to mean the long-run increase in aggregate demand.

3. The reason that international goals were not specified in the

Employment Act of 1946 is that the international sector of the economy was unimportant then.

4. Economic policy can always be chosen so as to achieve all of our goals at once.

5. There are other social goals besides the macroeconomics goals outlined here that are important to the economy.

6. Energy policies can solve all our economic problems at once.

7. Lags exist and are important in international policies.

8. Other nations have the same international goals as the United States; that is why they intervene in exchange markets.

9. Policies which achieve short-term goals often are detrimental to the long-run goal of economic growth.

10. Policies which fight unemployment often prevent the achievement of a balanced budget.

ECONOMIC CONTROVERSIES VIII: DEFENDING THE DOLLAR

The value of the dollar is of much concern to us these days. Hardly a newscast passes that does not include the most recent change in the dollar's value on international exchange markets. Falling dollar values are viewed with a combination of alarm and despair, while rising dollar prices are seen as a source of national pride and evidence of economic achievements at home. Much importance is attached to changes in the dollar's value, perhaps more than is justified by the economics of the situation.

In our analysis, we have discovered that a falling dollar can be caused by a number of things: rising costs for imports like oil, inflation at home, falling U.S. interest rates, or simply changing comparative advantages which alter import and export flows. A falling dollar has many economic impacts. It encourages exports, raises the price of imports, and affects business de-

cisions around the world. Monetary and fiscal policies in the United States and elsewhere are likely to be influenced by changes in the value of the dollar.

Should we "defend" the dollar—take actions designed to increase the dollar's value on the foreign exchange market? Economists and policy makers disagree concerning this issue. Some view the declining dollar as a problem to be solved. Others feel that it is a symptom of other problems. Still others view the changing exchange rate as a natural adjustment process which should be allowed to function freely. Some of the arguments follow:

DEFEND THE DOLLAR!

The dollar must be defended using economic policy tools because the decline is detrimental to the economy. A falling dollar is inflationary. Import prices rise and many imports are important to the production process. As a result, the falling dollar causes cost-push inflation. This inflation produces still more depreciation of the dollar, creating a cycle of inflation and depreciation. Jobs and incomes suffer.

As the dollar falls, foreign exchange traders are inclined to speculate against U.S. currency, causing it to fall even more. The ultimate devastating event would occur if the largest foreign holders of the dollar—the OPEC nations—should become disappointed with that currency and move to unload it all at once. The billions of dollars that would flood the exchange markets would drive the value of the dollar through the floor and thoroughly disrupt foreign exchange activities. A "dollar panic" would follow as everyone with dollars rushed to unload them before they fell even more. International trade and commerce would grind to a halt, and an international crisis would ensue.

The dollar must be defended precisely because it is such an important international currency. Dollar depreciation has undesirable national and international consequences. A return to fixed exchange rates, in fact, may be the ultimate answer to this problem.

FIGHT INFLATION FIRST

The real cause of the declining dollar is the rapid price inflation in the United States. The falling dollar is merely a symptom of this. As inflation makes each dollar worth less, this fact is reflected in the dollar's international value. To take actions to change the dollar's value

without getting to the cause of the problem—inflation—will not solve our problems.

Since domestic monetary and fiscal policies are at the heart of the inflation problem, they are also the cause of the dollar's demise. High levels of government spending, monumental budget deficits, and rapid increases in the money supply are the true causes of our current problems. Solutions should be sought here.

Reduced government spending and a slower rate of increase in the money supply would perhaps have the temporary impact of increasing unemployment. In the long run, however, the economy would rebuild on the basis of its natural strength. Without the burden of inflation, economic recovery would be rapid. The value of the dollar would rise as a natural consequence of the lessened inflation rates.

LET THE DOLLAR FALL

The falling dollar is nothing to be concerned about. The dollar is merely a price that adjusts in the market in order to bring the forces of demand and supply into equilibrium. As the dollar falls, the quantity of dollars (and U.S. goods) demanded will rise, and the quantity of imports (and foreign currencies) demanded will fall. A natural balance is available here, if only we allow the market to adjust by itself.

The goal of the increasing value of the dollar is rather silly, in fact, in that a rising dollar hurts employment in the United States by making U.S. exports more expensive. Other nations take actions in order to *reduce* the price of their currencies. The actions taken by the Japanese and West German central banks, in fact, have resulted in a falling price for their currencies as they have bid up the dollar. They obviously are aware of the importance of exports to their economies. We seem to have a silly notion that our national dignity is tied to the value of our currency. Hence, we take actions which help national pride by defending the dollar, but which result in unemployment at home. Leave the dollar alone and it will fall to its real value. Defending it will just serve to create other economic problems and may make us worse off in the long run.

DISCUSSION QUESTIONS

1. Is inflation the cause of the declining dollar, or does a falling dollar cause inflation? How can you tell which is which?

2. Suppose that the inflation/depreciation cycle exists. How would it be possible to stop this cycle? What policies would be needed?

3. How real is the threat of a "dollar panic" if we choose not to defend the dollar? What would happen if the dollar were to suddenly fall in price?

4. Evaluate the argument that the dollar's value should be allowed to find its "natural value." If this argument is true, then what are the impacts of keeping the dollar from finding its true value through intervention?

Suggestions for Further Reading

This section gives a chapter-by-chapter listing of readings which may be used to supplement or expand the treatment of economic problems, theories, and policies given in the text. These readings include articles from magazines, books, economics journals, and Federal Reserve Bank publications which should be available at most good college libraries. Many of the articles also appear in books of readings for introductory economics courses.

In addition to the specific article references here, certain periodicals can be counted upon for understandable presentations of current economic events. These include *Time*, *Newsweek* and *U.S. News* magazines, *The New York Times* and *The Washington Post*, and, most particularly, the *Wall Street Journal*.

Those articles which are particularly difficult are marked with an asterisk (*).

CHAPTER 1: MACROECONOMIC PROBLEMS

1. The *Wall Street Journal* is perhaps the best source of material dealing with current economic problems. Some of the best discussions are found in "The Outlook" column which appears on the front page every Monday.

2. The President's Council of Economic Advisors prepares the *Economic Report of the President* each year (volumes generally appear toward the end of January). These economic reports present a vast array of statistics concerning the performance of the economy and, more importantly, a readable analysis of current problems and potential solutions.

3. The Brookings Institution also prepares an annual survey of economic problems. These volumes, entitled *Setting National Priorities* are well written and deal with a variety of current problems.

*4. A more technical discussion of the Great Depression and the years since is contained in an article by Peter Temin, "Lessons for the Present from the Great Depression," *American Economic Review* (May 1976).

CHAPTER 2: SUPPLY AND DEMAND

1. Any good microeconomics text will expand on the treatment of supply and demand presented here. Good expositions are found in *Microeconomics* by James D. Gwartney (Academic Press, 1977) and *Introductory Microeconomics* by Michael Veseth (Academic Press, forthcoming).

2. An informative — and fun — illustration of how markets work is found in an article by R. A. Radford, "The Economic Organization of a P.O.W. Camp," *Economica* (1945). (This old but good article is also reprinted in most economics readings books.)

CHAPTER 3: THE PROBLEM OF UNEMPLOYMENT

1. A good discussion of the causes of current unemployment problems is found in an article by Steven P. Zell, "Recent Developments in the Theory of Unemployment," *Federal Reserve Bank of Kansas City Monthly Review* (September – October 1975).

2. Another modern discussion of the unemployment problem is "The Economics of the New Unemployment" by Martin Feldstein, *The Public Interest* (Fall 1973).

*3. A slightly more technical treatment, also by Martin Feldstein, is "The Private and Social Costs of Unemployment," *American Economic Review* (May 1978).

4. A more detailed introduction to the economics of the job market is a book by Richard B. Freeman, *Labor Economics* (Prentice-Hall, 1972).

CHAPTER 4: UNDERSTANDING INFLATION

1. The best overall discussion of the problem of inflation is an article by Robert Solow, "The Intelligent Citizen's Guide to Inflation," *The Public Interest* (Winter 1975).

2. The reader who is concerned about how inflation is calculated and the meaning and use of price indexes is advised to consult *Measuring Price Changes* (3rd ed.) by William H. Wallance and William E. Cullison (Federal Reserve Bank of Richmond, 1976).

3. Three articles which have appeared in the *Federal Reserve Bank of St. Louis Review* make good reading: "Are You Protected from Inflation?" by Nancy Ammon Jianakopolos (January 1977); "The Effects of Changes in Inflationary Expectations" by Rachel Balbach (April 1977) and "So What, It's Only a Five Percent Inflation" by Leonall C. Anderson (May 1977).

4. Indexation is an important topic these days. Good articles here are "Inflation and the 'Brazilian Solution'" by Ronald A. Krieger, *Challenge* (Sept.–Oct. 1974) and "Indexation and Inflation" by George W. Cloos, *Federal Reserve Bank of Chicago Economic Perspectives* (May–June 1978).

5. An interesting view of inflation is presented in Lindley H. Clark's well-written book *The Secret Tax* (Dow Jones Books, 1976).

CHAPTER 5: MEASURING ECONOMIC ACTIVITY

1. Students who are interested in more detail of the GNP accounts are counseled to consult recent issues of the *Survey of Current Business* for a more in-depth view of the GNP.

2. The use of GNP as a tool to measure anything other than production and income is discussed in a paper by Edward F. Dennison, "Welfare Measurement and the GNP," *Survey of Current Business* (January 1971).

3. International income comparisons are discussed in the article by Jai-Hoon Yang, "Comparing Per Capita Output Internationally: Has the United States Been Overtaken?" *Federal Reserve Bank of St. Louis Review* (May 1978).

CHAPTER 6: AGGREGATE DEMAND

1. Many of the newer intermediate macroeconomics texts provide good explanations of aggregate demand. Examples are *Macroeconomics* by Robert J. Gordon (Little, Brown, 1978) and *Macroeconomics* by Rudiger Dornbusch and Stanley Fisher (McGraw-Hill, 1978).

*2. Students interested in the Keynesian 45-degree-line model presented in the appendix to Chapter 6 are advised to read *A Guide to Keynes* by Alvin Hansen (McGraw-Hill, 1953).

CHAPTER 7: AGGREGATE SUPPLY AND THE ECONOMY

*1. The importance of aggregate supply to the economy is emphasized in a speech by Lawrence R. Klein published as "The Supply Side," *American Economic Review* (March 1978).

2. Intermediate macroeconomics texts

provide a good treatment of the material discussed in this chapter. See, for example, Chapter 11 of Rudiger Dornbusch and Stanley Fisher's *Macroeconomics* (McGraw-Hill, 1978).

3. The role of inventories is stressed in an article by John A. Tatom, "Inventory Investment in the Recent Recession and Recovery," *Federal Reserve Bank of St. Louis Review* (April 1977).

4. Wage and price controls are often discussed during periods of high inflation. A good reading here is "The Legacy of Phase II Price Controls," *American Economic Review* (May 1974) by Robert F. Lanzilloti and Blaine Roberts.

CHAPTER 8: FISCAL POLICY

1. Interesting and useful descriptions of current fiscal policies are contained in the annual issues of the *Economic Report of the President* and the Brookings Institution's *Setting National Priorities*.

*2. A more theoretical analysis of fiscal policies is found in an article by Robert J. Gordon, "What Can Stabilization Policy Achieve?" *American Economic Review* (May 1978).

3. Taxation is an important matter always. A good look at tax policy is found in *Federal Tax Policy* (3rd ed.) by Joseph Pechman (Brookings Institution, 1977).

4. The distribution of the tax burden is a matter of national concern. This is analyzed in detail in *Who Bears the Tax Burden?* by Joseph A. Pechman and Benjamin A. Okner (Brookings Institution, 1974).

CHAPTER 9: MONEY AND BANKING

1. John Kenneth Galbraith has written

an interesting and understandable history of money and banking. It is called *Money: Whence It Came, Where It Went* (Houghton Mifflin, 1975).

2. A more detailed analysis of money and banks can be found in almost any money and banking text. Especially good is *Principles of Money and Financial Markets* (Basic Books, 1977) by Lawrence S. Ritter and William L. Silber.

3. Another book by Ritter and Silber rates a mention here. Their *Money* (Basic Books, 1977) is an amusing introduction to the topic.

4. A short but informative primer to interest rates is "Prime Rate Update" by Randall C. Merris, *Federal Reserve Bank of Chicago Economic Perspectives* (May–June 1978).

CHAPTER 10: MONEY, CREDIT, AND THE ECONOMY

1. A good general discussion of credit markets is found in a short book called *Instruments of the Money Market* (Federal Reserve Bank of Richmond, 1974) edited by Jimmie R. Monhollon and Glenn Picou.

2. A slightly longer introduction to the credit market is found in *Macro-Finance* by Frank J. Jones (Winthrop Publishers, 1978), especially part 3.

3. A recent problem in credit markets is discussed in "Disintermediation Again?" by Eleanor Erdevig, *Federal Reserve Bank of Chicago Economic Perspectives* (May–June 1978).

CHAPTER 11: MONETARY VERSUS FISCAL POLICY

1. Two books give especially good "insider" views of how economic policy is made. They are *Making Monetary and Fiscal Policy* by G. L. Bach (Brookings Institution, 1971) and Sherman J. Maisel's *Managing*

the Dollar (W. W. Norton and Co., 1973).

2. The problem of "crowding out" is discussed in "The 1975–76 Federal Deficits and the Credit Market" by Richard W. Lan, *Federal Reserve Bank of St. Louis Review* (January 1977).

CHAPTER 12: THE MONETARISTS

1. A classic analysis of monetarism is contained in *A Monetary History of the United States, 1867–1960* by Milton Friedman and Anna Jacobson Schwartz (Princeton University Press, 1963); see especially chapter 13.

2. The monetarist evaluation of fiscal policies is summarized in "The Myth of Fiscal Policy: The Monetarist View" by Ira Kaminow, *Federal Reserve Bank of Philadelphia Business Review* (1969).

*3. Another treatment of the monetarist policy recommendations is found in "The Monetarist Controversy, or Should We Foresake Stabilization Policies?" by Franco Modigliani, *American Economic Review* (March 1977).

*4. A more difficult but still interesting article is "Monetarism: A Historic-Theoretic Perspective" by A. Robert Nobay and Harry G. Johnson, *Journal of Economic Literature* (June 1977).

CHAPTER 13: INTERNATIONAL TRADE

1. More detailed analysis of the motives for and gains from international trade can be found in any good international economics text. Typical is *International Trade and Investment* (4th ed.) by Franklin R. Root (Southwestern Publishing Co., 1978).

2. Trade restrictions are a hotly debated topic. Tariffs and quotas are discussed in "The New Protectionism" by Walter Adams, *Challenge* (1973) and "The Current Case for Import Limitations" by Irving Kravis in *Changing Patterns in Foreign Trade and Payments* (3rd ed.) edited by Bela Balassa (W. W. Norton and Co., 1978).

3. Two articles which appeared in the *Federal Reserve Bank of St. Louis Review* provide insights into trade and comparative advantage. They are "Free Trade: A Major Factor in U.S. Farm Income" by Clifton B. Luttrell (March 1977) and "The Recent U.S. Trade Deficit—No Cause for Panic" by Geoffrey E. Wood and Douglas R. Mudd (April 1978).

CHAPTER 14: THE FOREIGN EXCHANGE MARKET

1. International economics texts generally give a good account of the foreign exchange market. A good example is *International Economics: Concepts and Issues* by Klaus Friedrich (McGraw-Hill, 1974), chapter 9.

2. A discussion of flexible and fixed exchange rates is contained in the book by Sidney E. Rolfe and James L. Burtle, *The Great Wheel: The World Monetary System* (McGraw-Hill Paperbacks, 1975).

3. To see how exchange intervention is implemented, read "The Mechanics of Intervention in Exchange Markets" by Anatol B. Balbach, *Federal Reserve Bank of St. Louis Review* (February 1978).

CHAPTER 15: INTERNATIONAL ECONOMICS

1. The best source for information

concerning international economics these days are the pages of the daily newspaper, especially the *Wall Street Journal*.

2. Many of the impacts discussed in this chapter are presented in different forms in an article by Clifton B. Luttrell, "Imports and Jobs: The Observed and the Unobserved," *Federal Reserve Bank of St. Louis Review* (June 1978).

3. The relationship between exchange rates and economic policy is discussed in "Interdependence, Exchange Rate Flexibility, and National Economics," by Donald L. Kohn, *Federal Reserve Bank of Kansas City Monthly Review* (April 1975).

CHAPTER 16: PROBLEMS, GOALS, AND TRADE-OFFS

1. A good discussion of the trade-offs in economics is found in *Equality and Efficiency: The Big Tradeoff* by Arthur Okun (Brookings Institution, 1975).

2. A new kind of fiscal policy is reviewed in "A Tax-Based Incomes Policy (TIP): What's It All About?" by Nancy Ammon Jianakopolos, *Federal Reserve Bank of St. Louis Review* (February 1978).

3. Also good reading is "Oil Imports and the Fall of the Dollar," by Douglas R. Mudd and Geoffrey E. Wood, *Federal Reserve Bank of St. Louis Review* (August 1978).

Glossary

Absolute advantage: the advantage enjoyed by a country which is more efficient in production of a particular good

Accommodating monetary policy: FRS actions which are chosen to complement fiscal policies

Ad valorem tariff: a traiff levied according to the value of an imported item

Ad valorem taxation: taxation according to the value of an item (e.g., sales and property taxes)

Administrative costs: a component of the interest rate which depends on the cost of setting up and administering credit transactions

Aggregate demand (AD): the desired total purchases of goods and services in an economy; the AD curve shows how total demand varies with the price level

Aggregate supply (AS): the total production of goods and services in an economy; the AS curve shows how total output is related to the price level

Allocation function: government activities designed to provide the appropriate amounts and mix of private and public goods

Appreciation: a gain in value of any asset (e.g., stock, bond, house, or currency)

Arbitrage: the practice of buying currencies on one foreign exchange market and reselling them on another, for profit, which tends to stabilize exchange rates

Automatic stabilizers: government spending, taxation, and transfer programs which automatically (i.e., without legislative action) act to increase AD during economic downturns and decrease AD during periods of prosperity

Average propensity to consume (APC): the fraction of total income which goes to consumption spending

Balance of payments: an accounting of total inflows and outflows (including imports and exports, investment flows, and transfer payments) of an economy

Balance of payments deficit: a country's total money outflows exceed its total money inflows

Balance of payments surplus: a country's total money inflows exceed its total money outflows

Balance of trade: an accounting of the imports and exports of an economy

Balanced-budget multiplier: the multiple impact on AD of equal changes in government spending and taxation, generally equal to 1

Balanced federal government budget: total federal government expenditures equal total federal tax collections

Balanced growth: increases in demand accompanied by increasing supply; allows the larger quantities demanded to be satisfied without price increases

Barriers to occupational entry: institutional factors which limit or restrict employment in various occupations

Barter: a system where goods and services are exchanged for one another without the use of money

Base year: an arbitrarily chosen year that all other years are compared with in the construction of a price index for measuring inflation

Bond market: the financial market where bonds (i.e., IOUs issued by governments, businesses, and others) are exchanged

Bottleneck AS: the AS situation which prevails when there is substantial, but not severe, unemployment in an economy

Business cycle: periods of economic expansion followed by high levels of unemployment which have prevailed at various times in history

Capacity: the physical ability of the economy to produce, normally measured by the amount of plants, equipment, machinery, and the like available for use

Circular flow model: a description of the economy which highlights the circular flow of spending and income between the business and household sectors of the economy; built on the concept that spending creates income

Closed economy: an economy that has no economic interaction with the rest of the world

Collateral: assets which are held as security for a loan and may be seized if repayment is not made

Command economy: an economy where production and distribution decisions are made by central planners

Commercial banks: banks which issue demand deposits

Comparative advantage: the advantage enjoyed by a country which can produce a particular good at lower opportunity cost

Complement: goods which are used together (e.g., toast and jam, coffee and sugar, hamburgers and french fries)

Complete crowding out: an increase in government borrowing causes an equal decrease in private sector borrowing due to fixed credit supplies

Conflicting policies: monetary and fiscal policies that work in opposite directions, often with undesirable side effects

Consumer Price Index (CPI): a measure of inflation based on a market basket of goods and services purchased by urban households

Consumer's burden: the proportion of a tariff that is passed along to a consumer in terms of higher import prices

Consumption spending: spending by households on consumer items

Contractionary monetary policy: FRS actions designed to decrease the supplies of money and credit in the economy

Corporate income tax: a federal tax levied against the profits of corporations

Cost-push: price increases which are brought about through a decrease in supply typically caused by increased costs of production

Credit: the temporary exchange of money among individuals, as when loans are made

Credit market: the financial market, made up of borrowers and lenders, where loanable funds are exchanged

Cyclical unemployment: unemployment resulting from decreases in AD

Deadweight loss: a loss due to wasted resources

Decrease in demand: a change in income, tastes, and preferences or some other determinant of demand causing the quantity demanded to be lower at every price (shown by a shift to the left of the demand curve)

Decrease in supply: a change in costs of production, technology, or some other determinant of supply causing the quantity supplied to be less at every price (shown by a shift to the left in the supply curve)

Deficit spending: spending in excess of tax revenues

Deflation: a substantial, sustained decrease in the general level of prices

Demand: a description of the buyer side of the market; examines how the amounts and kinds of goods and services people wish to buy are determined

Demand curve: a curve which shows the quantity of a good or service that buyers wish to purchase at every possible price

Demand deposits: deposits in checking accounts in commercial banks

Demand-pull: price increases which result from an increase in demand

Deposit-expansion process: the process by which banks create money by loaning out funds acquired through deposits

Depreciation: a fall in value; the wearing out of machines and other productive resources

Depression AS: the AS situation which prevails when there are large amounts of unemployed resources in the economy, making increased production possible without higher prices

Derived demand: a property of a good that is desired because of the demand for a complementary good (e.g., the demand for foreign exchange is derived from the demand for foreign goods and services)

Devalue: the lowering of the official value of a currency in a fixed-exchange-rate system

Diminishing returns: the phenomenon that prevails when, as more and more resources are used in production, their average productivity tends to fall

Direct relationship: the relationship that exists between A and B if they increase or decrease together; that is, an increase in A implies an increase in B

Discount: the difference between the face value and the selling price of a bond; the interest rate on a bond

Discount rate: the interest rate charged by the FRS on short-term loans to member banks

Discouraged workers: people who become discouraged with employment prospects and leave the labor force

Disintermediation: the process whereby savers take funds out of financial intermediaries and invest directly in credit markets in order to achieve higher returns

Disposable income: income actually available for spending (gross income minus direct taxes)

Distribution function: government activities designed to produce an acceptable distribution of income

Dividends: corporation profits which are paid to stockholders

Division of labor: a way of increasing productivity by breaking a complicated process into a number of simple steps and then treating each step as a specialized job; the basis for the modern production line

Double-counting: a potential error in GNP statistics which occurs when production is counted more than once in compiling GNP

Economic Discomfort Index: a measure of the magnitude of national economic problems; the sum of the inflation and unemployment rates

Economics: a social science dealing with the production and distribution of goods and services in a world of scarce resources

Elastic demand: the property of a product when the quantity demanded changes substantially when price changes; generally goods having close substitutes or luxury items

Equation of exchange: an accounting identity associated with the monetarists; the equation of exchange states that $M \times V = P \times Q$ (where M is the money supply, V is the velocity of money, P is the price level, and Q is the level of real output)

Equilibrium price: the one price where the quantity supplied equals the quantity demanded

Equitable distribution of income: a more equal distribution of income among groups in the population

Equity: ownership of an asset

Eurodollars: dollar-denominated deposits in foreign banks

Excess demand: the quantity demanded at a particular price exceeds the quantity supplied at that price

Excess reserves: banks' holdings of reserves in excess of those required by law or FRS regulation

Excess supply: the quantity supplied at a particular price exceeds the quantity demanded at that price

Exchange rate: the ratio at which currencies or commodities can be traded for one another

Expansionary monetary policy: FRS actions designed to increase the supplies of money and credit

Exports: goods sold to the residents of other countries

Federal funds market: the financial market where banks lend excess reserves to each other

Federal Reserve System (FRS): national bank regulatory organization which has principal responsibility for monetary policy

Final good: a good which is purchased by its ultimate user; GNP measures the production of only final goods in order to avoid double-counting of intermediate goods

Financial investment: the purchase of stocks, bonds, and other financial instruments; involves an exchange of previously existing goods

Financial sector: the part of the economy which specifically deals with borrowing, lending, and exchanges of assets (e.g., banks, insurance companies, and stock exchanges)

First-order impact: the initial changes in the economy brought on by monetary or fiscal policies

Fiscal policy: economic policies involving government spending, taxing, and transfer payment activities

Fixed exchange rates: the relative values of the currencies of different nations are set by international agreement; the market is not allowed to function in setting exchange rates

Flexible exchange rates: a system where exchange rates are set through market forces

Float: occurs when two or more individuals temporarily own the same asset

Foreign exchange: foreign currencies

Fractional-reserve banking: the modern system of bank operation where only a fraction of deposits are held on reserve by the banking system while remaining funds are invested or loaned

Frictional unemployment: unemployment resulting from imperfections in the labor market such as poor information about jobs and lack of worker mobility

Full employment: the maximum possible employment rate in a healthy economy

Full-employment AS: the AS situation which prevails when all resources are in use; increases in total production are impossible and attempts to increase output result only in higher prices

Gross national product (GNP): the total market value (in current prices) of all final goods and services produced in a year; a basic measure of current market economic activity

Gross National Product Implicit Price Deflator Index (GNP Index): a measure of the prices of final goods, used to adjust the GNP statistics for inflation

Guidelines: announced governmental standards for wage and price increases designed to induce voluntary reductions in price increases

Hyperinflation: very high rates of price inflation

Identification lag: a problem in fiscal policies involving transfer payments caused by the time which must be spent identifying the proper transfer recipient groups

Immature creditor nation: a nation which has a surplus balance of payments resulting from high exports of raw materials

Immature debtor nation: a less developed country which has a deficit balance of payments resulting from imports of goods and services and high investment and transfer inflows

Impact lag: the lag in fiscal policy equal to the time it takes a change in spending, transfers or taxes to have its full impact on the economy

Implementation lag: the lag in fiscal policy equal to the time it takes for a decision to change spending transfers or taxes to be implemented

Imports: purchases of goods from foreign countries

Incidence: the actual distribution of the burden of a tax

Income: the receipts of a firm or household, derived from wages, rents, or business profits

Income effect: changes in demand behavior which result from changing prices; as the price of an individual good rises (or falls) buyers find that their fixed incomes are less (or more) able to purchase that good and all others

Increase in demand: a change in income, tastes, or some other determinant of demand which causes the quantity demand of some good to rise at every price (shown by a shift to the right in the demand curve)

Increase in supply: a change in the costs of production, technology, or some other determinant of supply which causes the quantity supplied to increase at every price (shown by a shift to the right in the supply curve)

Indexation: programs which tie wages, values, and/or taxes to a price index

Induced consumption expenditures: changes in consumption spending caused by changes in government spending, taxes, and so on; a part of the multiplier process

Inelastic demand: the property of a product when quantity demanded does not change very much relative to price changes; generally necessity items or goods with few close substitutes

Inflation: a substantial, sustained increase in the general level of prices

Inflation premium: a component of the interest rate resulting from changing anticipated inflation rates

Inflation rate: the rate of increase in prices as measured by a price index

Injections: factors which increase spending flows such as investment, government, and export spending; inputs into the circular flow of spending and income

Inputs: factors of production; goods and services which are used in the production of other goods and services (e.g., labor, raw materials)

Interdependence: mutual dependence

Intermediate good: items produced at one stage in production that are then used to produce other goods

Intervention: a situation which prevails when third parties (central banks) enter foreign exchange markets in order to increase or decrease the value of a currency

Intranational: within one nation

Inventories: stocks of goods which firms keep on hand in anticipation of future sale or use in production

Inverse relationship: the relationship that is said to exist between A and B if an increase in A results in a decrease in B (A and B move in opposite directions)

Investment in human capital: investments in training and education which increase worker productivity

Investment rule: tendency of firms to invest in opportunities whenever the anticipated return on investment exceeds the interest rate

Investment spending: economic or GNP investment spending refers to purchases of plant equipment, machinery, and other items which increase a firm's ability to produce

Investment tax credits: tax programs which lower tax rates on new investments and so encourage investment spending by increasing after-tax returns

Jawboning: governmental actions designed to hold down wages or prices by pointing out unwarranted increases and applying public pressure to reduce price increases

Keynesian 45-degree-line model: a model of economic activity based on the ideas of John Maynard Keynes which uses a 45° line to show the macroeconomic equilibrium

Keynesian model: the model of macroeconomic activity developed by John Maynard Keynes which concentrates on total spending as the determinant of the equilibrium level of national income

Labor force: all those involved in the labor market; those working plus those actively seeking work

Leading indicators: economic statistics which foretell future changes in the economy

Leakages: factors which tend to reduce total spending such as saving, taxes, and imports; outflows from the circular flow of spending and income

Legislative lag: a lag in fiscal policy equal to the time it takes legislative bodies to decide the proper governmental actions

M1: one level of the money supply; currency plus demand deposit balances

M2: currency and demand deposit balances plus time deposits held by commercial banks

M3: currency and demand deposits plus time deposit balances held at both commercial and savings banks

Macroeconomic equilibrium: the equilibrium which occurs when desired total spending equals income; at this point total spending and income neither rise nor fall

Macroeconomics: the study of the functioning of the national economy

Marginal propensity to consume (MPC): the proportion of any change in income which becomes a change in consumption; the MPC is constant in the short run and is generally assumed to be less than 1

Market: a general term describing the economic institutions where exchanges of goods and services are made

Market basket: a list of kinds and quantities of goods and services which is used in the calculation of the inflation rate

Market economy: an economic system where production and distribution decisions are made in decentralized markets

Mature creditor nation: a nation which has a balance-of-payments surplus resulting from exports of finished goods

Mature debtor nation: a country which has a balance-of-payments deficit resulting from high investment and transfer out-flows

Microeconomics: the study of individual economic decisions focusing on markets, production, and consumer behavior

Minimum-wage laws: federal laws which specify a minimum legal wage for workers in a variety of job categories

Models: simplified descriptions of real-world processes designed to increase the understanding of real-world behavior

Monetarists: members of a school of economics that hold that money is the most important factor in macroeconomic analysis

Monetary policy: policies designed to affect the economy by regulating the availability of money and credit

Monetary transmission mechanism: the process whereby monetary policies affect AD and AS through their impact on interest rates and investment spending

Money: anything which is generally accepted in exchange for goods and services and in payment of debt

Money supply: the amount of money available in an economy (depends on the exact definition of money used)

Money value: the value of an item as measured by the amount of current dollars required to purchase that item

Mortgage credit market: the financial market where loans are made for homes, buildings, and so on

Near-money: assets such as time deposits which have moneylike properties or can act as money substitutes

Negative income effect: less demand for a product as a result of an increase in income

Negotiable order of withdrawal (NOW account): a special type of bank account (often offered by savings banks) which allows depositors to

earn interest on what are essentially checking accounts

Net exports: the net injection from the foreign sector of the economy; exports minus imports

Net investment: total investment spending minus the amount of investment which went to keep existing capacity in use (i.e., total investment minus depreciation); the amount of investment which goes to expand total production

Nominal interest rate: the interest rate unadjusted for inflation

Nominal value: same as *money value;* the number of current dollars required to purchase an item

Open economy: an economy which has free economic interaction with the rest of the world

Open market operations: FRS sales and purchases of bonds designed to affect the money supply

Opportunity cost: the cost of an economic action as determined by the value of the opportunities foregone

Outputs: the goods and services which firms produce

Overvalued: a currency when it trades at an exchange rate above the market equilibrium

Partial crowding out: the phenomenon that occurs when increased government borrowing results in a reduction in private sector borrowing (the fall in private borrowing is less than the increase in government borrowing)

Payroll tax: a tax, like the Social Security tax, which is collected directly from pay checks

Per capita RGNP: a measure of production available for each person in a country; RGNP divided by total population of a country

Personal income tax: the federal income tax collected in the United States every April 15

Phillips Curve: a curve showing an inverse relationship between inflation and unemployment; suggesting that lower unemployment accompanies higher inflation, and vice-versa

Price-ceiling: a maximum legal price (set by the government, not by market forces)

Price floor: a minimum legal price

Price index (indices): mathematical estimators of inflation which compare the price of a fixed market basket of items for different years

Price stability: a national economic goal; a situation where inflation rates are close to zero

Prime rate: the lowest interest rate that a bank charges on short-term loans

Private sector: the nongovernment part of the economy; private industry

Producer's burden: the reduction in net selling price caused by the imposition of a tariff

Production: the act of using inputs (such as land, labor, and machinery) in order to produce goods and services

Production possibility curve (PPC): a graph showing the different possible combinations of two goods which can be produced with limited resources

Productivity: the relative ability of a resource to produce goods and services; often measured by the amount of production per man-hour

Progressive tax: a tax that imposes higher tax burdens on groups with higher incomes

Property tax: a tax collected by state and local governments based on the value of the property (land, houses, business property) that people and firms own

Proportional tax: a tax which imposes

equal tax burdens on all groups

Public goods: goods which, once produced, yield benefits which are (or can be) shared by all

Public sector: the government part of the economy; includes federal, state, and local governments

Purchasing power: the value of money as measured by the amount of goods and services that the money will buy

Quota: physical limitation on the amount of a good that can be imported

Real-balance effect: a change in the quantity of AD which occurs when price levels change; results from prices changing the real value of savings, thus inducing a change in saving and spending habits

Real gross national product (RGNP): a measure of the total annual production in an economy; the GNP adjusted for inflation by use of the GNP Index

Real income: a measure of the amount of goods and services that income will buy; income adjusted for the impact of rising prices

Real-income effect: a change in the quantity of AD which results from a change in the price level altering real incomes

Real interest rate: the interest rate adjusted for the effect of inflation

Real value: values adjusted for the impact of rising prices so as to allow the comparison of values over time

Recession: a sustained period of falling national production (falling RGNP)

Regressive tax: a tax which imposes higher tax burdens on groups with lower incomes

Reserve requirement: the proportion of total deposits that a bank must hold on reserve; determined by the FRS or by state law (for non FRS banks)

Risk premium: a component of the

interest rate which depends upon the relative risk of different forms of credit

Rules policy: a policy whereby the money supply is constantly expanded at a uniform rate according to a 'rule' or formula

Sales tax: taxes levied on the value of consumer purchases

Scarcity premium: a component of the interest rate which depends upon the relative scarcity of credit at different times

Sectors: parts of the economy which respond differently to economic events or are related by similar problems or activities

Shortage: quantity demanded exceeds quantity supplied

Social Security tax: the payroll tax which finances the Social Security program

Special drawing right (SDR): an international form of reserve which acts like gold in terms of transactions involving international central banks; 'paper gold'

Specialization: the principle of having a person or industry perform just one or a few tasks and so become very good at that task, which tends to increase productivity

Spending multiplier: the multiple impact of a change in a spending component on AD

Stabilization function: government activities designed to promote full employment, stable prices, and economic growth

Stagflation: the phenomenon of high inflation rates accompanied by high unemployment rates; a stagnant economy with inflation

Sticky wages: inflexible wages; wage rates that do not change in response to changing labor market conditions

Stock market: markets like the New

York Stock Exchange where shares representing ownership of corporations are bought and sold

Structural unemployment: unemployment resulting from a poor matching of worker skills and job needs

Substitutes: goods which perform the same function (e.g., coffee and tea, hamburgers and hot dogs, and pens and pencils)

Substitution effect: changes in demand behavior which result from changing prices; as prices change buyers substitute more of relatively cheaper goods and buy less of those with relatively higher prices

Supply: a description of the seller side of the market; looks at the factors which determine the amounts and kinds of goods and services offered for sale

Supply curve: a graphical device showing the relationship between price and the quantity supplied, all other factors held constant

Surplus: the quantity supplied exceeds the quantity demanded

Tariff: a tax on imports

Tax-based incomes policy(TIP): a program which attempts to use tax incentives to accomplish macroeconomic policies

Tax burden: the proportion of income that goes to pay a tax or taxes (tax payment divided by total income)

Tax expenditures: tax reductions or 'loopholes' designed to encourage certain types of private sector activities

Technology: the process by which inputs are combined to produce goods and services (changes in technology involve changes in the processes)

Time deposit: savings account balances

Time preference: a component of the interest rate which results from simple preference for present over future consumption

Total production: a measure of the amount of goods produced and the prices paid for those goods

Trade-off: the situation which occurs when one item or goal must be given up in order to obtain another item or goal

Transfer payments: payments from one group to another with no payment of goods or services in return

Underemployed workers: part-time workers who seek full-time jobs or people employed at occupations that do not use their training or skills

Undervalued: a currency when it trades at an exchange rate below the market equilibrium

Unemployed worker: a person willing and able to work, actively seeking work, but unable to find a job at the going wage rate

Unemployment rate: a measure of unemployment calculated by dividing the number of unemployed individuals by the size of the labor force

Unintended inventory accumulations: increases in inventories which occur when demand falls behind production

Unintended inventory reductions: decreases in inventory levels which occur when demand rises above supply

Unit tariff: a tariff levied according to the number of units of an item imported

Usury laws: state laws which set maximum legal interest rates on credit

Value-added: the amount of value added by the productive process; sale price of an item minus the costs of production

Variable lag: the lag between the implementation of monetary policy and the time when its impact is felt in the economy (can vary from a few months to several years)

Velocity of money: the average number of times that the money supply is exchanged (spent) is a period of time

Wage and price controls: government programs which attempt to fight inflation by regulating price and wage increases

Wage floor: minimum-wage rate caused by minimum-wage laws or sticky wages in a particular labor market

Wage-lag theory: used to explain the Phillips Curve; holds that wages do not rise as fast as prices (i.e., they lag behind prices), temporarily increasing employer profits and therefore inducing employers to hire more workers

Wholesale Price Index (WPI): a measure of the prices of goods used in business

Answers to "Test Yourself"

CHAPTER 1: MACROECONOMIC PROBLEMS

1. False
2. True
3. True
4. False
5. False
6. False
7. False
8. True
9. False
10. True

CHAPTER 2: SUPPLY AND DEMAND

1. False
2. True
3. False
4. False
5. False
6. False
7. False
8. True
9. False
10. False

CHAPTER 3: THE PROBLEM OF UNEMPLOYMENT

1. False
2. True
3. False
4. False
5. True
6. False
7. True
8. True
9. True
10. False

CHAPTER 4: UNDERSTANDING INFLATION

1. False
2. False
3. True
4. False
5. False
6. True
7. True
8. True
9. False
10. False

CHAPTER 5: MEASURING ECONOMIC ACTIVITY

1. False
2. False
3. True
4. True
5. False
6. True
7. True
8. True
9. False
10. False

CHAPTER 6: AGGREGATE DEMAND

1. True
2. True
3. False
4. True
5. False
6. False
7. True
8. False
9. True
10. True

CHAPTER 7: AGGREGATE SUPPLY AND THE ECONOMY

1. False
2. False
3. True
4. False
5. True
6. False
7. True
8. True
9. True
10. False

CHAPTER 8: FISCAL POLICY

1. False
2. False
3. True
4. False
5. False
6. True
7. False
8. False
9. True
10. True

CHAPTER 9: MONEY AND BANKING

1. False
2. True
3. False
4. True
5. False
6. True
7. True
8. True
9. False
10. False

CHAPTER 10: MONEY, CREDIT, AND THE ECONOMY

1. False
2. True
3. False
4. True
5. False
6. True
7. False
8. True
9. True
10. True

CHAPTER 11: MONETARY VERSUS FISCAL POLICY

1. True
2. False
3. False
4. True
5. False
6. True
7. False
8. True
9. False
10. False

CHAPTER 12: THE MONETARISTS

1. False
2. False
3. False
4. True
5. True
6. True
7. False
8. False
9. True
10. True

CHAPTER 13: INTERNATIONAL TRADE

1. False
2. False
3. True
4. False
5. True
6. True
7. False

8. False
9. True
10. True

CHAPTER 14: THE FOREIGN EXCHANGE MARKET

1. True
2. False
3. False
4. False
5. True
6. True
7. False
8. False
9. False
10. True

CHAPTER 15: INTERNATIONAL ECONOMICS

1. False
2. False
3. False
4. True
5. True
6. False
7. True
8. True
9. False
10. True

CHAPTER 16: PROBLEMS, GOALS, AND TRADE-OFFS

1. True
2. False
3. False
4. False
5. True
6. False
7. True
8. False
9. True
10. True

Index

A 9
B 0
C 1
D 2
C 3
E 4
F 5
G 6
H 7